Los Angeles Dodgers
Transactions,
1958–2024

AF088663

ALSO BY LYLE SPATZ
AND FROM MCFARLAND

*Brooklyn Dodgers Transactions, 1890–1957:
A History and Analysis* (2025)

*New York Yankees Openers: An Opening Day History
of Baseball's Most Famous Team, 1903–2017*, 2d ed. (2018)

Dixie Walker: A Life in Baseball (2011)

*Yankees Coming, Yankees Going: New York Yankee
Player Transactions, 1903 Through 1999* (2009 [2000])

*Bad Bill Dahlen: The Rollicking Life and Times
of an Early Baseball Star* (2004)

Los Angeles Dodgers Transactions, 1958–2024

A History and Analysis

LYLE SPATZ

McFarland & Company, Inc., Publishers
Jefferson, North Carolina

ISBN (print) 978-1-4766-9744-4
ISBN (ebook) 978-1-4766-5566-6

Library of Congress cataloging data are available

Library of Congress Control Number 2025017269

© 2025 Lyle Spatz. All rights reserved

No part of this book may be reproduced or transmitted in any form or by any means, electronic or mechanical, including photocopying or recording, or by any information storage and retrieval system, without permission in writing from the publisher.

Front cover images: Los Angeles Dodgers players (highlighted from left to right—top row) Shohei Ohtani, Sandy Koufax, Clayton Kershaw; (second row) Mike Piazza, Steve Garvey, Don Drysdale, Dusty Baker; (third row) Fernando Valenzuela, Mookie Betts, Don Sutton; (fourth row) Davey Lopes, Maury Wills, Tommy Davis, Ron Cey

Printed in the United States of America

*McFarland & Company, Inc., Publishers
Box 611, Jefferson, North Carolina 28640
www.mcfarlandpub.com*

Table of Contents

Preface — 1

1. 1958–1959 — 5
2. 1960–1964 — 12
3. 1965–1969 — 30
4. 1970–1974 — 44
5. 1975–1979 — 57
6. 1980–1984 — 78
7. 1985–1989 — 92
8. 1990–1994 — 115
9. 1995–1999 — 141
10. 2000–2004 — 171
11. 2005–2009 — 202
12. 2010–2014 — 224
13. 2015–2019 — 245
14. 2020–2024 — 264

Chapter Notes — 295
Selected Bibliography — 307
Index — 309

Preface

The trading, drafting, buying, and selling of players has forever been a part of the quest to create better baseball teams. These transactions are also a major contributor to the game's history and folklore. But perhaps the most important role may be their ability to stir the interest and passion of fans. Whether it is the purchase of a veteran star during the heat of a pennant race, a multi-player trade made during the dead of winter, or the off-season scramble for desirable free agents, player transactions engender more interest and heated debate among fans than almost any other aspect of the game. In no other sport but baseball are the movements of players from one team to another so eagerly anticipated and analyzed. Additionally, baseball fans love trade rumors: they love to hear about them, to read about them, and to talk about them. They even love those that are rumored but don't get made.

Ostensibly, there is in every trade the assumption that the combination of current players, future players, or money a particular team is getting is approximately equal in value to what it is giving up. Of course, it rarely works out that way. Furthermore, some trades that seem one-sided when they are made often turn out to be so but not necessarily in favor of the team that appeared to have the advantage initially.

This book included the trades, drafts, sales, purchases, and movement of free agents of the Los Angeles Dodgers following their move from Brooklyn in 1958 through the 2024 season. Because it is space- and time-prohibitive to detail every transaction, each year includes a section called "Also in," which lists many of the other transactions made that year. I do not include deals where the Dodgers acquired a player who never played for them or was not part of a subsequent deal that did involve a Dodgers player. Some lifelong Dodgers appear in the narratives only in their relation to other transactions.

For those transactions I deem meaningful, I have attempted to put it and the players involved in historical perspective. I describe why the Dodgers and the other team(s) made the deal. Using the newspapers of the time, I quote the expectations the owners, general managers, and managers of the respective teams had for their new players. I show what the players moving to and from Los Angeles thought about their old and new teams. The description and analysis of each transaction vary from a few sentences to several paragraphs.

This book focuses primarily on the baseball aspects of these transactions; for the most part, it deliberately excludes extensive discussions of money and length of contracts, including those details only when they were believed essential to the story. The business aspects of baseball transactions obviously are important, especially in the age of free agency; however, it is a subject adequately covered elsewhere.

The team names I use are the ones that were current at the time of the transaction. For minor league teams, the league in which they played will be identified, and often its classification. Mention of a player as a minor leaguer in the title of a transaction means that he had never before appeared in a major league game. And unless noted, the ending of a player's career refers specifically to his major league career.

Because this is primarily a reference book, each trade is treated as if the reader is looking at it without necessarily having read what came before. This makes it necessary to repeat certain facts pertaining to individual players and front office personnel, for which I beg your forbearance. For instance, within a chapter Walter Alston might be called "Walter Alston," "Alston," "Dodgers manager Walter Alston," "manager Walter Alston," or "manager Alston."

The basic building blocks for these transactions come from *Retrosheet* and the database built by the late and sorely missed Tom Ruane. During my research I came across several dates that differed from Tom's. Given that many newspapers often had multiple editions, some of the dates might be off by a day or so. Some perhaps even more, as the date the trade is made and the date a contract is signed might differ. This often occurs when a physical exam is required for one or more players. Sometimes I have used one and sometimes the other, as the specific date does not affect the analysis of the trade.

The primary source for information and quotes relating to these transactions was the newspapers of the day. Biographies from the SABR BioProject were also a valuable source of information for many players. The statistics I used are from three sources treasured by researchers: *Baseball-Reference*, founded by Sean Forman; *Baseball Almanac*, founded by Sean Holtz; and *Retrosheet*, founded by David Smith and currently under the direction of Tom Thress. While measures of performance like batting average, runs batted in, won-lost records, and earned run average have come under attack in recent years, I believe they still tell a story, and so I use them.

Preface

I also use newer and perhaps more meaningful measures, like OPS+ for batters and ERA+ for pitchers. OPS+ is the player's OPS (the sum of his on-base average [OBA] and slugging percentage [SLG]) adjusted for that season's OPS league average and the player's home ballpark. ERA+ is a pitcher's earned run average (ERA) adjusted for that season's league average ERA and the pitcher's home ballpark.

Finally, I thank Gary Mitchem, McFarland's senior editor, for his encouragement, advice, and cooperation. As with my previous books, members of the Society for American Baseball Research were there to answer whatever obscure fact I asked them to verify. I thank Andy McCue for lending his expertise on the Dodgers ownership history. But most of all I thank Maury Bouchard. Maury read and fact-checked the entire manuscript, saving me from numerous potential embarrassments. Any errors that slipped through are because I missed Maury's correction.

1

1958–1959

The franchise relocated to Los Angeles for the 1958 season and played home games in the Los Angeles Memorial Coliseum. Walter O'Malley and James and Dearie Mulvey bought the 25 percent of the team owned by John Smith's widow.

The Opening Day roster of the 1958 Los Angeles Dodgers, who continued to be managed by Walter Alston, was almost identical to the one that played in Brooklyn the year before. These twenty-five players were with Brooklyn for all or part of the 1957 season.

> PITCHERS: Don Bessent, Jackie Collum, Roger Craig, Don Drysdale, Carl Erskine, Fred Kipp, Sandy Koufax, Clem Labine, Danny McDevitt, Don Newcombe, Johnny Podres, Ed Roebuck
> CATCHERS: Joe Pignatano, John Roseboro, Rube Walker
> INFIELDERS: Jim Gilliam, Gil Hodges, Randy Jackson, Charlie Neal, Pee Wee Reese, Don Zimmer
> OUTFIELDERS: Gino Cimoli, Carl Furillo, Duke Snider, Elmer Valo

The other five were in the Dodgers minor league system: pitchers Ron Negray and Larry Sherry; infielders Dick Gray and Norm Larker; and outfielder Don Demeter.

1958

June 15, 1958: Traded Pitcher Don Newcombe to the Cincinnati Redlegs for First Baseman Steve Bilko, Pitcher Johnny Klippstein, Pitcher Charlie Rabe, and a Player to be Named

Branch Rickey had signed pitcher Don Newcombe and catcher Roy Campanella as undrafted free agents on April 4, 1946. Although both had played at a high level in the Negro leagues, Rickey assigned them to the Nashua (NH) Dodgers of the Class B New England League. When Bob Finch, a Rickey assistant, was asked what Newcombe, a 20-year-old right-hander, who stood 6'4" and weighed 220 pounds, had on the ball, "Everything" Finch replied. "Speed, fine curves, change of pace."[1]

Newcombe was dominant in his two seasons at Nashua, going 14–4 in 1946 and 19–6 in 1947, when he led the New England League in wins and strikeouts. After he was promoted to the Triple A Montreal Royals in 1948, his 17–6 record earned him advancement to the Dodgers in 1949. Newcombe pitched a shutout in his first start, the first of his league-leading five shutouts. Overall, he won 17 games and lost eight, was selected to the National League's All-Star team, and earned Rookie of the Year honors and an eight-place finish in the voting for the Most Valuable Player.

Newcombe went on to be the Dodgers best right-hander since Dazzy Vance, compiling a 123–66 record and a 116 ERA+. This despite missing the 1952 and 1953 seasons to army service. Newcombe's 1956 season was one of the best by a Dodgers' pitcher: a 27-7 record and a 131 ERA+, while allowing fewer than nine batters to reach base via a hit or walk per game. He was the league's MVP and the winner of the first Cy Young Award, when there was only one winner for both leagues.

But Newcombe, now 32, was having a terrible season in 1958, an 0–6 record and a 53 ERA+. "The Cincinnati organization will sure get everything I have," he said, while adding he would miss the Dodgers. "After all, you can't be with a club that long and not miss them"[2]

Reds general manager Gabe Paul called the trade a "calculated risk" but said manager Birdie Tebbets had watched Newcombe on Cincinnati's recent visit to Los Angeles and believed he will win again. "Newcombe could do a real big job for us," said Tebbets, "and if he can regain the form he had in 1956, he can win the pennant for us. Newcombe is sound, and we feel the change will do him good."[3] Newcombe split 14 decisions for the Reds in 1958 and had a 13–8 record in 1959.

Steve Bilko, a 6'1" mostly overweight minor-leaguer, had never lived up to the expectations the St. Louis Cardinals had for him when he reached the major leagues in 1949. He had only one full season with the Cardinals, 1953, when he hit 21 home runs but struck out 125 times—a league high. Bilko became a Pacific Coast League legend in 1955–1957, when he hit 37, 55, and 56 home runs, playing for the Los Angeles Angels in cozy Wrigley Field. He was the league's MVP in each of those years.

Playing 31 games for the Reds this season, the 29-year-old Bilko had a .264 batting average, four home runs, and a 110 OPS+. In Bilko, the Dodgers were getting a drawing card and a right-hand slugger, who was expected to profit from the lopsided LA Coliseum's short distance to left field. He did not. Bilko's numbers for the 1958 Dodgers were disappointing, a .208 average, seven home runs, and an 85 OPS+ in 47 games as a pinch-hitter and backup to Gil Hodges. He spent 1959 with the Dodgers PCL affiliate, the Spokane Indians, batting .305 with 26 home runs. After the season, he was taken by the Detroit Tigers in the rule 5 draft.

Johnny Klippstein, a 30-year-old right-hander, had been Dodgers property ten years earlier, when they acquired him from the St. Louis Cardinals in the 1948 minor league draft. A year later the Dodgers lost him to the Chicago Cubs in the 1949 rule 5 draft. Klippstein was in his ninth major league season, split between the Cubs and the Reds. He had a 63–85 record, including a 3–2 mark and a 4.91 earned run average this season. Pitching for the Dodgers in the second half of 1958 and all of 1959, Klippstein had a 7–5 record with 11 saves in 73 games, all in relief. On April 11, 1960, the Dodgers sold him to the Cleveland Indians for a reported $25,000.

Charlie Rabe, a 26-year-old left-hander, had an 0–4 record with Cincinnati over the last two seasons. The Dodgers sent him to Montreal, and he remained in the minor leagues through 1963.

The deal was completed on June 23, when the Reds sent 35-year-old right-hander Art Fowler, the player to be named, from their PCL team in Seattle to the Dodgers PCL team in Spokane. Fowler had a 3–4 record in 36 relief appearances with the Dodgers in 1959 and a 13–10 record, mostly as a starter, with the 1960 St. Paul Saints. On May 26, 1961, the Dodgers sold him to the expansion Los Angeles Angels of the American League.

August 4, 1958: Sold Third Baseman Randy Jackson to the Cleveland Indians

Randy Jackson had played in only 35 games this season, with a .185 batting average and a 35 OPS+. So, he was pleased when he learned he had been sold to Cleveland for the $20,000 waiver price. "I'm delighted," he said, with a touch of bitterness. "There was no reason for me to be happy on this club. It's no fun to sit around and be the forgotten guy."[4]

In a way Jackson hated to leave the Dodgers because he had lots of good friends on the team, yet he was glad to go to Cleveland where he would get a chance to play. "It'll probably take me three weeks to get into shape," he said. "I got pretty tired of sitting around."

On July 27, manager Walt Alston had started him at third base after declaring, "I haven't given him a fair shot at the job. I'm going to keep him in for five or six games and see if he can help us."[5] But Jackson had to leave the game after pulling a leg muscle in the fourth inning, ending his chance for a full-time role. He finished his Dodgers career with a .243 batting average and a 74 OPS+ in 184 games.

December 4, 1958: Traded Outfielder Gino Cimoli to the St. Louis Cardinals for Outfielder Wally Moon and Pitcher Phil Paine

Dodgers GM Buzzie Bavasi and Cardinals GM Bing Devine had been discussing a Gino Cimoli for Wally Moon trade since the 1958 World Series. The Dodgers wanted a pitcher included, and when Devine agreed to give them Phil Paine, the deal was made. Generally considered an even swap of outfielders by the press, the Dodgers were given a slight edge by having added Paine.

Signed as an amateur free agent in 1949, the right-handed hitting Gino Cimoli, who would turn 29 in two weeks, did not reach the Dodgers until 1956. In three seasons, he had a composite .269 batting average and an 81 OPS+ in 324 games. He also had the distinction of being the first batter in a major league game played on the West Coast, when he led off against the San Francisco Giants' Rubén Gómez at Seals Stadium on April 15, 1958.

"I felt I deserved a better shake in 1958," said Cimoli, who was often accused of moodiness and lack of commitment. "Maybe I was sullen. But I'm not getting any younger, and if I'm going to have some good years they'd better be right now. Maybe it will do both clubs some good," he said. "I can sit next to Stan Musial and pick up some hitting pointers. Another thing the Cards will be closer to the pennant next year. The Dodgers are rebuilding, and I don't think they're going to reach the first division too quickly."[6] (Cimoli proved to be a poor prognosticator, as the Dodgers won the National League pennant in 1959.)

Wally Moon, a left-handed batter who would be 29 when the 1959 season began, broke in with the Cardinals in 1954. He batted .304 with 12 home runs and was voted the National League's Rookie of the Year. During his first four seasons in St. Louis, Moon never played in fewer than 142 games, but this last season, manager Freddie Hutchinson had given more outfield playing time to Curt Flood and Joe Cunningham. Moon played in only 108 games, batting .238, with seven home runs and an 84 OPS+. Despite that poor 1958 season, his batting average for 702 games in St. Louis was .291 with a 116 OPS+.

"Every time a player moves," Devine said, "you hope it will be an incentive to him. Wally played for me at Rochester, too, and I have a lot of respect for his ability, but I think Cimoli's all-around talent will strengthen our club."[7]

Phil Paine, a twenty-eight-year-old right-hander, had a career record of 10–1, spread over five seasons with the Boston and Milwaukee Braves and St. Louis. Five of the wins and one of the losses came with the Cardinals this past season. It was Paine's last big-league action. The Dodgers sent him to their PCL team in Spokane.

Moon played the final seven seasons of his career with the Dodgers, batting .286 with a 120 OPS+. His best season was his first, 1959, when he helped the Dodgers win their first pennant and world championship in Los Angeles. Moon batted .302, with 19 home runs, a 129 OPS+, a league-leading 11 triples, and a fourth-place finish in the voting for MVP.

Also in 1958:

Traded: Minor League Second Baseman Sparky Anderson to Philadelphia Phillies for Outfielder Rip Repulski, Pitcher Jim Golden, and Pitcher Gene Snyder

Purchased: Outfielder Solly Drake from Chicago Cubs; Minor League Third Baseman Ramón Conde from Philadelphia Phillies

Signed Amateur Free Agents: Willie Davis; Ron Fairly; Frank Howard; Earl Robinson; Pete Richert

Released: Shortstop Pee Wee Reese; Catcher Rube Walker

1959

June 15, 1959: Traded Third Baseman Dick Gray to the St. Louis Cardinals for Two Players to be Named and Cash

A doubleheader loss at Pittsburgh, which dropped the Dodgers to fifth place, led them to recall slugger Frank Howard from the Victoria (TX) Rosebuds, of the Class AA Texas League. The addition of Howard, who was batting .371 with 27 home runs in 63 games, necessitated the Dodgers removing a player from their roster. They did so by trading third baseman Dick Gray to the St. Louis Cardinals for two players currently in the minor leagues and cash.

Gray, 27, batted .249 with nine home runs and 30 runs batted in as a rookie in 1958. But when the Dodgers moved Jim Gilliam to third base this season, Gray lost his job. He had appeared in only 21 games with a .154 batting average.

Two days later, the Cardinals sent Chuck Essegian, a 27-year-old outfielder from their Rochester Red Wings team in the International League, to the Dodgers Spokane Indians team in the Pacific Coast League. The right-handed-hitting Essegian, who played in 39 games for the Phillies in 1958, had a .297 average in 10 games with the Red Wings this season.

The second player to be named was Lloyd Merritt, a 26-year-old right-hander. Merritt, who appeared in 44 games for the 1957 Cardinals, was also sent from Rochester to Spokane.

October 19, 1959: Traded First Baseman Jim Gentile to the Baltimore Orioles for Two Players to be Named and Cash

Slugging first baseman Jim Gentile, now 25, had spent years in the minor leagues stuck behind Gil Hodges. With Hodges now nearing the end of his career, the Dodgers appeared content to go into the 1960 season with 29-year-old Norm Larker as his replacement. Gentile, a left-handed-hitter, had been in the Dodgers system since 1952. He received brief trials with Brooklyn in 1957 and Los Angeles in 1958 and was on the opening day roster this spring but was later assigned to St. Paul.

The 6'3", 205-pound Gentile hit 208 home runs in eight minor league seasons, an average of 26 a year, and he never had fewer than 25 doubles in any season. He had his best year in 1956, with the Fort Worth Cats of the Texas League, when he hit 40 home runs and drove in 115 runs, while batting .296. Gentile spent most of his last three seasons at the Triple A level, with Montreal, Spokane, and St. Paul.

Gentile cost the Orioles a reported $50,000 and two players to be named in the spring of 1960. The move by the Orioles was another try at getting more long-ball power at first base, where Bob Boyd had been playing for most of the last four years. Gentile would be a resounding success in his four years in Baltimore, with 124 home runs, 398 runs batted in, and an OPS+ of 145. He was an All-Star in each of his first three seasons with the Orioles, finished second in Rookie of the Year voting in 1960, and third in MVP voting in 1961, the year he led the American League with 141 runs batted in.

In March 1960, the two players to be named were sent by the Orioles to a Dodgers minor league team to complete the deal. Veteran shortstop Willy Miranda went to St. Paul, and career minor league outfielder-first baseman Bill Lajoie went to the Atlanta Crackers of the Southern Association.

Also in 1959:

Traded: Minor League Pitcher Dick Hanlon to Cincinnati Reds for Pitcher Chuck Churn; Third Baseman Jim Baxes to Cleveland Indians for Infielder Fred Hatfield and Cash; Pitcher Ron Negray and Outfielder Bob Wilson to Toronto Maple Leafs of the International League for Second Baseman Mike Goliat; Pitcher Lloyd Merritt, Pitcher Phil Paine, and Infielder Fred Hatfield to Baltimore Orioles for First Baseman Frank Kellert and Outfielder Joe Frazier

Sold: Outfielder Solly Drake to Philadelphia Phillies

Signed Amateur Free Agents: Al Ferrara; Nate Oliver; Phil Ortega; Larry Miller; Nick Willhite.

Released: Outfielder Elmer Valo; Pitcher Leo Cristante; Second Baseman Dick Young

2

1960–1964

1960

April 5, 1960: Traded Pitcher Fred Kipp to the New York Yankees for Outfielder Gordon Windhorn and Minor League Third Baseman-Outfielder Dick Sanders

Left-hander Fred Kipp pitched in one game for the Dodgers in September 1957, the team's last month in Brooklyn. He was 6–6 as a rookie with Los Angeles in 1958, then spent most of 1959 with St. Paul, where he had a 14-11 record. He also appeared in two games with the Dodgers.

Kipp had never been, nor would he ever be, a successful major league pitcher. Nevertheless, the Dodgers thought highly of his baseball knowledge and had offered him a job in their organization after his playing days were over. Kipp was in four games for the 1960 Yankees (his final major league appearances) losing his only decision.

Both Gordon Windhorn, whose Yankees career consisted of 11 hitless at-bats in 1959, and Dick Sanders, who had never played (or ever would play) in the major leagues, had been with Richmond of the International League in 1959. The Dodgers kept them in the International League, assigning both to the Montreal Royals. Windhorn played in 34 games for the Dodgers in 1961, batting .242. After the season, he was traded to the Kansas City Athletics.

April 8, 1960: Traded Infielder Don Zimmer to the Chicago Cubs for Third Baseman John Goryl, Minor League Pitcher Ron Perranoski, Minor League Outfielder Lee Handley, and Cash

Don Zimmer lost his shortstop job to rookie Maury Wills in 1959. During spring training of 1960, Zimmer told the Dodgers to play me or trade me, so the Dodgers traded him. In return they received a reported $25,000 and three minor leaguers, all of whom they sent to their Triple A team at St. Paul. One was Lee Handley, an outfielder who never reached the majors. Another was Johnny Goryl, an infielder who batted .230 in parts of three seasons with the 1957–1959 Cubs. Goryl never played for the Dodgers, but he later would play three seasons with the Minnesota Twins, after they obtained him in the 1961 rule 5 draft. The third man was Ron Perranoski, a 24-year-old left-hander. Perranoski spent the 1960 season pitching for Los Angeles's Triple A clubs in St. Paul and Montreal. He would join the Dodgers in 1961, where he would become one of the great relief pitchers in franchise history.

The 29-year-old Zimmer had been battling Wills and Bob Lillis for the starting shortstop job. He felt no ill will toward the Dodgers. "I think I'm leaving the greatest organization in baseball," he said. "I still think I could have helped the Dodgers in spots. I'm not that bad. But I've felt this coming for a long time, and maybe it will be a break for me."[1]

In his six years as a Dodger, the 5'9", 165-pound Zimmer played second base, shortstop and third base, mostly as a backup. He was the starting shortstop in only one season, 1958, when he appeared in 127 games and batted .262 with 17 home runs and 60 runs batted in.

May 7, 1960: Traded Outfielder Sandy Amorós to the Detroit Tigers for First Baseman Gail Harris

Sandy Amorós was 22 when he played 20 games for the 1952 Dodgers. Sent to Montreal in 1953, the 5'7" Amorós led the International League in batting (.353), runs (128), and hits (190). He split the 1954 season between Brooklyn and Montreal. The Dodgers kept the speedy Cuban-born Amorós for all of 1955 through 1957. Being a left-handed fielder as well as batter allowed him to make a game-saving (and World Series–saving) catch in Game Seven of the 1955 World Series against the Yankees.

It was back to Montreal for Amorós in 1958 and 1959, except for five 1959 games with Los Angeles. He was the Dodgers leading hitter during spring training this year and was on the opening day roster. At the time of the trade, he had been in nine games with two hits in 14 at bats. His career totals for the Dodgers in Brooklyn and Los Angeles were a .260 batting average and a 110 OPS + in 452 games.

Twenty-eight-year-old Gail Harris was a left-handed-hitting first baseman who played three seasons for the New York Giants (1955–1957) and the last three for the Detroit Tigers. He had a composite batting average of .240 with an 88 OPS+ in 437 games. The Dodgers assigned Harris to St. Paul. He never returned to the major leagues.

June 15, 1960: Traded Pitcher Clem Labine to the Detroit Tigers for a Pitcher to be Named and Cash

Clem Labine had been in 13 games this season, with one decision, a loss that came in his last game as a Dodger. Labine was walking through the clubhouse after the game, when he heard an announcement coming from the press box that the club had traded him to the Detroit Tigers. Labine was 33, had not pitched well, and a roster spot had to be made for Roger Craig, who was coming off the disabled list. Yet it was an unceremonious way of informing one of the franchise's best relievers he was being traded.

Allowing him to learn he was being traded in this manner was not nearly as shameful as the release of Carl Furillo a month earlier, and Labine handled it in a graceful way. He wrote a note addressed to his teammates and taped it on a locker room wall: "Perhaps the most difficult thing in the world is putting into words what has been purely an emotion all my adult life," he wrote. "Wearing a Dodger uniform has become almost synonymous with my life. The wonderful association that I've had with all you fellows is something that I'll always cherish. Believe me, with all my heart I wish you all success, for deep within I'm sure I'll always remain a Dodger." After reading the note, Dodgers manager Walter Alston paid tribute to Labine. "When Clem had it, you couldn't ask for a better competitor."[2]

In his 11 seasons with the Dodgers, Labine had a 70–52 record, with 81 saves and a 113 ERA+. He set the franchise record for most appearances in a season, with 60 in 1955, and led the National League in saves in 1956 (19) and 1957 (17). While only 37 of his 425 appearances as a Dodger were as a starter, he pitched two of the most memorable shutouts in team history. Labine shut out the Giants in the second game of the 1951 National League playoff, 10–0, and he pitched a 10-inning 1–0 shutout against the Yankees in Game Six of the 1956 World Series.

The Tigers sent 29-year-old right-hander Ray Semproch to Los Angeles as the pitcher to be named. The Dodgers sent Semproch to the Spokane Indians of the Pacific Coast League, where he won 11 and lost two.

December 16, 1960: Sold Pitcher Danny McDevitt to the New York Yankees

A week earlier the New York Yankees lost three second-line pitchers—Eli Grba, Duke Maas, and Bobby Shantz—in the expansion draft held to stock the American League's new Los Angeles and Washington franchises. To fill one of those spots on the staff, they purchased left-hander

Danny McDevitt, a 28-year-old native New Yorker and boyhood Yankees fan. The Yankees had not been the only team looking to trade for McDevitt. The Kansas City Athletics, the expansion Washington Senators, and the Milwaukee Braves wanted him as well.

In four years with the Dodgers, one in Brooklyn and three in Los Angeles, McDevitt had a record of 19–22, with a 98 ERA+. He is best remembered for his 2–0 shutout of the Pittsburgh Pirates on September 24, 1957, the Dodgers final game at Ebbets Field.

McDevitt often was out of favor with manager Alston. Despite his 10–8 record and 107 ERA+ in 1959, he was the only Dodgers pitcher Alston did not use in the World Series against the Chicago White Sox. McDevitt made 23 appearances this past season, losing his only four decisions. His departure left the Dodgers with just two experienced left-handers, Johnny Podres and Sandy Koufax.

Also in 1960:

Traded: Outfielder Rip Repulski to Boston Red Sox for Pitcher Nelson Chittum

Sold: Pitcher Johnny Klippstein to Cleveland Indians; Outfielder Earl Robinson to Baltimore Orioles

Signed Amateur Free Agents: Ken McMullen; Joe Moeller; Jim Barbieri; Thad Tillotson; Hector Valle; Johnny Werhas

Signed Free Agents: Outfielder Irv Noren

Released: Outfielder Carl Furillo; Pitcher Tom Lasorda; Outfielder Irv Noren

1961

February 1, 1961: Sold Catcher Joe Pignatano to the Kansas City Athletics

His sale to the Kansas City Athletics ended 30-year-old catcher Joe Pignatano's four-year stint with the Dodgers. Signed as an amateur free agent in 1948, Pignatano spent seven seasons in the minor leagues and two in the army before playing eight games for the Dodgers in 1957, their last season in Brooklyn. Pignatano served as the backup to John Roseboro in 1958 and 1959 and split that role with Norm Sherry in 1960. A better defender than he was a hitter, he batted .229 with an 80 OPS+ in 181 games as a Dodger.

While Kansas City general manager Frank Lane acknowledged Pignatano's offensive weakness, he was pleased with the acquisition: "I now feel much better about our catching. We have in Pignatano a catcher who can at least throw and get somebody out. He is not only a good thrower, but he runs well and is a good receiver. I know he is not considered a good hitter, but he does have some power."[3] Lane hinted that he paid $30,000 for Pignatano, a figure Los Angeles general manager Buzzie Bavasi claimed was too high.

February 1, 1961: Sold Outfielder Chuck Essegian to the Baltimore Orioles

On the day they sold Joe Pignatano to the Kansas City Athletics, the Dodgers also sold outfielder Chuck Essegian to the Baltimore Orioles. The Orioles second-place finish in 1960—their highest since moving to Baltimore in 1954 and their best since winning the pennant as the St. Louis Browns in 1944—had them believing they could win the American League pennant in 1961. They had an excellent young pitching staff, led by Chuck Estrada, Milt Pappas, and Steve Barber. All that was missing, felt general manager Lee MacPhail, was more punch in their offense, which he hoped Essegian would provide.

"What we need is a right-handed hitter with power," said MacPhail. "Essegian certainly has the physical ability and, at times, has looked like he was ready to make it big. You never know. Stranger things have happened."[4]

Yet, Essegian, who hit .215 for the Dodgers in 1960, primarily as a pinch-hitter, had been available for $25,000 in last November's draft, and nobody took him. He cost the Orioles an estimated $20,000, but there was a condition attached to the sale. If the 29-year-old slugger was on Baltimore's opening day roster, the deal would stand. If not, he would go back to the Dodgers and the Orioles would get their money back.

Essegian, whom the Dodgers acquired in a June 1959 trade with the St. Louis Cardinals, played in 76 games with LA. He had a .248 batting average with just four home runs. Essegian is best remembered for setting a World Series record when he had two pinch-hit home runs in the 1959 World Series against the Chicago White Sox.

May 4, 1961: Traded Outfielder Don Demeter and Third Baseman Charley Smith to the Philadelphia Phillies for Pitcher Turk Farrell and Shortstop Joe Koppe

After several blown leads, culminating in Milwaukee's Joe Adcock game-ending grand slam off Jim Golden, dropped the Dodgers into fourth place it spurred them to seek bullpen help. The result was a trade of outfielder Don Demeter and infielder Charlie Smith to the Philadelphia Phillies, which brought them relief pitcher Turk Farrell and shortstop Joe Koppe.

Walt Alston was not sure how much the addition of Farrell would help his club's pennant chances. "We'll have to wait and see about this," he said. "We needed a little more help in the bullpen. It has been a little overworked. Ed Roebuck is out, and we want Larry Sherry to have more help."[5]

Farrell, a 27-year-old right-hander, had a 10–6 record with 11 saves and a 2.70 earned run average in 59 appearances with the Phillies in 1960. He was 2–1 with no saves in five games this season. Farrell started and lost his debut game in the major leagues, with the 1956 Phillies. It was his only appearance of the season and the only start of his career, to date. He had a career record of 31–25 with 48 saves.

Farrell split 12 decisions and had 10 saves for the Dodgers in 1961. In October, the Houston Colt .45s selected him with the fourth pick in the National League's expansion draft.

Thirty-year-old Joe Koppe, who broke in with the 1958 Braves, was in his third season in Philadelphia. He had a .237 batting average in 206 games, all but 16 with the Phillies. The Dodgers sent him to Spokane, and on May 16 traded him to the St. Louis Cardinals for outfielder Duke Carmel. They then sent Carmel, who had been playing with the Pacific Coast League's Portland Beavers, to Spokane.

The Dodgers, then in Brooklyn, signed Don Demeter as an amateur free agent in 1953. His 41 home runs and 128 runs batted in for the 1956 Fort Worth Cats of the Texas League earned the 21-year-old a three-game promotion to Brooklyn late that season. His home run hitting for St. Paul in 1957 and the first half of 1958 made the right-handed-hitting Demeter the apparent heir to Duke Snider as the Dodgers' center fielder. He did not hit enough to earn that mantle over 264 games with the club. He compiled a .247 batting average and an 85+ OPS, though he did hit 34 home runs.

Phillies general manager John Quinn said, "Demeter is one of the best fielding center fielders around and he might have 20 home runs in him." An excellent guess. Demeter, 26, hit exactly 20 home runs for the Phillies in 1961, and 51 more for them in 1962–1963. Quinn was also high on the 23-year-old Smith, saying he has "real good power and he may be the answer to our third base problems."[6] Smith, who hit .322 with 20 home runs for Spokane in 1960, batted .190 in 27 games over the past two seasons with Los Angeles.

May 30, 1961: Traded Shortstop Bob Lillis and Outfielder Carl Warwick to the St. Louis Cardinals for Shortstop Daryl Spencer

This trade had been agreed to a few days earlier, when the Dodgers were in St. Louis. Administrative problems prevented Dodgers general manager Buzzie Bavasi and Cardinals general manager Bing Devine from making it official until now.

"I wanted Spencer because we need right-handed power in the Coliseum," said manager Walter Alston. His new acquisition, who would turn 33 in July, was also pleased with the trade. "It's nice to jump a few notches in the standings overnight," said Spencer, who was moving from the sixth-place Cardinals to the third-place Dodgers. "The Cards treated me very well, but I like the idea of shooting at that [left field] screen more than 11 games a year. I'm curious to see how other pitchers besides the Dodgers work on me here." Cardinals manager Solly Hemus called Spencer "an aggressive, intelligent player."[7] Spencer had spent most of his career at shortstop, but Alston said he would play him at third base and move Tommy Davis from third to the outfield.

Spencer had hit well in the Los Angeles Coliseum as a member of the Cardinals, and before that with the San Francisco Giants. He had a .295 batting average with 10 home runs in 34 games there. Now in his eighth big league season, he had played in 904 games and hit 94 home runs. (He missed 1954 and 1955 because of army service.) Spencer had been in 37 games this season, with a .254 batting average and four home runs.

Appearing in 144 games over three seasons with the Dodgers, Spencer had a .237 batting average, 10 home runs, and an 89 OPS+. Los Angeles released Spencer in May 1963. Cincinnati signed him but released him in July, ending his major league career.

Carl Warwick was a 24-year-old rookie who had one hit and two walks in 13 plate appearances. However, he had hit well and with power in three minor league seasons. With the American Association's St. Paul Saints in 1960, he had a .293 batting average with 19 home runs and 75 runs batted in. Playing for the Victoria (TX) Rosebuds of the Texas League in 1959, he batted .331 with 35 home runs and 94 runs batted in.

Hemus called Warwick the key man in the deal. "We took all the gamble," he said. "We gave up an established winning-type player. Warwick figures in our long-term plans. He hit with power in the minors, and we know he's got good speed. Right now, though, Curt Flood remains in center field because he's been getting on base a lot." The Cardinals manager said he also liked what he had seen of Lillis. "He adds speed and defense to our infield, and that'll make our good pitching just that much better."[8]

The Dodgers signed Lillis, who would turn 31 in three days, as an amateur free agent in 1951. While they used him mainly for defensive purposes, he batted an impressive .296 for them over four seasons. Like Warwick, he had been used sparingly this season, one hit and one walk in 11 plate appearances. Lillis called the trade "a good deal for his wife. I'm in a better mood when I play."[9]

October 10, 1961: Lost First Baseman Gil Hodges, First Baseman Norm Larker, Pitcher Roger Craig, Pitcher Turk Farrell, Pitcher Jim Golden, and Infielder Bob Aspromonte in the National League Expansion Draft

Having voted to expand to ten teams for the 1962 season, the National League held a draft of its players to stock the new Houston Colt .45s and New York Mets. The Dodgers lost six players in the draft: first baseman Gil Hodges and pitcher Roger Craig to the Mets; and first baseman Norm Larker, pitcher Turk Farrell, pitcher Jim Golden, and infielder Bob Aspromonte to the Colt .45s.

Future Hall-of-Famer Gil Hodges (1943, 1947–1961) had been one of the greatest, and perhaps the most popular, players the Dodgers ever had. In addition to being an outstanding defensive first baseman, he remains among the team's top 10 in these offensive categories: games, 2,007 (4th); runs, 1,088 (5th); hits, 1,884 (9th); doubles, 294 (10th); home runs, 361 (2nd); runs batted in, 1,254 (2nd); and walks, 925 (3rd). He was an eight-time All-Star and received MVP votes in nine seasons.

Roger Craig (1955–1961) had a 49–38 record with an ERA+ of 110 in 187 games with the Dodgers. He led the league with four shutouts in 1959.

Norm Larker (1958–1961) had a .294 batting average and a 100 OPS+ in 437 games.

Turk Farrell (1961) had a 6–6 record with 10 saves in 50 games.

Jim Golden (1960–1961) had a 2–1 record with a 73 ERA+ in 29 games.

Bob Aspromonte (1956, 1960–1961) had a .211 batting average and a 36 OPS+ in 69 games.

Dodgers vice president Fresco Thompson felt the club was not badly hurt by the loss of the six players. "We have good young pitchers to bring up," he said, mentioning right-handers Phil Ortega and Joe Moeller and left-hander Pete Richert. "It's tough to lose good first basemen like Gil Hodges and Norm Larker, but we feel Tim Harkness is a real comer. To plug the loss of Bob Aspromonte there are boys like Larry Burright, a second baseman at Atlanta, and Dick Tracewski, an Omaha shortstop."[10]

Thompson commented on each of the departing Dodgers:

Aspromonte: "Of all the players we gave up, I hated to lose Bobby the most. He has fine potential and could be a very good hitter."

Larker: "He's as fine a hustler as any in the league. He has great desire and is out to beat you but lacks power."

Farrell: "Having a young club mainly, we felt he wasn't our kind of player." He can throw hard, but like Leo Durocher used to say, "You never knew when you put him in a game whether he'd slept nine hours or 20 minutes the night before."

Golden: "He has a fair fastball but didn't live up to our expectations."

Hodges: "This is like losing an old friend. Next spring will mark the first time Gil hasn't been in our training camp in 15 years. At Brooklyn, he had 100 runs batted and over 30 home runs for us several seasons but lost his batting eye in Los Angeles. He'll he back among friends In New York and should have a good season"

Craig: "Roger seemed lose the zip on his fastball and that pinpoint control he used to have. He could come back strong, however, as a reliefer."[11]

December 15, 1961: Traded Second Baseman Charlie Neal and a Player to be Named to the New York Mets for Outfielder Lee Walls and Cash

The first time Casey Stengel saw Charlie Neal was during the spring of 1956, when his Yankees played the Brooklyn Dodgers in four exhibition games. Stengel was so impressed with Neal, he called the 25-year-old rookie "the best second baseman the Dodgers have had since I managed them back in the thirties."[12] The Dodgers' second basemen in 1934–1936, when Stengel managed them, were Tony Cuccinello and Jimmy Jordan. The new Mets manager was obviously up to his old game of spoofing the writers. Among those who had played the position for the Dodgers since they fired Stengel were Hall of Famers Billy Herman and Jackie Robinson, plus Eddie Stanky and the current second baseman, Jim Gilliam.

In his six years with the Dodgers, Neal batted .265, with 73 home runs and a 93 OPS+. His OPS+ was above average only in 1958 (102) and in his best year, 1959 (106). That season he batted a career-high .287, with 19 home runs, a league-leading 11 triples, and an eight-place finish in the MVP voting. When skeptics questioned how good a player Neal was, pointing out the Dodgers never gave up a player for only money (in this case a reported $100,000) unless they knew something no one else did, Stengel brushed them aside. "I go by what I see with my own eyes," he said.[13]

Lee Walls, a 29-year-old outfielder, who could also play the infield, had played previously for the Pirates, the Cubs, the Reds, and the Phillies. A 6'3" right-handed-hitter, he batted .280 in 91 games for the Phillies this past season. The Mets obtained him in the player draft held to stock the two new National League franchises.

"Lee Walls is the type of player we wanted," Buzzie Bavasi said. "He can do whatever is needed of him, playing either in the infield or the outfield. And he can fill in whenever he is needed without losing any of his hitting ability."[14]

Walls played in 161 games for Los Angeles over the next three seasons. He had a .242 batting average and a 76 OPS+. The Dodgers released him in October 1964, ending his major league career.

On May 25, 1962, the Dodgers completed the trade by sending left-handed pitcher Willard Hunter to the Mets. Hunter, a rookie, had allowed 9 earned runs in two innings in his one game with the Dodgers. He went 1–6 in 27 games for the expansion Mets.

Also in 1961:

Traded: Pitcher Ed Rakow to Kansas City Athletics for Pitcher Howie Reed and Cash; Pitcher Ed Palmquist and Minor League First Baseman Joe Altobelli to the Minnesota Twins for Minor League Outfielder Ernie Oravetz and Cash; Outfielder Gordon Windhorn and Minor League Outfielder-First Baseman Bill Lajoie to Kansas City Athletics for Outfielder Bobby Prescott, Outfielder Stan Johnson, and Minor League Infielder Jay Ward,

Sold: Pitcher Art Fowler to Los Angeles Angels

Signed Amateur Free Agents: Jack Billingham; Cleo James; Roy Gleason; Dick Nen; Bart Shirley; Bill Singer

Signed Free Agents: First Baseman Joe Altobelli

1962

In 1962 the team moved from the Los Angeles Memorial Coliseum to Dodger Stadium.

November 26, 1962: Traded Pitcher Stan Williams to the New York Yankees for First Baseman Bill Skowron

Although the trade of pitcher Stan Williams to the Yankees for first baseman Bill Skowron was concluded on November 26, 1962, the deal had been set in motion two weeks earlier. Dodgers' general manager Buzzie Bavasi had written to his Yankees counterpart, Roy Hamey, informing him of the availability of Williams, a 26-year-old right-hander. Hamey said he was interested and that they would talk later at the winter meetings.

"We got the pitcher we wanted, and we're all set now," Hamey said after it became official. "This is it—as far as major deals for us is concerned." Yankees manager Ralph Houk said: "Williams fits into our plans perfectly. He's young, he can throw hard, and he won 14 games for the Dodgers this year. If he does the same for us next year, I'll be more than satisfied."

Bavasi was equally pleased. "Our first need was a right-handed long ball hitter, and we feel Skowron can be the man. We plan to platoon Skowron with Ron Fairly," he said, "and that will help us maneuver more. Last season they pitched too many left-handers against us."[15]

The Dodgers signed Williams as an amateur free agent in 1954. He had been with them since 1958, their first season in Los Angeles. The 6'5", 230-pound Williams had a 57–46 won-lost record with a 106 ERA+. Forty-three of his wins had come in the last three seasons: 14 in both 1960 and 1962, and 15 in 1961.

Williams said that if he had to be traded away from the Dodgers, he could not think of a club he would rather go to than the Yankees. "It hurts a little to be traded," he said. "I've been with the Dodgers organization for nine years. And we've built a new home here, which also makes it tough. But a change of pace might be a help to me. The Yankees are a fine baseball club. I got to know Ralph Houk when I was in the American Association."[16]

Signed out of Purdue University, Bill Skowron was voted Minor League Player of the Year in 1952 as a member of the American Association's Kansas City Blues. He had been the Yankees' full-time first baseman since 1955, except for 1959 when a bad back limited him to 74 games. Skowron batted better than .300 in each of his first four seasons with New York and five times overall. Always a dangerous hitter, he had a .294 lifetime batting average, with 165 home runs and 672 runs batted in. But he was now 32, and Joe Pepitone, ten years younger, was waiting to take over. "I hate to go, but that's baseball," Skowron said. "I'll do the best I can for the Dodgers. That's the only way I know how to play."[17]

November 30, 1962: Traded First Baseman Tim Harkness and Second Baseman Larry Burright to the New York Mets for Pitcher Bob Miller

The Dodgers made their second trade at the winter meetings with New York's other team, the Mets. They sent 24-year-old first baseman Tim Harkness [he would turn 25 in a month] and 25-year-old second baseman Larry Burright to the Mets for 23-year-old right-hander Bob Miller.

Miller, who split 18 decisions in four years with the Cardinals, was the Mets' first choice in the player pool when the league expanded this past year. He appeared in 33 games for New York in 1962, as a starter and a reliever. Miller made 21 starts, but had only one complete game, which came on the next-to-last day of the season and was his only win. He had a 1–12 record, with an ERA+ of 85.

But Bavasi recognized that the Mets, who won only 40 games, were a terrible team in 1962 and had no qualms about trading for Miller. "I've liked Miller for three or four years, and I know the Giants and Tigers were after him," he said.[18] Miller was expected to replace Stan Williams, with the hope he could match Williams's 14 victories of 1962.

Burright, a rookie, started the past season well, but finished with a .205 batting average in 115 games. The Dodgers expected to replace him at second base with rookie Nate Oliver, who batted .317 in 124 games with Spokane.

Harkness appeared in in 92 games for the Dodgers in 1962 but had just 73 plate appearances with a .258. batting average. Manager Alston used him primarily as a defensive replacement for Ron Fairly. Now that the club had Fairly and newly acquired Bill Skowron available for first-base duty, there was no room for Harkness.

Also in 1962:

Traded: Minor League Third Baseman Ramón Conde and Minor League Outfielder Jim Koranda to Chicago White Sox for Third Baseman Andy Carey; Minor League Infielder Jay Ward to Minnesota Twins for Minor League Pitcher Bert Cueto

Sold: Catcher Norm Sherry and Minor League Outfielder Dick Smith to New York Mets

Signed Amateur Free Agents: Dick Calmus; Jim Campanis; Derrell Griffith; Jim Lefebvre

Released: Third Baseman Andy Carey

1963

April 1, 1963: Sold Outfielder Duke Snider to the New York Mets

New York Mets president George Weiss had been trying all spring to engineer a deal that would bring them Duke Snider, a seven-time All-Star in Brooklyn. But the Dodgers wanted their former pitcher Roger Craig in return, and the Mets wanted only a straight sale. In the third week of March, the Dodgers put Snider, now 36, on the waiver list. He was immediately claimed by the Yankees and the Mets, but Buzzie Bavasi said he would deal only with the Mets.

Bavasi withdrew Snider from the waiver list on March 26, hoping to negotiate a deal with the Mets for more than the $20,000 waiver price; he hoped to get $40,000. March passed and still no deal had been made. "I talked to Buzzie Saturday night, and he still wasn't sure if I'd go. But if I go Buzzie will be doing me a favor. It'll be tough to leave a club I've been with all my life, and it'll be tough to go to a losing club," Snider said, referring to the Mets. "It's even tougher though to sit on the bench when you know you're still able to play. The way I've felt all spring, I can play in at least 110 games. My knee isn't as strong as it used to be, but it hasn't been sore."[19]

The next day, April 1, the deal was announced. Snider was sold to the Mets for $40,000. A Dodger since 1947, Snider was one of the club's most popular and productive players when the Dodgers were based in Brooklyn. He hit 40 or more home runs in each of his last five seasons there, but fell off badly after the move to Los Angeles, slowed by age and injuries.

Like Gil Hodges, another Brooklyn hero who preceded him to the Mets, Snider ranks high in almost every Dodgers offensive category. He is the leader in home runs (389) and runs batted in (1,271) and in the top 10 in games, 1,923 (7th); runs, 1,199 (3rd); hits, 1,995 (4th); doubles, 343 (2nd); and walks, 893 (4th). Snider received MVP votes in nine seasons, including second, third, and fourth-place finishes. He played in six World Series, batting .286 with 11 home runs and a 945 OPS. Snider remains the only player to have four home runs in two different World Series.

July 30, 1963: Traded Pitcher Ed Roebuck to the Washington Senators for Second Baseman Marv Breeding

The trade of Ed Roebuck to the lowly Washington Senators, for second baseman Marv Breeding, left the Dodgers with only three pitchers who had played in Brooklyn—Don Drysdale, Sandy Koufax, and Johnny Podres. An unhappy Roebuck put the blame for his departure on manager Walter Alston.

"I think the Dodgers will win the pennant this year in spite of Alston," he said. "It's sort of sad to leave but in another way it's almost like getting out of prison—getting away from Alston." Roebuck said he felt he had been treated very poorly this season and his manager was to blame. "The first part of the year it was Roebuck every day. Every game I've lost so far has been on errors, not that I've pitched that well. Then they didn't use me for two- or three-weeks sort of sloughed me aside. And nobody said a word. Somebody could have told me, look, you did a job for us last year so don't worry about it."[20] Last year (1962), Roebuck had a 10–2 record with a 118 ERA+ in a career high 64 games. This season he was 2–4 and his ERA+ had fallen to 71.

Roebuck, a 32-year-old right-hander, had been a fixture in the Dodgers' bullpen since 1955. He appeared in 322 games (all but one in relief) and had a 40–22 record, 43 saves, and a 113 ERA+.

Marv Breeding, 29, played with Baltimore for three seasons before he was traded to Washington in December 1962. He batted .248 with a 65 OPS+ in 337 games for the Orioles and had a .274 average in 58 games for the Senators this season. Primarily a second baseman, he also could play third base and shortstop. Breeding batted .167 in 20 games for the 1963 Dodgers. He was playing for Spokane in 1964, when the Dodgers sold him to Baltimore in August. The Orioles sent Breeding to the Rochester Red Wings of the International League. He never returned to the major leagues.

December 6, 1963: Sold First Baseman Bill Skowron to the Washington Senators

The sale of Bill Skowron was announced as a straight cash deal for slightly over the $20,000 waiver price. Acquired from the New York Yankees in November 1962, the 33-year-old Skowron batted .203, with four home runs and 19 RBIs in 89 games, far below the production the club had expected. Skowron did his best work in the 1962 World Series sweep of the Yankees. Appearing in all four games, he had five hits, including a home run, in 13 at-bats and drove in three runs.

Skowron became the fourth Dodger sent to the Senators since Gil Hodges became Washington's manager, joining pitcher Ed Roebuck, infielder Don Zimmer, and catcher Mike Brumley. Buzzie Bavasi denied that a two-way street existed between Los Angeles and Washington, like the one between the Yankees and the Kansas City Athletics a few years earlier. "That's a lot of nonsense," the Dodgers GM said. "A lot of clubs were interested in Skowron, but Washington made me the first and the best offer."[21]

Also in 1963:

Traded: Minor League Pitcher Scott Breeden to Cincinnati Reds for Infielder Don Zimmer; Pitcher Dick Scott to Chicago Cubs for Pitcher Jim Brewer and Catcher Cuno Barragan
Sold: Don Zimmer to Washington Senators; Mike Brumley to Washington Senators
Signed Amateur Free Agents: Wes Parker; Jeff Torborg
Released: Third Baseman Daryl Spencer

1964

April 9, 1964: Traded Pitcher Larry Sherry to the Detroit Tigers for Outfielder Lou Johnson and Cash

The Dodgers were still in Brooklyn, in 1953, when they signed Los Angeles native Larry Sherry out of high school. Six years later, in 1959, Sherry, now 23, won seven and lost two as a starter and reliever following his midseason call up from the St. Paul Saints. He topped off the 1959 season with a sensational display of relief pitching to help the Dodgers win their second World Series and their first in Los Angeles. Appearing in relief in four games against the Chicago White Sox, he had two wins and a 0.71 earned run average over 12⅔ innings. Sherry's performance earned him the Series' Most Valuable Player Award.

Over the next three seasons, the 6'2" right-hander was the workhorse of the Dodgers bullpen, pitching in 168 games with 25 wins and 33 saves. Sherry's effectiveness declined in 1963—a 2–6 record and only three saves. After appearing in more than 50 games in each of the 1960, 1961, and 1962 seasons, he was used just 36 times in 1963, and not at all in that year's World Series sweep of the Yankees. A few days before the 1964 opener, the Dodgers traded Sherry to the Detroit Tigers for outfielder Lou Johnson and a reported $20,000. Johnson had some major league experience but had spent the 1963 season with three different minor league teams.

The Dodgers assigned him to the Spokane Indians of the Pacific Coast League.

Manager Alston said he was sorry to see Sherry go. "Without him, we never would have won the pennant and the World Series in 1959," Alston said. "He's a hard worker and always puts out 100 percent." However, Alston added "it could be a nice break for Larry, because he'll probably get to pitch more often for the Tigers."[22]

Sherry had mixed feelings about the trade. "I hate to leave L.A. and the Dodgers, but I've never been content to sit idle," he said. "[Tigers manager] Chuck Dressen phoned me this morning and told me he had some plans for me as a relief pitcher."[23] When asked if he thought Sherry could still be an effective pitcher, Dressen said, "I think so. We've been trying to get him for a long time."[24] (Sherry would have 18 wins and 36 saves for Detroit over the next three seasons.)

The favorite to replace Sherry in the Dodgers' bullpen was Jim Brewer a 26-year-old left-hander. Brewer came to the Dodgers from the Chicago Cubs in December 1963, along with catcher Cuno Barragan in exchange for left-hander Dick Scott. In his four seasons with the Cubs, Brewer had a 4–13 record and zero saves. Currently on the Dodgers Spokane roster he had been impressive as a relief pitcher during spring training. "He has control and keeps the ball down, which is what you're looking for in a relief pitcher." Alston said. "We have until Monday midnight to decide who we'll put on the roster, so there's no point in rushing into a decision now."[25]

Alston did decide to bring Brewer to Los Angeles, which proved to be a wise decision. Brewer spent 12 seasons with the club. He appeared in 474 games (fourth all-time for the Dodgers), with a 61–51 record, 126 saves (fifth all-time for the Dodgers), and a 2.62 earned run average. The Dodgers traded him to the California Angels on July 15, 1975, for a player to be named. A week later they received pitcher Dave Sells. Sells was 0–2 over the remainder of the season and never pitched again in the major leagues.

December 4, 1964: Traded Outfielder Frank Howard, Third Baseman Ken McMullen, Pitcher Phil Ortega, Pitcher Pete Richert, and a Player to be Named to the Washington Senators for Pitcher Claude Osteen, Infielder John Kennedy, and Cash

The Dodgers had completed several transactions with the Washington Senators since ex-Dodger Gil Hodges became Washington's manager early in the 1963 season. They had been minor deals, but not this one, concluded on the final day of the winter meetings in Houston. The Dodgers sent four young players, including power-hitting outfielder Frank Howard, to Washington for pitcher Claude Osteen, infielder John Kennedy, and a reported $100,000.

Howard, a $108,000 bonus baby, had been in the Dodgers organization since 1958. A 6'7" right-handed slugger, he hit a combined 80 home runs in his two seasons in the minors. His manager with the Class AA Victoria (TX) Rosebuds in 1959 was Pete Reiser, the former Brooklyn outfielder. Reiser had this to say about Howard: "In 25 years in baseball I've never seen anyone hit the ball like Howard. And I saw [Ralph] Kiner when he came up and [Hank] Greenberg in his prime and I saw [Babe] Ruth at the tail end at his career. If he keeps improving this kid will break Ruth's home run record and he'll hit .380 doing it."[26]

The Dodgers brought Howard to Los Angeles in 1960, where he won the Rookie of the Year Award. He had his best season in 1962, when he batted .296, hit 31 home runs, drove in 119 runs, and had a 146 OPS+. Howard batted only .226 this past season but still had 24 home runs and an OPS+ of 111. Overall, Howard hit 123 home runs and had a 125 OPS+ in 624 games as a Dodger. He would win two American League home run titles with Washington and finish his 16-year career with 382 home runs and a 142 OPS+.

"I wasn't sure how he would take it," Hodges, his former teammate, said. "He took it wonderfully. Frank was very enthused about coming to us. His attitude was excellent. We talked for a while and he said, 'You know me Gilly. I'll give you 100 percent'"[27]

The deal was the Senators second of the day. Earlier, they traded outfielder Chuck Hinton to the Cleveland Indians for outfielder Woodie Held and first baseman Bob Chance. The additions moved Hodges to say, "I believe we now have as much power as any club in the American League."[28] (Washington would have 136 home runs in 1965, sixth best in the 10-team AL.)

For the past three seasons, Ken McMullen, a right-handed hitting third baseman, moved between the Dodgers and several of their minor league affiliates. Over that span, he appeared in only 109 games at the major league level. He was in the army for part of this past season, batting .209 in 24 games when he returned.

Pete Richert, a 25-year-old left-hander, had also spent the last three seasons moving between the Dodgers and their various minor league affiliates. He had a 12–10 record in 47 games for Los Angeles. His 1964 record was 2–3 with LA and 7–8 with Spokane. Right-hander Phil Ortega, 25, won seven and lost nine for the Dodgers in 1964. Richert and Ortega would pitch well for poor Washington teams over the next few seasons. Richert would win 29 games over the next two seasons, and Ortega would win 34 over the next three seasons.

Claude Osteen was 22 when the Cincinnati Reds traded him to Washington in September 1961. A member of the Reds for parts of four seasons, he appeared in only 26 games, and his one decision was a loss. The Senators put the 5'11" left-hander into their rotation and he quickly became the ace of their staff. Pitching for teams that finished tied for nineth, tenth, tenth, and nineth, he won 33 games with a 111 ERA+. He had 15 wins this past season for a team that won only 62.

Buzzie Bavasi believed the addition of Osteen gave the Dodgers the best four-man rotation in the major leagues. "Where will you find a starting staff better than Sandy Koufax, Don Drysdale, Johnny Podres, and Osteen," he said.[29]

John Kennedy, a 23-year-old infielder, had spent partial seasons with Washington in 1962 and 1963 and a full season in 1964. Playing shortstop and third base, he batted .230 with a 68 OPS+ in 148 games.

On December 15, the Dodgers sent first baseman Dick Nen to the Senators as the player to be named.

Also in 1964:

Traded: Pitcher Larry Miller to New York Mets for Outfielder-First Baseman Dick Smith

Sold: Pitcher Ken Rowe to Baltimore Orioles; Second Baseman Marv Breeding to Baltimore Orioles; Pitcher Nick Willhite to Washington Senators; Catcher Doug Camilli to Washington Senators

Signed Amateur Free Agents: Willie Crawford; Tommy Dean; Mike Kekich; John Purdin; Bill Sudakis; Don Sutton; Chuck Goggin

Signed Free Agents: First Baseman Tom Hutton

Released: Outfielder Lee Walls

3

1965–1969

1965

In 1965, Major League Baseball instituted a draft for amateur players.

December 15, 1965: Traded Infielder Dick Tracewski to the Detroit Tigers for Pitcher Phil Regan

The Brooklyn Dodgers signed 18-year-old Dick Tracewski as an amateur free agent in 1953. He made his major league debut in 1962, when the Dodgers were in Los Angeles, and had been a weak-hitting backup infielder for the past four seasons. Tracewski appeared in 303 games, with a .231 batting average and an OPS+ of 76. After the trade he became an even weaker-hitting backup infielder in his four seasons with the Tigers.

Six-foot-two right-hander Phil Regan had been a journeyman pitcher for Detroit the past six seasons. He was in 170 games (101 as a starter) with a record of 42–44 and an ERA+ of 86. Regan had his best season in 1963, when he led the Tigers in wins, with 15 (15–9), but he had only six wins and 15 losses over the past two seasons.

Arthur "Red" Patterson, of the Dodgers front office, said Regan, who would be 29 in 1966, would be the team's fourth starter behind Sandy Koufax, Don Drysdale, and Claude Osteen. "Tracewski is a top shortstop," Patterson said. "But we want to strengthen our pitching staff."[1]

Also in 1965:

  Purchased: Pitcher Nick Willhite from Washington Senators
  Chosen in Amateur Free Agent Draft: Jim Fairey; Alan Foster; Gary Moore; Leon Everitt
  Released: Outfielder Wally Moon

1966

May 10, 1966; Traded Pitcher Johnny Podres to the Detroit Tigers for a Player to be Named or Cash

The trade of Johnny Podres to Detroit left only four Dodgers remaining from when the team played in Brooklyn: Jim Gilliam, Don Drysdale, Sandy Koufax, and John Roseboro.

"I had an idea it was coming," said Podres, who had pitched in only one game this season. "When they don't use you, you have to suspect that something is coming. I'm glad I'm going somewhere where I can pitch."[2]

The 33-year-old left-hander was going to Detroit, where Charlie Dressen was the manager. It was Dressen who managed the Dodgers in 1953 when Podres broke in. "Buzzie [Bavasi] gave me a chance to choose among three clubs. I picked Charlie's over Kansas City and Boston."[3]

Podres had eight double-digit win seasons for the Dodgers, with a high of 18 in 1961, the year his .783 winning percentage led the National League. Elbow surgery had slowed him the last two seasons, and rookie Don Sutton's impressive spring training had earned him a spot in the starting rotation, replacing Podres.

In his 13 years as a Dodger Podres won 136 and lost 104, with an ERA+ of 107. His most memorable win was his 2–0 shutout of the Yankees in Game Seven of the 1955 World Series, earning the Dodgers their first world championship. He remains in the Dodgers' top ten in wins, starts, strikeouts, and shutouts. "It's tough to see Podres go," said manager Walt Alston. "He's been a real money pitcher. While his record may not have been outstanding the last few years, he could rise to the occasion."[4]

September 10, 1966: Traded Minor League Pitcher Thad Tillotson and Cash to the New York Yankees for Shortstop Dick Schofield

The Dodgers were in a battle for the National League pennant with the Pittsburgh Pirates and the San Francisco Giants. They wanted Dick Schofield, a 14-year veteran, for insurance should shortstop Maury Wills' troublesome right knee keep him from playing. The Yankees had purchased Schofield from the Giants in May, but now that they were on their way to a tenth-place finish, they had no use for a .155-hitting utility infielder.

Manager Walter Alston would use Schofield mostly at third base in the season's remaining weeks. Schofield batted .257 for the pennant-winning Dodgers and then stayed around the major leagues with various teams for another five years.

Right-hander Thad Tillotson had been in the Dodgers system since 1960 but had yet to pitch for the parent club. He pitched for the Pacific Coast League's Spokane Indians the past three seasons, winning 33 and losing 32.

November 29, 1966: Traded Outfielder Tommy Davis and Outfielder Derrell Griffith to the New York Mets for Second Baseman Ron Hunt and Outfielder Jim Hickman

According to GM Buzzie Bavasi, he had been discussing trades with the New York Mets for about a month. The Dodgers first expressed interest in veteran third baseman Ken Boyer, who had just finished his first season in New York after 11 seasons with the St. Louis Cardinals. While nothing came of that, the Mets asked Bavasi if he would be willing to trade outfielders Tommy Davis and Derrell Griffith for All-Star second baseman Ron Hunt. Bavasi said he needed another outfielder to offset the loss of Griffith. The Mets offered to include Jim Hickman and the deal was made.

Tommy Davis was playing golf with friend and teammate Willie Davis when he got the news he had been traded. "Tommy didn't let on too much as to whether he felt bad or good," Willie told a radio station. "He said his mother would be happy because that [New York] is his home."[5]

Tommy Davis had put together an excellent career with the Dodgers, including back-to-back batting championships in 1962 and 1963. Davis also led the league in hits and RBIs in 1962. He fell off some in 1964 and missed almost all of 1965 with a broken ankle. Playing in 100 games this past season, at age 27, he batted .313, but his power numbers were greatly reduced. His overall batting average as a Dodger was .304 with a 117 OPS+ in 821 games.

When Walter Alston was asked why someone as good a hitter as Davis was not playing every day, he said: "I had a choice, and Lou Johnson was pretty consistent. In the big outfield, Johnson covered more ground."[6]

Derrell Griffith was a 23-year-old left-handed batter who could play in the outfield and at third base. In 1964, his rookie season, Griffith played in 78 games and batted .290 with a 111 OPS+ but spent most of the past two seasons in the minor leagues. Mets manager Wes Westrum said he would work Griffith "a lot at third base and also in the outfield. I'm interested mostly in his bat."[7] However, Griffith would never play for the Mets as they traded him to the Houston Astros in March 1967. But he never played for Houston either; his major league career was now over.

In four seasons with the Mets, Ron Hunt had a .282 batting average and a 107 OPS+. He finished second to Pete Rose in 1963's Rookie of the Year voting and had twice been an All-Star. Hunt said he had heard rumors that he would be traded but hoped to stay with the Mets. "I started with the Mets ... but we can't get everything we want."[8]

The acquisition of Hunt, a 26-year-old second baseman, would allow the Dodgers to move Jim Lefebvre from second to third, and John Kennedy from third to shortstop. Kennedy would replace Maury Wills, who was expected to be traded.

Twenty-nine-year-old Jim Hickman, a right-handed-hitting outfielder, was an original member of the 1962 expansion New York Mets. He was a regular in their outfield from 1962 to 1965, but a broken finger limited him to just 58 games this past season.

December 1, 1966: Traded Shortstop Maury Wills to the Pittsburgh Pirates for Third Baseman Bob Bailey and Shortstop Gene Michael

Two weeks after Sandy Koufax announced his retirement, the Dodgers traded Maury Wills, their second biggest star, to the Pittsburgh Pirates. Dodgers GM Buzzie Bavasi had talked to several clubs about his 34-year-old shortstop before concluding the deal with his Pirates counterpart, Joe L. Brown.

Wills, a switch-hitter, was 26 when he broke in with the Dodgers in 1959. Beginning in 1960, he led the National League in stolen bases for the next six seasons. (He also led in being caught stealing seven times.) His 104 steals in 1962 broke the long-standing season record held by Ty Cobb and helped earn him the Most Valuable Player Award. Wills is the franchise leader in career steals, with 490. His speed on the bases made him a drawing card in Los Angeles and around the league. But he stole only 38 bases in 1966—down from 94 in 1965—and he had angered owner Walter O'Malley by leaving the team during a postseason tour of Japan.

Wills had mentioned a preference to go to the Yankees, saying he might quit if he did not like where he was traded. He initially balked at going to Pittsburgh, but quickly reconsidered. "Pittsburgh has a great club," he said. "They might have had the best team in the National League last season. No player should feel bad about going to a contender. Leaving the Dodgers is by no means the end of the world."[9]

Brown said Wills probably would bat first or second. "We should have additional offensive strength because we're going to have Wills hitting ahead of all those other good hitters," he said. "Also, I think Wills will stimulate aggressiveness on the part of others on our team who have latent base-running ability."[10]

The Pirates signed 18-year-old Bob Bailey in 1961, giving him a bonus reported to be anywhere between $125,000 and $175,000. Bailey played briefly for the Pirates at the end of 1962 and had been their third baseman and part-time left fielder since 1963. He had a .257 batting average and a 99 OPS+ in 596 games with Pittsburgh.

Bailey was ecstatic about coming to the Dodgers. "The chance to play at home is the best thing that could happen to my career," said Bailey, a native of Long Beach. "How do I feel about leaving a potential pennant winner in the Pirates? I'll tell you. I think the Dodgers are a potential pennant winner, too, and I want to make them so."[11]

Gene Michael, a 28-year-old rookie this past season, batted only .152 with a 15 OPS+ in 33 plate appearances. But he was an excellent shortstop, and the Dodgers saw him as Wills' replacement.

Also in 1966:

Traded: Pitcher Howie Reed to California Angels for Pitcher Dick Egan and a player to be named; Pitcher Nick Willhite to California Angels for Pitcher Bob Lee

Chosen in Amateur Free Agent Draft: Charlie Hough; Bill Russell; Billy Grabarkewitz; Ted Sizemore; Ray Lamb; Bob Stinson

Signed Amateur Free Agents: John Duffie

Signed Free Agents: Outfielder Wes Covington; First Baseman Dick Stuart

Chosen in Major League Draft: Pitcher Bruce Brubaker

Released: Third Baseman Jim Gilliam; Outfielder Wes Covington; First Baseman Dick Stuart

1967

April 3, 1967: Traded Infielder John Kennedy to the New York Yankees for Pitcher Jack Cullen, Outfielder John Miller, and Cash

Yankees manager Ralph Houk had been disappointed with the mobility afield of both his shortstops, Ruben Amaro and Dick Howser. Houk felt

Amaro did not have the range he had had before his 1966 knee operation, and Howser, the backup, just lacked the physical skills to play the position. So, with the exhibition season nearing its end, the Yankees made a deal for the Dodgers John Kennedy. Although 25-year-old Kennedy had played mostly at third base in his five-year career with the Washington Senators and the Dodgers, Houk planned to use him at shortstop. Kennedy played in 229 games in his two seasons in Los Angeles. He batted .171 and .201 and had a combined OPS+ of 47.

While acknowledging Kennedy's poor hitting, manager Walt Alston paid tribute to his contributions. "John never did get to play regularly with us," he said, "but he went in defensively for us in spots and did a helluva job. It was not one of the most pleasant assignments, but he did it willingly. And he helped us win a couple of pennants."[12]

Right-handed pitcher Jack Cullen and outfielder John Miller were Yankees farmhands, each of whom had made brief appearances with the club. Cullen had a 4–4 record in 19 games spread over three years (1962, 1965, and 1966), while Miller batted .087 in six games in 1966. The Dodgers sent them both to their Pacific Coast League team at Spokane.

The Yanks also sent a reported $25,000 to Los Angeles and transferred outfielder-second baseman Roy White to the Dodgers' Spokane club on option. White had a disappointing rookie season in 1966 after batting .333 in 14 late-season games in 1965. He would return to the Yankees later in the 1967 season.

May 10, 1967: Traded Third Baseman Johnny Werhas to the California Angels for Outfielder Len Gabrielson

Fittingly, in this trade with their American League neighbors, the Dodgers and California Angels traded players who had been teammates on coach Rod Dedeaux's 1959 University of Southern California's varsity. The Dodgers had signed Johnny Werhas, now 29, after his graduation from USC in 1960. He spent most of the next five years in Los Angeles's minor league system, including several fine seasons at Triple A Spokane.

Werhas, a 6'2" right-handed batter, was the Dodgers' third baseman on Opening Day 1964, but played only 29 games and spent most of the season back at Spokane. He played in four games for Los Angeles in 1965 and had been in seven games this season. His combined batting average for those 40 games was .183 and his OPS+ was 51. Over the rest of what would be his final major league season, Werhas batted .160 in 49 games with the Angels.

Twenty-seven-year-old Len Gabrielson was a 6'4" left-handed hitter who had played for the Milwaukee Braves, Chicago Cubs, and San

Francisco Giants before being traded to the Angels for outfielder Norm Siebern this past winter. In only three of those seasons did he appear in more than 100 games. Gabrielson played in 324 games in his four seasons with the Dodgers, his final four as a major leaguer. He had a .262 batting average with a 111 OPS+. Gabrielson had his best season in 1968, when he batted .270 with a 137 OPS+ in 108 games.

November 28, 1967: Traded Catcher John Roseboro, Pitcher Ron Perranoski, and Pitcher Bob Miller to the Minnesota Twins for Pitcher Jim Grant and Shortstop Zoilo Versalles

This was the first major trade at the winter meetings in Mexico City, and it was a big one. The Dodgers gave the Minnesota Twins catcher John Roseboro and pitchers Ron Perranoski and Bob Miller. In return they received shortstop Zoilo Versalles and pitcher Jim "Mudcat" Grant.

"The deal helps both clubs where they were hurting the most," said the Dodgers' Buzzie Bavasi. "They needed relief pitching and a catcher and we needed a shortstop." The key man for the Dodgers was Versalles, the American League's Most Valuable Player in 1965. Bavasi said he first offered Roseboro and Perranoski for Versalles, but Twins president Calvin Griffith turned him down. "Calvin Griffith asked me to give them Miller, too," Bavasi said. "I said I couldn't do that, give up two relief men and Roseboro, too. He asked if I'd have an interest in Grant and I said I would. So, we had a deal. Cal is very easy to do business with. I think this is the easiest deal I ever made."[13]

"We feel all three of the people we've picked up are going to be instrumental in helping us," said Twins manager Cal Ermer. "We got a guy who can catch and a good right-handed and left-handed relief pitcher. I think we're going to be more than adequate at shortstop. We have Cesar Tovar and Jackie Hernandez." As for the players he gave up, Ermer said: "I think Grant is still a very competent pitcher. One reason we made this deal was that we didn't want to trade him to any other club in the American League. We feel he is going to come back and have a good year. Versalles is still young and has great ability." Asked about reports of a personality conflict with Grant, Ermer said: "It's a long story. But he did ask to be traded at one point in the season because he wasn't pitching."[14]

In getting Grant and Versalles, the Dodgers were getting two of the stars on the Twins team they played in the World Series two years earlier. Grant led the American League in wins that year, while Versalles had been the league's Most Valuable Player. Grant, 32, had not come close to his 1965 performance since, and in 1968, his one season in LA, Alston used him almost exclusively in relief. Grant had a 6–4 record with a 2.08 earned run average and three saves.

Versalles, 28, had followed his MVP season with another good season in 1966, but had had a terrible season in 1967. Nevertheless, for the last two years the Dodgers had been looking for a shortstop to replace Maury Wills and hoped they had found him in Versalles. Unfortunately, they had not. Versalles would have an even worse season as a Dodger in 1968, batting a lowly .196, and he and Grant would both be gone after the season. The National League would be adding franchises in Montreal and San Diego in 1969, and both were taken in the expansion draft—Grant by the Expos and Versalles by the Padres.

Getting Ron Perranoski for Don Zimmer in April 1960 ranks as one of the Dodgers best trades. This was one of their worst. Perranoski pitched in 457 games for Los Angeles—all but one in relief—from 1961 through 1967. He had a 54–41 record and 100 saves. His best season was with the 1963 World Series winners, a league leading .842 winning percentage (16–3) and an ERA+ of 179. While pitching strictly in relief, Perranoski won 24 games for the Twins over the next three years and led the American League in saves in 1969 and 1970.

John Roseboro had been the Dodgers first-string catcher ever since the team moved to LA ten years earlier. He played in 1,289 games, with .251 batting average and a 97 OPS+ and was an excellent defensive catcher. And, although he was now 35, he would be Minnesota's first-string catcher for the next two seasons.

Roseboro and Perranoski were philosophical about leaving the Dodgers. "Any time you leave an eighth-place club for a contender, it's like writing home for five dollars and getting ten," said Roseboro. Perranoski said all the players were aware the club would be making changes. "The seven years here have been the finest in my whole life. Now I'll try my best to help Minnesota win the pennant next year."[15]

Bob Miller spent five years with the Dodgers. He pitched in 275 games, including a league leading 74 in 1964. He won 29 and lost 33, had 24 saves, and an ERA+ of 104. Miller spent two years with the Twins and then played for several other teams, ending his career with the 1974 New York Mets

November 30, 1967: Traded Outfielder Lou Johnson to the Chicago Cubs for Infielder Paul Popovich and Minor League Outfielder Jim Williams

Lou Johnson began his major league career with the 1960 Chicago Cubs. The Dodgers acquired him in an April 1964 trade that sent pitcher

Larry Sherry to the Detroit Tigers. Johnson had been the Dodgers left fielder the past three seasons and helped them win pennants in 1965 and 1966. Overall, he played 387 games in his three seasons in LA, with a .267 batting average and a 111 OPS+.

Johnson broke an ankle while sliding home on April 27 this season, but still managed to get into 104 games and bat .270. "He scored 13 winning runs for us," said Dodgers vice president Arthur Patterson, "and he drove in eight winning runs." Cubs manager Leo Durocher said Johnson would be his right fielder. "Finally, I'll be able to write one right fielder into the lineup. Last season, we used about 11 guys out there." When asked about Johnson's age (33), Durocher said, "do I care what his age is? Age is relative. He's a swinging 23."[16]

His departure was less than sweet for "Sweet Lou," as the fans called him. "I got traded for personal reasons for a couple of things that happened—and not for my ball-playing," he said without revealing what the "personal reasons" were. "In this game I long since learned to expect the ordinary and the extraordinary." "I'll say one thing," he added, "it sure doesn't pay for a Dodger to break his ankle."[17]

Paul Popovich, 27, appeared in 49 games for the Cubs last season and hit .214 with an OPS+ of 43. "Our shortstop (Don Kessinger) and second baseman (Glenn Beckert) were both in the [military] reserve program," said Chicago's general manager John Holland, "and Popovich filled in very well for them. He is an outstanding glove man." Walter Alston agreed. "I saw Popovich at short, and I was quite impressed."[18]

Jim Williams, a 20-year-old right-handed hitter, batted .248 for the Quincy (IL) Cubs of the Midwest League this year. He hit 17 home run and drove in 70. Williams reached the major leagues with San Diego in 1969 and played two seasons with the Padres.

November 30, 1967: Sold Shortstop Gene Michael to the New York Yankees

Two days earlier the Dodgers thought they had solved their shortstop problem when they traded for Minnesota's Zoilo Versalles. That allowed them to part with the two men who had filled the position this past season. They sold 29-year-old journeyman Gene Michaels to the Yankees and released his backup, Dick Schofield. Serving as Maury Wills' replacement in 1967, Michael batted a measly .202 with an OPS+ of 41 and no home runs in 98 games for the Dodgers.

Baltimore's Luis Aparicio was the shortstop the Yankees had targeted, but Aparicio's original team, the Chicago White Sox, outbid them.

Instead, for a reported $30,000, they settled for Michael. Although never much of a hitter—his lifetime average was just .229—Michael would spend seven years with the Yankees, five of them (1969–1973) as the club's regular shortstop.

Also in 1967:

Traded: Outfielder-First Baseman Dick Smith to the Minnesota Twins for Pitcher Jerry Fosnow; Pitcher Dick Calmus to Chicago Cubs for Pitcher Fred Norman
Sold: Pitcher Bob Lee to Cincinnati Reds
Chosen in Amateur Free Agent Draft: Steve Yeager
Signed Amateur Free Agents: Von Joshua; Tim Johnson
Chosen in Major League Draft: Pitcher Vicente Romo
Chosen in Minor League Draft: Pitcher Mike Strahler
Released: Third Baseman Dick Schofield

1968

February 13, 1968: Traded Second Baseman Ron Hunt and Second Baseman Nate Oliver to the San Francisco Giants for Catcher Tom Haller

The Dodgers and Giants had not made a trade with one another since 1956, when both teams were still in New York. That was the trade of Jackie Robinson from Brooklyn to the Giants for pitcher Dick Littlefield, a trade that was voided when Robinson chose to retire. But Los Angeles needed help behind the plate and San Francisco needed help at second base, so this trade figured to help both teams.

For San Francisco, Ron Hunt would be a big improvement over Tito Fuentes at second base, the Giants weakest infield position. Hunt, who batted .263 with an OPS+ of 107 for the Dodgers in 1967, had a .278 batting average in his five seasons in the National League. Twenty-six-year-old Nate Oliver, who could also play shortstop, spent five years with the Dodgers. Appearing in 329 games, he had a .234 batting average and a 69 OPS+.

For Los Angeles, manager Walt Alston was pleased at getting Tom Haller, an experienced and knowledgeable catcher to replace the departed John Roseboro. Haller was a 6'4" left-handed hitter who had been with the

Giants for seven seasons. He had a .248 batting average with 107 home runs and a 114 OPS+. Haller, 30, hit .251 for the Giants this past season, including 23 doubles five triples and 14 home runs. His 117 OPS+ was his sixth consecutive season with an above average OPS+

"We also have added some sock," Alston said. "Haller is a good all-around catcher, and it is good to have a catcher of this experience to handle the many fine young pitchers we have coming along on our staff." Giants vice president Charles "Chub" Feeney said: "We are sorry to see Tom go, but we had to do something to strengthen our infield."[19]

April 23, 1968: Traded Pitcher Phil Regan and Outfielder Jim Hickman to the Chicago Cubs for Outfielder Ted Savage and Pitcher Jim Ellis

The feeling In the Dodgers clubhouse ranged from surprise to shock when they learned that general manager Buzzie Bavasi had traded pitcher Phil Regan to the Chicago Cubs for journeyman outfielder Ted Savage. "It's like getting a knife in the back," said first baseman Wes Parker. "I'm too shocked to react properly," said Regan. "All I can say is it's a good trade for the Cubs." Don Drysdale said: "It shocked me. I don't understand it. There has to be something else cooking." Coach Preston Gomez also thought this trade was a forerunner to another trade. "We were able to give up Regan because we are confident that [rookie Jack] Billingham can do the job. Maybe they can use Savage in another deal."[20]

Savage, a 32-year-old right-handed hitter, had a .226 batting average in five years with the Phillies, Pirates, Cardinals, and Cubs. He had his best season as a Phillies rookie in 1962, a .266 batting average and a 96 OPS+. Savage played in 61 games for LA in 1968, with a .206 batting average and an OPS+ of 83. In March 1969, the Dodgers traded him to Cincinnati for catcher Jimmie Schaffer.

Phil Regan had been a starter with the Tigers, but when the Dodgers acquired him for the 1966 season, manager Walter Alston turned him into a reliever. Regan spent only two years with the Dodgers but that first one, 1966, was spectacular. He had a 14–1 record and a league-leading 21 saves, to help lead the Dodgers to a pennant. Regan's ERA+ that year was 203. His number of saves dropped to six in 1967, as Ron Perranoski took over the role of what soon would be called "the closer." After joining the Cubs, Regan had a 10–5 record and again led the NL in saves, with 25.

Jim Hickman was glad to leave the Dodgers, who sent him from Spokane in the Pacific Coast League to Tacoma, the Cubs affiliate in the PCL. Hickman called his November 1966 trade from the Mets to Los Angeles the worst thing that ever happened to him. "I didn't play at all," he said. "I had about 90 at-bats last year [1967] and that's not many in six months."[21] Jim Ellis, a 23-year-old left-hander, went the other way, from Tacoma to Spokane.

October 14, 1968: Lost Pitcher Jim Grant, Pitcher Jack Billingham, Shortstop Zoilo Versalles, Outfielder Al Ferrara, Outfielder Jim Fairey, and Minor League Outfielder Jim Williams in the National League Expansion Draft

Having voted to expand to twelve teams for the 1969 season, the National League held a draft of its players to stock the new Montreal Expos and San Diego Padres. The Dodgers lost six players in the draft: pitcher Jim Grant, pitcher Jack Billingham, and outfielder Jim Fairey to the Expos; and shortstop Zoilo Versalles, outfielder Al Ferrara, and minor league outfielder Jim Williams to the Padres.

December 4, 1968: Traded Pitcher Mike Kekich to the New York Yankees for Outfielder Andy Kosco

In 1968, 27-year-old Andy Kosco's one season in New York, he batted .240, with 15 home runs and 59 runs batted in. Those home run and RBIs totals were higher than any Dodger had in 1968. Kosco was a right-handed-hitting outfielder who occasionally filled in for Mickey Mantle at first base. He had played exceptionally well at times, and while Yankees manager Ralph Houk was sorry to see him go, the Dodgers were glad to have him.

"We have filled a little gap," said Dodgers owner Walter O'Malley, "but we still need an established right-handed hitter." Manager Alston said: "He'll give us more maneuverability and beef up our hitting against left-handed pitchers."[22] Alston was expected to platoon Kosco in left field with Willie Crawford.

Los Angeles signed left-hander Mike Kekich as an amateur free agent in 1964. Although he had gone 2–10 as rookie in 1968, for a seventh-place Dodgers team, he was young, just 23, and had made a favorable impression on several Yankees scouts.

Also in 1968:

Traded: Minor League Shortstop Frederick Moulder to Detroit Tigers for Pitcher Hank Aguirre; Pitcher Jim Ellis to St. Louis Cardinals for

Pitcher Pete Mikkelsen; Catcher Jim Campanis to Kansas City Royals for Future Considerations

Purchased: Outfielder Rocky Colavito from Chicago White Sox

Sold: Second Baseman Luis Alcaraz to Kansas City Royals; Third Baseman Bob Bailey to Montreal Expos

Chosen in Amateur Free Agent Draft: Davey Lopes; Doyle Alexander; Bobby Valentine; Bill Buckner; Tom Paciorek; Geoff Zahn; Joe Ferguson; Ron Cey; Steve Garvey; Sandy Vance

Signed Free Agents: Third Baseman Ken Boyer

Chosen in Major League Draft: Pitcher Bobby Darwin

Released: Outfielder Rocky Colavito; Pitcher Hank Aguirre

1969

June 11, 1969: Traded Outfielder-First Baseman Ron Fairly and Second Baseman Paul Popovich to the Montreal Expos for Shortstop Maury Wills and Outfielder Manny Mota

Shortstop Maury Wills returned to Los Angeles in a trade that sent veteran Ron Fairly and utility infielder Paul Popovich to the Montreal Expos. The Dodger also received outfielder Manny Mota. Expos GM Jim Fanning and Dodgers Director of Player Personnel Al Campanis had spoken earlier, while Montreal was playing in Los Angeles, without reaching agreement on a deal. Originally, the Expos wanted at least two pitchers (Joe Moeller and either Alan Foster or John Purdin) for Wills and another player.

Wills came to the Dodgers from their Spokane team in the Pacific League in 1959. He helped lead the Dodgers to pennants that year and again in 1963, 1965, and 1966. Following the 1966 season the Dodgers traded him to the Pittsburgh Pirates for third baseman Bob Bailey and shortstop Gene Michael, neither of whom were still with the team.

The Dodgers, who had been looking for a shortstop to replace Wills since 1967, finally found him—in Maury Wills. He would play through the 1972 season before the club released him in October. At 39, Wills' playing days were ended. In his two stints with the Dodgers, covering 12 seasons, Wills batted .281 with an OPS+ of 87. In addition to being the franchise leader in stolen bases, he is tenth in hits and runs scored.

Manny Mota, 31, came to the major leagues with the 1962 San Francisco Giants. He spent the next six seasons with Pittsburgh, but like Wills, he went to Montreal in the expansion draft. Mota, a right-handed hitter with little power, had a .297 batting average and a 110 OPS+ for the Pirates. He would have even greater success in his 13 years with the Dodgers—a .315 batting average and a 117 OPS+. Mota was batting .315 in 31 games for the Expos at the time of the trade.

Paul Popovich played in 162 games in his season-and-a half with the Dodgers, mostly at second base. He was a reliable defender but batted just .229 with a 67 OPS+. He had 10 hits in 50 at-bats this season. The Expos quickly traded Popovich to the Chicago Cubs for outfielder Adolfo Phillips and relief pitcher Jack LaMabe. Glenn Beckert, the Cubs regular second baseman, had been out with a broken finger and former Dodger Nate Oliver had been playing second for Chicago. "Popovich will start at second base as soon as he gets here" said Cubs manager Leo Durocher.[23]

Thirty-year-old Ron Fairly played 12 years with the Dodgers, as an outfielder and a first baseman. His composite batting average was .260 but he had an excellent 111 OPS+. Wes Parker had long since replaced Fairly at first base, and Walt Alston was using newcomer Andy Kosco in right field. Fairly had played in only 30 games this season, with a .219 batting average. He would play five seasons in Montreal and continue his major league career through 1978.

Also in 1969:

Traded: Outfielder Ted Savage to Cincinnati Reds for Catcher Jimmie Schaffer; Shortstop Tommy Dean and Minor League Pitcher Leon Everitt to San Diego Padres for Pitcher Al McBean; Minor League Second Baseman Chuck Goggin and Minor League Outfielder Ron Mitchell to Pittsburgh Pirates for Pitcher Jim Bunning

Purchased: Pitcher Jack Jenkins from Washington Senators

Chosen in Amateur Free Agent Draft: Lee Lacy; Bob O'Brien; Terry McDermott; Stan Wall

Signed Amateur Free Agents: Ivan de Jesus; Eddie Solomon

Chosen in Major League Draft: Pitcher José Peña

Released: Third Baseman Ken Boyer

4

1970–1974

1970

On March 17, 1970, Peter O'Malley replaced his father, Walter O'Malley, as team president. Walter remained as Chairman of the Board.

October 5, 1970: Traded Second Baseman Ted Sizemore and Catcher Bob Stinson to the St. Louis Cardinals for First Baseman Dick Allen

The Dodgers hit 87 home runs in 1970, the lowest total in the major leagues. That spurred Vice President Al Campanis to initiate a search for a player to boost that total. In Dick Allen, he was getting one of the game's prime offensive weapons. "We've looked for a long time because we knew what we needed more than anything was a big bat in the middle of our lineup. We believe we have it in Richie Allen," Campanis said.[1]

In 1960 Allen, who would turn 29 next March 8, received a $60,000 bonus to sign with the Philadelphia Phillies. As a rookie in 1964, he batted .318 with 29 home runs, 91 runs batted in and an OPS+ of 162. Allen led the league with 125 runs, 13 triples, and 352 total bases and was the runaway winner of the Rookie of the Year Award. He batted over .300 in his first four seasons with Philadelphia but there was almost constant discord with his manager, Gene Mauch.

The Phillies fired Mauch in mid-1968 and Mauch's successor, Bob Skinner, a year later. Both managers lost their jobs mainly because of their inability to handle Allen. After the 1969 season Philadelphia traded Allen to St. Louis in the deal in which the Cardinals' Curt Flood refused to report to the Phillies and challenged the game's antitrust laws. Allen had 34 home runs, 101 RBIs, and a 146 OPS+ for St. Louis this past season.

And while he had no apparent problems with manager Red Schoendienst, someone close to the club said: "They knew they weren't going to change him, so they just left him alone. He never indicated he wasn't happy."[2]

Allen played first base and third base for St. Louis, but Campanis said manager Walter Alston would decide in March where to play him. Campanis said first base was out because the team was happy with their incumbent, Wes Parker. It seemed likely Alston would use Allen at third base or left field.

Ted Sizemore, 25, had been a catcher and an outfielder in the minor leagues, but in the Arizona Instructional League following the 1968 season, the Dodgers switched him to the infield. Sizemore played in 159 games in 1969, mostly at second base, batted .271 and was voted Rookie of the Year. Injuries limited him to 96 games with a .306 batting average this past season. The Cardinals reportedly wanted Sizemore as a replacement for 34-year-old second baseman Julian Javier, a 12-year veteran who was threatening to retire.

The trade came at an inopportune time for Sizemore who had just moved his family into a new home. "At first I was really disappointed," he said. "My wife was really upset. You know, the house and all. But after thinking about it for a while, it's a great thing prestige-wise to be traded for a player the caliber of Richie Allen."[3]

The Dodgers considered Bob Stinson, who would turn 25 in a few days, a promising prospect. Like Sizemore, the switch-hitting Stinson had also had his position switched, in his case from the outfield to catcher. He spent most of the past two seasons with the Spokane Indians of the Pacific Coast League, while appearing in a total of eight games with the Dodgers

December 11, 1970: Traded Pitcher Alan Foster and Pitcher Ray Lamb to the Cleveland Indians for Catcher Duke Sims

Duane "Duke" Sims had been a catcher for Cleveland since his major league debut in 1964. This past season he had also filled in at first base and the outfield, after Ray Fosse had replaced him as the Indians number one catcher. Sims was unhappy at being shifted and generally displeased with Cleveland's manager-general manager, Alvin Dark. "This club has been mismanaged and underfinanced," Sims had said recently. "I really don't want to be a part of it any longer." Sims's statements made the trade possible, said Dodgers vice president Al Campanis. "They put him on the market after and, next to [Indians pitcher] Sam McDowell Duke, is the man we have talked about the most."[4]

The Dodgers expected the 30-year-old Sims to challenge Tom Haller, 34, for the top spot behind the plate in 1971. Although Haller was the more experienced catcher, Sims was considered to have the better throwing arm. Along with the recent addition of Dick Allen, Sims was expected to add power to a team that finished last in home runs in the National League in 1970. This past season the left-handed-batting Sims hit a career-high 23 home runs with a .264 batting average and an .859 OPS. In his 536 games with the Indians, Sims had 76 home runs and a 118 OPS+. "We made up our minds to find some slugging strength in our winter deals," said Campanis. "And we're very happy with the results."[5]

Of the two pitchers the Dodgers gave up, right-hander Alan Foster, selected in the second round of the 1965 amateur free agent draft, had shown the most promise. After brief stays with the Dodgers in 1967 and 1968, Foster had spent the last two seasons full-time with the club. He made 33 starts in 1970, with a 10–13 record and a 90 ERA+. Foster, 24, would pitch another six seasons in the major leagues, with four different clubs. His best year was with the 1973 St. Louis Cardinals, when he was 13–9 with a 117 ERA+.

Right-hander Ray Lamb, 26, was the Dodgers' 40th pick in the 1966 amateur free agent draft. Lamb lost his only decision in 1969 but had a 6–1 record with a 101 ERA+ this past season.

Also in 1970:

Traded: Pitcher Bruce Brubaker to Milwaukee Brewers for Pitcher Jerry Stephenson
Sold: Catcher Jimmie Schaffer to Baltimore Orioles; Pitcher John Purdin to California Angels; Pitcher Fred Norman to St. Louis Cardinals
Chosen in Amateur Free Agent Draft: Lance Rautzhan; Greg Shanahan; Doug Rau
Signed Amateur Free Agents: Orlando Álvarez; Jerry Royster
Signed Free Agents: Pitcher Camilo Pascual
Released: Pitcher Al McBean; Pitcher Camilo Pascual

1971

February 10, 1971: Traded Outfielder Andy Kosco to the Milwaukee Brewers for Pitcher Al Downing

The Dodgers had gone into the offseason looking to add a left-handed pitcher. Frank Lane, the new general manager of the Milwaukee Brewers, offered them Al Downing and agreed to take outfielder Andy Kosco in return. After Downing and Kosco, who were teammates with the Yankees in 1968, cleared waivers the deal was made. "We think that Downing can be the answer to our search," said Al Campanis. "This does not mean we aren't still interested in another left-hander. I'm still looking for one more."[6]

In 1969, his first year in Los Angeles, Kosco had what would be the best season of his career, hitting 19 home runs and driving in 74 runs. He started slowly this past year, and his playing time was further limited after he pulled a hamstring muscle in late May. Kosco hit .228 with eight home runs and 27 RBIs. With spring training ready to begin, the Dodgers had several outfielders vying for playing time. Dick Allen in left and Willie Davis in center seemed set, with Kosco, Willie Crawford, Manny Mota, Bill Buckner, and Tom Paciorek battling to be the right fielder. At 29, Kosco was the most expendable.

The 5'11" Downing, who would not turn 30 until June, pitched for Oakland and Milwaukee in 1970, compiling a 5–13 record with a 3.52 earned run average. The Dodgers were hoping he could regain the form he had shown with double-digit wins during five consecutive seasons (1963 to 1967), with the Yankees. Downing pitched in two World Series and one All-Star game, and the Dodgers hoped he would join Bill Singer, Claude Osteen, and Don Sutton in their 1971 rotation. "It's a great break coming here from Milwaukee, and I'm going to make the most of it," Downing said. "This club needs pitching, I know that. My arm is sound. All I need is the work."[7]

Downing not only joined the Dodgers rotation in 1971, but he was also the team's ace, with a 20–9 record, a 2.68 earned run average, a league-leading five shutouts, and a third-place finish in the voting for the Cy Young Award. He would pitch for the Dodgers until they released him in July 1977, but never came close to that first-year success. His final numbers for LA were 46 wins, 37 losses and an ERA of 107+. He is best remembered for giving up Hank Aaron's 715th home run that allowed Aaron to pass Babe Ruth as the all-time home run king.

March 13, 1971: Sold Catcher Jeff Torborg to the California Angels

Los Angeles signed Jeff Torborg as an amateur free agent in 1963. He made his major league debut the next year and spent seven seasons with the Dodgers. All were as a backup catcher, to John Roseboro the first four seasons and to Tom Haller the last three. The recent trade for catcher Duke

Sims and the presence of rookie catcher Joe Ferguson left no place for the 29-year-old Torborg on the 1971 club. California Angels GM Dick Walsh purchased him for what he said was a bit more than the $20,000 waiver price. Torborg was an excellent defensive catcher, but he never was able to hit major league pitching. In 358 games with the Dodgers, he batted .214, with seven home runs and an OPS+ of 60.

"This is a great organization," Torborg said of the Dodgers, "but this is also a great opportunity. It's like someone just shoveled a load of dirt off my career. I was just bogged down here." But Torborg would again assume the familiar role of backup catcher with his new club, this time to Jerry Moses. When Torborg asked Walsh if he had a chance to be the No. 1 catcher, Walsh was honest with him. "I told him that at the present time Jerry Moses was our No. 1 catcher and that Moses was the man he would have to dislodge."[8]

Angels manager Lefty Phillips, who worked with Torborg when Phillips was a coach with the Dodgers, was visibly pleased with the new acquisition. "When I was with the Dodgers, their pitching staff was almost unanimous in requesting that Jeff be allowed to catch them," Phillips said. "Pitchers have faith in his ability."[9]

December 2, 1971: Traded Outfielder-Third Baseman Dick Allen to the Chicago White Sox for Pitcher Tommy John and Infielder Steve Huntz

The Dodgers went to the winter baseball meeting in Phoenix in search of a starting pitcher and a right-handed-hitting outfielder. They came home with both while retaining their four best young players: Bill Buckner, Bobby Valentine, Bill Russell, and Joe Ferguson. In the first of the three trades they would make this day, they sent Dick Allen to the Chicago White Sox for left-hander Tommy John and infielder Steve Huntz.

In 1971 Allen had provided the power the Dodgers had hoped for when they traded for him in October 1970. He batted .295, led the team in home runs (23) and runs batted in (90), and had an OPS+ of 151. But his behavior had forced manager Walt Alston to adopt two sets of rules, one for the other 24 players and one for Allen. And while team officials avoided criticizing Allen in public, they were annoyed by, among other things, his tardiness for games. He would arrive at the park at 6:30 p.m., while the other players were required to report at 5 p.m. As far back as July, team president Peter O'Malley told one club official: "I've made up my mind that Allen will have to be traded. He's been an unsettling influence on the club."[10]

But White Sox manager Chuck Tanner did not foresee any problems with Allen, his fellow Pennsylvanian. "Richie is a wonderful person and a good friend as well," Tanner said. "The White Sox will judge Allen on what he does on the field. I know he's going to make us more exciting next year."[11]

Tommy John was a 28-year-old left-hander with nine years of major league experience, two with Cleveland and the last seven with the White Sox. John had been a mainstay of Chicago's rotation since joining them in 1965, winning 82 and losing 80, with an impressive 117 ERA+. He had 21 shutouts for the Sox and led the American League in that department in 1966 and 1967.

Twenty-six-year-old Steve Huntz batted .209 in 35 games for Chicago in 1971. The Dodgers assigned him to the Albuquerque Dukes of the Pacific Coast League for the 1972 season. He would never play for Los Angeles, but he did play in 22 games for the 1975 San Diego Padres.

December 2, 1971: Traded Pitcher Doyle Alexander, Pitcher Bob O'Brien, Infielder-Outfielder Royle Stillman, and Catcher Sergio Robles to the Baltimore Orioles for Outfielder Frank Robinson and Pitcher Pete Richert

Of the three trades Los Angles made this day, the trade for Frank Robinson was the big one. Trading for Robinson had been on their radar since August, when Baltimore scout Jim Russo let them know the 11-time All-Star was available; the Orioles wanted to make room for highly regarded young outfielders Don Baylor and Terry Crowley.

Robinson, even at 36, was one of the game's biggest stars. He was the National League's Rookie of the Year with the Cincinnati Reds in 1956 and is still the only man to win the Most Valuable Player Award in both leagues: with Cincinnati in 1961 and with Baltimore in 1966. Robinson batted .281 for the Orioles this past season, with 28 home runs. That boosted the right-handed slugger's home run total to 503, making him (at that time) one of the few players to have hit 500 career home runs.

"I know I can do it again next year," Robinson answered when asked about his future. "Beyond that I can't say. At my age you play one year at a time. The Dodgers were so close last year that I can't help but feel that if I go in and do my part, they will have a real chance to win it." He said about being traded: "I expected it, but when it came, I went numb; I guess you're never ready for it. I just went blank, but I can tell you now that I have a very good feeling. I'm very happy."[12]

"We've been hesitant to deal Frank Robinson—for four years, we've been hesitant," said Orioles manager Earl Weaver. "I know the names we got are not known now, but those names will explain themselves in a few years."[13] Weaver gave another reason for the trade. In praising Don Baylor, he said: "I feel that by 1980, he'll be recognized as another Robinson. I realize that's a long way off, but Baylor is that young, that capable of giving us a dozen great years."[14]

Pete Richert, now 32, was returning to Los Angeles ten years after he broke in with the Dodgers in 1962 and seven years after he was traded to the Washington Senators in 1965. Richert had two strong seasons as a starter for mediocre Washington teams in 1965 and 1966. He was traded to the Orioles in May 1967 and made a combined 29 starts that year, but in 1968 the Orioles made him a reliever. In that role, Richert was a contributor to the Orioles pennant-winning teams of 1969, 1970, and 1971. He was a combined 14–6 with 25 saves in 1969–1970 before slipping to a 3–5 record and four saves in 1971.

Going from Los Angeles to Baltimore in exchange for Robinson and Richert were four relative unknowns, with a combined total of 31 games in the major leagues: pitcher Doyle Alexander, 21; pitcher Bob O'Brien, 22; catcher Sergio Roble, 25; and outfielder-first baseman Royle Stillman, 20. The key man for the Orioles, they said, was Alexander, a 6'3" right-hander with a 6–6 record in 17 games for the Dodgers this past season. O'Brien was 2–2 in 14 games. Robles and Stillman were in the minor leagues in 1971. Robles batted .265 with Spokane and Stillman batted .267 at Albuquerque.

December 2, 1971: Traded Catcher Tom Haller to the Detroit Tigers for a Player to be Named and Cash

In the Dodgers third trade of the day, one that lacked the pizazz of a big name like Dick Allen or Frank Robinson, they sent 34-year-old catcher Tom Haller to the Detroit Tigers for a player to be named. The left-handed-hitting Haller spent four seasons with the Dodgers. He was their No. 1 catcher in the first three but shared the role with Duke Sims in 1971. Haller played in 474 games with the Dodgers, batting .276 with an OPS+ of 116. Tigers manager Billy Martin was expected to use Haller as a backup to perennial All-Star Bill Freehan.

The player to be named was announced on March 31, 1972. It was left-hander Bernie Beckman, who had 7–12 record in 1971 for the Class A Rocky Mount (NC) Leafs of the Carolina League. The Dodgers assigned

Beckman to the El Paso Dodgers of the Class AA Texas League. Beckman remained in the Minor Leagues for the rest of his career.

Also in 1971:

   Traded: First Baseman Tom Hutton to Philadelphia Phillies for Outfielder Larry Hisle; Outfielder Bobby Darwin to Minnesota Twins for Outfielder Paul Powell
   Purchased: Chris Cannizzaro from Chicago Cubs
   Chosen in Amateur Free Agent Draft: Rick Rhoden; John Hale; Rex Hudson; Kevin Pasley
   Signed Amateur Free Agents: Henry Cruz; Greg Heydeman
   Signed Free Agents: Pitcher Hoyt Wilhelm

1972

November 28, 1972: Traded Outfielder Frank Robinson, Pitcher Bill Singer, Infielder Billy Grabarkewitz, Infielder Bobby Valentine, and Pitcher Mike Strahler to the California Angels for Pitcher Andy Messersmith and Third Baseman Ken McMullen

Four days short of one year ago, the Dodgers traded Dick Allen to the White Sox after one season. In his first season in Chicago Allen was voted the American League's Most Valuable Player. Undeterred, they did the same here, trading superstar slugger Frank Robinson after only one year in the first major deal with their neighbors and rivals, the California Angels. The trade reunited Robinson with Angels general manager Harry Dalton, who made the trade that brought Robinson to Baltimore in 1966 and launched an Orioles dynasty. A hand injury limited Robinson to 103 games in his one season with the Dodgers. He batted .251 with 19 home runs and 59 runs batted in. Robinson did better for the 1973 Angels, but not close to what Allen had done for the White Sox in 1972.

The Dodgers had been after Andy Messersmith for more than a year. "At least eight or ten clubs expressed genuine interest in Messersmith," said Dalton. "He was our main avenue of tradeability [*sic*]." According to new Angels manager Bobby Winkles, "Everyone we talked to was interested in our starting pitchers. Everybody was available except Nolan Ryan. But Ryan wasn't the one the Dodgers wanted. They specifically asked for Messersmith." The Dodgers original offer was Robinson, Bill Singer, and Bobby Valentine for Messersmith. But Dalton wanted one more player, either infielder Billy Grabarkewitz or pitcher Mike Strahler. When the Dodgers said the Angels could have both if they threw in third baseman Ken McMullen, the deal was made.[15]

Messersmith was a 27-year-old right-hander who won 20 games (20–13) in 1971 with a 2.99 earned run average and a fifth-place finish in voting for the Cy Young Award. A finger injury that eventually required surgery limited him to 25 games and only eight wins (8–11) this past season, although his ERA dropped to 2.81.

"I've always wanted to play in the National League, and I've wondered about the difference," said Messersmith. "There are probably more good clubs in the National, but I'm not worried about facing better hitters a pitcher can get up for any team. Besides, the challenge might make me a better pitcher."[16]

New Angels pitcher Bill Singer said, "I think the Dodgers gave up too much and it's up to us to prove it. We got four guys under 30 in the trade."[17] Singer won 20 games with a 142 ERA+ for the Dodgers in 1969 but had only 24 wins with 38 losses in the last three seasons. His record in 1972 was 6–16 with an ERA+ of 92. The Angels were counting on Singer to regain his form of 1969 and make up for the loss of Messersmith.

Billy Grabarkewitz, 26, and Bobby Valentine, 22, were talented young players, but the Dodgers were strong at the infield positions and were willing to part with them to get Messersmith. Mike Strahler had a 2–3 record in parts of three seasons with Los Angeles and would not be missed.

"It's not really fair to compare five men to two," said Ken McMullen, who was returning to the Dodgers after an interlude of eight seasons as the regular third baseman for the Senators and the Angels. "I look at it this way," McMullen said, "the Dodgers plugged two positions which they feel can help them win a pennant while the Angels received five players who will likely be regulars. To me it appears both teams will benefit."[18]

Also in 1972:

Purchased: Catcher Dick Dietz from San Francisco Giants
Sold: Third Baseman-Catcher Bill Sudakis to New York Mets; Catcher Duke Sims to Detroit Tigers
Chosen in Amateur Free Agent Draft: Dennis Lewallyn; Glenn Burke

Signed Amateur Free Agents: Rafael Landestoy
Signed Free Agents: Pitcher Ron Perranoski
Released: Pitcher Hoyt Wilhelm; Pitcher Ron Perranoski; Shortstop Maury Wills; Second Baseman Jim Lefebvre

1973

December 5, 1973: Traded Outfielder Willie Davis to the Montreal Expos for Pitcher Mike Marshall

Willie Davis was not surprised to hear he had been traded, in a deal that sent him to the Montreal Expos for relief ace Mike Marshall. "I knew I was going to be dealt," Davis said, "because I told [president] Peter [O'Malley] at the end of the season that I wanted to go. The reason I asked to be traded is personal and I'd rather not go into that," Davis replied when asked if he had differences with manager Walter Alston. "I have no disappointment with the Dodger organization. They treated me great. I feel just great about the deal. I feel like a rookie again."[19] Davis admitted to having financial problems during his career in Los Angeles but said they had been his fault.

Los Angeles had signed the now 33-year-old Davis out of high school in 1958. With much expected of him, he joined the Dodgers in 1960 but never fully lived up to his advance notices. Still, he had an excellent 13 seasons with the Dodgers. Davis had a .279 batting average and is among the franchise's top-ten career leaders in almost every offensive category and in the top four in hits (3rd), triples (2nd), extra-base hits (4th) total bases (4th), and stolen bases (3rd). His best season was 1969, when he batted .311 with a 134 OPS+ and compiled a 31-game hitting streak, the longest in franchise history. This past season, Davis batted .285 in 152 games.

Montreal general manager Jim Fanning and manager Gene Mauch were ecstatic over the acquisition of Davis. "Willie Davis will save more games for us than Mike Marshall and he'll probably win a few more, too," Mauch said. "It's rare when you get an opportunity to get a player of Willie's caliber. There aren't many players—maybe none—who can do all the things he can." Marshall's public criticism of the fielding of teammates Ron Hunt and Bob Bailey may have helped motivate the Expos to trade him. Alston was equally delighted in adding Marshall to his staff. "We've always relied on pitching, and we know this will help us."[20]

Marshall, 31, was coming off a 1973 season in which he set a major league record by appearing in 92 games, while leading the National League in saves, with 31. In his four seasons with the Expos, the 5'10" right-hander threw 471 innings in 192 games, all but five in relief, winning 36 and saving 75. (The rules at this time made it more difficult for a pitcher to earn a save.) In an era when voters for the Cy Young Award were beginning to recognize the value of relief pitchers, they voted Marshall fourth in 1972 and second to Tom Seaver this year.

Marshall, who often rebelled against the baseball establishment, said there was a possibility he would not show up to play in Los Angeles. He said he would wait until March "when I have all the facts before me" to decide. Marshall was working on his doctorate in physiology at Michigan State University and said if an "attractive offer" to teach came along he would have to decide based on what is best for his family. "I have ties here in East Lansing that are fairly firm. I feel I am performing a function that makes me feel vital as a human being while teaching," he said.[21] Marshall did sign, but declared at spring training in 1974: "I'm an educator and baseball is my hobby. I enjoy throwing a baseball. The money is nice, but it won't dictate my life."[22]

December 6, 1973: Traded Pitcher Claude Osteen and Minor League Pitcher David Culpepper to the Houston Astros for Outfielder Jim Wynn

Dodgers vice president Al Campanis, who negotiated the trade with Astros GM Spec Richardson, explained his reason for trading Claude Osteen. "We felt Osteen was expendable because of his age and the development of Doug Rau. Walt (Alston) and I feel that Rau will be one of our starters next season."[23]

The 34-year-old Osteen, who approved the trade, said: "I'm very excited about it. The Astros have solid hitting, an outstanding defense, and a manager (Preston Gomez) I respect. It's all up to me. It's a real challenge." Osteen said he did not mean to imply that he was happy to be leaving the Dodgers. "I hate leaving," he said. "I can't say enough good things about the organization. I had the thrill of pitching on a world champion and two pennant winners. I had the opportunity of pitching in the same rotation with Sandy Koufax, Don Drysdale, and Johnny Podres. My pride in being a Dodger will never rub off."[24] In his nine season with the Dodgers, Osteen won 147, lost 126, with an ERA+ of 106. He was a double-digit winner in all those seasons, including two where he was a 20-game winner.

Jim Wynn, 31, was glad to be leaving the Astrodome, which he called "one of the toughest home run parks in baseball. They say the same thing about Dodger Stadium, but I don't buy it. I think I'll benefit a great deal by playing outdoors. I expect to hit more than 25 home runs and drive in more than 80 runs. This is why the Dodgers traded for me."

Known as The Toy Cannon for his explosive power coming from his 5'9", 165-pound frame, Wynn averaged 20 home runs, 65 RBIs and a batting average of .255 in his 11 seasons with Houston. Astros manager Leo Durocher had moved him to the leadoff spot this season, and he batted only .220 with 20 home runs and 55 RBIs. "I hated batting leadoff," said Wynn. "I'd have driven in a lot more runs if I had been hitting lower in the batting order."[25] Wynn was expected to compete with Tom Pacoriek and newly acquired Tommie Agee to replace the traded Willie Davis in center field.

David Culpepper was a minor league pitcher, whom the Astros sent to the Denver Bears of the American Association. He pitched for Houston's minor league teams the next two seasons but never reached the major leagues.

Also in 1973:

Traded: Pitcher Pete Richert to St. Louis Cardinals for Outfielder Tommie Agee; Minor League Shortstop Tim Johnson to Milwaukee Brewers for Shortstop Rick Auerbach; Outfielder Jim Fairey and Minor League Outfielder Mike Floyd to Minnesota Twins for Outfielder Charlie Manuel and Minor League Catcher Glenn Ezell

Purchased: Pitcher George Culver from Houston Astros; Rick Auerbach from Milwaukee Brewers

Sold: Catcher Dick Dietz to Atlanta Braves; Pitcher George Culver to Philadelphia Phillies; Shortstop Rick Auerbach to Milwaukee Brewers

Chosen in Amateur Free Agent Draft: Joe Simpson

Signed Amateur Free Agents: Jeffrey Leonard

Signed Free Agents: Outfielder Jim Fairey

Released: Catcher Chris Cannizzaro, First Baseman Wes Parker

1974

Traded: Minor League Pitcher Bruce Ellingsen to Cleveland Indians for Minor League Infielder-Outfielder Pedro Guerrero

Purchased: First Baseman Gail Hopkins from Hawaii Islanders of Pacific Coast League
Chosen in Amateur Free Agent Draft: Steve Shirley; Rick Sutcliffe
Released: Outfielder Tommie Agee; First Baseman Gail Hopkins

5

1975–1979

1975

Walter O'Malley bought out the Mulvey family's share of the team to become sole owner.

January 29, 1975: Sold Outfielder Von Joshua to the San Francisco Giants

Von Joshua had been requesting a trade for the past two seasons. Joshua made his feelings known in a personal meeting with club president Peter O'Malley, who told him he would honor that request. After failing to find a trading partner during the winter meetings, the Dodgers put Joshua on waivers shortly after New Year's. On January 29, 1975, vice president Al Campanis announced the club had sold Joshua to the San Francisco Giants for the $20,000 waiver price. "If a guy doesn't want to play for us," Campanis said, "we try to accommodate him. I told Von we'd do our best to trade him. I didn't say which club. We put him on waivers and the Giants were the only club to claim him."[1]

The 27-year-old Joshua felt he deserved more playing time than manager Walter Alston had given him. After the left-handed hitting outfielder played in 97 games for Los Angeles in 1969–1971, they sent him to Albuquerque for the 1972 season. Joshua batted .337 for the Dukes to win the Pacific Coast League batting title and a return to the Dodgers. He hit very well during the exhibition seasons of 1973 and 1974, but he was injured in the opening weeks of both seasons and lost his place in the lineup. Joshua appeared in only 75 games in 1973 and 81 in 1974, batting .252 and .234 respectively.

May 2, 1975: Traded Pitcher Geoff Zahn and Pitcher Eddie Solomon to the Chicago Cubs for Pitcher Burt Hooton

Right-hander Burt Hooton was a three-time All-American at the University of Texas, where he had a 35–3 career record and a 1.14 earned run average in 291 innings. The Chicago Cubs drafted him with the second pick of the first round of the June 1971 amateur free agent draft. In 1972 Hooton pitched a no-hitter against Philadelphia in only his fourth major league start. Yet he failed to fulfill the promise the Cubs had for him. In 129 games for Chicago, Hooton, 25, compiled a 34–44 record with a 104 ERA+. He was 7–11 last season, and 0–2 with an 8.18 ERA this season. Hooton was pleased to be going to Los Angeles, having long admired the Dodgers system and particularly coach Tom Lasorda. He had pitched for Lasorda in winter ball in Venezuela and this past winter pitched for Licey of the Dominican League, managed by Lasorda.

Geoff Zahn, a 29-year-old left-hander, was 3–5, with an outstanding 2.03 ERA for Los Angeles as a rookie in 1974 but appeared in only two games in 1975. "Zahn is the guy we've been after," said Cubs assistant GM Blake Cullen. "He's a good solid lefty we need to balance off our staff."[2] Zahn had mixed emotions about leaving the Dodgers. "I'm torn emotionally because I've been blessed by the Dodger organization," he said, "but this will give me a chance to pitch."[3]

Eddie Solomon, 24, a right-hander, pitched in four games for the Dodgers in both 1973 and 1974, without a decision. At the end of this season's spring training, they had assigned him back to Albuquerque, where he was 11–4 last season.

July 15, 1975: Traded Pitcher Jim Brewer to the California Angels for Pitcher Dave Sells and Cash

Left-hander Jim Brewer came to the Dodgers in a little-noted December 1963 trade with the Chicago Cubs. He was used sporadically until early in the 1968 season, after the Dodgers traded their top reliever, Phil Regan, to the Cubs. Brewer, who had developed an effective screwball, took over that role and pitched in 54 games, with an 8–3 record, a 2.49 earned run average, and 15 saves. He remained manager Walt Alston's top reliever until Mike Marshall replaced him in 1974. After six consecutive seasons of appearing in 50 or more games, Brewer's appearances dropped to 24. This season, the now 37-year-old Brewer had been in 21 games, with a 3–1 record. A recent terrible outing against San Diego had raised his earned run average to 5.18. Overall, Brewer pitched in 474 games for the Dodgers (fourth all-time) with 61 wins, a 127 ERA+, and 126 saves (fifth all-time).

In addition to $20,000 from the Angels, the Dodgers received Dave Sells, a 28-year-old right-hander. Sells had pitched briefly for California this season, as well as the previous three, with an 11–5 record. He was currently with the Salt Lake City Gulls of the Pacific Coast League. The Dodgers kept him in the PCL by transferring him to Albuquerque. Sells pitched in five games for the Dodgers later in the season, the last games of his major league career.

November 17, 1975: Traded Outfielder Jim Wynn, Outfielder Tom Paciorek, Outfielder Lee Lacy, and Infielder Jerry Royster to the Atlanta Braves for Outfielder Dusty Baker and First Baseman Ed Goodson

When 23-year-old Dusty Baker batted .321 with a 142 OPS+ in 1972, his first full season with the Atlanta Braves, there were some who thought the Braves had found a new Hank Aaron. Baker, a 6'2" right-handed-batter, had not approached that lofty position but had followed with three solid seasons. His best was 1973, when he hit .288 with 99 runs batted in and 21 home runs. Baker's Atlanta, and career, totals for 628 games were a .278 batting average, 77 home runs, and a 115 OPS+. Dodgers GM Al Campanis said the trade for Baker and Ed Goodson would satisfy his club's primary needs: a defensively sound center fielder with power and a left-handed pinch-hitter.

"He can run, throw, field, and hit with power," Campanis said of Baker. "And it's our feeling that he has yet to reach his peak. Our scouting reports on him have always been good." Campanis said he "hated giving up the two young players, particularly [Jerry] Royster, but both [manager Walter] Alston and I believe that Baker has the ability to more quickly make us better or equal to [defending World Series winner] Cincinnati."[4] Moreover, Baker, a Southern California native, had not been happy in Atlanta and had asked to be traded to a West Coast team.

Ed Goodson, 27, was traded to the Braves this past June after five and a half seasons with San Francisco. His .208 average in 86 games last year was the worst of his career. In addition to his value as a pinch-hitter, Goodson also could fill in at first and third. He would play two seasons with Dodgers, appearing 144 games, 109 as a pinch hitter, while batting .207 with a 53 OPS+. He was released in March 1978 and signed a minor league contract with Cleveland. Goodson was playing for the Indians

PCL team, the Portland Beavers, that year when a beaning ended his career.

In 1974, Jim Wynn's first year in Los Angeles, the Dodgers were National League champions. Wynn was a major contributor, batting .271, with 32 home runs and 108 runs batted in. But his average fell to .248 this past season, with only 18 home runs and 58 RBIs. However, it was more for Wynn's defense that the Dodgers felt they required a new center fielder. "Jimmy displayed defensive weaknesses even in '74," Campanis said, "and we felt that his arm never really came back from the surgery last winter." Not surprisingly, Wynn disagreed: "There is no doubt my mind but that I can still play center on a regular basis," he said. "My arm is strong, and I can still get around. I don't really understand why the Dodgers feel otherwise. I went into a rut last year when I began pressing in an attempt make up for all the injuries. Then found myself out of the lineup and felt that they had given up on me … given up on me just one year after I had helped them win a pennant. Yet I still considered myself a fixture and I'm surprised to be traded. But I don't want to sound bitter. You live one season, die the next and are traded. I have no differences with the Dodgers. They treated me right."[5]

It was several months before the start of spring training, but Braves manager Dave Bristol was working on the construction of his 1976 lineup. Wynn, he said, would be his left fielder, with Roland Office in center and Ralph Garr in right. Bristol planned to move Darrell Evans from third base to first base and play newcomers Lee Lacy at second base and Jerry Royster at third base.

Lacy, 27, batted .314 with a 129 OPS+ in 101 games this season, but the Dodgers felt he lacked the defensive skills of Davey Lopes and had moved him to left field in midseason. Royster, 23, played 29 games for the Dodgers over the past three seasons. He was the Pacific Coast League's batting champion in 1975, with a .333 average for the Albuquerque Dukes, but the Dodgers had Lopes at second, Bill Russell at short, and Ron Cey at third. Royster was not likely to unseat any of them. Tom Paciorek, a 29-year-old outfielder, whose career had been hampered by knee injuries, played in 264 games for the Dodgers over six seasons, with a .237 batting average and a 79 OPS+. The 1975 season had been his worst, a .193 batting average and a 48 OPS+.

The Dodgers' trade for Jim Wynn two years earlier had turned out to be one of their best. What made it so was that after two seasons they were able to package him in a deal that sent him to Atlanta for Dusty Baker. Not that the players the Dodgers sent away had little value. Tom Paciorek, Lee Lacy, and Jerry Royster all had a lot of baseball left, especially Paciorek. However, Baker was an outstanding player and would be an outfield fixture for LA for the next eight seasons.

Also in 1975:

Traded: Minor League Second Baseman Bob Randall to Minnesota Twins for Outfielder Danny Walton
Chosen in Amateur Free Agent Draft: Dave Stewart, Brad Gulden, Myron White, Mark Bradley
Signed Amateur Free Agents: Rudy Law
Signed Free Agents: Pitcher Juan Marichal; Outfielder Leron Lee

1976

March 2, 1976: Traded Outfielder Willie Crawford to the St. Louis Cardinals for Second Baseman Ted Sizemore

The 6'1" left-handed-hitting Willie Crawford had been a Dodger since 1964, when they signed him for a $100,000 bonus. For the past few seasons, he had been platooned in right field, and despite OPS totals well above the league average, he never reached the heights they had envisioned for him. His combined batting average for his 989 games with Los Angeles was .268 with a 118 OPS+. In 1975 Crawford hit .263 in 124 games.

St. Louis Cardinals general manager Bing Devine said the trade was made at second baseman Ted Sizemore's suggestion after Sizemore was told the club planned to shift shortstop Mike Tyson to second base for the 1976 season. However, in a conversation this past winter, Devine said Sizemore told him he wanted to stay in St. Louis and believed he could win back his position. Several days before the start of spring training, Sizemore called Devine again to say he wished to be traded back to the Dodgers.

Sizemore was returning to the team he won Rookie of the Year honors with in 1969. He was traded to St. Louis for Dick Allen following the 1970 season. Sizemore had been the Cardinals regular second baseman since, batting .260 in 679 games. "Having Ted Sizemore on our club gives us excellent protection in many positions," said Al Campanis. "He was a catcher throughout his minor league career, but he has also played shortstop, third base, and the outfield in the major leagues. However, the fact that he has outstanding utility value does not preclude the fact that he has a very good opportunity to win a starting job with the club for the 1976 season."[6]

Andy Messersmith played the 1975 season with the Los Angeles Dodgers without a signed contract. After the season he challenged Major League Baseball to have him declared a free agent, now that his option year had expired. Fellow pitcher Dave McNally, who had retired from the Montreal Expos in mid-season, joined him in the legal action. The owners argued that Messersmith was bound by an indefinite reserve clause, which allowed a team to renew a player's contract indefinitely, even without the player's consent. On December 23, 1975, a three-member panel headed by arbitrator Peter Seitz ruled in favor of the two players. They were declared free agents because the standard line in player contracts could only be interpreted to allow the clubs to renew a contract unilaterally for one year and one year only.

April 10, 1976: Free Agent Pitcher Andy Messersmith Signed with the Atlanta Braves

Andy Messersmith had a 53–30 record in his three years with the Dodgers, including a league-leading 20 wins and a second-place finish in Cy Young Award voting in 1974. This past season, he won 19, had a 149 ERA+ and led the league in games started (40), complete games (19), and innings pitched (321⅔).

When Messersmith declared himself a free agent in March, eight teams showed interest. But only the New York Yankees, Atlanta Braves, and San Diego Padres made serious offers for him. On April 10, the Braves won out, signing the 30-year-old right-hander to a three-year contract. Messersmith would receive $200,000 for each of the three years, plus a $400,000 signing bonus. His agent, Herb Osmond, called the agreement a "lifetime contract. It's a three-year contract with renewal clauses every year. Messersmith will play as long as he can pitch." Braves owner Ted Turner said: "He'll never be traded. He'll be a Brave as long as I am."[7]

(In December 1977, after Messersmith spent two seasons with Atlanta, Turner sold him to the Yankees.)

Before signing with the Braves, Messersmith had turned down a $1.1 million offer from the Padres. "For my part, he (Messersmith) can go wash cars," said angry Padres' owner Ray Kroc. Messersmith said Kroc's statement helped convince him to become a Brave. "Kroc has not endeared himself to me with his remarks. When Ted called to reopen talks, it took me just ten minutes to make up my mind I was going to sign with Atlanta."[8]

June 15, 1976: Traded Catcher Joe Ferguson, Minor League Outfielder Bob Detherage, and Minor League Shortstop Freddie Tisdale to the St. Louis Cardinals for Outfielder Reggie Smith

With less than two hours remaining before the midnight trading deadline, the Dodgers traded 29-year-old catcher Joe Ferguson to the St. Louis Cardinals for 31-year-old outfielder Reggie Smith. While both men were established major leaguers, neither was having a good season; Ferguson was batting .222 and Smith .218.

"Forget that," Ted Sizemore said regarding Smith's batting average. "Reggie can play," he said when informed the Dodgers had landed Smith. "He's a super hitter and he gives us plenty of punch" said Sizemore who was Smith's teammate with St. Louis before he was traded back to the Dodgers this past March. Al Campanis, who had been trying to obtain the switch-hitting Smith for two years, agreed. "He is an outstanding hitter," the Dodgers vice president said. "He has been hurt most of the year and hasn't been hitting. But you don't get guys like Reggie Smith if they're hitting .335. All our people believe he's one of the finest power hitters in the game."[9]

Smith, who came up with the Boston Red Sox, got the only vote that Rod Carew did not in the balloting for the Rookie of the Year in 1967. For the next six years he was a fixture in center field for Boston, leading the league in doubles twice and total bases once. His overall batting average with the Red Sox was .281 with 149 home runs, and an OPS+ of 129. The Cardinals moved him to right field after they traded for him after the 1973 season. He had two excellent seasons in St. Louis: a .309 batting average with 100 RBIs and a 155 OPS+ in 1974, and a .302 batting average with 76 RBIs and a 137 OPS+ in 1975.

Ferguson was the Dodgers first-string catcher in 1973. He shared the position with Steve Yeager in 1974, while also playing right field in both seasons. He split his time between the two positions in 1975, while batting a lowly .208 in just 66 games. Ferguson's reduced playing time was due partly to his poor performance and partly to the broken arm he suffered on July 1. The slump carried over to this season, though there were signs he had begun to regain his form.

Ferguson was pleased with the trade. "I'm very happy about it," he said. "I want to be able to catch more and the Cardinals say I'll be able to do that. Sure, I've got a lot of friends on the Dodgers, and we've got a chance to win. The tough part was hearing all the stuff and still trying to play. Every time a deal is rumored it seems my name is in it. At least that's over with."[10]

Bob Detherage and Freddie Tisdale were both in the minor leagues. Detherage would reach the big leagues in 1980, playing in 20 games for the Kansas City Royals. Tisdale would never play in the major leagues.

June 23, 1976: Traded Pitcher Mike Marshall to the Atlanta Braves for Second Baseman Lee Lacy and Pitcher Elias Sosa.

The Dodgers knew they were getting an often-difficult player to deal with when they traded Willie Davis to Montreal for pitcher Mike Marshall in December 1973. They also knew they were getting an outstanding relief pitcher, which Marshall demonstrated in 1974. He set a still-standing record by pitching in 106 games. He won 15 (15-12), led the league in saves (21) for the second consecutive season and in gamed finished (83) for a fourth consecutive season. Marshall's performance earned him the Cy Young Award, the first ever given to a relief pitcher, and a third-place finish in voting for the league's Most Valuable Player.

Marshall was an All-Star in 1975, as he was in 1974, but his production fell off sharply: from 15 wins to 9; a 2.42 ERA to 3.29; 106 games to 58; 83 games finished to 46; 21 saves to 13; 208⅓ innings pitched to 109⅓. He had been erratic this season, with eight saves and a 4.45 ERA, and more and more Walter Alston was using Charlie Hough in the tough situations he had formerly used Marshall.

"[Marshall] was late for spring training in 1976 because of court appearances and soon angered Dodgers management in his role as a player representative," wrote biographer Warren Corbett. "He aired grievances about hotel accommodations in several cities and demanded that sportswriters be banned from the team bus."[11]

In June, Marshall, now 33, said he wanted to clarify his now nationally celebrated derogatory statement about the infielders who played behind him. "I look around and see four infielders resembling cigar store Indians." In his clarification, he said: "Those were my words but because I've had the pressure of this Michigan State thing on my mind, I did not express myself in a coherent fashion. What I meant to say was that they resemble cigar store Indians because they were deadened and dispirited by the booing that I've received every time I come into a game. It saps everyone's enthusiasm." When asked about Marshall's clarification, Steve Garvey said: "I hope this doesn't go over your head, as someone else might say, but I think Marshall could have come up with a better lesson plan."[12]

President Peter O'Malley had heard enough and instructed vice president Al Campanis to get rid of Marshall. The deal was explained to the press this way. Marshall was sold to the Braves for the $20,000 waiver price. The Dodgers then bought outfielder Lee Lacy and pitcher Elias Sosa from Atlanta for an undisclosed amount of money.

Marshall was unemotional in his reaction to the trade. "I have nothing to support the way I feel, but I do believe that when I was going well, the Dodgers felt there was nothing they could do about it. But as soon as I stumbled and Charlie [Hough] began to do well, it was my feeling that the club began to look for ways to move me," he said. "I don't know the reasons for this. The only thing that has come down to me from second-hand sources is that the Michigan State incident was of great concern to the management of the Dodgers. I have also explained that it is of great concern to me, that my education, my future, my candidacy for a doctor's degree was being threatened. I refuse to be pushed around."[13]

Lacy, whom the Dodgers traded to Atlanta last November, was batting .272 with three home runs and 20 runs batted in. He was not happy about returning to Los Angeles. "I had begun to like to live in the South," he said. "I looked at a house here just yesterday."[14]

Elias Sosa, 26, was 4–4 this season with 21 appearances, all in relief. He was in his second season with the Braves, having pitched three seasons with the Giants and a half-season with the Cardinals.

December 20, 1976: Traded Second Basemen Ted Sizemore to the Philadelphia Phillies for Catcher Johnny Oates and a Player to be Named

Ted Sizemore, 31, was the National League's Rookie of the Year with the Dodgers in 1969. They traded him to St. Louis two years later, but after five years with Cardinals he was traded back to the Dodgers in 1976 and batted .241 in 84 games. The Phillies had lost second baseman Dave Cash to the Montreal Expos via free agency, and they expected Sizemore to compete for the job with Terry Harmon and rookie Fred Andrews. "Sizemore gives us some infield depth," said Paul Owens, the Phillies director of player personnel. "He's a battler. The guy knows how to play the game. I think he'll definitely help us."[15]

Thirty-one-year-old Johnny Oates was a left-handed-hitting catcher who would serve as the backup to Steve Yeager. Oates had played for Baltimore and Atlanta before being traded to Philadelphia in May 1975. He opened the 1976 season as the Phillies number-one catcher but broke his collar bone on Opening Day and did not return until June 1. He played in 37 games and batted .253 in 1976. Oates played in 126 games for the

Dodgers from 1977 through 1979. He batted .256 with an OPS+ of 70 before being released in March 1980.

On January 4, 1977, the Dodgers received minor league pitcher Quency Hill as the player to be named. Hill was sent to Albuquerque and remained in the minor leagues until his career ended a year later.

With four games remaining in the 1976 season, Tom Lasorda replaced Walter Alston as manager.

Also in 1976:

Traded: Outfielder Orlando Álvarez to California Angels for Catcher Ellie Rodríguez; Minor League Catcher Steve Patchin to Kansas City Royals for Minor League Shortstop Ron Washington
Chosen in Amateur Free Agent Draft: Dave Patterson, Ted Power
Signed Free Agents: Outfielder Jim Lyttle
Chosen in Major League Draft: Infielder-Outfielder Ted Martínez
Released: Third Baseman Ken McMullen; Outfielder Jim Lyttle; Outfielder Leron Lee

1977

January 11, 1977: Traded Outfielder Bill Buckner, Shortstop Ivan De Jesus, and Minor League Pitcher Jeff Albert to the Chicago Cubs for Outfielder Rick Monday and Pitcher Mike Garman

Dodgers vice president Al Campanis said the Dodgers had been trying to trade for Rick Monday for close to four years. They finally landed the 31-year-old, 11-year veteran when the Cubs realized he had become too expensive for them to keep. "Rick was simply asking for more than we were able to pay," said Cubs general manager Bob Kennedy. "We traded him strictly as a matter of dollars and cents." Kennedy said Monday had asked for a multiyear deal and had brought up the possibility of a trade to the West Coast. Monday's response was, "I had not asked to be traded and I never would simply because of my appreciation for the way the Cubs treated me and because of my regard for friends and teammates in Chicago. At the same time, since I have the right of approval over any trade, I had told the Cubs that I would not disapprove of a trade to the West Coast, to the Dodgers."[16]

In 1965 Monday was taken by the Kansas City Athletics with the first pick of the newly installed amateur free agent draft, receiving a $104,000 bonus from A's owner Charles Finley. Monday, a left-handed batter and an excellent defensive center fielder, played six seasons with the A's, in Kansas City and Oakland, and for the Cubs the past five seasons.

Kennedy indicated that 24-year-old Ivan De Jesus would likely be Chicago's shortstop in 1977. De Jesus batted .304 at Albuquerque, in 1976, but only .171 in 22 games with the Dodgers. Kennedy was also high on Jeff Albert, a 23-year-old right-hander. This past season, Albert's first as a professional, he had an 8–3 record and a 2.82 ERA with the Bellingham Dodgers of the Class A Northwest League.

While Monday was pleased to be going to the Dodgers, the man he was basically traded for, Bill Buckner, was said to be shocked, disappointed, and emotionally stressed at leaving the Dodgers. "I feel I had a good year in 1976. I thought they were satisfied. I thought I was wanted where I was. I'm going from a contender to a non-contender, from a city I love to a city I dislike. It's a real drag. I'm very upset about it." "I feel like a piece of meat," he said. "They use you for what they can and get rid of you in the same way." Buckner was particularly critical of new manager Tom Lasorda. "Being traded was totally unexpected, especially since Tommy had become the manager. He's been like a father to me. He was the one who first scouted me. He managed me at Ogden and Spokane. I've lived at his home. Now he becomes the manager and I'm traded. It's hard to understand and it's a real disappointment, especially since he hasn't called me. He had to know about the trade before it was announced."[17]

Lasorda said he knew of the negotiations, but he was not informed of the trade until it had been made. "The toughest part of it," Lasorda said, "is giving up a player who is like a son to me." Campanis defended the trade, saying he regretted giving up a player of Buckner's ability, but the club needed a center fielder. "You have to trade quality to get quality."[18] Campanis said Monday was a better outfielder than Buckner and would provide the club with more runs batted in than Buckner would. Buckner had played in 773 games in his eight years with Los Angeles. He batted .289 with a 99 OPS+.

Accompanying Monday to LA was Mike Garman, a 27-year-old right-handed relief pitcher, who had pitched previously for the Red Sox and the Cardinals. Lasorda said he had always liked the 6'2", 200-pound Garman who had a 2–4 record, with a 4.95 ERA and one save in 1976. Lasorda believed that Garman's weight was preventing from being a successful pitcher, and the club would work on a weight reduction regimen with him at spring training.

August 31, 1977: Traded Two Players to be Named and Cash to the New York Mets for Catcher Jerry Grote

During the Dodgers 5–0 shutout of the Chicago Cubs, Al Campanis announced the club had acquired catcher Jerry Grote from the New York Mets for a "nominal" amount of cash and two minor leaguers to be named later. As a player with ten years in the major leagues and the last five years with the same team, Grote's approval was necessary before the trade could be made. To make room for Grote, the Dodgers asked for unconditional waivers on Boog Powell, whom they had signed as a free agent in April. Used mostly as a pinch-hitter, Powell had 10 hits in 41 at bats.

"I still feel I can play, and I still want to play," Powell said. "I still feel that to be effective, to generate any kind of power, I have to play regularly." Powell went unclaimed, ending his illustrious 17-year career, 14 of which were with Baltimore.

"In my 32 years, I've never met any finer person, any more popular guy on a team, than Boog," said Tom Lasorda. "This was a difficult decision, but we felt we needed the protection of three catchers and a man who might be more adaptable to pinch-hitting than Powell." Campanis said: "When Steve Yeager was hurt in Pittsburgh, it convinced us that we had to have three catchers down the stretch, that we had to have three if we made the playoffs and Series."[19]

Grote, 34, was in his 14th big league season, the last 12 with the Mets. He began this season with a .250 career batting average. Bothered by back problems, he had appeared in 42 games for New York with a .270 batting average. Grote was a two-time National League All-Star and had established a reputation as one of the game's finest defensive players. Two months earlier, the Mets had traded Tom Seaver to Cincinnati, breaking up the battery of Seaver and Grote that was a major contributor to their championship teams of 1969 and 1973. Over the rest of this season and the next, Grote played in 59 games for LA and batted .268. In November 1978, he left as a free agent.

After the 1977 season, the Dodgers sent minor league shortstop Randy Rogers and minor league pitcher Don Smith to the Cubs.

November 18, 1977: Signed Free Agent Pitcher Terry Forster

The postseason market for free agents had been around for three seasons, but the Dodgers had not yet signed one. That changed with the signing of left-handed pitcher Terry Forster for five years, reportedly for

$850,000. "It was the feeling of our front office staff, manager, and scouting staff that we needed a veteran left-handed pitcher for the bullpen," said vice president Al Campanis. "We feel we have obtained a very good relief pitcher in Forster to fill our need."[20] Campanis added that the signing of Forster would not preclude the club from trying to sign one of two free agent right-handers—either Pittsburgh's Rich Gossage or St. Louis's Rawly Eastwick—to strengthen their disappointing bullpen of 1977.

"I'm extremely happy to be with the Dodgers," Forster said. "They have a first-class organization and a first-class club. I'm ready to go. I had arm trouble years ago, but I feel I can come back and have the kind of success I had in 1972 and 1974. I'm not afraid of anybody or any situation. The Dodgers have the type of club that if I give up two runs, they can come back with five or six."[21]

The 25-year-old Forster spent six seasons with Chicago White Sox, appearing in 263 games, mostly in relief. He had a 26–42 record with 75 saves and a 111 ERA+. Forster had 29 saves in 1972 and a league-leading 24 in 1974, when he was voted the American League's Fireman of the Year. In December 1976 the White Sox sent Forster, along with Rich Gossage, to Pittsburgh as part of the trade for Richie Zisk. Forster was 6–4 in 33 games with a 4.43 earned run average in his one season with the Pirates.

Also in 1977:

Traded: Shortstop Rick Auerbach to New York Mets for Pitcher Hank Webb and Minor League Pitcher Richard Sander; Outfielder Danny Walton to Houston Astros for Infielder Alex Taveras and Minor League Outfielder Bob Detherage; Pitcher Rex Hudson to Minnesota Twins for Pitcher Bill Butler

Purchased: Pitcher Bobby Castillo from Kansas City Royals; Outfielder Vic Davalillo from Aguascalientes of Mexican League

Sold: Outfielder Henry Cruz to Chicago White Sox; Outfielder John Hale to Toronto Blue Jays; Catcher Kevin Pasley to Seattle Mariners

Chosen in Amateur Free Agent Draft: Bob Welch; Joe Beckwith; Mickey Hatcher; Bobby Mitchell; Ron Roenicke

Signed Amateur Free Agents: German Rivera

Signed Free Agents: First Baseman Boog Powell; Outfielder Ron Kittle

Released: Pitcher Al Downing; Catcher Ellie Rodríguez

1978

May 16, 1978: Traded Outfielder Glenn Burke to the Oakland Athletics for Outfielder Bill North

Shortly after a game in which the Dodgers defeated the Pirates, Al Campanis announced he had traded reserve outfielder Glenn Burke to the Oakland A's for veteran center fielder Bill North. The 30-year-old North had clashed on several occasions with A's owner Charles Finley. In addition, he was playing out his option and would be declaring for free agency after the season. Under instructions from Finley, A's manager Bobby Winkles used North only in a reserve role. The switch-hitting North, who was in his sixth season with Oakland, was noted for his speed and had twice been the American League's leader in stolen bases. In 24 games this season, he had a .212 batting average with just three steals.

"I have not talked to North," Campanis said, "but I have talked to his agent, and it was his feeling that North would be happy coming here." "When he sees the type manager we have, the type players and the type environment, I think he may like it well enough to sign for two or three years." North verified that he was both happy to leave Oakland and happy to be coming to Los Angeles. "I couldn't sleep last night after I had heard," he said. "I was elated. It was a total plus. When you think of organizations, you think this one (the Dodgers). To be wanted by the Dodgers is very good for my ego."[22] North played in 110 games for the 1978 Dodgers, batting .234. In March 1979 he signed as a free agent with the San Francisco Giants.

In explaining the reason for trading Burke, Campanis said: "We're playing for today. Our future is now. Burke has potential but it's in the future. We've obtained a player who can help us immediately with his experience and ability, who can help us more than Burke." The 25-year-old Burke, who was brought up in the Oakland area, said, "yea, I'm going home but the team's going to move to Denver next year. Still, I want to play, and this is probably a break for me."[23] (Charles Finley's plan to move the A's from Oakland to Denver was an often-heard rumor at the time.) Burke finished his two-plus seasons as a Dodger with a .248 batting average and a 60 OPS+ in 124 games.

July 1, 1978: Traded Two Players to be Named to the Houston Astros for Catcher Joe Ferguson

Two years after the Dodgers traded Joe Ferguson to the St. Louis Cardinals, they brought him back. After a half season with St. Louis, the

Cardinals traded him to the Houston Astros in November 1976. Ferguson was the Astros first-string catcher in 1977, batting .257 with 16 home runs and an OPS+ of 127. He was batting .207 at the time of this trade, and Houston had rookie catchers Bruce Bochy and Luis Pujols ready to replace him.

Houston general manager Tal Smith told his Los Angeles counterpart, Al Campanis, "Fergy never lost his Dodger blue, never got over leaving Los Angeles. I think it's a significant reason he didn't do as well as had been expected in St Louis and Houston." Campanis said there were several factors prompting interest in the 31-year-old Ferguson, including Steve Yeager's .192 batting average. "For one thing," he said, "we don't know if [Jerry] Grote will be back next year." (Earlier in the day, the Dodgers learned that Grote had a fractured wrist and would have to go on the disabled list for at least four weeks.) "Secondly," Campanis said, "Ferguson is a plus since he also can play the outfield and each of our outfielders has been out at times with injuries. Third, [Lee] Lacy may play out his option."[24] It appeared likely that Lacy, 30, would test the free agent market. He had recently rejected a Los Angeles offer of three-years that would have nearly doubled his salary of $70,000. The offer included a provision whereby the club would pay off Lacy's new home. However, Lacy thought the acquisition of Ferguson meant his playing days with the Dodgers were over.

"When Ferguson and Yeager were on the same teams the competitive situation worked to their advantage," said manager Tom Lasorda. "They seemed to push each other. I'm very pleased to have Fergy back. He can play two or three positions and should be able to play five or six more years. The fact that Yeager has been struggling had a lot to do with it, though Yeager is still my regular catcher, still the best defensively I've ever seen." Yeager said: "The way I'm hitting I could understand being set down. At the same time, I can't get any hits sitting on the bench. I also think it would be a bad move because I can help a club hitting .190 as I proved in Atlanta the other night (he picked two runners off first base). But I certainly think the trade was a good move. He's a hell of a player and a valuable property since he can play two or three positions, Yeager said of Ferguson: We've always been friends. There's never been ill feelings." Asked if anyone in authority had explained the move to him, Yeager smiled and said, "No, but then I'm only a player."[25]

The two players to be named going to Houston were infielder Rafael Landestoy and outfielder Jeffrey Leonard. Landestoy, who was sent to the Astros on July 7, batted .278 in 15 games with the Dodgers in 1977. He had played in 66 games with Albuquerque this season with a .274 batting average. Leonard, who appeared in 11 games for the Dodgers in 1977, went to

Houston on September 11. He, too, was at Albuquerque this season, where he led the Pacific Coast League in batting (.365) and hits (183). He also had 93 runs batted in, 36 stolen bases and was voted the PCL's Player of the Year.

After the 1978 season Lacy and Grote declared their free agency. Lacy signed with the Pittsburgh Pirates in January 1979. Grote was out of baseball in 1979 and 1980; he signed with the Kansas City Royals in April 1981.

November 14, 1978: Signed Free Agent Infielder-Outfielder Derrel Thomas

Manager Tom Lasorda said the signing of 27-year-old, free agent infielder-outfielder Derrel Thomas would offset the loss of Lee Lacy and Bill North, both of whom had left as free agents. Thomas signed a five-year contract at undisclosed terms with the Dodgers. The switch-hitting Thomas batted just .227 in 352 at-bats with the San Diego Padres in 1978. He blamed his poor season on the pressure of playing out his option and his futile negotiations with the Padres. After a brief appearance with Houston in 1971, Thomas played three seasons for the Padres, three for the San Francisco Giants, and this last season back in San Diego.

"It would be a dream come true to play center field regularly for the Dodgers," Thomas said, "but with a Rick Monday out there, that's unlikely. I'm happy enough being with the Dodgers. I'll do what the manager asks." His new teammates, however, were not happy with his acquisition. Their animosity dated back to August, when Thomas, attempting to break up a double play, slid hard into second base injuring shortstop Bill Russell. "He exceeded the limits of aggressiveness," Russell said.[26] It was a play Lasorda and several of his players said would not be forgotten.

"I enjoy playing baseball," Thomas had once said. "Call it hot-dogging. Call it flashy, conceited, cocky. Call it whatever you want. We get paid to entertain people. I try to entertain the best way I can." Reggie Smith, a leader of the Dodgers on and off the field, said: "The two of us are going to sit down and talk about it. He does things that make it easy to hate him," Smith had said at the time. "He's one of the most irritating players I've ever seen. I wouldn't mind if he was a good player but he's not. He's not a quality player. I don't like the guy and I don't know too many people who do." Now that Thomas was his teammate, Smith softened a bit. "If he puts his mind to it, he can be a good player. If he puts his mind to it, he can make a hell of a contribution. It'll be up to all of us to help him…. Dusty, Cey, Lopes, Garv, myself. It'll be up to all of us to put personalities and the things that have happened in the past aside. He's with a first-place club now and he can be as much a part of it as anyone."[27]

Lasorda said he did not believe the Russell incident would have a lasting effect. "He's as tough as anyone. He can dish it out and he can take it. I was as upset as anyone," Lasorda said. "I challenged Derrel and called him every name I could think of. Reggie even tried to steal third and break his leg. That's the nature of the game. I'd get into fights as a player and the next year the guy would be my teammate. It's all forgotten when he puts on the same uniform. As far as I'm concerned, Derrel Thomas is now one of my boys."[28]

The versatile Thomas spent five years with Dodgers, playing the infield and the outfield. He played in 522 games with a .257 batting average and a 90 OPS+. In 1984 he signed as a free agent with the Montreal Expos.

November 22, 1978: Free Agent Pitcher Tommy John Signed with the New York Yankees

George Steinbrenner of the New York Yankees had been the most active owner in the free agent market since its inception. This year was no different. Steinbrenner, who declared his interest in Tommy John as soon as the 35-year-old left-hander became a free agent, signed him to a three-year, $1.4 million contract. Along with Pete Rose, John was the most sought-after free agent in this year's crop. John said three teams offered him more money than the Yankees, but the winning tradition of the defending world champions was the overriding factor.

"I took less money from the Yankees," John said, "but it's not very often you have an opportunity to play for a team like the Yankees. I said when I was traded from the White Sox to the Dodgers for Dick Allen (in 1971) that it was like going from a Chevy to a Cadillac. This is like going from a Cadillac to a Rolls-Royce.... It's an opportunity to come to the big city and play for the best team. Cincinnati, Atlanta, and Kansas City offered me substantially more money, but they're not New York." Yankees president Al Rosen said: "In signing John we have taken a giant step toward obtaining a third straight world championship. He is one of the truly fine left-handed pitchers in the game today."[29]

John said he could pitch for another five or six seasons. "My arm is only 4 years old," he joked, referring to his eponymous 1974 surgery where Dr. Frank Jobe performed a tendon transplant in his left elbow. Despite his relationship with the front office, which had worsened over the last year, John said he held no bitterness toward the club. "I had a great seven years with the Dodgers, but that's water over the dam now. That chapter is closed and a new chapter in the life of Tommy John has begun."

John compiled an 87–72 record with a 2.97 ERA in his six active seasons with Los Angeles. He twice led the league in winning percentage and finished second twice and fourth once in voting for the Cy Young Award. John won 20 games in each of his first two seasons in New York and continued to pitch through the 1989 season, when he was 46 years old.

Also in 1978:

    Traded: Pitcher Mike Garman to Montreal Expos for Pitcher Larry Landreth and Pitcher Gerry Hannahs
    Sold: Pitcher Elias Sosa to Pittsburgh Pirates
    Chosen in Amateur Free Agent Draft: Brian Holton; Mike Marshall; Steve Sax, Gary Weiss
    Signed Amateur Free Agents: Candy Maldonado; Dave Sax; Alejandro Peña; Leo Hernández
    Signed Free Agents: Shortstop Enzo Hernández
    Released: Outfielder Bob Detherage; Outfielder Ed Goodson; Outfielder Ron Kittle; Shortstop Enzo Hernández
    Left as Free Agents: Outfielder Lee Lacy; Outfielder Bill North; Catcher Jerry Grote

1979

February 15, 1979: Traded Catcher Brad Gulden to the New York Yankees for Outfielder Gary Thomasson

New York Yankees general manager Cedric Tallis called the trade that sent outfielder Gary Thomasson to the Dodgers for catcher Brad Gulden a sensible deal for both clubs. The Dodgers needed an extra outfielder, and the Yankees needed a backup catcher for Thurman Munson, specifically one who was better defensively than the incumbent, Cliff Johnson. The 22-year-old Gulden, a left-handed batter, had an outstanding year with Albuquerque in the Pacific Coast League in 1978. He batted .294, and led all PCL catchers in assists, putouts, and double plays. Late in the season he played in three games with the Dodgers.

Thomasson, 27, once was considered a bright prospect in the San Francisco Giants organization. He played six seasons with the Giants before they traded him to Oakland in March 1978 in the deal that brought them Vida Blue. In June the A's traded Thomasson to the Yankees. Although he batted .276 and played well in his half season in New York, he was just one of many surplus outfielders on the roster and easily expendable. Thomasson had a career batting average of .251 in 705 games. He had his best season in 1977, with the Giants, when he drove in 71 runs, hit 17 home runs, and had a .256 batting average.

George Genovese, the Giants scout who signed Thomasson, thought the Dodgers helped themselves with the acquisition of the left-handed-hitting outfielder. "They need outfield help," he said. "Gary has yet to come into his own, but I think he'll fit in well with the Dodgers. Also, he gives them some insurance at first base, and he can play any position in the outfield."[30]

Thomasson batted .239 in 195 games over the next two seasons. As Genovese predicted, he played all three outfield positions and first base. In December 1980, the Dodgers sold Thomasson to the Yomiuri Giants of the Japan Central League.

April 7, 1979: Traded Pitcher Rick Rhoden to the Pittsburgh Pirates for Pitcher Jerry Reuss

Right-hander Rick Rhoden had a 42–24 in his five seasons in Los Angeles. He became a starter in in 1976, his first full season in the big leagues. Rhoden won his first nine decisions that year and finished with a 12–3 record. He pitched in 58 games for the Dodgers in 1976–1977, 57 as a starter. He won 28 and lost 13 in those two seasons. However, Rhoden's inconsistency and a troublesome shoulder in 1978 led manager Tom Lasorda to move him to the bullpen and replace him in the rotation with Bob Welch. Rhoden was unhappy with the demotion, and as a five-year man he had the right to demand a trade at the end of the season. If he was not traded, he said, he would become a free agent.

Rhoden, who would turn 26 in May, said this about the Dodgers dropping him from the starting rotation. "They do what they think is best for them. I don't know whether it was a matter of them giving up on me or if they just felt the others were more capable. I hate to leave but I want to get a chance to pitch for a good team in Pittsburgh."[31] Rhoden and the Pirates agreed to a five-year extension of his current contract.

Jerry Reuss, 29, was a 6'5" left-hander with a 108–94 record in 10 seasons with St. Louis, Houston, and Pittsburgh. He was a starter throughout his career (he led the league with 40 starts for the 1970 Astros), with the Pirates moving him to a relief role in 1978. Like Rhoden, Reuss objected to the demotion. The Dodgers made no statement regarding his role, but it was expected to be relief pitcher. According to Al Campanis, Reuss said he would accept either role. "I've always wanted to be a Dodger," he was quoted as saying. "Ever since my high school days, I looked forward to playing for them and now it's a dream come true."[32]

On August 9, 1979, Walter O'Malley died. Peter O'Malley replaced his father, Walter, as the team's Chairman of the Board. Peter shared ownership with his sister Teresa O'Malley Seidler.

November 14, 1979: Signed Free Agent Pitcher Dave Goltz

When it became clear that Nolan Ryan would not be available to the Dodgers, team president Peter O'Malley pursued another free agent—the right-handed pitcher Dave Goltz of the Minnesota Twins. The Dodgers outbid the Milwaukee Brewers, signing Goltz to a six-year contract worth $3 million. They had not spent that much money in the free agent market previously, and the signing surprised many baseball people. Among them was Goltz's agent, Larue Harcourt. "Based on their history, I didn't think the Dodgers would be willing to pay out that kind of money," Harcourt said. "We had a void to fill to get an otherwise very good team back into first place, back into the World Series," said O'Malley. After two successive National League pennants, the Dodgers had a 79–83 record in 1979. "We are actively filling whatever voids need to be filled."[33] (Their greatest need was a quality relief pitcher.)

Milwaukee was Goltz's first choice, but the Brewers were unwilling to match the Dodgers offer of up-front money and a large signing bonus. As a Minnesota native, Goltz had hoped to stay with the Twins. "Money isn't that important to me," he said, but Harcourt confirmed that it was money that made the difference. "All things being equal you look at the money." Free agency had changed baseball and Goltz saw it for himself. "I went out and saw what the rest of the (baseball) world looked like," he said. "It was a lot different than Minnesota…. I tried to negotiate with the Twins, but they never even gave me a counteroffer."[34]

Goltz had a 96–79 record and a 112 ERA+ in eight seasons with the Twins. He was a 20-game winner only once and never an All-Star, but he was reliable starter, logging more than 220 innings in each of the past five seasons. Goltz was now the highest-paid player on the team, which was a potential source of problems. Burt Hooton, arguably a better pitcher than Goltz, had signed a five-year contract prior to last season for approximately half of what Goltz received. When asked about it, O'Malley said he did not think it would be an issue.

Also in 1979:

Purchased: Outfielder Von Joshua from Tabasco of Mexican League; Pitcher Lerrin LaGrow from Chicago White Sox; Pitcher Fernando Valenzuela from Yucatán of the Mexican League

Sold: Outfielder Joe Simpson to Seattle Mariners; Pitcher Lance Rautzhan to Milwaukee Brewers; Outfielder Von Joshua to San Diego Padres

Chosen in Amateur Free Agent Draft: Greg Brock, Don Crow; Orel Hershiser; Steve Howe

Signed Amateur Free Agents: Rich Rodas; Tony Brewer

Signed Free Agents: Pitcher Andy Messersmith; Pitcher Ken Brett; Pitcher Don Stanhouse; Outfielder Jay Johnstone

Released: Pitcher Andy Messersmith; Outfielder Manny Mota; Outfielder Vic Davalillo

Left as Free Agents: Pitcher Lerrin LaGrow

6

1980–1984

1980

July 11, 1980: Sold Pitcher Charlie Hough to the Texas Rangers

Knuckleballer Charlie Hough was in his eleventh season with the Dodgers. He had been in 401 games, all but 16 in relief, with a 47–46 record, 60 saves, and a 102 ERA+. Fourteen of Hough's sixteen starts were in 1979, when several of the team's regular starters suffered injuries. He managed a 7–5 record, but his ERA ballooned to 4.76, and his ERA+ was 76, his career worst for a full season. Hough seemed to bear the blame for the failures of the Dodgers bullpen. While he maintained his popularity among his teammates, the fans had taken to booing him.

"I could handle the criticism," said the 32-year-old right-hander. "I'm not 20 years old. I've had my ups and downs before."[1] Tony Attanasio, Hough's agent, said the 6'2" right-hander was ecstatic over being sold by the Dodgers to the Rangers. Manager Tom Lasorda was happy, too. "Charlie has been with me for a long time. He helped me win pennants in Ogden, Spokane, Albuquerque, the Dominican, Venezuela, and in L.A. It was hard to see him go but it was the best for him."[2]

Hough would go on to spend 11 years with the Rangers, two with the Chicago White Sox, and two with the Florida Marlins. He was a starter almost all that time, including starting the first game for the expansion Marlins in 1993. Overall, Hough pitched for 25 seasons, compiling 216 wins and 216 losses.

December 4, 1980: Free Agent Pitcher Don Sutton Signed with the Houston Astros

Don Sutton left the Dodgers as their all-time wins' leader, with 233. He was also first in games started (533), innings pitched (3,816⅓) and shutouts (52). Larue Harcourt, his agent, said the four-year contract Sutton signed with Houston would make him one of baseball's "top 5 or 10" salaried players. The Astros beat out the New York Yankees for the 35-year-old Sutton's services with a package that included a signing bonus, business loan, and incentive provisions.

Sutton said Milwaukee had been his first choice, but the Brewers were unable to satisfy his contract needs. "I just had a gut feeling that I wanted to play in Milwaukee," Sutton explained. "I like [GM] Harry Dalton and I like the way his club scores runs. I've also always had the feeling about Milwaukee that it was a conservative, laid-back, blue-collar town where there was no pressure to be a star. The people there can recognize and appreciate a good effort regardless of the result. I've always had the same feeling about Houston." He said he chose the Astros over the Yankees for a variety of reasons, most dealing with comfort and environment "You can wear your jeans here without people thinking you're trying to be stylish. I've frequently said I wouldn't mind retiring in Texas, and I'm sure that played a subconscious role in my decision. I knew my family would be more comfortable here than in New York."[3]

In leaving, Sutton took a parting shot at Dodgers manager Tom Lasorda. When he was asked about Bill Virdon, who would be his manager in Houston, Sutton said: "Virdon is a stable and honest man, like the Walter Alston I used to know."[4]

Also in 1980:

Traded: Shortstop Ron Washington to Minnesota Twins for Minor League Infielder Wayne Caughey; Pitcher Dennis Lewallyn to Texas Rangers for Shortstop Pepe Frías
 Sold: Gary Thomasson to Yomiuri Giants of Japan Central League
 Chosen in Amateur Free Agent Draft: R.J. Reynolds; Larry See; Ricky Wright
 Signed Amateur Free Agents: Gil Reyes; Jose Gonzalez; Tom Niedenfuer; Ed Amelung
 Signed Free Agents: Outfielder Vic Davalillo; Outfielder Manny Mota
 Released: Pitcher Ken Brett; Catcher Johnny Oates; Infielder-Outfielder Ted Martínez; Outfielder Vic Davalillo, Outfielder Manny Mota

1981

March 30, 1981: Traded Outfielder-Third Baseman Mickey Hatcher, Minor League Pitcher Matt Reeves, and Minor League First Baseman Kelly Snider to the Minnesota Twins for Outfielder Ken Landreaux

The Dodgers had been seeking to add a left-handed batter all winter. They failed in their attempt to get Fred Lynn from the Red Sox and to re-acquire Bill Buckner from the Cubs. With Opening Day nearing they worried that Reggie Smith, their only left-handed hitting regular, would not be ready to open the season. Two days after the Buckner negotiations fell apart, the Dodgers traded 26-year-old right-handed-hitting Mickey Hatcher and two minor leaguers to the Minnesota Twins for centerfielder Ken Landreaux. General manager Al Campanis had spoken to the Twins about Landreaux at the Dallas winter meetings, but the Twins were asking for third baseman Hatcher, outfielder Pedro Guerrero (an emerging star), and minor leaguers in return. "A day ago, they asked for just Guerrero and the minor leaguers," Campanis said. "We said no. When they asked for Hatcher, we said we'd think about that.... It wouldn't have been fair to the ballclub not to protect ourselves in the eventuality one of our ballplayers can't play. We wanted a left-handed batter."[5]

Hatcher appeared in a combined 90 games for the Dodgers in 1979 and 1980. Based on his .359 batting average in 43 games at Albuquerque in 1980, he was thought to have high potential. Tom Lasorda loved Hatcher's style of play. "If anybody ever put on the uniform with more determination and more desire, who loved the game of baseball more, then I haven't seen him. We're going to miss him." Hatcher took the deal philosophically. His agent had asked the Dodgers to trade him if they did not intend to play him. "I have no bad feelings for the Dodgers," Hatcher said. "How could you? It's a great program, a great team. I'll miss them. I don't know if the Twins will kid each other the way this team does. The Twins don't have a (Jay) Johnstone, a (Jerry) Reuss, a (Don) Stanhouse. Now they have a Hatcher, though."[6] The two minor leaguers going to Minnesota were Kelly Snider, a first baseman who hit .303 and drove in 77 runs at Albuquerque last season, and left-handed pitcher Matt Reeves, who was 5–11 with a 6.62 ERA for the Lodi Dodgers of the Class A California League. Neither one ever reached the major leagues.

Landreaux, 26, came to the Twins from the California Angels in the

February 1979 trade for Rod Carew. He batted .305 with 15 home runs and 83 RBIs in his first season in Minnesota, and .281 with a 31-game hitting streak in 1980. The Dodgers players approved of the trade, including Smith, who had advised against re-acquiring Buckner. "I'm not knocking Buck," second baseman Davey Lopes said, "but ever since his ankle injury, he's been basically a first baseman, and he can't play first base for this club. (Not with Steve Garvey there.) Kenny is five or six years younger than Buck."[7]

Twins manager Gene Mauch said: "There are very few players in the American League as talented as Ken Landreaux. He's in the upper echelon. I don't think he's fully realized his potential.... If you went out looking for major league potential and you saw Ken Landreaux, it wouldn't go beyond that." Landreaux was thrilled with the trade. "It's like a dream come true. Dodger Blue. I get a chance to play at home," said the Los Angeles native.[8]

Landreaux spent the next seven seasons with the Dodgers. He batted .263 with a 98 OPS+ in 868 games. His best season was 1983, when he batted .281 with 17 home runs, 66 runs batted in, and a career-high OPS+ of 115. Landreaux was replaced by Reggie Williams in center field in 1986 and by John Shelby in 1987, a season in which he batted .203 and his OPS+ fell to 57. He declared for free agency after the season, but Landreaux's major league career was over.

December 9, 1981: Traded Pitcher Rick Sutcliffe and Second Baseman Jack Perconte to the Cleveland Indians for Second Baseman Jorge Orta, Minor League Pitcher Larry White, and Minor League Catcher Jack Fimple

The Dodgers traded two players who had grown disillusioned with the team and with manager Tom Lasorda. Rick Sutcliffe, a 6'7", 215-pound right-hander, was the team's first choice in the 1974 amateur free agent draft. He was the National League's Rookie of the Year in 1979, when he won 17 games (17–10) and had an ERA+ of 105. It had been downhill for Sutcliffe ever since. Struggling to throw strikes with his curve ball, he was 3–9 with a 64 OPS+ in 1980 and 2–2 in 14 games this past season. Lasorda removed him from the rotation in May. After the midseason player strike ended, Sutcliffe injured his foot and pitched infrequently the rest of the season. With the Dodgers on their way to the playoffs, Sutcliffe promised two things if they dropped him from the postseason roster: He would not go quietly, and if he ever pitched against the Dodgers a lot of them would be going down.

"I don't want to leave," he said in late September. "Everyone who leaves the Dodgers always talks about how they'd like to come back. But if they're not going to use me, I have to." A week later, he was called into Lasorda's office to be told he would not be on the playoff roster. According to the *Los Angeles Times*, Sutcliffe was enraged. He began screaming at Lasorda and used his arm to sweep everything off the manager's desk. He picked up a chair and started smashing the rows of autographed pictures of Frank Sinatra hanging on the wall. "I know one thing, I'm never going to challenge Sutcliffe," said Cleveland manager Dave Garcia.[9] Sutcliffe said he was embarrassed by the incident and called it childish on his part.

Jack Perconte, 27, was a sixteenth-round choice in the 1976 amateur free agent draft. In the past three seasons at Albuquerque, the left-handed-hitting Perconte, hit .322, .326, and .346 and averaged 40 stolen bases. But the Dodgers questioned his fielding, and because they were grooming 22-year-old Steve Sax as Davey Lopes' replacement at second base, Perconte wanted out. He was expected to be (and was) the Indians' second baseman in 1982.

Jorge Orta, 31, spent eight years as a good-hitting, poor-fielding second baseman for the Chicago White Sox. For the past two seasons, he had been a good-hitting, adequate-fielding right fielder for Cleveland. A left-handed hitter, he had a .282 career batting average and was a two-time All-Star. "We've always liked Jorge Orta," Al Campanis said. "He appears to be a natural kind of hitter. He plays more than one position."[10]

Accompanying Orta to Los Angeles were two minor leaguers, pitcher Larry White and catcher Jack Fimple. The Dodgers considered White a good prospect and Fimple a throw-in. Orta spent one season with Dodgers, batting .217 with a 72 OPS+. In December they traded him to the New York Mets for pitcher Pat Zachry. Orta never played for the Mets. In February 1983 he was traded to the Toronto Blue Jays.

Also in 1981:

Chosen in Amateur Free Agent Draft: Dave Anderson; John Franco; Sid Bream; Lemmie Miller; Sid Fernandez; Stu Pederson
Signed Amateur Free Agents: Balvino Galvez
Signed Free Agents: Catcher Jerry Grote; Shortstop Mark Belanger
Released: Pitcher Doug Rau; Pitcher Don Stanhouse; Catcher Joe Ferguson; Shortstop Pepe Frías; Catcher Jerry Grote

1982

February 8, 1982: Traded Second Baseman Davey Lopes to the Oakland Athletics for Minor League Infielder Lance Hudson

Davey Lopes, the Dodgers captain for the last two seasons, had been the team's starting second baseman for nine of the ten seasons he was with the club. Yet it had become apparent late in the 1981 season the Dodgers were ready to replace the 36-year-old Lopes with 22-year-old Steve Sax. While the "official line" was that the two men would compete for the position this spring, Dodger officials hinted often that they expected Sax to prevail. After his August 1981 debut, Sax, a rookie, batted .277 as a replacement for the injured Lopes. When Lopes was ready to return, Lasorda continued to play Sax. But Lasorda returned Lopes to the lineup for the playoffs and the World Series, where he helped lead the Dodgers to a world championship. "They can do anything they want with us now!" Lopes yelled in the Dodgers dressing room after the six-game victory over the Yankees. "I've got the ring! They can't take that away from me!"[11]

"What you've got to realize," Al Campanis said in early September, "is Davey took someone else's job when he became the regular second baseman. This same thing holds true. Here we have an aggressive, enthusiastic, double-play-making, pretty-good-hitting young man and I would say that Davey has to look and say, 'Hey this guy may be for real, he may be taking my job.'"[12]

Lopes, an articulate, outspoken man, had this to say about losing his job. "People said I was running away from a challenge. I'm not running away from a challenge. The Dodgers told me the job would be up in the air, but everything told me otherwise. Other people I know are telling me otherwise, people I trust, teammates, guys I respect. They didn't feel I'd get a fair shot." Lopes said what hurt him most was that Tommy (Lasorda, who has been with Lopes since managing him at Spokane in 1970) didn't call and say, "Stay and fight for it." "If he would have said, 'Stay and fight for it,' I would have stayed. When he didn't call, I knew. That was very disappointing to me, when he didn't call, but I can deal with anything."[13]

Lopes played in 1,207 games for Los Angeles, with a .262 batting average and 105 OPS+. His 418 stolen bases as a Dodger is second only to Maury Wills' 490. In return for Lopes, the Dodgers received a 19-year-old Class A infielder named Lance Hudson, who hit .225 for San Jose in the

California League last season. Players his age are divided into "definite prospects" and those thought to have a chance. Campanis said Hudson is a "has a chance." However, Hudson never reached the major leagues. Meanwhile, Lopes played another six seasons, for Oakland, the Chicago Cubs, and Houston.

March 30, 1982: Traded Outfielder Rudy Law to the Chicago White Sox for Outfielder Cecil Espy and Minor League Pitcher Bert Geiger

Center fielder Rudy Law batted .260 with 40 stolen bases as a 23-year-old rookie in 1980. But the Dodgers, loaded with outfielders, sent the left-handed-hitting Law to Albuquerque in 1981, where he hit .335 and stole 56 bases. He was out of options, so rather than keep him, the Dodgers traded him to the Chicago White Sox a week before opening day. They received next to nothing in return. Outfielder Cecil Espy had 11 at bats for them in 1983, and pitcher Bert Geiger never reached the major leagues.

"I'm happy this is what I wanted," Law said when he heard he had been traded. "It was obvious they didn't have the kind of plans I was hoping for. But I think I showed them something the past couple of weeks. From what I understand there's a chance I'll play center field for the White Sox. I don't care whether it's left, center, or right as long as I get a shot."[14]

It was an excellent deal for Chicago, one that paid immediate dividends. Law batted .318 with 36 stolen bases in 1982 and .283 with 77 stolen bases in 1983.

December 1, 1982: Free Agent Pitcher Terry Forster Signed with the Atlanta Braves

In his five seasons with the Dodgers, Terry Forster pitched in 150 games, all in relief. He had 22 saves in 1978, his first year with the club, but only five since. His overall record was 11 wins and 13 losses, but with a fine 116 ERA+. Forster declared for free agency after the Dodgers best offer to him was a three-year contract worth $900,000. When the Atlanta Braves matched the three years and raised the money amount to $1.5 million, the 31-year-old left-hander agreed to join them.

"Going into the offseason, our two most important needs were a prime addition to the starting rotation and a left-hander for the bullpen," said Braves general manager John Mullen. "If we can get both, great. But now we've got half of what we need."[15] (The "prime addition to the rotation they were pursuing was Seattle free agent Floyd Bannister who signed with the Chicago White Sox two weeks later.")

As Forster and everyone else knew the Braves' weakness was its starting pitching. But Forster said Mullen and team owner Ted Turner "assured me they're going to do everything they can to strengthen the starting pitching."[16]

December 21, 1982: Free Agent First Baseman Steve Garvey Signed with the San Diego Padres

Steve Garvey had been the Dodgers most productive player since 1974, when he was selected to the National League's All-Star team and voted its Most Valuable Player. It was the first of eight consecutive seasons he would be an all-star and get consideration for the MVP Award. Garvey had declared for free agency after the 1982 season, although he allegedly wanted to stay in Los Angeles. Dodgers president Peter O'Malley allegedly wanted to keep him and began negotiations with Garvey and his agent, Jerry Kapstein. A few days later O'Malley was outraged at suggestions that he had not really tried to sign Garvey. The last negotiating session, reported the *Los Angeles Times*, was said to have been heated and to have included some name-calling. A friend of Garvey's said that Garvey, the man who never gets angry, later called O'Malley "a fragile, insecure man."

"Final offers had to be made," Garvey said. "[Peter O'Malley] said his final offer was $5 million for four years, no incentives. We drew the line at $6 million for four years."[17] On December 21, the day before his 34th birthday, Garvey signed a five-year, $6.6 million contract with the San Diego Padres. "Despite all the good taste and good manners in public," wrote Mark Heisler in the *Los Angeles Times*, "despite the mutual declarations of respect, sources close to the parties suggest that the storybook Garvey-Dodger association ended badly."[18]

"They [San Diego] got a good player," said Al Campanis. "We'd like to wish him the best of luck. He's a fine gentleman. I understand he did pretty well monetarily. We made him a good offer and we had to stay with it. I don't know what he got, but I understand it was better than our offer." Padres manager Dick Williams said. "This is an early Christmas present. I'm elated. We're already up one notch in the standings before he even dons a uniform." Padres president Ballard Smith believed the acquisition of Garvey made his team a pennant contender. "I don't see how anyone can say anything else. The only thing we want to do is win. I believe in 1983 we can win the division title. When the Dodgers didn't sign Steve Garvey," Smith said, "I didn't really think we had much opportunity. I had some idea what the Dodgers offered, and it was very substantial." Garvey called it the toughest decision of his professional life. He talked of respect and fans and contracts and chemistry and then said: "One of the most important factors is that my heart is here in Southern California."[19]

Garvey played in 1,727 games over 14 seasons with Los Angeles. He had a .301 batting average and a 122 OPS+. He remains third in doubles on the Dodgers all-time list, fifth in hits and runs batted in, and sixth in home runs. He left ten games short of breaking Cubs outfielder Billy Williams's National League record of 1,117 consecutive games played. He broke that record in San Diego's 11th game of the 1983 season and extended it to 1,207 games before a broken thumb ended the streak. That record still stands.

Also in 1982:

Traded: Pitcher Bobby Castillo and Outfielder Bobby Mitchell to Minnesota Twins for Minor League Third Baseman Scotti Madison and Minor League Pitcher Paul Voigt; Minor League Third baseman Leo Hernández to Baltimore Orioles for First Baseman José Morales; Pitcher Ted Power to Cincinnati Reds for Minor League Outfielder Mike Ramsey; Outfielder Jorge Orta to Cincinnati Reds for Pitcher Pat Zachry

Purchased: Pitcher Vicente Romo from Coatzacoalcos of Mexican League

Chosen in Amateur Free Agent Draft: Jeff Hamilton; Ken Howell; Franklin Stubbs; Reggie Williams; Tim Meeks

Signed Amateur Free Agents: Mariano Duncan

Signed Free Agents: Outfielder Manny Mota

Released: Pitcher Dave Goltz; Outfielder Jay Johnstone; Outfielder Manny Mota

1983

January 19, 1983: Traded Third Baseman Ron Cey to the Chicago Cubs for Minor League Pitcher Vance Lovelace and Minor League Outfielder Dan Cataline

The Dodgers infield of first baseman Steve Garvey, second baseman Davey Lopes, shortstop Bill Russell, and third baseman Ron Cey had played together for eight seasons, three seasons longer than any other major league infield had done. But with the trade of Cey, a month away from turning 35, preceded by the February trade of Lopes, then 36, and the 34-year-old Garvey signing as a free agent with San Diego a month ago, only Russell remained. To further emphasize the Dodgers youth movement, only Russell and left fielder Dusty Baker were left from the 1980 opening day starting lineup. (The Dodgers would release Russell after the 1986 season.) Cey had been a Dodger for 12 seasons, the last ten as their third baseman. He played in 1,481 games, with a .264 batting average and a 125 OPS+. His 228 career home runs were at the time the most hit by a Los Angeles Dodger.

"We got a guy we think we can depend on," said Chicago Cubs GM Dallas Green. "He's tickled to death, and we are too. He said, 'It's kind of neat to feel wanted again.' He doesn't feel he was appreciated there the last two years.... He was dropped to sixth in the batting order and benched a couple of times. He recognized the Dodgers were undergoing a youth movement." Dodgers vice president Al Campanis explained the thinking behind the movement of Cey and his other veterans: "We appreciated the fine work he did for us over the years. He was a true Dodger ballplayer. But we had to make a turnover. You build a club for a decade not one year.... Ten years ago, we did the same things with no-names like Garvey, Lopes, Cey, Ferguson, and Yeager. This is the direction we are going. We had to start thinking about doing something and fortunately we have some talent."[20]

Cey, however, had been angry about the youth movement and depressed by suggestions that his time with the Dodgers would soon be ending. During the season-ending series in San Francisco, he told a friend he thought he was gone. He gave the Dodgers a deadline: they had until January 15 to move him. When the Dodgers and the Cubs got close to a deal a week ago, Cey relaxed his deadline and gave them another week. The Dodgers asked the Cubs for reliever Lee Smith in return for Cey. When Green rejected that offer, they asked for Joe Carter, a Class AA prospect and a former No. 1 draft choice. Green, wisely, said no to that too. So Campanis took what he could get, two raw prospects. Six-foot-five left-hander Vance Lovelace, 19, was the Cubs' second choice on the first round of the 1981 draft. In two seasons, one in the Rookie League and one in Class A, he had 138 strikeouts in 124 innings; he also had 120 walks and a combined 4–11 record. Dan Cataline hit 18 homers last season at Class A Salinas, with a .246 batting average. Cataline would never reach the big leagues. Lovelace would, with the Angels five years later, but never had a win or a loss.

"I'm extremely pleased to be going to the Cubs and to a new organization," Cey said. "It represents a challenge for me. I'm also looking forward to playing in front of the great Chicago Cubs fans."[21] Cey had five seasons as the Cubs' third baseman. One of the reasons the Cubs got him was because they thought rookie Ryne Sandberg, who played third for them in 1982, might be a better second baseman and getting Cey would allow them to move him there.

August 19, 1983: Traded Pitcher Dave Stewart, a Player to be Named, and Cash to the Texas Rangers for Pitcher Rick Honeycutt

The Dodgers saw the acquisition of Texas left-hander Rick Honeycutt as a major step to winning the National League West championship. After outbidding division rival Atlanta and the Philadelphia Phillies, they signed the 29-year-old Honeycutt to a five-year contract worth an estimated $3.75 million. Dodgers' scouts rated Honeycutt, who was leading the American League in earned run average (2.42), and ERA OPS+ (1.65), and was third in victories (14), the league's best pitcher this season.

"This could be a blockbuster," said Al Campanis. "This could really mean something to our club. We're really excited. Embarking on this season our thoughts focused on our youngsters and a turnover year, but we believe in trying to win now and with the addition of Honeycutt we feel we have bolstered our hopes of winning the Western Division title."[22]

Campanis said Honeycutt would immediately move into the Dodgers' five-man starting rotation, taking the place of a struggling Burt Hooton. "We have to do what's best for the ballclub," Campanis said. "We did this because we felt we would improve our pitching. We felt this trade would give us one more good starter The only reason we did this was that Texas felt they couldn't sign him."[23] Honeycutt was eligible for free agency at the end of this season.

Dave Stewart a 26-year-old right-hander, was in his third year with the Dodgers; he had gone 18–13 with a 106 ERA+ over that time, including 5–2 with a 122 ERA+ this season.

Stewart didn't do much with Texas, or the Phillies, and Honeycutt spent a few years in LA, where he was a sub-.500 pitcher. But in 1988 they both landed in Oakland, along with another ex–Dodgers pitcher, Bob Welch, and were teammates on the A's three consecutive pennant winners from 1988 to 1990. A's manager Tony LaRussa turned Honeycutt into a relief pitcher, mostly as a set-up man for Dennis Eckersley. Stewart, on the other hand, really blossomed with the A's, where he was a 20-game winner for four consecutive seasons. (1987-1990) . On September 16, the Dodgers sent pitcher Ricky Wright to Texas to complete the trade.

December 8, 1983: Traded Pitcher Sid Fernandez and Minor League Shortstop Ross Jones to the New York Mets for Pitcher Carlos Diaz and a Player to be Named

Within a week, Commissioner Bowie Kuhn would rule on the immediate future of Steve Howe for his use of illegal drugs. The Dodgers suspected Howe, their best relief pitcher, would be suspended for a minimum of half of the 1984 season and perhaps for all of it. (It would be a year.) Needing a left-handed reliever to take Howe's place, they traded 21-year-old pitcher Sid Fernandez and minor league shortstop Ross Jones to the New York Mets for 26-year-old left-handed reliever Carlos Diaz and a player to be named.

A year ago, the Dodgers were touting Fernandez, a hard-throwing left-hander, as the next Sandy Koufax. He was in two games for them in 1983, pitching poorly while losing his only decision, a start on the last day of the season. "We still like Sid Fernandez," Al Campanis said. "It's not that we don't like him we just recognized we have a need." Campanis pointed out that the Dodgers had three left-handed starters—Jerry Reuss, Fernando Valenzuela, and Rick Honeycutt—and no left-handed relievers. Unmentioned was the Dodgers awareness of a weight problem with Fernandez. Mets general manager Frank Cashen was also aware of Fernandez's weight. "He's as big as a bread box," said Cashen, while adding Fernandez had a good chance to be on the Mets roster in 1984.[24]

Fernandez would not be another Koufax, but he would have a successful 15-year career, winning 114 games with a 111 ERA+ for the Mets, the Orioles, the Phillies, and the Astros. Ross Jones played three major league seasons for three different teams, the Mets, the Seattle Mariners, and the Kansas City Royals. He batted .221 with a 45 OPS+ in 67 games.

Unlike Fernandez, Carlos Diaz did not throw hard; his best pitches were a curve ball and a screwball. Diaz appeared in 54 games for the 1983 Mets, with a 3–1 record and a 2.05 earned run average. Tom Lasorda thought the Fernandez-Diaz trade might be the first in major league history where one Hawaiian-born player was traded for another.

Neither team would reveal the identity of the player to be named going to Los Angeles. It was expected to be (and was) infielder-outfielder Bob Bailor. The Dodgers planned to use Bailor as a utility man, replacing Derrel Thomas who had declared for free agency. Bailor played in 139 games for LA over the 1984 and 1985 seasons. He batted .261 with an OPS of 69. The Dodgers released him in April 1986, ending his major league career.

Also in 1983:

Traded: Outfielder Mark Bradley to New York Mets for Minor League Pitcher Steve Walker, Minor League Pitcher Jody Johnstone, and Cash; Minor League Pitcher John Franco and Minor League Pitcher Brett Wise to Cincinnati Reds for Infielder Rafael Landestoy; Pitcher Joe Beckwith to Kansas City Royals for Minor League Pitcher Jose Torres, Minor League Pitcher John Serritella, and Minor League Catcher Joe Szekely
Chosen in Amateur Free Agent Draft: Luis Lopez
Signed Amateur Free Agents: Dennis Powell
Released: Outfielder Ron Roenicke

1984

January 13, 1984: Signed Free Agent Outfielder Terry Whitfield

After brief appearances with the 1974–1976 Yankees, outfielder Terry Whitfield spent the next four seasons with the San Francisco Giants. The 6'1" left-handed hitter batted .289 with an OPS+ of 108, but despite his size he showed little power, 26 home runs in 1,529 at-bats. Whitfield left the Giants after the 1980 season to play for the Seibu Lions of the Japan Pacific League. There he took up martial arts training, which along with facing lesser-quality pitchers turned him from a slap hitter into a slugger. He had 22, 25, and 38 home runs in his three seasons with the Lions. The 38 home runs in 1983, along with his 109 RBIs were league highs.

The Seibu club had informed Commissioner Bowie Kuhn's office of Whitfield's free agency, thus making him eligible to sign with an American team. He chose the Dodgers, one of four teams interested in him. Whitfield said he had some regrets about leaving Japan but wanted to be closer to his aging parents and his five-year-old son. He exercised his right to buy out his option with Seibu and agreed to a cut in pay to sign with the Dodgers, who reportedly gave him $300,000 a year for three years. Al Campanis said Whitfield would give the Dodgers the additional left-handed hitter they needed, along with someone who could play all three outfield positions.

Whitfield said that while he may not have been totally accepted in Japan, "I was respected there. I was always treated first-class," and his leaving Seibu, "is probably headlines all over Japan." He said, "I'm a lot better ballplayer now. I feel I'm good enough to start anywhere."[25] Whitfield batted .242 with seven home runs in 185 games over three seasons with Los Angeles. He was released in May 1986, ending his major league career.

December 20, 1984: Free Agent Pitcher Burt Hooton Signed with the Texas Rangers

Burt Hooton had been a reliable starter for the Dodgers from 1975 to 1983. He was a double-digit winner in seven of those seasons and had his best year in 1978. Hooton won 19 and lost 10 with a 2.71 earned run average in 236 innings. He finished second (a distant second) to Gaylord Perry in voting for the Cy Young Award. But Hooton had never been the same since he was hit in the knee by a line drive during spring training in 1982. He was 3–6 with a 3.44 earned run average this past season. Hooton's totals for his 10 years in LA were a 112–84 record and a 113 ERA+.

With last season's emergence of rookie Orel Hershiser, the Dodgers had six starting pitchers on their staff, not including Hooton. As a result, they had little interest in re-signing a pitcher who would turn 35 in February. Hooton turned down their perfunctory offer and declared for free agency. He had hoped to stay in the Los Angeles area, but when the California Angels also showed no interest, he signed with the Texas Rangers. It was a two-year contract, loaded with incentive clauses. Hooton's hope was that the Rangers would give him a chance as a starter. "The biggest thing in coming to Texas was their interest in me," he said. "This is a chance to perform. The Dodgers weren't offering that chance." Tom Grieve, the Rangers new general manager, said: "He will be an important member of our pitching staff in 1985."[26]

Also in 1984:

Chosen in Amateur Free Agent Draft: Shawn Hillegas; Tracy Woodson; Jeff Edwards

Signed Amateur Free Agents: Ramón Martínez; Craig Shipley; Carlos Hernández; William Brennan; Darren Holmes

Signed Free Agents: Outfielder Mike Vail; Pitcher Tom Brennan

Released: First Baseman José Morales; Outfielder Rick Monday; Infielder Rafael Landestoy

Left as Free Agents: Infielder-Outfielder Derrel Thomas

7

1985–1989

1985

July 10, 1985: Traded Minor League Pitcher Rafael Montalvo and a Player to be Named to the Houston Astros for Infielder-Outfielder Enos Cabell

Dodgers Vice President Al Campanis had been seeking to add Houston Astros infielder-outfielder Enos Cabell to his roster for months. This past winter he had unsuccessfully offered outfielder Candy Maldonado to Houston for Cabell. Campanis got him now for minor league pitcher Rafael Montalvo and a player to be named. To make room for Cabell, the Dodgers returned first baseman Sid Bream to their Albuquerque farm club. The 35-year-old Cabell was in his fourteenth major league season, with a lifetime .277 batting average. He was in his second stint with Houston and had also played for Baltimore, San Francisco, and Detroit.

"I'm very satisfied with what Enos Cabell can do for our ball club" Campanis said. "He can play regularly or come off the bench. He's a contact hitter who puts the ball in play and he's a leader…. Cabell's still a good runner and he's a good team man. We're fortunate we were able to maneuver where we could get him for two minor leaguers and not hurt the big club."

Manager Tom Lasorda was equally pleased with getting Cabell. "There's nothing definite yet on how we'll use him" he said. "We can play him at third, he can fill in at first or play in the outfield…. We'll put Cabell in the lineup in different places and see what he can do. He gives us an extra overall dimension."[1]

Cabell admitted to being a little nervous. "I grew up in Los Angeles. Even though the Giants were my favorite team—I hate to say it—I always had a lot of respect for the Dodgers, and I learned most of my baseball from Tommy Davis," he said. "Mr. Campanis told me to hurry up and get myself here, so I did. It's a good feeling to be wanted. I hope I can justify the Dodgers' feeling in me and produce."[2]

Cabell, played mostly at first base and third base in his two seasons with the Dodgers. He batted .292 in 57 games in the second half of the 1985 season, and .256 in the 1986 season. Cabell declared for free agency after the 1986 season, but no club signed him, ending his major league career.

The correctly rumored player to be named going to the Astros was third baseman German Rivera. Rivera played in 107 games for the 1983–1984 Dodgers with a .266 batting average.

Right-hander Rafael Montalvo's major league career consisted of one inning pitched for the 1986 Astros.

August 31, 1985: Traded Three Players to Be Named to the Pittsburgh Pirates for Third Baseman Bill Madlock

The trade for Pittsburgh's Bill Madlock ended the Dodgers' season-long search for a full-time third baseman. Pedro Guerrero played the position early in the season, but he was unhappy there and moved back to the outfield. Since then, manager Lasorda had used Dave Anderson, Bill Russell, Bob Bailor, and most recently Enos Cabell at third. The Dodgers had traded with Houston for Cabell a month earlier, after trade talks for Madlock had broken down. To get the 34-year-old, four-time league batting champion, the Dodgers gave up three players to be named. According to one Dodgers source one of the players would be utility outfielder R.J. Reynolds, who had been designated for assignment to make roster room for Madlock. The other two were expected to be minor league first baseman Sid Bream and minor league infielder-outfielder Cecil Espy. Within a week Reynolds, Bream, and Espy were sent to Pittsburgh.

"I was in Pittsburgh July 22 to talk to Joe (Pirates general manager Joe L. Brown) about a deal for Madlock," said Al Campanis. "I felt their demands for Madlock were too high, and I told the press we were out of the running. But Thursday, when I returned from lunch, there was a message that Joe had called. This time, we started talking from our offer. Before the deal could be completed, we had to talk to Madlock. He had a contract with the Pirates through the next two years. Unless we signed him to another contract, he could have become a free agent next March. We reached agreement on a new two-year contract."[3] The trade had to be completed by midnight August 31 for Madlock to be eligible for postseason play.

Campanis believed Madlock would add leadership to a mostly young and inexperienced team. The 13-year veteran started his major league career with Texas in 1973, played three years with the Chicago Cubs, was traded to San Francisco in 1977, and sent to Pittsburgh in 1979. Madlock entered the 1985 season with a career batting average of .312. His elbow and shoulder surgery in August 1984 had likely contributed to his subpar batting this season. In 110 games with the Pirates, he hit .251 with 10 home runs and 41 runs batted in.

As the Pirates captain and team leader, Madlock had been unhappy with the team's trading of high-priced players George Hendrick, Kent Tekulve, and John Candelaria earlier this season. He told the club six weeks ago he would not object to a trade. "I always said that a player, before he retires, should have a chance to play with two clubs the Dodgers and the Yankees. I think it was time for me to move on."[4]

Madlock batted a torrid .360 in 34 games for the 1985 Dodgers. He followed with a .280 average and a 110 OPS+ in 111 games in 1986. He was batting .180 after 21 games in 1987 when the Dodgers released him in May.

December 11, 1985: Traded Catcher Steve Yeager to the Seattle Mariners for Pitcher Ed Vande Berg

Steve Yeager, a Dodger for the past 14 years, had caught more games (1,181) than any Los Angeles Dodgers catcher other than John Roseboro (1,199). But the team's need for a left-handed relief pitcher led to them trading the 37-year-old Yeager to the Seattle Mariners for 27-year-old left-hander Ed Vande Berg. Primarily a defensive specialist, Yeager batted .228 in 1,219 games with the Dodgers. His best season was 1977, when he batted .256 with 21 doubles and 16 home runs. He did, however, bat .298 over 21 games in four World Series. A broken leg limited him to just 74 games in 1984 and 53 in 1985 as the backup to Mike Scioscia.

The Mariners were hoping Yeager could catch between 80 and 100 games in 1986, while sharing the position with Bob Kearney. Mostly they wanted him for his leadership qualities and to serve as a teacher for Seattle's promising young pitching staff. "Our guys have no confidence in Kearney," a Seattle scout said. "We need leadership. Just having Yeager in the clubhouse should help our kids." Dodgers manager Tom Lasorda said he felt about the trade the way he did when Steve Garvey and Ron Cey and Davey Lopes departed. "I told the Seattle people that Yeager had been with me in the Rookie League, in Triple A, in the Puerto Rico Winter League and in the major leagues, and every time he put the uniform on, he played with all the drive and the determination you would want in a player."[5]

According to Al Campanis, the addition of Vande Berg would allow Lasorda to use Carlos Diaz in a middle-inning emergency, saving Vande Berg for the eighth and ninth innings as a complement to right-handers Ken Howell and Tom Niedenfuer. "We had a dire need for a pitcher of Vande Berg's capability," Lasorda said: "All of our reports indicate he was among the best southpaws available." Vande Berg said: "The Mariners told me at the end of the season that I might be traded, so it's not really a surprise. But Los Angeles ... wow. That's big time. That's a team that's in the playoffs all the time. I just hope I can help the Dodgers. I'm confident I can."[6]

Vande Berg had appeared in 272 games for the Mariners over the past four seasons, the fifth most by any major league pitcher during that time frame. He had a 21–21 record with 20 saves and a 111 ERA+.

December 11, 1985: Traded Outfielder Candy Maldonado to the San Francisco Giants for Catcher Alex Trevino

In conjunction with the Steve Yeager trade made earlier in the day, the Dodgers announced they had traded Candy Maldonado, once considered their center fielder of the future, to the San Francisco Giants for catcher Alex Trevino. "I've been working my way across the country for this" said the 28-year-old Trevino, who would be joining his fourth team in five years. "I'm thankful to God that He has done this." Before playing for San Francisco this past season, Trevino, a seven-year veteran, had played for the New York Mets, the Cincinnati Reds, and the Atlanta Braves. "Every team I've been with, they've cleaned house after I've left," he said. "I don't think this will happen with the Dodgers. They've been doing too well for too many years. To me winning is everything."[7]

Trevino, a right-handed hitter, who was acquired to replace Yeager as the backup to catcher Mike Scioscia, was content to accept that role. "By winning I can compensate for not playing every day," he said. "As you know the Dodgers have been very good about playing everybody so I'm not too worried about that."[8]

Candy Maldonado had been with the Dodgers since 1981. A 25-year-old right-handed-batter, he never had lived up to expectations. He left with a .237 batting average and an 81 OPS+ in 296 games. He would play in the major leagues for another 10 seasons.

Also in 1985:

Traded: Pitcher Pat Zachry to Philadelphia Phillies for Outfielder-First Baseman Al Oliver; Outfielder-First Baseman Al Oliver to Toronto Blue Jays for Outfielder-First Baseman Len Matuszek

Chosen in Amateur Free Agent Draft: John Wetteland; Chris Gwynn; Jack Savage; Mike Devereaux; Mike Huff
Signed Amateur Free Agents: Henry Rodríguez; Juan Guzmán
Signed Free Agents: Pitcher Bobby Castillo; Outfielder Jay Johnstone; Infielder Mike Ramsey
Released: Infielder Mike Ramsey; Pitcher Steve Howe; Outfielder Jay Johnstone
Left as Free Agents: Catcher Dave Sax; Pitcher Tom Brennan

1986

December 10, 1986: Traded Pitcher Dennis Powell and Minor League Second Baseman Mike Watters to the Seattle Mariners for Pitcher Matt Young

Still looking for bullpen help, the Dodgers traded pitcher Dennis Powell and minor league infielder Mike Watters to the Seattle Mariners for left-handed short reliever Matt Young. Powell, a 23-year-old left-hander, had a 3–8 record and a 77 ERA+ in two seasons with the club. Still, the Dodgers were reluctant to lose him. "I think Powell's an outstanding young pitcher," said Al Campanis. "He could have been a starter for us."[9] Mike Watters, 23, batted .285 for Albuquerque in 1986. He would never reach the major leagues.

In 1983 Young, then 24 years old, won 11 games for Seattle and was selected to the American League All-Star team. He was mostly a starter in his four years with the Mariners, until last season. Moved to the bullpen by manager Dick Williams, Young had an 8–6 record and a team-leading 13 saves. "We've wanted Young for some time, but we didn't have a shot at him last year," Campanis said in explaining the trade. "We've filled our need for a short man. We were fortunate to get a left-hander of his ability."[10]

Two of the best hitters in the American League, Don Mattingly of the Yankees and Wade Boggs of the Red Sox, rated Young as the best left-hander in the league. The Mariners had timed every pitcher in the AL this past season, and the only two who threw fastballs at more than 95 m.p.h. were Young and Boston's Roger Clemens. The Dodgers made it known they were aware that since 1984, Young had required medication to control his arthritis. Neither they, nor Young, saw it as a problem. "Too much was made about it in the first place," Young said. "I haven't had a problem for 2½ years."[11]

December 10, 1986: Traded First Baseman Greg Brock to the Milwaukee Brewers for Pitcher Tim Leary and Minor League Pitcher Tim Crews

Al Campanis followed up the trade for Matt Young, by sending disgruntled first baseman Greg Brock to the Milwaukee Brewers for two young right-handers: Tim Leary and Tim Crews. Brock, who grew up dreaming of playing first base for the Dodgers, realized his dream when he replaced Steve Garvey in 1983. Thought to be the team's best left-handed power hitter since Duke Snider, Brock, to this point, had fallen short of those hopes. He batted just .233 over four-plus seasons, with 71 home runs and 219 runs batted in.

Campanis said he did not know why Brock and the organization gave up on each other. "When a guy says he wants to be traded you begin to feel he's lost some of his confidence in us," he said. "The Dodgers don't have many players who ask to be traded." There wasn't that much of a market for him. Franklin Stubbs would be the new first baseman, Campanis added. "There may have been some pressure on Brock from replacing Steve Garvey. This could be the best thing that ever happened to him. Brock has great potential, but you come to a point when you have to make a move, especially when you have a guy like Stubbs."[12]

Brock said he did not think things went the way they should have for him, or did the Dodgers get what they expected. "Maybe this will be the best thing for both of us," he said. "There's just a lot of pressure in playing in the major leagues. I can't weigh what was involved, Steve Garvey or the pressures of playing. I got in a rut a few years ago. Then I wasn't playing every day I never got out of the rut. By no means am I downgrading the Dodgers I just hope this works out for the best for both of us."[13] Brewers manager Tom Trebelhorn said Brock would be his first baseman, replacing Cecil Cooper who would become Milwaukee's designated hitter.

The New York Mets chose Tim Leary with the second overall pick in the June 1979 amateur free agent draft. He was limited by arm problems with the Mets, who traded him to the Brewers in 1985. Leary had a 12–12 record and a 104 ERA+ in 33 games, 30 of them starts, for the 1986 Brewers. "I remember facing him when I was 19 and 20 years old," said Dodgers outfielder Mike Marshall, "and he was the best arm I had ever faced. At that time, I put him up there with the Dwight Goodens and Nolan Ryans. Later after the arm problems it was a different story. But I hear that he's back."

Leary, who grew up as a Dodgers fan, said he "was starting to feel at home with the Brewers, but if you're going to be traded this is the best place to go. I just hope I get a chance to start."[14]

Tim Crews, 25, was considered a "has chance" prospect. He would be a relief pitcher for the Dodgers from 1987 to 1992, with an 11–13 record, 15 saves, and a 104 ERA+. In January 1993, Crews signed as a free agent with the Cleveland Indians. During spring training that year, he and Indians pitcher Steve Olin were killed in a boating accident in Florida.

Also in 1986:

Purchased: Pitcher Joe Beckwith from Toronto Blue Jays
Chosen in Amateur Free Agent Draft: Dave Hansen; Mike Munoz; Billy Bartels; Mike James
Signed Amateur Free Agents: Jose Vizcaino; Jose Offerman
Signed Free Agents: Outfielder César Cedeño; Infielder Brad Wellman
Chosen in Minor League Draft: Pitcher Mike Hartley
Released: Infielder-Outfielder Bob Bailor; Pitcher Bobby Castillo; Outfielder Terry Whitfield; Outfielder César Cedeño; Pitcher Carlos Diaz; Pitcher Joe Beckwith; Shortstop Bill Russell; Catcher Jack Fimple; Pitcher Ed Vande Berg
Left as Free Agents: Infielder-Outfielder Enos Cabell

1987

For the 1987 season, Fred Claire replaced Al Campanis as general manager.

May 22, 1987: Traded Pitcher Tom Niedenfuer to the Baltimore Orioles for Outfielder John Shelby and Pitcher Brad Havens

Mike Ramsey's excellent defense during spring training had won him the starting center field job as a non-roster player. But the Dodgers were not satisfied with Ramsey, who after 48 games was batting just .232 with no home runs and a 57 OPS+. Desperate to upgrade the position, they traded one of their best relief pitchers, veteran right-hander Tom Niedenfuer, to the Baltimore Orioles for centerfielder John Shelby and Brad Havens, a left-handed long reliever. Both Shelby, 29 and Havens, 27, were currently with the Rochester Red Wings, the Orioles' Triple A team in the International League. To make room for Shelby, the Dodgers optioned Ramsey to Albuquerque. (He would never return to the major leagues.)

"I see it as a good opportunity for us," said Dodgers vice president Fred Claire, after completing his first trade in his new job as director of player personnel. Claire said it took two weeks of evaluation and negotiation to get the deal done. "We're getting a center fielder who is very good on defense and has major league experience."[15]

Shelby, a switch-hitter with a .239 batting average and a 75 OPS+ in seven seasons in Baltimore, did not appear to be a significant offensive upgrade from Ramsey. He was hitting only .188 in 21 games this season when the Orioles demoted him to Rochester two weeks earlier. Shelby said he was surprised he was not sent to Albuquerque. "I heard that the trade was Jim Dwyer [another Orioles outfielder] and myself for Niedenfuer," said Shelby. "That's all I kept hearing. I heard they wanted a left-handed hitter, and Jim is that. I thought I'd go to Albuquerque or wherever their minor league team is. I had heard about Baltimore and Boston last week, and I knew the Dodgers had some holes to fill."[16] Shelby played with Los Angeles into the 1990 season, before being released on June 2. He batted .247 with an 88 OPS+ in 393 games. He was granted free agency after the 1990 season and signed with the Detroit Tigers.

Tom Niedenfuer was in his seventh season with Los Angeles. He had appeared in 310 games with a 30–28 record, but with 64 saves and an ERA+ of 128. He had pitched in at least 60 games each of the last two seasons and three of the last four. His departure left the Dodgers with only Ken Howell as a right-handed short reliever. "When I was told to go to Fred's suite at New York's Grand Hyatt, I walked in and asked which team," said Niedenfuer.[17] He emphasized that he had not requested a trade but seemed happy to go. "I don't know yet whether I'll like it," he said. "I'll like the chance to pitch. It's going to be strange. I've never played in the American League and only played for one manager (Tom Lasorda)."[18]

Brad Havens was a starter for the Minnesota Twins in this first three major league seasons (1981–1983), but a reliever for the Orioles in 1985 and 1986, with an overall record of 21–32. He would spend the rest of this season and the early part of 1988 with the Dodgers, appearing in 40 games with no decisions and one save. Havens was released in May 1988 and signed as a free agent with the Cleveland Indians.

August 29, 1987: Traded Pitcher Rick Honeycutt to the Oakland Athletics for a Player to be Named

Oakland was leading the American League's West Division and looking to add a left-handed pitcher. Los Angeles was out of the race in the National League's West Division and had been seeking to trade Rick Honeycutt for several months. Honeycutt had endured a frustrating fifth season with the Dodgers, with a 2-12 record that led to his removal from the rotation. He had set a Los Angeles team record of 11 consecutive losses, three short of Jim Pastorius' franchise record set in 1908. Honeycutt appeared in 128 games as a Dodger with 33 wins, 45 losses, and a combined 100 ERA+. After Honeycutt was switched from a starter to a reliever, Tom Reich, his agent, met with Fred Claire to find the best deal for both the player and the team. The A's would assume the remainder of his $775,000 contract this season and all his $825,000 salary for the 1988 season.

"I didn't demand anything," the 33-year-old Honeycutt said. "I just felt like, for myself, it would be a good move to get traded. I feel like this is an opportunity to wash away everything that has happened this season. I'm excited to go to a contending club. In one day, I picked up about 12 games in the standings." Honeycutt's last appearance as a Dodger came a few days earlier in New York, when he was called in only to issue an intentional walk. "That kind of tops my year off right there," he said.[19]

Claire said the Dodgers would receive a "prospect" within a few days. "It's obviously somebody the Dodgers covet highly," said Sandy Alderson, the A's vice president. "But we don't consider him a top echelon prospect." Claire said: "It is a player who certainly figures to be a prominent player in our future. Otherwise, we would not have made the deal, because, in Rick Honeycutt, we gave up a prominent major league pitcher."[20]

On September 3, the Dodgers received Tim Belcher, a 25-year-old right-hander who was 9-11 with a 4.42 earned run average this season with the Tacoma Tigers of the Pacific Coast League. Belcher pitched for the Dodgers the last month of the season, winning four and losing two with a 2.38 earned run average. Despite Alderson's assessment, Belcher would prove to be "top echelon prospect," winning 146 major league games.

December 11, 1987: Traded Pitcher Bob Welch and Pitcher Matt Young to the Oakland Athletics and Pitcher Jack Savage to the New York Mets in a Three-Way-Deal that brought them Pitcher Jay Howell and Shortstop Alfredo Griffin from Oakland and Pitcher Jesse Orosco from New York

In all, this was a three-team, eight-player transaction in which the Dodgers sent pitcher Jack Savage to the New York Mets and pitchers Bob Welch and Matt Young to the Oakland Athletics; Oakland sent pitchers Kevin Tapani and Wally Whitehurst to the New York Mets; the Mets sent pitcher Jesse Orosco to the Dodgers; and Oakland sent shortstop Alfredo Griffin and pitcher Jay Howell to the Dodgers.

The trade of Welch, the biggest name in the deal, came as a surprise. The 31-year-old right-hander had been with the club 10 years; his 115 wins were the fifth highest in Los Angeles Dodgers history; and he was coming off a 15–9 season. Several teams were after Welch, most of all the Mets, but after a week of negotiations he ended up in Oakland.

"You know that I have a stomach of iron, but it's been in a knot since last night at the thought of Bob leaving," Tom Lasorda said. "He's meant so much to us. He's helped us to so many playoff and World Series victories. He's our senior player since Billy Russell retired. You win 15 games with the type of team we had last year, and you know what he's going to do with a good team. We can't replace a pitcher of his caliber. You just insert someone in there to do the job. We have four or five guys to choose from."[21] Lasorda said he would consider returning Alejandro Peña to the rotation and that Shawn Hillegas, Tim Belcher, and Tim Leary would also be given opportunities to join Fernando Valenzuela and Orel Hershiser as starters.

Also leaving Los Angeles were pitchers Matt Young, 29, and Jack Savage, 23. The Dodgers had traded for Young in December 1986, hoping he would be the closer they had lacked since the loss of Steve Howe. But Young was a disappointment, with a 5–8 record, 11 saves, and a 90 ERA+. Savage, a 23-year-old right-hander, had been in the minor leagues before pitching for the Dodgers in three September games this past season. Savage was going to the Mets, while Young was accompanying Welch to Oakland.

The three players coming to Los Angeles were all veterans, Jay Howell was 32, and Alfredo Griffin and Jesse Orosco were 30. And all had physical problems. Howell had not pitched since he had bone chips removed from his right elbow in August. Griffin suffered a jammed left thumb in September and would have to wear a cast for four or five weeks. An undaunted Fred Claire dismissed those possible problems. He said Dr. Frank Jobe had investigated Howell's and Griffin's physical status and reported that neither man's injury represented a long-term threat.

Griffin was a switch-hitter with a .258 career batting average, 161 stolen bases, and a reputation for giving his all. "He plays hard, and he plays hurt," said Bill Rigney, an A's adviser. "His character? Top of the line." Claire said he had talked to several people about Griffin's character and competitiveness, and he looked for Griffin to be a positive influence on the organization's many other Dominican infielders, including Mariano Duncan. "I haven't seen him that much, but I hear he's a hell of a player. I looked at his record over the last six years and he's played all 162 games four times and more than 140 the other two. That's something we haven't had."[22] Griffin, who had asked the A's to trade him, said: "I wasn't unhappy in Oakland. To me, it makes no difference where I go. I have to play and behave the way I should anywhere. I'm excited about playing in L. A."[23]

Jay Howell, a hard-throwing right-hander, had played for four major league teams in eight years. Primarily a relief pitcher, Howell had saved 29, 16, and 16 games for the A's the past three seasons. He was expected to strengthen the Dodgers bullpen, but the team was still searching for a quality left-handed relief pitcher to replace Howe. They had traded for what they hoped would be that man in each of the past four season, but Carlos Diaz, Ed Vande Berg, and Matt Young had not been the answer. Jesse Orosco believed he was.

"They've got their guy now," Orosco said. "I hope I can make them forget. I'm not trying to be cocky, but the Dodgers chose me for a reason. I am going to be their short lefty. You guys will be the judge this time next year or midway through the season. I have confidence I can do the job. I like that role. I'm more than happy about this trade. I feel like a kid again. This is the greatest thing that's happened to me in a long time." Orosco also addressed the talk about him suffering from arm soreness. "Everybody always asks about that," he said. "But I can tell you that it's 100. Well, maybe 99.9 because, you know, any reliever who pitches a lot is going to have a little something. But I've felt no pain at all for two years."[24]

The Dodgers had led both leagues in errors for the past two seasons and had lost 32 games by one run last season and were last in the league in saves. Something had to be done. "We've filled the holes that we desperately needed to fill," said Lasorda. "The last two years, we've had a very, very poor bullpen and a very, very poor defense. We tried every way possible not to deal Welch, but it couldn't be done. He was the pitcher everyone wanted, and we had to improve our defense and bullpen." Claire said: "From my view, from the point of what we wanted to achieve here after surveying the market, I think we've achieved the maximum. It's one step."[25]

So, what did the Dodgers get out of the trade? Orosco spent one mediocre season in Los Angeles before becoming a free agent. Griffin, the man they were after, was their shortstop for four years, but never batted above .247. He became a free agent after the 1991 season when the club, anxious to make room for 23-year-old Jose Offerman at shortstop, chose not to pursue him. The Dodgers did much better with Howell, who was their closer for several seasons and saved 28 games in 1989. But numerous injuries limited his effectiveness the next three seasons and the Dodgers cut him loose after the 1992 season, when they chose not to offer him arbitration.

And what did they give up? Welch pitched another seven seasons for Oakland, in which he won 106 games and lost only 60. Along with ex–Dodger Dave Stewart, he was very influential in the A's winning three consecutive pennants (1988–1990). In 1990, Welch won 27 games and lost only 6. He easily won the Cy Young Award, although by most measures the award should have gone to Boston's Roger Clemens.

A footnote to this trade on the misjudgments in so many trades made by those who make them. Joe McIlvaine, who engineered this deal for the Mets, evaluated the three minor league pitchers he got, by saying that Savage was the key guy. When their careers were over, their major league win totals read, Kevin Tapani, 143; Wally Whitehurst, 20; and key guy Jack Savage, zero.

Also in 1987:

Traded: Pitcher Balvino Galvez to Detroit Tigers for Catcher Orlando Mercado; Minor League Catcher Jeff Edwards to Houston Astros for Infielder Phil Garner; Minor League Catcher Tim Meeks to Oakland Athletics for Pitcher Bill Krueger; First Baseman Larry See to Texas Rangers for Minor League Infielder José Mota; Minor League Pitcher Billy Bartels to Boston Red Sox for Shortstop Glenn Hoffman; Minor League Pitcher Juan Guzmán to Toronto Blue Jays for Second Baseman Mike Sharperson

Chosen in Amateur Free Agent Draft: Darrin Fletcher; Rafael Bournigal

Signed Amateur Free Agents: Pedro Astacio; Steve Green

Signed Free Agents: Outfielder-First Baseman Mickey Hatcher; Outfielder Danny Heep; Outfielder Tito Landrum; Pitcher Ron Davis; Outfielder Mike Davis

Released: Pitcher Jerry Reuss; Third Baseman Bill Madlock; Catcher Orlando Mercado; Pitcher Bill Krueger; Shortstop Glenn Hoffman

Left as Free Agents: Outfielder Ken Landreaux

1988

January 29, 1988: Signed Free Agent Outfielder Kirk Gibson

The Detroit Tigers selected former Michigan State football star Kirk Gibson with the twelfth pick in the June 1978 draft of amateur free agents. Following his major league debut in September 1979, the left-handed-hitting Gibson developed into one of the most productive players in the American League. After missing the first three weeks of this past season with a rib injury, he batted .277 with 24 home runs and 79 runs batted in. He had a career batting average of .276 and over the last four years had averaged 27 homers, 88 RBIs, and 30 stolen bases. Gibson, who would turn 31 in May, declared himself a free agent after the 1987 season. He found the Tigers offer to keep him well short of the Dodgers offer of a $1 million signing bonus and salaries of $1.5 million in 1988 and $1 million in both 1989 and 1990.

"My first choice was Detroit, hands down," Gibson admitted. "We tried so many different contract scenarios, but the Tigers just weren't going to budge. I looked at my financial picture all day today, and as much as I tried to make Detroit work out, it didn't make sense. I was only fooling myself. The way L.A. structured the contract, I'd have been an idiot to turn it down…. I had good times and bad times in Detroit. Obviously, there are a lot of mixed emotions involved. I spent eight years with the Tigers and have grown up a lot. But I look on this as a challenge, a fresh start. We're all excited about it."[26]

Dodgers GM Fred Claire said, "Our goal has been to improve the club. Gibson should help us accomplish that. There have been few players who combine his power and speed. When you're coming off the type year we had (73–89), I'm not concerned about having too much talent and competition. We've not only done a lot to change the personnel this winter, we've done a lot to strengthen the character." Tom Lasorda said he was elated about the addition of the competitive Gibson. "This is another indication that Peter O'Malley is doing everything he can to bring the fans a good club again."[27]

August 16, 1988: Traded Outfielder-Third Baseman Pedro Guerrero to the St. Louis Cardinals for Pitcher John Tudor

With six weeks to go in the season, the Dodgers felt they needed a quality left-handed starter to win the National League West title. They got their man by trading veteran slugger Pedro Guerrero to the St. Louis Cardinals for 34-year-old John Tudor. Tudor had been around for 10 seasons, the last four with the Cardinals whom he helped win pennants in 1985 and 1987. He had an overall 105–61 record and had finished a distant second in the 1985 Cy Young Award race to the Mets' Dwight Gooden. He was 21-8 that season with a league-leading 10 shutouts and a 185 ERA+. Tudor had missed most of spring training this year while recovering from arthroscopic shoulder surgery. Yet at the time of the trade, he had a 6–5 record with an earned run average of 2.29, the best in the National League.

"I'm very surprised [GM] Fred [Claire] could make this big a deal this late in the season," said catcher Rick Dempsey. "It's a miracle. It's fantastic. It gives everyone a lift. No one has to wonder anymore if we have enough to win the division. We know now we do. We know we'll have a 20-game winner out there every four or five days. Tudor has to come out here and do the job, but his credentials say he will. It takes a lot of the pressure off. It helps everyone relax."[28]

Pedro Guerrero came to the Dodgers in an April 1974 trade with the Cleveland Indians. It was one of the most profitable deals the Dodgers ever made, a trade that barely made the fine print in the newspapers. Pitcher Bruce Ellingsen had been in the Dodgers farm system for five years and had gone 5–10 at Albuquerque in 1973. He would win a game and lose one for the Indians in 1974, but that would be the sum of his major league career. Like Ellingsen, Guerrero was also a minor leaguer. He had spent only one year in organized baseball, and he would not reach the Dodgers for another four years. But when he did, he would spend 11 years with them and be recognized as one of the top hitters in the National League.

While he was a below average fielder, Guerrero had contributed greatly to the team's offense, a combined .309 batting average and an outstanding 149 OPS+. He was, however, moody, and some members of the Dodger organization believed he had become a disruptive influence in the clubhouse. Moreover, Guerrero would have been a free agent at the end of the season.

"Of course, I feel kind of bad," the 32-year-old Guerrero said about leaving. "But, of course, I knew before the season this would probably be my last here. It's all business. I think it was time for me to get out of here. Or they thought it was time for me to go. I think I'll have a new life in St. Louis. I'm playing with new guys and new people. Probably, it'll be a little hard for a while. I hope to come back next year and win it all with St. Louis."[29]

Guerrero said he knew the Dodgers would not re-sign him when Claire declined to negotiate a contract extension with his agent, Tony Attanasio, "I wish I could've stayed here, but I couldn't. They didn't want me. They were trying to trade me during the winter, so I knew," Guerrero said. "They didn't offer me a contract early in the season. You really don't want to be where nobody wants you. It was time for me to get out. If they didn't want me here, I didn't want to be here. I'm out of here tomorrow. I won't look back."[30]

Tudor appeared in a total of 15 games in his two seasons with the Dodgers. He declared free agency after the 1989 season and signed with the Cardinals in 1990, where he won 12 and lost 4 in his final major league season. Meanwhile, Guerrero led the Cardinals in RBIs in 1989 and finished third in voting for the National League's Most Valuable Player Award.

November 23, 1988: Free Agent Second Baseman Steve Sax Signed with the New York Yankees

Steve Sax said there were two factors that led him to leave Los Angeles for the New York Yankees. One, not surprisingly, was money. He had been willing to re-sign with the Dodgers for $3.95 million for three years, but they would not go above $3.5 million. The extent of the Yankees package was significantly different from what the Dodgers were offering. It included a $500,000 signing bonus, a $1.1 million salary in 1989, $900,000 in 1990, $1.5 million salary in 1991, and several no-trade provisions. The second factor, Sax said, was the difference in attitudes of Fred Claire and Yankees GM Bob Quinn. Sax and his agent, Jerry Kapstein, had met with Quinn in New Jersey last week and then flown to Florida to meet with Yankees owner George Steinbrenner. Both, Sax said, convinced him he was respected and wanted, but "there was a great difference in tone. I thought I'd be treated special by the Dodgers after we won the World Series, but I felt like I was just another number and that was the biggest reason I left," he said. "It was a turn-off. Bob Quinn made me feel welcome and respected. Fred Claire talked down to me. He was aloof. He made me feel like a punk kid. I'll miss the manager, the coaches, the camaraderie of my teammates and the fans, but that's all I'll miss," Sax said.[31]

"He's free to respond in any way he wants but I certainly feel we made a number of efforts to sign him. I made a point to tell him on several occasions that he was important to the club and that we had a real desire to sign him. I'm surprised and disappointed," said Claire. "We didn't turn over a blank contract and say, 'fill in the amount,' but we made a number of moves and showed a determination to negotiate in good faith.... We called Steve this morning in the hope of continuing negotiations, but he had obviously made up his mind. We wish him the best. We appreciate what he has done for us," Claire added.[32] Sax had done a lot. He was the Rookie of the Year in 1982 and a fixture at second base ever since. He batted .282 in 1,091 games and had 290 stolen bases, fifth highest in franchise history,

Dallas Green, the Yankees' new manager, said Sax would bat second behind Rickey Henderson. Green said he had encouraged Steinbrenner and Quinn to pursue Sax. "Any manager would jump at the opportunity to sign Steve Sax," Green said. "He's a .285 career hitter who plays 150 to 155 games every year, is aggressive, knows how to hit and run, cares about winning and knows how to do it. He's what every player should be."[33]

December 4, 1988: Traded Pitcher Ken Howell, Pitcher Brian Holton, and Minor League Infielder Juan Bell to the Baltimore Orioles for First Baseman Eddie Murray

On the first day of the winter meetings in Atlanta, Dodgers GM Fred Claire engineered a trade with the Baltimore Orioles for future Hall of Fame first baseman Eddie Murray. In return, the Orioles received minor-league shortstop Juan Bell and relief pitchers Brian Holton and Ken Howell. Claire and Orioles vice president Roland Hemond had been discussing a trade for Murray since October. The talks continued in Oakland during the World Series, in Palm Springs during the general managers' meetings in November, and in a Chicago meeting last week. The original deal was Bell, Howell and outfielder Mike Devereaux to Baltimore for Murray. But Claire, not wanting to lose two promising prospects, Bell and Devereaux, offered an either-or proposition and for the first time made Holton available. Baltimore could take either Bell or Devereaux; either Holton or another reliever, Tim Crews; plus, Howell. "As much as I wanted Eddie Murray, I was prepared to walk if I had to give up more than I wanted," Claire said. Murray did not come cheap. He stood to earn about $8 million over the next three seasons and $1.57 million in deferred salary for 20 years, beginning in 1992. The Orioles agreed to pay $1 million of that deferred money. "I couldn't be happier," Claire said. "I think we've acquired a player who's headed for the Hall of Fame, whose potential is unlimited."[34]

In Murray the Dodgers, who had been without a power-hitting first baseman since Steve Garvey left as a free agent six years earlier, were getting one of the best. The 32-year-old Murray had slugged 333 home runs in his 12 years with the Orioles, at the time the most home runs by any switch-hitter except Mickey Mantle. He also had, a .295 batting average, 1,190 runs batted in, and more than 2,000 hits. Murray was the American League's Rookie of the Year in 1977 and had finished in the top five for the Most Valuable Player Award five times, including back-to-back second place finishes in 1982 and 1983.

Yet much of the blame for the Orioles poor showings the past few seasons had been directed at Murray. He was unhappy in Baltimore, believing he had unfairly become the main target of blame for the Orioles' losing. "It was pretty hard the last couple of years," he said.

Murray also reportedly claimed that much of the abuse he heard was racist in nature. He refused to confirm that belief after the trade, but he did not deny it, either. "I was unhappy," he said. "It was tough here. When the fun leaves, it becomes a tough job. You have to turn your ears off to certain things."[35]

Of the three Dodgers leaving, only 29-year-old middle reliever Brian Holton fit into their 1989 plans. He had an overall 13–9 record but had been a star out of the bullpen in 1988, a 7–3 record and a 1.70 earned run average in 45 games. Ken Howell, 28, had a 10–1 record at Albuquerque in 1988 as he attempted to come back from shoulder surgery. His overall record in five seasons with the Dodgers was 18–29 with an 89 ERA+. Juan Bell, a 20-year-old switch-hitter, had the most potential of those going to Baltimore. He was the younger brother of the Toronto Blue Jays' George Bell, the 1987 American League's Most Valuable Player. Juan was not the power hitter his brother George was, although he was said to share some of his older brother's reputation for being difficult to handle. "It's not a must that he be our shortstop in 1989," said Orioles manager Frank Robinson, an obvious statement considering Cal Ripkin, Jr., was at the peak of his career. "I think he'll be our shortstop in the near future," which turned out to be wishful thinking.[36]

December 10, 1988: Signed Free Agent Second Baseman Willie Randolph

It was almost like a trade. Seventeen days after second baseman Steve Sax signed as a free agent with the New York Yankees, Yankees second baseman Willie Randolph signed as a free agent with the Dodgers. Randolph had not been the Dodgers first choice. In his search to find a replacement for Sax, Fred Claire had made offers to free agents Tom Herr and Ron Oester and approached the Mets about a trade for Wally Backman. None of those efforts were successful, so Claire signed Randolph to a two-year guaranteed contract in which Randolph would reportedly receive about $1.8 million. That was well below the $4-million, 3-year deal Sax had signed with the Yankees on November 23.

Following the trade for first baseman Eddie Murray six days earlier, the arrival of Randolph gave the Dodgers a completely new look on the right side of their infield. Agent Ron Shapiro, who represented both players, said Murray had been instrumental in Randolph's decision to choose the Dodgers over the Montreal Expos. The Expos wanted Randolph to either start or platoon with the left-handed hitting Tom Foley. Murray called Randolph and urged him to sign with the Dodgers. The deal was not made final until Randolph passed a medical examination in New York earlier in the day. "We're satisfied with the findings of the physical reports on his knee," Claire said. "He also had a little problem with his wrist, it's fine now. There's no problem."[37]

Comparisons between the second baseman coming and the one going were inevitable. The 34-year-old Randolph, a Yankee for 13 seasons, was five years older than Sax who would turn 29 next month. And Randolph was coming off a season in which he played in only 110 games and hit a career-low .230, while Sax played in a career-high 160 games, batted .277, and was fourth in the NL in hits, with 175. But Claire pointed to Randolph's .373 career on-base average, which he said suited him to be the Dodgers' leadoff hitter. He also cited the one-time Yankees captain's good reputation. "I must have talked to 100 people about Willie Randolph," Claire said, "and he must have more supporters than just about anybody in baseball." When asked about the comparisons, Randolph said: "Both Sax and I have to make adjustments. I'm not looking to compete with Steve Sax. He made the decision to come to New York. Everything is speculation now." Randolph said he saw no reason why he could not approach his numbers from two seasons ago, when he hit .305, had 82 walks, and finished fourth in the AL with a .411 on-base percentage. "When healthy, I produced," he said. "The statistics speak for themselves. In my heart and soul, I know I can show I'm still one of the best second basemen in baseball." Randolph said he was glad the Dodgers planned to use him as their leadoff hitter. "Leading off is one of my strengths."[38]

Also in 1988:

Traded: Infielder Craig Shipley to the New York Mets for Catcher John Gibbons; Outfielder Reggie Williams to Cleveland Indians for Minor League Pitcher Greg LaFever; Pitcher Shawn Hillegas to Chicago White Sox for Pitcher Ricky Horton; Pitcher Bill Krueger to Pittsburgh Pirates for Minor League Pitcher Jim Neidlinger

Chosen in Amateur Free Agent Draft: Billy Ashley; Jerry Brooks; Eric Karros; Mike Piazza; Jim Poole; Eddie Pye; Brian Traxler

Signed Amateur Free Agents: Raul Mondesi; Pedro Martínez

Signed Free Agents: Pitcher Bill Krueger; Pitcher Don Sutton; Catcher Rick Dempsey; Pitcher Ray Searage

Released: Pitcher Ron Davis; Catcher Alex Trevino; Outfielder Tito Landrum; Pitcher Brad Havens; Pitcher Don Sutton; Outfielder Danny Heep

1989

March 11, 1989: Traded Outfielder Mike Devereaux to the Baltimore Orioles for Pitcher Mike Morgan

Although he had been traded from the world champion Dodgers to the Baltimore Orioles, the team with the worst record in the major leagues last season, Mike Devereaux was pleased. Devereaux, who would turn 26 in a month, was once one of the Dodgers' top prospects. But with the 1988 outfield of Kirk Gibson, John Shelby, and Mike Marshall returning in 1989, and with Mike Davis and Franklin Stubbs available as backups, there was no room for someone who batted .222 and .116 in his limited playing time the last two years. Devereaux knew he would get a chance for a starting berth with the lowly Orioles. And he could put his mind at ease after suffering through trade rumors for three months. Trade speculation involving Devereaux began when the Dodgers were negotiating the deal that brought first baseman Eddie Murray from the Orioles in December.

"I thought I was in that deal," Devereaux said. "When I wasn't, I started hearing about this one. It was a little distracting. Now that this is over, I can concentrate on baseball. I'd like to be playing in L.A., but I just want to be playing in the major leagues. I could see the opportunity to play every day wasn't going to come soon," he said. "It's hard to say I didn't get a shot, but I would have liked to play more than I did." Fred Claire and Tom Lasorda both had good things to say about Devereaux. Claire said, "He has a good chance to have a long major league career, and I hope he does." Lasorda added: "It's hard to give up a person of the caliber of Mike Devereaux. Sometimes you have to trade guys you think the world of."[39]

Right-hander Mike Morgan, then 18, was the Oakland A's first-round pick (fourth overall) in the June 1978 amateur free agent draft. He made his major league debut days later. Since then, the 6'3", 195-pound Morgan had pitched for the Blue Jays, the Yankees, and the Mariners before coming to the Orioles in 1988. He had a combined record of 34–68 (1–6 in 1988) and had never posted a winning season. Nevertheless, he was recommended highly by Dodgers scout Phil Regan, his former pitching coach with Seattle. The deal was made after Dodgers physician Frank Jobe examined Morgan's right foot. Morgan had undergone surgery last August for an abnormal bone growth on his big toe. Dr. Jobe found he had fully recovered.

Morgan, now 29, said he was glad to be with a winner after pitching for losers in Seattle and Baltimore. "I was disappointed that I didn't get a chance to be a starter with the Orioles, but I'm excited about going to a winning environment. Maybe I can start winning now." Lasorda was unsure if he would use the lifetime American Leaguer as a starter or a reliever. "I can't tell you anything about the guy because I've never seen him. I wouldn't know him if he walked in right now." Claire, however, was enthusiastic about the deal. "We feel that he has an outstanding arm and major league ability," he said.[40]

July 18, 1989: Traded Pitcher Tim Leary and Shortstop Mariano Duncan to the Cincinnati Reds for Infielder Lenny Harris and Outfielder Kal Daniels

A need for offensive help led the Dodgers to trade pitcher Tim Leary and shortstop Mariano Duncan to Cincinnati for outfielder Kal Daniels and infielder Lenny Harris. Leary gave the Reds a starting pitcher to replace the injured José Rijo, and Duncan gave them a shortstop to fill in for the injured Barry Larkin. Leary had a 17–11 record with a 2.91 ERA and six shutouts in 1988 in helping the Dodgers to the world championship. He was named the National League's Comeback Player of the Year, but he was only 6–7 this season and had been moved to the bullpen. Overall, in Leary's three seasons with Los Angeles, he was 26–29 with a 102 ERA+. Duncan, a slick fielder but a weak hitter, had a .234 batting average and a 71 OPS+ in four seasons with Dodgers. He had been in 49 games this season, with a .250 batting average.

Leary was not unhappy about the trade, although as the father of a newborn he called the timing of it emotionally upsetting. "But I'd rather go somewhere and start," he said. "I'm feeling some sadness, but I was here in 1987 and I wasn't too pleased when I was in the bullpen then. The overriding factor is can I start? Being able to start in LA, my home, and winning it all last year, that's what I'll always remember. But I don't like the bullpen, so if there's no room here for me to start, it's better to move on."[41]

Kal Daniels, a 25-year-old left-handed hitter, gave the Dodgers another offensive weapon. Daniels had a .311 batting average and a 154 OPS+ over three previous three seasons with Reds but was hitting a disappointing .218 in 44 games this year. Until recently, Daniels had been on the disabled list while recovering from arthroscopic surgery on his right knee. It was his fourth knee operation, but Fred Claire was not concerned. "We've watched Kal closely the last few games," he said. "He's run well, stolen bases. We didn't do a physical examination on him, but Dr. Frank Jobe talked to their team physician. I trust both of them. I'll take full responsibility for his health." Manager Lasorda already had plans for his new outfielder. "We're going to put Daniels in left field, and we hope to bat him leadoff. I'm hoping he will make an impact, give us some punch. I always thought he was a good ballplayer."[42]

Reds manager Pete Rose once said he considered Daniels a potential batting champion but had changed his mind. "The more I've watched him the last couple of weeks against left-handed pitching the more I'm starting to doubt that," Rose said. "He looked to me like he had great potential but with men in scoring position it looked to me like he was too selective." Daniels claimed he was unappreciated in Cincinnati. "I don't feel I got the publicity I deserved," he said. "But what do you expect when you're playing with Eric Davis and Dave Parker one year and Eric Davis the next? I guess this trade is good for me. I get to play on grass because of my knees."[43]

Harris, 24, who was batting .223 in 61 games, became expendable when second baseman Ron Oester returned from the disabled list earlier this week. Harris had been unhappy with his play this season. "When I saw a lot of guys go down (with injuries) I tried to step it up and do too much," he said. "That's the reason I played like I did. I made mistakes, lots of mistakes rookie mistakes."[44]

Harris played with the Dodgers until declaring free agency following the 1993 season. Appearing in 578 games, mostly at second or third base and as a left-handed pinch-hitter, he had a .279 batting average and a 91 OPS+

November 28, 1989: Free Agent Shortstop Dave Anderson Signed with the San Francisco Giants

When the Dodgers chose Dave Anderson with their first pick in the 1981 amateur free agent draft, they envisioned him as their shortstop of the future. Anderson, now 29, never fulfilled that vision. Often bothered by back problems, he played in 100 games or more in only three of his seven seasons with the team, while compiling a .232 batting average in 662 games. As a free agent, Anderson signed a two-year guaranteed contract with the San Francisco Giants worth $1.1 million in salary, a $100,000 signing bonus, and various incentive clauses. The Dodgers top offer had been a one-year contract for the same $420,000 he made in 1989 and was contingent on him making the club in spring training. Fred Claire said he was interested in keeping Anderson but would agree only to a one-year contract.

"We gave the Dodgers and Giants the same offer," Anderson said. "The Giants bettered our offer. After the Giants made their offer, we gave the Dodgers a chance to better it. But they only wanted to do a one-year deal and I don't even know if that was guaranteed. So, we went elsewhere."[45] After two seasons with the Giants, Anderson returned to the Dodgers in 1992 to play his final major league season.

December 20, 1989: Traded Outfielder Mike Marshall and Pitcher Alejandro Peña to the New York Mets for Infielder-Outfielder Juan Samuel

Fred Claire had two goals this offseason, to find a center fielder and a leadoff hitter, and to do so without giving top young pitchers Ramón Martínez or John Wetteland. The man he got was Juan Samuel, whom he acquired from the New York Mets in exchange for outfielder Mike Marshall and right-handed reliever Alejandro Peña. "It was our hope and goal to be able to do that," said Claire about keeping his league-best starting rotation intact. "There were many times I didn't think it was possible. But then that door finally opened, and this was just what we were looking for. This is the best possible fit."[46]

Samuel, 29, was a speedy right-handed batter who spent his first full five seasons with the Philadelphia Phillies. He had at least 33 stolen bases in each of his six major league seasons, including 72 in 1984. A free swinger, Samuel also led the league in strikeouts in four of those six seasons. As for being the "best possible fit," as Claire described him, Samuel seemed anything but. He had played the outfield for only one season and preferred getting back to his normal position, second base. And he had twice been tried in the leadoff spot and found wanting. Still, he was a two-time All-Star who had 80 extra-base hits in 1987, only the third second baseman in major league history to reach that level. Samuel had been unhappy about moving to center field following his 1987 midseason trade to the Mets. After batting a combined .235 with 11 home runs and 48 RBIs for the season, he asked to be traded.

"Juan is very excited about playing for the Dodgers," Claire said. "He said he'd be happy to play any place we wanted him to. He's excited about the trade." Tom Lasorda was excited as well. "This is the answer to what we've needed. We knew we needed a center fielder in order to be able to compete This guy has all the ability to be a quality center fielder and he'll play there for us. He might have said he doesn't like playing center field in New York. Plus, he'll be an ideal leadoff man," said the always optimistic manager.[47]

Samuel played mostly at second base for the Dodgers in 1990, 1991, and part of 1992. He batted .258 with a 97 OPS+ in 343 games. The Dodgers released him in July 1992, and the Kansas City Royals signed him a week later.

Mike Marshall, who would turn 30 in 1990, had been bothered by a bad back throughout his career. Marshall batted .260 in 1989 with 11 home runs and 42 RBIs in 377 at-bats. His best year with the Dodgers was 1985, when he batted .293 with career-highs in home runs (28) and runs batted in (95). Overall, Marshall batted .271 with 137 home runs, 484 RBIs, and a 117 OPS+ in his nine seasons with the Dodgers.

Alejandro Peña was 4–3 in 1989 with a 2.13 earned-run average and five saves in 53 appearances. He was 38–38 with 32 saves and a 122 ERA+ in his nine seasons and 281 games with Los Angeles. Peña, 30, was a starter earlier in his career, and had a 12–6 record in 1984, while leading the NL in earned run average (2.48) and shutouts (4).

Also in 1989:

Traded: Catcher Gil Reyes to Montreal Expos for Pitcher Jeff Fischer; Minor League Outfielder Steve Green and Minor League Outfielder-First Baseman Domingo Michel to Detroit Tigers for Outfielder Billy Bean; Third Baseman Tracy Woodson to Chicago White Sox for Pitcher Jeff Bittiger

Chosen in Amateur Free Agent Draft: Tom Goodwin; Garey Ingram; Eric Young

Signed Amateur Free Agents: Dave Walsh; Felix Rodriguez; Henry Blanco; José Parra

Signed Free Agents: Pitcher Jim Gott; Pitcher Mike Maddux; Outfielder Hubie Brooks

Chose in Minor League Draft: Pitcher Mike Christopher

Released: Pitcher Ricky Horton

Left as Free Agents: Outfielder Mike Davis; Pitcher John Tudor

8

1990–1994

1990

April 1, 1990: Traded Outfielder-First Baseman Franklin Stubbs to the Houston Astros for Minor League Pitcher Terry Wells

Franklin Stubbs, the Dodgers number-one draft choice in June 1982, had spent the last six seasons with the club. Used as an outfielder and first baseman, he hit 23 home runs in 1986 and 16 home runs in 1987. Stubbs was primarily a first baseman in those two seasons, but the arrival of Eddie Murray in 1989 reduced him to a part-time player. Last winter, the 29-year-old Stubbs asked the Dodgers to trade him, after they signed Murray. But Stubbs was coming off knee surgery and teams were reluctant to take a chance on him. His play in 1989 showed his knee had healed. He batted .291 in 69 games in 1989, but his overall average in 542 games with the Dodgers was .227 with a 94 OPS+.

Stubbs was pleased the Dodgers had agreed to trade him. "I've had good times and bad times with the Dodgers, but I've got a World Series ring and a big trophy, and the good times have been more than the bad," he said. "I'm just lucky they are giving me a chance to go somewhere and play."[1] The Astros were expected to use Stubbs as a backup to first baseman Glenn Davis and to outfielders Glenn Wilson and rookie Eric Anthony.

In Terry Wells the Dodgers were getting a 6'3", 26-year-old hard thrower whom they hoped would eventually fill their need for a left-handed bullpen closer. Wells split the 1989 season between the Double A Columbus (GA) Mudcats and the Triple A Tucson Toros, going 2–8 with a 5.21 ERA and 67 walks in 95 innings. Scouts liked him because of his strikeout totals, 458 in 532⅓ career innings. The Dodgers sent Wells to their Triple A team in Albuquerque to begin the season.

"Major league arm, major league head, but control problems," said Dodgers catcher Darrin Fletcher, who caught Wells when both were at the University of Illinois. "But, who knows, it seems like everybody with control problems who comes to the Dodgers, they get with the pitching coaches and put on that blue and something happens. It could happen again." Fred Claire, the Dodgers vice president for player personnel, said: "He has had control problems, but he has a good arm. There is always a risk, but we think he is worth it."[2]

Wells' major league career would consist of five start and a 1-2 record in 1990. Stubbs would play 403 games for Houston, Milwaukee, and Detroit over the next four seasons.

May 13, 1990: Traded Second Baseman Willie Randolph to the Oakland Athletics for Outfielder Stan Javier

In trading second baseman Willie Randolph to Oakland, for switch-hitting utility outfielder Stan Javier, the Dodgers were improving their speed and defense while losing a veteran leader, popular with his teammates. The move allowed them to move Juan Samuel from center field, a position he neither liked nor played well, back to second base. The Dodgers hoped that by returning Samuel to his natural position, he would become a more relaxed hitter and make up for Randolph's loss. The 26-year-old Javier would play center field until Kirk Gibson returned from rehabilitating last summer's knee surgery. "There are a number of factors that went into this trade," said Fred Claire. "First of all, we feel we are getting a fine young player in Javier. He will add speed to our ball club. We also have to look ahead to the return of Kirk Gibson to our outfield. Kirk is making good progress. We feel he will be ready soon."[3] Javier continued his role as a backup outfielder with the Dodgers until they traded him to the Philadelphia Phillies in July 1992. He batted .257 in 281 games.

Last season, his first with the Dodgers, Randolph batted .282 and was voted the team's most valuable player. "It would be terrible if they traded Willie," said one Dodger when he heard rumors of the possible trade. "Willie doesn't just have ability, he has heart." Juan Samuel would miss him, as well. "I was hoping Willie would stay, he was good batting behind me, protecting me with my stolen bases," Samuel said. "And I haven't taken a ground ball at second base in two years … but I can play there. I'll be fine." But the Dodgers were concerned about Randolph's legs. He would turn 36 this summer, and they worried about the effects of age on his speed and his defensive range. Randolph had already committed four errors in 26 games at second base, after committing just nine in 140 games last season. However, he was still an effective second-place hitter, with a .271 batting average. "I can't say enough good things about Willie's contribution," said Claire. "From the day he signed with us, he has been an outstanding player and representative."[4]

The trade did not come as a surprise to Randolph. He expected he would likely be traded to make room at second base for Samuel. "I understand how the game works, it is a business," he said. "I figure I could make the move from New York to Los Angeles, so anything else will be easy. I like the Dodgers, but if I have to go, I have to go. I understand that, and don't get too caught up in it."[5]

November 7, 1990: Signed Free Agent Outfielder Darryl Strawberry

Darryl Strawberry, the biggest prize in this year's free agent market, signed a five-year, $20.3 million contract with the Dodgers. The 28-year-old Strawberry was chosen with the first overall pick by the New York Mets in the 1980 amateur free agent draft. A 6'6" left-handed slugger, he hit 252 home runs and drove in 733 runs and had a 145 OPS+ in eight years with the Mets. He was the Rookie of the Year in 1983, a seven-time All Star, and had earned second and third place finishes in the voting for the National League's Most Valuable Player. The second-place finish came in 1988, when Strawberry led the NL in home runs (39), slugging percentage (.545), and OPS+ (165). This past season Strawberry batted .277 with 37 home runs and a then club-record 108 runs batted in.

The Mets never made him a significant offer, Strawberry claimed. "It seemed like we were making no progress with the Mets, who were my first choice," he said. "It's tough to make a change, but they left me no choice but to make the change. It hurts me a lot to walk away from players I've had a relationship with for so long. Eventually, I'll get over it." Strawberry said the Mets' best offer was $15 million over four years. But he was looking for a contract more like José Canseco's five-year, $23.5 million deal with the Oakland Athletics. Mets spokesman Jay Horwitz said: "The New York Mets made Darryl an offer, but he wanted to go back home. We knew the Dodgers posed a serious threat." Strawberry disputed Horwitz's claim: he said he would have stayed in New York had the Mets made what he considered to be a serious offer. "They never called and talked to me," he said. "It was like they were waiting for me to call them, which I wouldn't do. They never made any offer like they were interested in me. It was a choice the Mets had to make, and it shows me it wasn't in their interest. I can't understand it. They just let me walk away."

Dodgers general manager Fred Claire was happy to take advantage of the Mets' seeming disinterest. "Darryl is one of the premier players in baseball, and we welcome him to our organization," Claire said.[6] Meanwhile, Strawberry's departure stunned several of his Mets teammates. "Oh my God," said Dave Magadan. "I still don't believe it." Dwight Gooden, Strawberry's closest friend on the Mets, said: "I might not believe it until next year when we get to Shea and see his locker with somebody else in it. Even then, I won't." Having lost their team's most valuable player, Magadan, Gooden and other of his teammates thought the Mets could have done more to keep him. But mostly they were happy for Strawberry. "It's probably the best for Darryl to leave," catcher Mackey Sasser said.[7]

Yet not every Mets player was sorry to see Strawberry go. "His leaving might be beneficial to us," said infielder Tim Teufel. "This team can use a gamer, a guy who wants to win and get the most out of his ability at all times. Those type of players are hard to find these days, but Cincinnati proved you can win with 25 guys. (The Reds were world champions in 1990.) When you don't have togetherness, you can't do it. I don't blame the Mets at all for taking a stand. The last two weeks of the season," Teufel continued, "the way Strawberry handled himself and didn't want to play in a pennant race … you're going to give a guy $20 million who wouldn't go out there in those games?" he asked.[8]

Teufel was referring to Strawberry missing several games near the end of the season due to a bad back. Players on the team questioned whether the injury was that serious. "Obviously, he was not going to jeopardize anything going into the offseason as a free agent," Teufel said. "He wanted to be healthy. He was thinking totally of himself, not the team. We still had a chance to win, and Darryl just wouldn't play…. If it was a true injury, and he was getting in early, taking treatment, taking the proper steps, then that's different. But just to shut it down, it left some of us wondering how he could do it."[9]

Strawberry had a strong 1991 season, his first with the Dodgers. He hit 28 home runs, had 140 runs batted in, a 140 OPS+, and was selected to the All-Star team for the eighth consecutive year. The next two seasons did not go well. An injured back, surgery, and stays on the disabled list from injury and drug-and-alcohol addiction limited him to a combined 75 games, with 10 home runs and 37 RBIs. The Dodgers released him in May 1994.

December 1, 1990: Free Agent Outfielder Kirk Gibson Signed with the Kansas City Royals

Even before the 1990 season ended, it had become apparent the Dodgers would not re-sign Kirk Gibson. Perhaps as early as a meeting prior to the All-Star break, in which Gibson and Fred Claire got into a shouting match. Claire tried to trade Gibson during the break but was unsuccessful. He then tried to trade him to Oakland before the August 15 inter-league trading deadline, but the White Sox put in a waiver claim to block the deal. Gibson, 33, was not activated until June 2, after he recovered from knee and hamstring injuries, but managed to hit .260 and steal 26 bases in 89 games. He reportedly told teammates he would give the Dodgers an opportunity to re-sign him to a one-year deal, but they never made an offer. The Kansas City Royals and Milwaukee Brewers did make offers, with the Royals winning out. Gibson signed a two-year contract for a reported $3.3 million.

Gibson was the National League's Most Valuable Player in 1988, his first season with the Dodgers. He capped off the season when he limped off the bench with two outs in the ninth inning of the first game of the 1988 World Series and hit a two-run game-winning homer against Oakland's Dennis Eckersley.

"I play very hard and with a lot of emotion," Gibson said after signing with the Royals. "You've got to stay focused on some of the days when things aren't going so good. All I can say is I promise you I will play as hard as I can and do everything I can to win ballgames." Royals manager John Wathan said he planned to use Gibson primarily as a left-handed designated hitter, while occasionally playing him in the outfield. "Being a DH on a sometime basis is appealing to me," Gibson said. "I think I'll see a lot of outfield play, though. I think I can be a great asset in the outfield."[10]

December 3, 1990: Signed Free Agent Pitcher Kevin Gross

In what some called an example of a free agent market out of control, the Dodgers signed pitcher Kevin Gross to a three-year $6.4 million contract. The contract called for a $650,000 signing bonus and salaries of $2 million in 1991 and 1992 and $1.75 million in 1993. This for a pitcher who had an 80–90 record in eight National League seasons—six with Philadelphia and the last two with Montreal—including a 9–12 mark with the Expos in 1990. Dodgers manager Tom Lasorda said: "I watched him at Montreal and Philadelphia and said to myself, 'This guy should be a winner.' The challenge is to make him believe that, to find out why he doesn't win more."[11]

Gross, a 6'5" right-hander, said he had hoped to join a West Coast team and was excited it turned out to be Los Angeles. "The Dodgers were the farthest thing from my mind because I didn't think they needed help, and I had some vibes from other teams," he said. "I'm overwhelmed. I've always considered Tom Lasorda to be an aggressive and inspirational manager and Dodger Stadium to be the best place in the world to play. Coming from Montreal it will be a major difference. It will be nice playing again in real baseball circumstances." Expos manager Bob Rodgers said of Gross: "He's a horse. He gives you a lot of innings and is a good guy on the team. But his stuff is too good to be a sub-.500, pitcher and I've told him that."[12]

December 14, 1990: Signed Free Agent Outfielder Brett Butler

The Dodgers, who had already spent $20.65 million on free agents Darryl Strawberry and Kevin Gross this winter, continued their shopping spree by signing former San Francisco center fielder Brett Butler. In outbidding the Atlanta Braves and Boston Red Sox for the 33-year-old Butler, they signed him to a three-year contract worth more than $3 million per year. It was a move that would give the Dodgers a proven leadoff batter and a Gold Glove center fielder. Butler, a left-handed batter, had played previously for Atlanta, Cleveland, and the last three years for the Giants. He batted .309 in 1990, with a league-leading 192 hits. The speedy Butler had also led his league twice in triples and once in runs scored.

"I'm really flabbergasted about the whole thing," Butler said. "It's a dream come true for me to be able to play for Tommy Lasorda and the Dodgers. They're a class organization. It's something that, boy, I still have to pinch myself. It's something I've longed for for many years."[13]

December 15, 1990: Traded Outfielder Hubie Brooks to the New York Mets for Pitcher Bob Ojeda and Minor League Pitcher Greg Hansell

When the Dodgers signed Darryl Strawberry in November, the plan was to have him play his natural position, right field. That left them with the choice of moving incumbent right fielder Hubie Brooks to left field and trading incumbent left fielder Kal Daniels or keeping Daniels in left and trading Brooks. The consensus among the players was that the 27-year-old Daniels would be traded because he was seven years younger than Brooks and would bring more in return. In addition, Brooks was popular with his teammates, many of whom expressed their admiration of his quiet leadership and clutch hitting. "Hubie didn't have one enemy, Hubie was one of our cornerstones," said outfielder Chris Gwynn. So, it came as a surprise when Brooks was traded to the New York Mets for left-handed pitcher Bob

Ojeda and right-handed pitching prospect Greg Hansell. As in previous transactions, popularity and team chemistry did not play a part in Fred Claire's personnel moves. Last season, during a losing streak, he traded team leader Willie Randolph. "Yes, I am concerned about chemistry," Claire said, "but we now have a ballclub that should produce victories and victories produce chemistry."[14]

Brooks had a 102 OPS+ in 153 games in 1990, his one season with the Dodgers. He was also third on the team in home runs (20) and runs batted in (91). "Hubie was one of the three or four people Tommy could always count on" Gwynn said. "He brought this team stability." Brooks, who signed a three-year contract with the Dodgers as a free agent from Montreal, was clearly disappointed. When told about yesterday's acquisition of Brett Butler, he said, "It does look like I've lost a job. I can't believe it." Gwynn said Brooks phoned him immediately after the trade. "Hubie was shocked," Gwynn said. "You could tell he was really disappointed." Claire said: "I loved Hubie. Trading him was one of most difficult things I ever have had to do." Meanwhile, Daniels was glad he was still a Dodger. "I feel bad for Hubie, and I thought I would be the one traded because my trade value was higher, but I am glad they didn't choose me. I am really happy to stay in Los Angeles. It looks like our puzzle is all coming together. We are looking like a championship team."[15]

Bob Ojeda, 6'1" left-hander, had spent the last five seasons with the Mets, following six years with the Red Sox. He had a 95–79 record with a 3.65 earned-run average. His best season was for the world champion Mets in 1986, when he led the league with a .783 winning percentage (18–5) and had a 140 ERA+. "I feel like a big kid being back home," said Ojeda, a Los Angeles native. "I grew up like everybody down there, watching Vin Scully and the Farmer John Hot Dog." Mets manager Davey Johnson had used Ojeda mostly as a reliever this past season, so Ojeda was overjoyed that Tom Lasorda planned to return him to a starting role. "That is music to my ears, Tommy," he said. "The bullpen, I don't like it. I'm not ready for it. When I'm 37, I'll be ready for it," said Ojeda, who would turn 33 in a week.[16]

Ojeda started 60 games for the Dodgers over the next two seasons. He went 12–9 and 6–9, with a 101 ERA+. Ojeda was a free agent after the 1992 season, but Claire chose not to re-sign him. He was the only left-handed starter the Dodgers had, but Claire wanted to move right-hander Pedro Astacio into the rotation. Ojeda signed with the Cleveland Indians, saying he wanted to pitch for a winning team. The Dodgers had finished last in the Western Division in 1992.

Greg Hansell was a 19-year-old right-hander who spent this past season in the Class A Florida State League. He was 7–10 with a 3.60 ERA for the Winter Haven Red Sox. Hansell was traded to the Mets during the season and had a 2–4 record and a 2.61 ERA for the St. Lucie Mets.

Also in 1990:

Traded: Catcher Darrin Fletcher to Philadelphia Phillies for Pitcher Dennis Cook; Pitcher Mike Munoz to Detroit Tigers for Minor League Pitcher Mike Wilkins; Shortstop Jose Vizcaino to Chicago Cubs for Second Baseman Greg Smith; Pitcher Darren Holmes to Milwaukee Brewers for Catcher Bert Heffernan; Pitcher Jim Poole and Cash to Texas Rangers for Minor League Pitcher Dave Lynch and Minor League Pitcher Steve Allen

Chosen in Amateur Free Agent Draft: Mike Busch; Todd Williams

Signed Amateur Free Agents: Omar Daal

Signed Free Agents: Pitcher Don Aase; Outfielder Butch Davis; Pitcher Pat Perry; Catcher Barry Lyons

Released: Outfielder John Shelby; First Baseman Luis Lopez; Pitcher Ray Searage

Left as Free Agents: Pitcher Don Aase; Pitcher Mike Maddux; Catcher Rick Dempsey; Pitcher Pat Perry; Pitcher Terry Wells

Lost in Minor League Free Agent Draft: Outfielder Mike Huff

1991

March 25, 1991: Signed Free Agent Pitcher John Candelaria

From the mid–1970s to the mid–1980s, the Pittsburgh Pirates' 6'7" left-hander John Candelaria was among the National League's top pitchers. Candelaria had double-digit win totals in eight of those seasons, with a high of 20 in 1977. His .800 winning percentage and 2.34 earned run average were the NL's best that season. Candelaria had moved around since then, playing for four different teams in the past two years. He became a free agent after the 1990 season, but, perhaps due to a history of injuries and battles with alcohol, he remained unsigned through the winter. The Dodgers saw him as a possible addition to their bullpen and invited him to spring training. He performed well and was signed to a one-year $500,000 contract.

"This closes the case on getting a left-handed reliever," manager Tom Lasorda said during spring training. Candelaria had struck out Atlanta's left-handed-hitting Dave Justice in a key situation that afternoon. "We wanted somebody to face the league's top left-handed hitters in the late innings, and we've got one." The 37-year-old Candelaria understood the situation. "I'm a reliever. My starting days are long over. What they are going to ask me to do, who knows? Maybe they can get a couple of more years out of me. This is an ideal situation."[17]

The Dodgers had also reached an agreement with free agent catcher Gary Carter but could not sign him until they cleared a space on their roster. The most likely candidates to go were left-hander Dave Walsh or right-hander Mike Morgan. "I have talked to Gary Carter, and we are anticipating a move," Fred Claire said. "It's not a move we necessarily want to make, but a move we have to make to clear up a spot for Gary on the roster."[18]

Walsh, who was 1–0 with a 3.86. earned-run average in 16 major league innings last year after eight seasons in the minors, said he wanted to remain with the Dodgers. But he understood the addition of Candelaria, also a left-hander, made him expendable. "I understand that it is out of my hands," he said. "I can't force them to do anything. I just hope I go somewhere that I can pitch in the major leagues. Because last year, I finally proved that I could do it." Morgan said if the Dodgers were going to trade him, he preferred they do it as soon as possible. "I don't want to join a team on April 8, where it would take me longer to get used to the team," he said. "But I feel I can be one of the Dodgers' five starting pitchers, and I don't want to stay here just to be in the bullpen as an insurance policy. I guess I'm used to this happening. Even though I felt I had a pretty good two seasons here, it seems my role is always the traded role. I'm always the guy to be traded."[19]

As he feared, Walsh was the man to go. He was designated for assignment and then sent to Albuquerque. He appeared in 14 games without a decision and never returned to the major leagues. Candelaria made 109 relief appearances with a total of 59 innings pitched in his two seasons in Los Angeles. He won three, lost six, and had a 107 ERA+. He declared free agency after the 1992 season and signed with his original team, Pittsburgh.

March 26, 1991: Signed Free Agent Catcher Gary Carter

After clearing a spot for him by sending pitcher Dave Walsh to Albuquerque, the Dodgers made the signing of free agent Gary Carter official. Carter was a 16-year major league veteran. He played eleven years for the

Montreal Expos and five for the New York Mets before signing as a free agent with the San Francisco Giants in 1990. He was the Rookie of the Year in 1975, an 11-time All-Star, and was 57th on the all-time home run list with 313. Carter batted .254 for the Giants in 1990, with nine home runs and 27 RBIs in 244 at-bats. But when the Giants decided to go with rookie Steve Decker as their backup catcher this season and chose not to re-sign Carter, the Dodgers invited him to spring training as a non-roster player. Carter, who would turn 38 in two weeks, showed enough to win a job and was signed to a one-year contract worth $500,000.

Tom Lasorda said he planned to use Carter primarily as a pinch-hitter and as a backup to catcher Mike Scioscia. "Gary Carter adds to our ball club experience and competitiveness," Lasorda said. "He can still swing the bat enough to get you some big hits." Carter said: "I wasn't really worried. I was prepared either way. I felt with the work I did in the offseason and my experience I was going to be a proven factor."[20]

Carter played in 101 games for the 1991 Dodgers, 61 as a backup to Scioscia. He batted .246 with six home runs and 26 runs batted in. When he chose not to file for free agency after the season, the club put him on waivers. The Expos claimed him, and Carter played his final season with Montreal.

May 20, 1991: Free Agent Pitcher Fernando Valenzuela Signed with the California Angels

Fernando Valenzuela was the talk of the baseball world in the shortened split-season of 1981. The 20-year-old left-hander had complete-game victories in his first eight starts and went on to lead the league in complete games, innings pitched, shutouts, and strikeout. The Dodgers won the World Series and Valenzuela became the first pitcher to win his league's Rookie of the Year and Cy Young Awards. The Mexican-born Valenzuela quickly became a fan favorite in Los Angeles, especially among the large number of Latins in the area. The phenomenon was called "Fernandomania," and it endured in Southern California for more than a decade. Valenzuela was an All-Star for his first six seasons, during which he added second, third, and fifth place finishes in the Cy Young Award voting. He won 141 games and had a 107 ERA+ as a Dodger, while finishing in their all-time top ten in wins, starts, innings pitched, strikeouts, and shutouts.

But the heavy load manager Tom Lasorda had Valenzuela carry wore him down, and he had not had a winning record since 1987. He had a win and two losses with a 7.87 ERA in spring training when the Dodgers released him on March 28. Valenzuela's agent, Tony DeMarco, said the pitcher no longer felt bitter toward the Dodgers for cutting him. He received $630,495 in termination salary after his release with less than a week before the team would have had to pay his full salary of $2.55 million. Teams in Japan and Mexico expressed strong interest in signing him, but DeMarco said Valenzuela wanted to wait in hopes a major league team would pick him up.

One did, the California Angels, which would allow him to remain in Southern California. Valenzuela signed a one-year contract that called for a specified number of minor-league starts, probably three, before he would join the Angels. "To play here makes a lot of sense for Fernando and a lot of sense for the Angels," DeMarco said, referring to Valenzuela's huge popularity in the area. Angels president Richard Brown said the contract included a number of incentives. "If we bring him up, that's when the incentives will kick in," Brown said. "If he has a good year, he'll make a lot of money." The Angels also had the option to renew the contract in 1992. "Hopefully, Fernando will fit right in with the other excellent pitchers on the staff," Angels manager Doug Rader said. "It doesn't matter if they're left- or right-handed. The thing I admire most is productivity and he certainly showed that with the Dodgers. Hopefully, he's got plenty left for us."[21]

July 3, 1991: Traded Outfielder Jose Gonzalez to the Pittsburgh Pirates for Outfielder Mitch Webster

By trading substitute outfielder Jose Gonzalez to Pittsburgh for substitute outfielder Mitch Webster, the Dodgers added a player from whom they expected increased production while ridding themselves of one who was disgruntled and frustrated. The 26-year-old Gonzalez had asked to be traded last season and had been repeating that request all this season. Gonzalez, a right-handed batter, was in his seventh season with Los Angeles. He had a combined .213 batting average with just seven home runs, 33 RBIs, and an OPS+ of 77 in 532 at-bats. This season Gonzalez was hitless in 28 at-bats, the only major leaguer who began the season on an active roster who had yet to get a hit.

The 32-year-old Webster was a speedy switch-hitter who could play every outfield position. Drafted by the Dodgers in 1977, although he never signed with them, Webster reached the major leagues with the Toronto Blue Jays in 1982. In addition to Pittsburgh, he had also played for the Montreal Royals, the Chicago Cubs, and the Cleveland Indians. Webster was batting .125 in 13 games with the Indians before being traded to the Pirates on May 16. He had not done much better there, batting .175 in 36 games, with one hit in his past 16 at-bats. But the Dodger were counting on

Webster returning to his early form. Entering this season, he had a career average of .270 and had stolen more than 20 bases four times.

Manager Lasorda planned to use Webster mostly as a pinch-hitter, pinch-runner, and late-inning defensive replacement. "We've heard that the guy plays hard and hustles all the time," said Brett Butler about Webster. "Sounds like a great guy to have." When Lasorda was asked about Gonzalez, he said, "There is an old saying: Talent which is used develops, and talent which is not used wastes away. Jose had his role, here and knew his role here, but he was unhappy with that."[22]

Webster played five seasons with LA, mostly as a backup. He did get into 135 games in 1992, with a 114 OPS+. Overall, Webster appeared in 417 games with a .256 batting average. He declared free agency after the 1995 season but went unsigned.

July 31, 1991: Traded Pitcher Mike Hartley and Minor League Outfielder Braulio Castillo to the Philadelphia Phillies for Pitcher Roger McDowell

Although the Dodgers were leading the National League West by 4½ games over Atlanta, they were concerned about their relief corps. Of particular concern was right-hander Jay Howell, recently back from a stay on the disabled list. To shore up their bullpen, they made a move just before the midnight trading deadline. They acquired Philadelphia Phillies reliever Roger McDowell in exchange for pitcher Mike Hartley and minor league outfielder Braulio Castillo. McDowell, a 30-year-old right-hander, was used as a closer and a set-up man with the Phillies and before that, the Mets. This season he had been replaced in that role by Mitch Williams. McDowell had a career total of 128 saves, including 20 or more in four of the last six seasons, and he was 3–6 with a 3.20 ERA and three saves in 38 games for the Phillies this season.

"I wasn't surprised at all," said McDowell, whose contract called for a $200,000 bonus if he was traded. "It's a great opportunity for me. Hopefully I'll be able to help the Dodgers win a pennant. I always liked to pitch in Dodger Stadium." Fred Claire believed the move from Philadelphia's Veterans Stadium's turf to Dodger Stadium's grass would help McDowell. "You look at his career and he's been a very good pitcher on grass," Claire said. "He's been a much better pitcher on grass than he's been on AstroTurf because he's a sinkerball pitcher and he's going to get more ground balls than anything else.... He's also had a great deal of success against right-handed hitters. I think Roger's only given up one home run the last three or four years. I hope that continues."[23] McDowell had a 17–19 record, with 23 saves and a 106 ERA+ in four seasons with Los Angeles. In 1995 he signed as a free agent with the Texas Rangers.

Right-hander Mike Hartley, 29, was 6–3 with a 2.95 earned run average as a rookie in 1990. He was 2–0 with a 4.42 ERA and a team-leading 40 appearances this season. Braulio Castillo was batting .302 with eight home runs and 48 RBIs in 86 games with the San Antonio Missions, the Dodgers Class AA team in the Texas League.

November 27, 1991: First Baseman Eddie Murray Signed as a Free Agent with the New York Mets

Eddie Murray had missed very few games in his three seasons as the Dodgers' first baseman. In 1990, he batted .330, with 26 home runs, 95 runs batted in ,and had an OPS+ of 159. Overall, he averaged 22 home runs and 93 RBIs, with an OPS+ of 126. But Murray soon would turn 36, and the contract Fred Claire offered him was for $3 million but only for one season. When the New York Mets offered a two-year deal worth $7.5 million, Murray accepted. Claire's decision to let Murray leave angered several Dodger veterans; it had removed a stabilizing influence from the club and the last measure of defensive stability from an unproven infield.

"I just don't understand the arrogance of letting him go like that," said pitcher Bob Ojeda. "I don't understand just letting a Hall of Famer out the door so easily. It's like they thought they could offer whatever they wanted, and he would come crawling back to them because they are the Dodgers. That's not the way it works anymore." Brett Butler said the Dodgers had lost their father figure. "Eddie was the papa bear in the clubhouse, Eddie was our glue. When I heard he was leaving, All I could say was, 'Wow.'"[24]

Murray said he was surprised the Dodgers had not offered him more than a one-year contract. "I never thought it would come to this," he said. "I knew I would have at least three years with the Dodgers, but I wanted to play longer than that." Claire said he respected Murray, but thought it was time to give younger players such as Eric Karros and Henry Rodríguez a chance. "No one could possibly have more respect for Eddie than I have, as a person and a player ... but this team is getting younger, there is no getting around that," he said.[25]

November 27, 1991: Traded Pitcher Tim Belcher and Pitcher John Wetteland to the Cincinnati Reds for Outfielder Eric Davis and Pitcher Kip Gross

Just hours after they lost slugger Eddie Murray to the New York Mets, the Dodgers traded for Cincinnati's Eric Davis, one of the top hitters in the National League. In return for Davis and right-hander Kip Gross, they sent the Reds right-handed pitchers Tim Belcher and John Wetteland. Davis had never fully lived up to the expectations the Reds had for him, partly due to his having missed so many games with injuries. He had never played more than 135 games in his six full seasons with Cincinnati. This past season Davis played in only 89 games because of a kidney injury suffered while making a diving catch during the 1990 World Series.

Davis, 30, was a Los Angeles native and a two-time All-Star who batted .271 in nine seasons with Cincinnati. He had 203 home runs and a 137 OPS+. Kip Gross, a 27-year-old right-hander, won six games for the Reds in 1991, but he won only one for the Dodgers in 1992—and that was his last major league win. In May 1994, the Dodgers sold him to the Nippon Ham Fighters of the Japan Pacific League.

Tom Lasorda said by acquiring the right-handed-hitting Davis, the team had picked a good cornerstone in their rebuilding process. "A couple of years ago, before the injury, somebody asked me who would be my first pick if I had to start a ballclub, and I immediately said Eric Davis. And we really need him here to give us more balance with left-handers. Last year teams were sending out all kinds of left-handers against us in the late innings. This will change that," said Lasorda. "I believe Eric brings to our ballclub one of the outstanding talents in the game today," said Fred Claire. "I know it is a significant risk. We now have an obligation to restructure our pitching staff. But to acquire talent, you have to give up talent. And Eric Davis has as much talent as anybody playing baseball." Davis was overjoyed at the trade, which would reunite him with his boyhood friend Darryl Strawberry. "This is a dream come true," he said. "Darryl and I have dreamed about it in the past, and it seemed so far-fetched at the time, we never thought it could come true. But here we are."[26]

Tim Belcher, 30, had a 50–38 record and a 2.99 earned run average in 138 games with the Dodgers, who were reluctant to trade him. They offered Bob Ojeda instead, but the Reds held out for Belcher, who would win another 96 games after leaving LA. Belcher did not think the Dodgers made a good trade. "Even though I respect Fred and thank him for bringing me to the Dodgers, I think he's made a mistake," Belcher said. "If I were to take a snapshot of the National League West right now, given the Dodgers' current situation, I would rank them far down the list, considerably below the Reds and Braves. And that is based on pitching alone." Belcher, who ranked fourth in the National League with a 2.62 earned-run average in 1991, added: "I'm just shocked. Fred told me he had to fill a need for a right-handed power hitter. I said, 'What are you going to do with the rotation now?'"[27] (At this time, the return of starters Orel Hershiser and Mike Morgan was still unclear.)

As with Kip Gross, John Wetteland was more-or-less a throw-in. The 25-year-old Wetteland had an 8–12 record and a 92 ERA+ in parts of three seasons with the Dodgers. The Reds thought so little of him, they traded him to Montreal two weeks later. Belcher's future success and what would turn out to be Davis's failure would have been enough to make this a terrible trade for Los Angeles. When you add what Wetteland went on to accomplish it makes it a lot worse. In the next nine years, with the Expos, the New York Yankees, and the Texas Rangers, Wetteland would record 329 saves.

December 3, 1991: Free Agent Pitcher Mike Morgan Signed with the Chicago Cubs

The Dodgers were willing to sign 32-year-old Mike Morgan to a three-year contract calling for $9 million, but they refused to give him a guaranteed fourth year. Morgan, who earned $650,000 in 1991, chose instead to sign a four-year contract worth $12.5 million with the Chicago Cubs. He would be paid $2.5 million in 1992, $3 million in 1993, $2.5 million in 1994, and $3 million in 1995. In addition, he received $1.5 million signing bonus. Morgan won 33 and lost 36, with a 117 ERA+ in his three seasons with the Dodgers. This past season, he led the club in innings pitched (236) while finishing second in victories (14) and earned run average (2.78).

Morgan was not pleased when he learned later in the day the amount of money the Dodgers had spent in retaining free agent pitcher Orel Hershiser and signing thirty-five-year-old pitcher Tom Candiotti. "I'm glad for Candiotti," he said, "but after all I've done for them, they spend the last two months saying they can't give me four years, then they turn around and give that guy four years. What college did these people go to? It's kind of ironic that I sign a four-year deal, then all of a sudden, they pop up and sign two more pitchers," he said.[28]

December 3, 1991: Signed Free Agent Pitcher Tom Candiotti

About an hour after pitcher Mike Morgan signed with the Chicago Cubs, the Dodgers re-signed Orel Hershiser to a three-year contract and signed knuckleball pitcher Tom Candiotti, a free agent from the Toronto Blue Jays. Candiotti, a 35-year-old right-hander, signed a four-year contract worth $15.5 million. He had spent eight years in the American

League, mostly with the Cleveland Indians before they traded him to Toronto last June. He pitched a combined 238 innings in 1991, while going 13–13 with a 2.65 earned run average. Perhaps because the knuckleball was not as hard on a pitcher's arm, Candiotti had totaled more than 200 innings for six consecutive years. During that stretch, he had only one losing season despite pitching for mostly poor Cleveland teams.

Although Candiotti had secretly visited Dodger Stadium a few days earlier, his agent, Rocky Lucia, said there were substantial gaps in the negotiations. Those gaps were closed shortly after Morgan joined the Cubs. According to Lucia, Candiotti, who grew up in Northern California but rooted for the Dodgers, was excited to join them. "Tom rooted for the Dodgers because everyone else rooted for the Giants" Lucia said. "That's just the way he is. During this whole process, he kept saying he couldn't believe it. When it comes to Dodgers trivia from the '60s and 70s, he knows as much as anybody." Candiotti would be the National League's first regular knuckleball pitcher since Phil Niekro. "I haven't broken the news to [Dodgers catcher] Mike Scioscia yet," said Fred Claire.[29]

Candiotti would be a member of the Dodgers rotation for six years. He appeared in 187 games, 159 of which were starts, winning 52 and losing 64 with an ERA+ of 106. Following the 1997 season he signed as a free agent with the Oakland Athletics.

December 11, 1991: Traded Outfielder Chris Gwynn and Minor League Infielder-Outfielder Domingo Mota to the Kansas City Royals for First Baseman-Outfielder Todd Benzinger

Chris Gwynn, now 27, was the Dodgers first-round choice in the 1985 amateur free agent draft. He spent most of his first three seasons with the club in the minor leagues and a good part of the last two on their bench. Gwynn batted .252 in 139 at-bats last season, mostly as a pinch-hitter, with five home runs and 22 runs batted in. He had asked for a trade earlier this offseason and was pleased to now have a chance to play regularly. "I'm outta here!" he said. "I had no chance to play with the Dodgers. I had been passed over for a few years. Either I was invisible, or the Dodgers didn't think I could do the job. I'm just glad Fred [Claire] had enough, I don't know what the word is, to trade me."[30] Also going to Kansas City was infielder-outfielder Domingo Mota. The 22-year-old Mota batted .343 for the Dodgers Gulf Coast League team in 1990 and .275 for Bakersfield in the Class A California League in 1991. Mota would never reach the major leagues.

8. 1990–1994

Eddie Murray's departure had left the Dodgers without a regular first baseman. The 29-year-old Benzinger, who could also play the outfield, had spent two seasons with the Boston Red Sox and three with the Cincinnati Reds, before his trade to the Royals this past July. The switch-hitting Benzinger had a .255 career batting average, with an average of 10 home runs and 72 runs batted in during his four full major league seasons. He had lost his starting job twice this season—to Hal Morris with Cincinnati and to the recently acquired Wally Joyner with Kansas City. The Dodgers hoped Benzinger could be their regular first baseman if rookie Eric Karros was not ready, or as a platoon player with Karros.

"He will certainly solidify the infield because he is one of the best defensive first basemen I have ever been associated with," said Eric Davis, a teammate of Benzinger's in Cincinnati. "Todd is a perfect fit. I think we have set our ballclub for the 1992 season," said Fred Claire. "He is going to save a lot of people a lot of errors. This will give us some breathing room," Claire said. "Eric Karros can compete for the first base job, and the weight of the world will not be on his shoulders. We can compete and win with this club." But some of the Dodgers' players were not so optimistic. "Benzinger is a good acquisition; he's got some ability defensively and Lenny Harris will be solid at second base," reliever Tim Crews said. "But I don't think Jose Offerman is ready at shortstop. As a pitcher, I don't feel comfortable with him behind me. And I don't think Dave Hansen will play all the time at third base because he is another left-handed bat. That leaves Jeff Hamilton, and if he has a wimpy attitude like he has had in the past, we're in deep trouble."[31]

Benzinger was pleased to be leaving the Royals, although he said it would take time adjusting to the Dodgers. "I grew up in Cincinnati hoping the Dodgers would lose to the Reds every game they played," he said. "I grew up hating the Dodgers, and when I became a member of the Reds, it intensified. But I am going to approach this like I approached Kansas City last year. I will have no preconceptions that will mess up my head.... Los Angeles is a good move for me regardless of what happens at first base," he said. "Platooning is better than not playing at all. I'm not in a position to demand anything or expect anything." Benzinger had a reputation for being one of baseball's most intelligent and personable athletes. "Todd is quiet, he doesn't show any emotion, and a lot of people don't understand him," said Lenny Harris, also a teammate of Benzinger's with the Reds. "But you have to realize all people in this game are not the same. The guy plays hard, and that's all that matters."[32]

Benzinger had only 313 at-bats in 1992, as Karros became the full-time first baseman. He batted .239 with a 76 OPS+. Benzinger declared for free agency after the season and signed with the San Francisco Giants in 1993.

Also in 1991:

Traded: Minor League Pitcher Jeff Hartsock to Chicago Cubs for Pitcher Steve Wilson; Pitcher Dennis Cook and Pitcher Mike Christopher to Cleveland Indians for Pitcher Rudy Seanez
Sold: Catcher Gary Carter to Montreal
Signed Amateur Free Agents: Roger Cedeño; Antonio Osuna; Ismael Valdez; Juan Castro; Eric Weaver; Wilton Guerrero; Rick Gorecki
Left as Free Agents: Catcher Barry Lyons; Outfielder Butch Davis
Lost in Minor League Free Agent Draft: Outfielder Billy Bean

1992

June 27, 1992: Traded Outfielder Kal Daniels to the Chicago Cubs for a Player to be Named

After Eric Davis came off the disabled list on June 19, Kal Daniels was designated for assignment, meaning the Dodgers could trade him, release him, or assign him to a minor league club, a move Daniels could veto. They preferred to trade him because of Daniels's $2.5 million guaranteed contract and had until midnight to do so. GM Fred Claire beat the deadline by sending Daniels to the Chicago Cubs for a player to be named within the next six months. Claire would receive a list of ten unnamed players from the Cubs. "I don't think Ryne Sandberg will be on the list," Claire joked. "I think a lot of clubs may have felt we would release Kal and then they could sign him for the pro-rated major league minimum ($109,000). I'm glad Kal is in a situation that's good for him. He should hit well in Wrigley Field; he knows National League pitchers and he will be on grass. And in that left field, he won't have to roam too far."[33]

Daniels had been with the Dodgers since July 18, 1989, when he was traded with Lenny Harris by Cincinnati for Tim Leary and Mariano Duncan. He appeared in 313 games with a .271 batting average and a 129 OPS+. His best year with LA was 1990, when he batted .296 with 27 home runs and 94 runs batted in. At the time of the trade, Daniels was batting .231 with two home runs in 35 games.

Cubs general manager Larry Himes said the Cubs traded for Daniels instead of waiting, knowing another club was also interested. "We needed a left-handed hitter, and he has hit well in Wrigley Field. Basically, we need a hitter." Because Daniels had a history of knee problems, Himes said he would play about five days a week. His addition would also allow the Cubs to rest right fielder Andre Dawson, who also had knee troubles. "This is his [Daniels] free agent year, and he has a chance to put up numbers in a ballpark where he has had success."[34] During his career, Daniels had a .319 batting average in Wrigley Field with five home runs and 20 RBIs.

On July 28, the Dodgers received minor league pitcher Mike Sodders, a 28-year-old right-hander who never would reach the major leagues.

December 5, 1992: Signed Free Agent Infielder-Outfielder Cory Snyder

In addition to re-signing free agent pitcher Roger McDowell, the Dodgers signed free agent Cory Snyder to a two-year contract worth $3 million. The Dodgers said they planned to use Snyder at third base or as a backup outfielder. Snyder expected it would be third base. "I'm looking at it like they want me to play third base and that's how I'm going into spring training, then if they want me to do something else, that's fine." Although he was signed by the Cleveland Indians as a third baseman, Snyder had played the outfield during most of his seven-year major league career. "Cleveland signed me as an infielder, and I played shortstop and third base through Triple A, then all of a sudden, they bring me up to the big leagues as an outfielder. I guess because they wanted to utilize my arm there." Snyder said. "But last year at San Francisco, I played a lot of third base. Every time Matt Williams went down with his bad back, I was there."[35]

Snyder, 30, played six seasons for Cleveland before they traded him to the Chicago White Sox after the 1990 season. In July 1991, Chicago traded him to the Toronto Blue Jays, who released him in late October. Snyder signed a minor league contract with San Francisco in 1992 and made the big-league roster based on a strong spring training. He batted .269 for the Giants in 124 games, with 14 home runs, 57 runs batted in, and a 117 OPS+. "He had some problems after Cleveland, but he bounced back with San Francisco," said Tom Lasorda. "He swung the bat well, and he can hit the ball out of the park."[36]

The Dodgers used Snyder mostly as an outfielder in his two seasons with them. In 1993 he was their regular right fielder. Overall, Snyder played in 216 games, with a .259 batting average, 17 home runs, 74 RBIs, and a 96 OPS+. He declared for free agency after the 1994 season and spent 1995, his final season, in the minor leagues.

December 9, 1992: Signed Free Agent Pitcher Todd Worrell

By signing free agent pitcher Todd Worrell, the Dodgers hoped they had added their first reliable closer since 1989, when Jay Howell saved 28 games. Worrell, a 33-year-old native Californian, agreed to a three-year contract worth $9.5 million, including a $1.25 million signing bonus. The Dodgers and the Atlanta Braves made comparable offers for the 6'5" right-hander who had spent his entire career with the St. Louis Cardinals. Worrell had missed the 1990 and 1991 seasons because of injuries to his right elbow and shoulder (he pitched in three minor league games in 1991), and the Braves wanted him to get a physical before they signed him. The Dodgers took the advice of team doctor Frank Jobe, who performed both of Worrell's surgeries, and did not ask for a physical.

"I offered to take a physical for both the Dodgers and the Braves, and I have nothing to hide, and everything was out in the open," the 32-year-old Worrell said. "But the Dodgers were hot on my trail from the first day that I became a free agent. I was trying to keep the Dodgers happy and interested and the physical would have put a decision off for another week and I felt I couldn't do that. I didn't want to jeopardize it. Not after all I have been through, that's the way it developed, and it pushed me over to the Dodgers."[37]

Worrell was St. Louis's first-round draft pick in 1982. In 1986 he established a rookie record for saves with a league-high 36 and was named Rookie of the Year. He had 33 saves in 1987, 32 in 1988, and 20 in 1989, despite injuring his right elbow in September. In 348 relief outings, Worrell had 129 saves, with a 33–33 record and a 2.56 earned run average. In 67 games this past season, mostly as the set-up man for Lee Smith, he had a 5–3 record with three saves and a 2.11 ERA.

"We watched Todd pitch, we saw him pitch late in the season and pitch in back-to-back games," said Fred Claire. "We know what kind of program he was on, what kind of player he is. He wants to be the person who is out there in the ninth inning with the game on the line and that's what we want. There are always concerns when a player has had surgery. We had to make the same call on Orel Hershiser last year and he went out and pitched in 30-plus games. Todd is the same type of player as Orel, his work ethic is the same." Worrell had already spoken with Tom Lasorda about overuse. "It's best for me and the team not to run me ragged," he said. "If I need a day off, I need to take it. Even before I got hurt there were days that I needed off."[38]

Worrell pitched five seasons for Los Angeles with a record of 17 wins, 19 losses, and 127 saves. He was the club's closer in his last three seasons, with save totals of 32 in 1995, a league-leading 44 in 1996, and 35 in 1997. The Dodgers granted Worrell free agency after the 1997 season, but he never again pitched in the major or minor leagues.

December 24, 1992: Traded Minor League Shortstop Tim Barker to the Montreal Expos for Third Baseman Tim Wallach

Spurred by a last-place finish in the National League West, the Dodgers had made several offseason moves designed to improve the team. The latest was the Christmas Eve addition of right-hand-hitting third baseman Tim Wallach from the Montreal Expos in exchange for minor league shortstop Tim Barker. "We are very pleased to acquire Tim [Wallach] in that he fills the needs of our club exceptionally well," said Fred Claire. "Tim gives us a proven third baseman, and I know he is anxious to help our ballclub. At the conclusion of last season, we wanted to improve our club at third base, second base, and getting a closer for our bullpen. With the addition of Tim, Jody (Reed) and Todd (Worrell), we have filled those needs, and the signing of Cory Snyder has given us added depth."[39]

Wallach, 35, spent 12 full seasons with Montreal, with an overall batting average of .259, 204 home runs, 905 runs batted in, and a 105 OPS+. In 150 games with the 1992 Expos, he hit .223 with nine home runs and 59 RBIs. Wallach, who was from nearby Huntington Beach, was excited about coming back home. "I'm certainly going to miss a lot of people in Montreal, fans and players," he said. "It's going to be strange after being there for 12 years, but it's nice to be coming home. It wasn't really a comfortable situation last year." Expos manager Tom Runnells had split Wallach's playing time between first base and his normal position at third. "It was a distraction from the start," Wallach said about moving between the two positions. "I knew it was the first sign that I was on my way out. I think I had one of my best years defensively in 1991. To be moved after that was a surprise." He said he knew the Expos were looking to trade him and he was glad it was to the Dodgers. "One thing about the Dodgers—they've always had a winning tradition. I wouldn't have gone to a team that didn't have a chance to win. They've always done the things they can do to make them a better team. I think I can help make them a better team."[40]

Dodgers manager Tom Lasorda told Wallach he would be the Dodgers' everyday third baseman. And he was for most of his three seasons in Los Angeles, the best of which was 1994, when he batted .280 with 23 home runs and a 127 OPS+. In December 1995, Fred Claire informed Wallach the Dodgers were getting ready to trade for third baseman Mike Blowers.

Wallach, a free agent, signed with the California Angels. He batted .237 in 57 games for the Angels before being granted free agency on July 19. The Dodgers signed him a week later. In his final hurrah, he batted .228 in 45 games.

Tim Barker, 24, had done well in his four seasons in the Dodgers minor league system, but he would never play in the major leagues.

Also in 1992:

Traded: Stan Javier to Philadelphia Phillies for Pitcher Steve Searcy and Outfielder Julio Peguero; Pitcher Rudy Seanez to Colorado Rockies for Second Baseman Jody Reed

Signed Amateur Free Agents: Matt Herges; Karim García; Ángel Peña

Released: Infielder-Outfielder Juan Samuel

Left as Free Agents: Shortstop Alfredo Griffin; Pitcher Tim Crews; Pitcher Steve Searcy; Pitcher Bob Ojeda; Shortstop Dave Anderson; Pitcher John Candelaria; First Baseman-Outfielder Todd Benzinger

Lost in Expansion Draft: Second Baseman Eric Young

1993

February 11, 1993: Free Agent Catcher Mike Scioscia Signed with the San Diego Padres

In his 13 seasons with the Dodgers, Mike Scioscia caught in 1,394 games, the most in franchise history. He was a superior defensive catcher with a .259 batting average and a 99 OPS+. Scioscia was coming off his worst season, a .221 batting average with a 63 OPS+. At 34, and with rookie Mike Piazza ready to take his position, the Dodgers saw no room for him in their future. When manager Tom Lasorda could not guarantee him significant playing time in 1993, Scioscia filed for free agency. Ten teams showed interest in signing him, with three in the final bidding. Scioscia chose the San Diego Padres, he said, because it was where he believed he had the best opportunity to win a job. With the Padres number one catcher, Benito Santiago, gone to the Florida Marlins, manager Jim Riggleman said he planned to carry three catchers this year. Scioscia believed he would be one of them.

"With the Dodgers, I could have hit .800 in spring training and it wouldn't have mattered. They made up their minds to go with the young guys. In San Diego, I was assured my playing time would depend on my performance in spring training. The chance is there to win a job. As a player, that's all you can ask for. I promise you." But there were no guarantees. "Playing time is up to the manager," said Padres general manager Joe McIlvaine. "But I know Mike will battle. He welcomes competition." McIlvaine said Scioscia would help the Padres in three areas. "He knows the National League, and he knows the pitchers. Second, he's a veteran guy, so he'll be able to help Riggleman (who had managed just 12 major league games). Third, he'll help [second-year catcher Dan]Walters. Mike can do nothing but help us. We have a young club, and you can't teach experience. This is a very positive move for us."[41]

Things did not work out as planned for Scioscia. He injured a rotator cuff during spring training and began the season on the disabled list. He never got to play any regular-season games and was released by the Padres after the season ended.

August 31, 1993: Traded Outfielder Eric Davis to the Detroit Tigers for a Player to be Named

"It doesn't matter what I think. It's done," said Eric Davis after the Dodgers traded him to the Detroit Tigers for a player to be named. "I'm looking forward to it. It's an opportunity to jump in a situation where they have a chance to win. You can't ask for more than that if you have to leave." Speaking of his new acquisition, Tigers general manager Jerry Walker said: "He can hit for power, he can run and he's an excellent defensive player."[42] The November 1991 trade with Cincinnati that brought Davis to Los Angeles in exchange for pitchers Tim Belcher and John Wetteland ranks among the worst the Dodgers ever made. While the two pitchers prospered after leaving LA, Davis, once touted as the next Willie Mays, continued his career history of missing time because of injuries. He also did not contribute offensively the way the team had expected. That he had some off-the-field problems and would be a free agent at the end of the season was further incentive for the Dodgers to trade Davis for whatever they could get, which was not much. On September 7, the Tigers sent right-handed pitcher John DeSilva to the Dodgers to complete the trade. DeSilva's Dodgers' career consisted of three 1993 late-season games without a decision. In his two seasons with LA, Davis batted .232, with 19 home runs, 85 RBIs, and an 89 OPS+ in 184 games.

"Under the circumstances, with the way things transpired, no, I'm not disappointed," Davis said of his time with the Dodgers. "Injuries are part of the game. It took me a while to get totally healed from my kidney injury. Then I had triple surgery last year. Now this is the best I've felt since 1990 when we (Cincinnati) won the World Series."[43]

"When you get older, there's more to think about," said teammate Cory Snyder in Davis's defense. "I think in Eric's case, he thought about baseball situations. If we needed a base hit, he'd think about that instead of hitting a homer. That's the sign of a mature player, although people view less homers as a lack of production."[44]

November 19, 1993: Traded Pitcher Pedro Martínez to the Montreal Expos for Second Baseman Delino DeShields

Free agent signee Jody Reed batted .276 in 1993, his one season with the Dodgers, and then declared again for free agency. The 31-year-old Reed wanted more money than the Dodgers were willing to pay, and he signed instead with the Milwaukee Brewers. Looking to replace him with someone younger and faster, the Dodgers traded promising young pitcher Pedro Martínez to the Montreal Expos for 25-year-old Delino DeShields. A left-handed speedster, DeShields had four seasons with the Expos, mostly as their leadoff batter. He had a combined .277 batting average, a 106 OPS+ and averaged more than 46 stolen bases per season. Despite a strained thumb ligament that forced him to miss five weeks this past season, he hit .295 and stole 43 bases.

Manager Tom Lasorda conceded that it was difficult to part with the 22-year-old Martínez. "Pedro did an outstanding job for us in the role that he played," Lasorda said. "But in order to get a player the caliber and the quality of a DeShields you have to give up something. We had to have this guy because we felt we needed speed in the lineup. As an everyday player we feel he will be more valuable to us than the relief pitcher." Lasorda said he did not plan to have DeShields replace Brett Butler in the leadoff spot. Still, Butler, who was perhaps a better judge of talent than his manager, was shocked by the trade. "In a nutshell, I guess I'm blown away that they traded probably one of the best pitchers we had on the staff."[45]

Because the Expos were unable to sign all their players eligible for arbitration, DeShields, who was one of them, expected to be traded. Speaking of the Dodgers, he said, "I really felt in the second half of 1993 they were one of the best teams in the league." Fred Claire said he first discussed the deal with Expos general manager Dan Duquette a few weeks earlier. Pitching mostly in middle relief, Martínez was 10–5 with a 2.61 earned run average in 65 games in 1993, his first full major league season. The Expos said they planned to use the 22-year-old right-hander as a starter and expected him to pitch 200 innings a year. Martínez said he and his older brother Ramón, a Dodger starter, were surprised he was traded. "I was more surprised than anyone. I thought I was someone really needed by the Dodgers," he said. "I'm going to be really sad about the situation of being without my brother. I talked to him, and I told him about me being traded and the only thing he said was '*You* got traded?' He was really surprised.... Nobody except Fred Claire was thinking about me being traded."[46]

No one realized at the time this would turn out to be the worst trade in Dodgers history. DeShields would be their second baseman for a few years and have a decent 13-year major league career. But they had given up a future Hall of Famer, one who would rank among the great all-time pitchers. In his four years with Montreal, and seven with the Boston Red Sox, Martínez had his league's lowest earned run average five times and led in winning percentage and strikeouts three times each. He won three Cy Young Awards, while compiling a career record of 219 wins and 100 losses, a 2.93 earned run average, and a 141 ERA+.

Also in 1993:

Traded: Minor League Pitcher Mike James to California Angels for Outfielder Reggie Williams
Purchased: Pitcher Ricky Trlicek from Toronto Blue Jays
Chosen in Amateur Free Agent Draft: Darren Dreifort; Paul Lo Duca
Signed Amateur Free Agents: Dennis Reyes; Noe Muñoz
Signed Free Agents: Shortstop Kevin Elster; Pitcher Rod Nichols; Catcher Tom Prince; Second Baseman Jeff Treadway
Released: Shortstop Kevin Elster
Left as Free Agents: Second Baseman Jody Reed; Infielder Lenny Harris; Pitcher Rod Nichols

1994

December 13, 1994: Free Agent Pitcher Kevin Gross Signed with the Texas Rangers

In December 1990, when Kevin Gross left the Expos to join the Dodgers, Montreal manager Bob Rodgers said Gross's stuff was too good for him to be a sub-.500, pitcher. But, as he had been before, that is what he was in his four seasons with the Dodgers. Appearing in 138 games, 95 as a starter, he had 40–44 record. He was 9–7 this past season and had the lowest earned run average (3.60) among the team's starters.

Gross, who would be 34 next season, signed a two-year, $6 million contract with the Texas Rangers. His deal included a $400,000 signing bonus, a 1995 salary of $2.5 million, and a 1996 salary of $3.1 million. He was also eligible for $300,000 in bonuses. "I have a lot of high goals and expectations of myself," Gross said. "I don't necessarily expect to be the number one starter. It's going to take a team effort from the whole staff."[47]

Also in 1994:

Traded: Minor League Pitcher Jimmy Daspit to Houston Astros for Pitcher Al Osuna; Minor League Third Baseman Eddie Lantigua to Cleveland Indians for Pitcher Brian Barnes; Pitcher John DeSilva to Baltimore Orioles for Pitcher John O'Donoghue; Minor League Pitcher Ben Van Ryn to Cincinnati Reds for Pitcher Will Brunson

Sold: Outfielder Tom Goodwin to Kansas City Royals; Pitcher Ricky Trlicek to Boston Red Sox; Pitcher Kip Gross to Nippon Ham Fighters of Japan Pacific League; Pitcher Brian Barnes to Florida Marlins

Chosen in Amateur Free Agent Draft: Paul Konerko; Gary Rath; Mike Metcalfe; Adam Riggs

Signed Amateur Free Agents: Chan Ho Park; Adrian Beltre; Luke Prokopec

Signed Free Agents: Pitcher Gary Wayne; Pitcher Rudy Seanez; Outfielder Chris Gwynn

Released: Second Baseman Mike Sharperson; Outfielder Darryl Strawberry; Outfielder Jerry Brooks

Left as Free Agents: Pitcher Jim Gott; Infielder-Outfielder Cory Snyder; Pitcher Roger McDowell; Pitcher Gary Wayne; Outfielder Mitch Webster

9

1995–1999

1995

February 8, 1995: Signed Free Agent Pitcher Hideo Nomo

The strike that shut down the 1994 season, which had not yet been settled, did not deter Japanese pitcher Hideo Nomo from signing a free agent contract with the Dodgers for the 1995 season. Nomo was considered the best pitcher in Japan, having compiled a 78–46 record with a 3.15 earned run average in five seasons with the Kinetsu Buffaloes of the Japan Pacific League. The 26-year-old right-hander signed a minor league contract that included a signing bonus of more than $2 million. If he were to make the Dodgers, Nomo would become the second Japanese-born player to reach the major leagues. (Masanori Murakami pitched for the 1964–1965 San Francisco Giants.) "The Dodgers over the years have had remarkable pitchers—a great black pitcher named Don Newcombe, a great Jewish pitcher in Sandy Koufax, and a great Mexican pitcher by the name of Fernando Valenzuela," said Dodgers broadcaster Vince Scully. "So, in retrospect, it's only right that we should have a great Japanese pitcher."[1]

Nomo, who spoke no English and would be given a full-time interpreter, said he had wanted to pitch in the major leagues ever since pitching in the 1988 Olympics. "This is very, very big news in our country," said Hiroto Shibatu, a Japanese reporter. "I know it's not a big story in the United States, maybe because they don't know him, but he's a star in Japan."[2] Several American players who faced Nomo in Japan predicted that he could become a consistent 15- to 18-game winner.

April 8, 1995: Free Agent Pitcher Orel Hershiser Signed with the Cleveland Indians

Orel Hershiser's 12-year career with the Dodgers came to an end when he signed as a free agent with the Cleveland Indians. Tom Lasorda, who was his manager for all those years, sent Hershiser his regards and congratulations on his one-year $1.45 million deal with the Indians. "He wore the Dodger uniform with pride, dignity, and character, and he was a good role model," Lasorda said. "I wish him well, nothing but the best. He deserves it."[3]

Hershiser had a record of 134–102 with a 3.00 ERA for the Dodgers. The best of his many good seasons was 1988, when he won the National League's Cy Young Award with a record of 23–8 and led the Dodgers to a World Series title. In 21 starts this past season, Hershiser was 6–6 with a 3.79 earned run average.

San Francisco Giants general manager Bob Quinn said he offered the 36-year-old Hershiser a package that would have been worth $4.1 million over two years, but Hershiser turned him down. "There were larger financial offers out there, but you don't always make decisions based on finances," he said. "I had a fantastic career in Los Angeles. That's one of the best organizations in professional sports. But I saw some of the same qualities of Los Angeles in the Cleveland Indians. I wanted to join another organization that has great things going for it."[4]

Cleveland's signing of pitcher Bud Black and slugger Dave Winfield influenced his decision to sign with them, Hershiser said. "Maybe in some ways it took some money out of the budget and left less for me. But signing guys like that put some sparkle in the other categories for me." John Hart, Cleveland's general manager, said: "We feel Orel was the best free agent pitcher on the market for us. He's been a staff leader, he's pitched in the postseason, and he's been involved in the last out in a World Series. That's a special quality."[5]

April 11, 1995: Free Agent Outfielder Brett Butler Signed with the New York Mets

The players' strike of 1994 remained unsettled, delaying the start of the 1995 season. A proposed salary cap was one of the major issues, and the owners took advantage of the non-agreement to drive hard bargains in signing this year's free agents. Several had signed for lower salaries than they made in 1994. One was Brett Butler, who was paid $3.5 million by the Dodgers in 1994 and signed with the New York Mets for a reported $1.5

million in 1995. "I got to be at a point," Butler said, "where I was fed up with what was going on. I said OK. I've got a number I'm going to play for and if the numbers out there are less, I'm going to retire. I'm financially secure."[6]

In addition to Butler being one of the top leadoff hitters in the game, the Mets felt he could provide leadership. "A winning team has to have the right kind of veteran leadership, especially a rebuilding club like us," said Mets manager Dallas Green. "He will lead by example. He will lead in the clubhouse. He will be a terrific mentor for our young players, like a Ryan Thompson." Butler said he expected to win with the Mets. "I'm not coming to New York to lose. I'm 37 years old. My days are numbered as a player."[7]

The best of Butler's four seasons with the Dodgers was his first, 1991. He batted .296, had an OPS+ of 114, and led the National League with 112 runs and 108 walks. Butler batted .314 in the shortened 1994 season, with eight home runs 33 runs batted in, and 27 stolen bases.

May 23, 1995: Traded Outfielder Henry Rodríguez and Second Baseman Jeff Treadway to the Montreal Expos for Outfielder Roberto Kelly and Pitcher Joey Eischen

Fred Claire had seen the Dodgers lose their last six games, in five of which they scored three or fewer runs. Realizing something drastic had to be done, he called Expos General manager Kevin Malone and consummated the Dodgers' biggest trade in four years. The two-for-two deal sent outfielder Henry Rodríguez and second baseman Jeff Treadway to Montreal and brought right-handed-hitting outfielder Roberto Kelly and left-handed pitcher Joey Eischen to Los Angeles. The Dodgers were extremely pleased with the trade. They considered Rodríguez a third or fourth outfielder who did not fit into their future, and they had been trying to dump Treadway all spring. Meanwhile, Kelly would give them speed at the top of the lineup, and Eischen would give them an additional left-handed reliever. "We're a much better team today than we were yesterday," Claire said. "I've always liked Kelly," said Tom Lasorda. "I think we'll be better offensively, defensively, and have much more speed. I've always liked him. I liked him when he was with Cincinnati, the Yankees, Atlanta, and, uh, where else was he?"[8]

The "where else," of course, was Montreal. But Lasorda's confusion raised the question of how a talented player, popular with his teammates, could be traded four times in the last four years. Kelly was a career .286 hitter with 195 stolen bases in his nine major league seasons. "If you figure it out, let me know," said the 30-year-old Kelly. "I'm starting to get used to this. I guess, if nothing else, it lets you know that you're wanted. I've learned to pack light. Once you're traded the first time, the rest aren't that tough. But this one came as a surprise. I had no idea until the general manager Malone came to my apartment. I just looked at him, and said, 'What team?'"[9] After Kelly batted .279 with an 87 OPS+ in 112 games for the 1995 Dodgers, he signed as a free agent with the Minnesota Twins for the 1996 season.

Expos manager Felipe Alou said he thought the 25-year-old Joey Eischen had a bright future and hated to lose him. Claire agreed and said the Dodgers had been after him for a while. The Expos had just recalled Eischen from Ottawa of the International League, where he had a 2–1 record with a 1.72 earned run average in 11 games.

Henry Rodríguez was in his fourth season with the Dodgers, as an outfielder and part-time first baseman. He batted .246 with an 83 OPS+ in 254 games. He was batting .263 in 21 games this season. The Expos, who lost first baseman Cliff Floyd for the season when he broke his hand, planned to use Rodríguez at first base.

In the strike shortened 1994 season, his first with the Dodgers, Jeff Treadway had 20 hits in 67 at-bats for a .299 average as a pinch-hitter and utility infielder. This season, the 32-year-old Treadway, had batted only 17 times, with two hits.

July 31, 1995: Traded Pitcher Greg Hansell, Pitcher José Parra, Minor League Third Baseman Ron Coomer, and a Player to be Named to the Minnesota Twins for Pitcher Kevin Tapani and Pitcher Mark Guthrie

New York Mets pitcher Bret Saberhagen was the man the Dodgers wanted, but the Mets traded him to the Colorado Rockies. With the 9 p.m. (Pacific Time) trading deadline approaching, the Dodgers engineered a six-player deal that brought them Minnesota Twins starter Kevin Tapani. Also coming to Los Angeles was left-handed reliever Mark Guthrie. The new pitchers would fill two of the team's most pressing needs—a fifth starter, in Tapani, and a left-handed reliever, in Guthrie. In exchange, the Dodgers sent pitcher José Parra, pitcher Greg Hansell, minor league third baseman Ron Coomer, and a player to be named to Minnesota.

Tapani, a 31-year-old right-hander, had led the Twins in wins in each of the past three seasons. He was struggling this season, with a 6–11 record and 4.92 earned run average in 20 starts. Guthrie, 29, was 5–3 with a 4.46 ERA in 36 games, all in relief. "I feel a whole lot better about it after hearing that," said Dodgers first baseman Eric Karros about the trade. "I was just going to bed when I caught ESPN Sports Center and saw the Rockies got Saberhagen. I'm thinking: 'You've got to be kidding me.' I'm excited that we did something. Tapani's got good stuff."[10]

Greg Hansell, 24, was 0–1 with a 7.45 earned run average with the Dodgers this season.

José Parra, a 22-year-old rookie, had made eight relief appearances for the Dodgers, without a decision. He was considered the best of the three prospects and was expected to replace Tapani in the Twins' rotation. Ron Coomer, 28, was the last player the Dodgers cut this past spring. He was batting .322 with 16 home runs and 76 runs batted in for the Triple A Albuquerque Dukes.

"Coomer fits in well with this team," said Twins general manager Terry Ryan. "We needed a right-handed bat at first base; he [Coomer] can also play third. I think he'll get his share of playing time. Parra will replace Tapani in the rotation. Hansell has to get some innings before we'll bring him up."[11] On October 30, 1995, the Twins received minor league outfielder Chris Latham as the player to be named.

November 29, 1995: Traded Minor League Second Baseman Miguel Cairo and Minor League Third Baseman Willis Otáñez to the Seattle Mariners for Third Baseman Mike Blowers

Looking to replace third baseman Tim Wallach, Fred Claire engineered a trade for Mike Blowers of the Seattle Mariners. The Mariners received two minor league infielders, third baseman Willis Otáñez, 22, and second baseman Miguel Cairo, 21. Blowers, 30, had been mostly a part-time player in his first six seasons, three with the New York Yankees and three with the Mariners. He was now coming off the best season of his career. As the fulltime third baseman for the 1995 American League West champions, Blowers had career highs for home runs (23), doubles (24), and runs batted in (96), while batting .257 with a 108 OPS+.

Mel Didier, the Dodgers' special assignment scout, predicted Blowers would add power to the lineup, while continuing to improve at third base. He thought Blowers would benefit by playing on a natural surface, which did not require the quickness of the Seattle Kingdome's synthetic field.

"I think I showed everybody in the league that I can come through in big situations," Blowers said. "I always felt my numbers would be very good if I had the opportunity to play every day, and I think I'll continue to grow if I continue to get that opportunity." Blowers, a longtime Seattle resident, said he was initially disappointed by news of the trade, but the more he thought about it, the more excited he became. "I've heard nothing but good things about the Dodgers. If I had to be traded, I couldn't think of a better place."[12]

The Mariners, which were attempting to maintain a $34 million budget, had already committed to paying Ken Griffey, Jr.; Jay Buhner; Randy Johnson; Edgar Martínez; Chris Bosio; and Greg Hibbard a combined total of about $29 million next season. "With the type numbers involved," Blowers said, "I knew that once the Mariners picked up the option on Edgar Martinez and the rumors started about Tino [Martinez] being traded, I might be traded as well. The only thing that surprises me is that it happened so soon." Lee Pelekoudas, Seattle's director of baseball administration, said finances are a hard reality with the Mariners, but "we felt we could make this move without depleting our nucleus or competitiveness."[13]

Blowers played in 92 games for the 1996 Dodgers. He batted .265 with six home runs and 38 runs batted in. In January 1997 he returned to Seattle as a free agent.

November 30, 1995: Signed Free Agent Shortstop Greg Gagne

A day after trading for Mike Blowers to play third base, the Dodgers continued the revamping of the left side of their infield by signing free agent Greg Gagne to replace Jose Offerman at shortstop. Gagne, who was coming off a three-year, $10.7 million contract with the Kansas City Royals, rejected a two-year offer from the St. Louis Cardinals in favor of a one-year, $2.6 million deal with Los Angeles. The Dodgers had offered him two years, but Gagne chose one. After spending 11 seasons with the small-market Royals and Minnesota Twins, Gagne wanted to see if he could adjust to Los Angeles. "In fairness to myself, my family, and the Dodgers, I want to see how it goes this year before making a decision about the future," Gagne said. "I'm excited and happy to be coming to L.A. I'm hopeful we'll like it there and the Dodgers will want to sign me for another year. Perhaps, I'll play the rest of my career on one-year contracts."[14]

The 34-year-old Gagne was a fair hitter, at best. He batted .256 with six home runs and 49 runs batted in with the Royals in 1995. His strong point was defense, which managers and coaches recognized by his many high finishes in voting by for the Gold Glove Award. Gagne averaged fewer than 16 errors in each of his 11 full seasons and made 40 in his three years with the Royals. By contrast, Offerman, who was displaced as the starter by Chad Fonville last September, made 35 in 1995 and 125 over the last four seasons. Gagne had played seven more full seasons than Offerman but made only 38 more errors.

"Gagne will make some plays Dodger fans haven't seen for a while," Kansas City manager Bob Boone said. "He'll be a real asset for them, and I'll miss him, but we can't play the big-money game with the Dodgers."[15]

Gagne was aware of the controversy that surrounded Offerman. "I know people are looking for me to step up and be the man defensively. I expect to be able to do that. I expect to provide some leadership, help the pitchers and be a stabilizing force in the field, maybe more than Jose was." Fred Claire called Gagne "an outstanding shortstop and leader." He said Gagne's decision to take one year over two speaks volumes about character. Gagne said he was attracted' to the Dodgers' tradition and reputation and felt he was joining a club that has a chance to return to the playoffs. "I was on two World Series winners in Minnesota," he said. "Not many players get a chance to play for a Series winner in both leagues. I feel I'll have that chance with the Dodgers."[16]

Gagne played two seasons with the Dodgers, batting .253 in 272 games. He left as a free agent after the 1997 season but chose to retire. Gagne's addition made Offerman expendable. On December 17, the Dodgers traded him to Kansas City for left-handed pitcher Billy Brewer.

Also in 1995:

Traded: Infielder Rafael Bournigal to Montreal Expos for Minor League Pitcher Kris Foster; Minor League Pitcher Dax Winslett to Chicago Cubs for Pitcher Willie Banks; Minor League Outfielder Dwight Maness and Minor League Outfielder Scott Hunter to New York Mets for Outfielder Brett Butler; Pitcher Todd Williams to Oakland Athletics for Minor League Pitcher Matt McDonald; Pitcher Omar Daal to Montreal Expos for Minor League Pitcher Rick Clelland

Purchased: Pitcher John Cummings from Seattle Mariners; Infielder-Outfielder Chad Fonville from Montreal Expos

Sold: Pitcher Willie Banks to Florida Marlins

Chosen in Amateur Free Agent Draft: Onan Masaoka

Signed Amateur Free Agents: Eric Gagne

Signed Free Agents: Outfielder Rick Parker; First Baseman Oreste Marrero; Outfielder Reggie Williams; Pitcher Rob Murphy; Shortstop Dick Schofield, Jr.; Pitcher Darren Hall

Released: Pitcher Al Osuna; Pitcher Rob Murphy; Shortstop Dick Schofield, Jr.

Left as Free Agents: Outfielder Mitch Webster; Outfielder Chris Gwynn; Outfielder Roberto Kelly; Third Baseman Tim Wallach

1996

On June 24, 1996, Bill Russell replaced Tom Lasorda as manager.

July 31, 1996: Traded Pitcher Joey Eischen and Pitcher John Cummings to the Detroit Tigers for Outfielder Chad Curtis

Two hours before the trading deadline, the Dodgers filled their need for a center fielder and for a leadoff hitter with one player—Chad Curtis. To get Curtis, they sent left-handed pitchers Joey Eischen and John Cummings to the Detroit Tigers. The acquisition of the 27-year-old right-handed-hitting Curtis ended the Dodgers search to replace Brett Butler, who left the club at the end of April to battle throat cancer. "He's a quality player who fills two needs," said Fred Claire. "There were really two keys to this trade. One, we found a player who fits our need and, two, the price we had to pay. We had no interest in trading pitching that was key to our organization. I felt this was our best opportunity."[17]

The Tigers were trying to cut payroll—they had traded first baseman Cecil Fielder to the New York Yankees earlier in the day—and had already told Curtis they did not plan to offer him a contract for the 1997 season. Curtis began his major league career with the California Angels in 1992 and was traded to Detroit in the spring of 1995. In his five major league seasons, he had a .267 batting average with 58 home runs, 259 runs batted in, and 159 stolen bases. He was hitting .263 this season, with 10 home runs and 37 runs batted in.

"Obviously I'm going into a better baseball situation this year," Curtis said. "I'll be in the middle of a pennant race. I've never been in one before. There's still more I can do that I haven't done yet. I still believe I can play. Obviously, there's another club out there that thinks so too." Curtis admitted he had mixed emotions about the trade. "The Tigers were the team I grew up cheering for, but I knew they really didn't want me back next year. That makes it easier."[18]

Joey Eischen, 26, was 0–1 with a 4.78 ERA in 28 relief appearances this season. He became expendable when right-hander Darren Dreifort was called up from Albuquerque the previous week. The Tigers said they would likely give Eischen a chance to become a starter. John Cummings, 27, was 3–1 as a reliever in 1995. He was 0–1 with a 6.75 ERA in four April games this season before he was sent to Albuquerque. "Both pitchers will pitch in the major leagues at some point," Claire said. "The big thing is we added a player who brings a lot of experience and will be very aggressive. It's a good fit."[19]

Curtis was not such a good fit. He played in 43 games, with a .212 batting average, two home runs and two stolen bases, and an OPS+ of 75. After the season he signed as a free agent with the Cleveland Indians.

November 20, 1996: Free Agent Second Baseman Delino DeShields Signed with the St. Louis Cardinals

Delino DeShields came to the Dodgers in the infamous November 1993 trade that sent pitcher Pedro Martínez to Montreal. After three seasons in Los Angeles, DeShields signed a $1.9 million contract to play for the St. Louis Cardinals in 1997. "After a certain point in your career, winning is the reason you're out there," DeShields said. "Basically, we're in the same situation. I've come up short a couple of years in the playoffs. They [the Cardinals] have done the same."[20] DeShields, 27, batted .241 with 114 stolen bases and a 79 OPS+ in 370 games for LA. This past season had been his least productive of the three. While he stole 48 bases, he batted just .224, struck out 124 times and had an OPS+ of 60. In addition, DeShields's .975 fielding percentage ranked him ninth among National League second basemen.

December 8, 1996: Signed Free Agent Third Baseman Todd Zeile

The Dodgers hoped their pursuit of a full-time third baseman—they had had 25 third basemen since 1986—ended when they signed Todd Zeile to a three-year contract worth more than $10 million. It was the club's most expensive free-agent contract for a position player since they signed Brett Butler and Darryl Strawberry in 1990. Zeile, 31, broke in with the St. Louis Cardinals as a catcher in 1989. He was in his seventh season with St. Louis when they traded him to the Chicago Cubs in June 1995. Zeile, split the 1996 season between the Philadelphia Phillies and Baltimore Orioles. He batted a combined .263 with 99 runs batted in and a 105 OPS+ in 163 games. His 25 home runs were a career high.

"He'll give us good power, good on-base percentage, and he's a good competitor," said GM Fred Claire. "He's going to fit this team fine." Zeile, a native of Van Nuys who lived 28 miles from Dodger Stadium, said he grew up a Dodgers fan. "My dad went to the first game ever in Dodger Stadium and still has his tickets."

"Eric and I have been talking back and forth," said Zeile, a reference to Dodgers first baseman Eric Karros. The two had been teammates at UCLA. "He's been pulling for this," Zeile said. "We always said it would be great to get back into the same infield together." There had been more lucrative offers, Zeile said, "but L.A. was the No. 1 place to go."[21]

Also in 1996:

Traded: Pitcher Billy Brewer to New York Yankees for Minor League Pitcher Mike Judd; Minor League Pitcher Carl South to Pittsburgh Pirates for Outfielder Dave Clark

Purchased: Outfielder Wayne Kirby from Cleveland Indians; Shortstop Tripp Cromer from St. Louis Cardinals; Second Baseman Nelson Liriano from Pittsburgh Pirates; Catcher Geronimo Gil from Mexico City Reds of Mexican League

Sold: Outfielder Milt Thompson to Colorado Rockies

Chosen in Amateur Free Agent Draft: Alex Cora; Jeff Kubenka; Ted Lilly

Signed Amateur Free Agents: Jeff Williams; Luke Allen, Ricardo Rodríguez; José Díaz

Signed Free Agents: Outfielder Reggie Williams; Outfielder Milt Thompson; Pitcher Scott Radinsky; Pitcher Mike Harkey; Third Baseman Tim Wallach; Infielder Chip Hale; First Baseman-Third Baseman Eddie Williams

Released: Outfielder Reggie Williams; Third Baseman Mike Busch

Left as Free Agents: Catcher Carlos Hernández; First Baseman Oreste Marrero; Pitcher Jim Bruske; Pitcher Rudy Seanez; Outfielder Dave Clark; Pitcher Felix Rodriguez

1997

August 18, 1997: Traded Pitcher Pedro Astacio to the Colorado Rockies for Second Baseman Eric Young

Trailing the San Francisco Giants by two games in the National League West, the Dodgers made their second trade in a week. On August 12 they sent minor league catcher Bobby Cripps to the Toronto Blue Jays for veteran center fielder Otis Nixon. Six days later they traded pitcher Pedro Astacio to the Colorado Rockies for second baseman Eric Young. The 30-year-old Young was drafted by the Dodgers in the 43rd round of the 1989 draft and began his career with them in 1992. He batted .258 in 49 games and was chosen by the Rockies in the expansion draft that followed the season. Young batted .295 with 180 stolen bases in his five seasons in Colorado. At training camp this spring, he was openly criticized by Rockies manager Don Baylor, but Young was having a strong season, with a .282 batting average and 32 stolen bases.

The Dodgers had been making do with rookie Wilton Guerrero and veteran Tripp Cromer at second base, but the position now belonged to Young. The right-hand-hitting Young would bat second, behind Nixon, giving the Dodgers great speed at the top of their lineup. Fred Claire, who had been reluctant to relinquish pitchers, said this deal was an opportunity to get an experienced player for the pennant drive. "I think this trade will really help us. We added a player we know very well. He came up in our system and he's one of the top second basemen in the game." Dodgers manager Bill Russell said: "We feel with Eric Young aboard we have experience at each position. With that experience and base stealing potential it's really big."[22]

Pedro Astacio, a 28-year-old right-hander, had a 48–47 record with an ERA+ of 104 in his six years with the Dodgers. He was 7–9 with a 4.10 earned run average this season, and when fellow starter Ramón Martínez came off the disabled list, Russell moved Astacio to the bullpen. Perhaps adding to Astacio's expendability was a much-publicized June dispute he had with Russell in the Dodgers' dugout. Including the Rockies, Astacio pitched for seven other major league teams after leaving Los Angeles, with a combined 81–77 record.

December 8, 1997: Signed Free Agent Shortstop Jose Vizcaino

Finding a replacement for shortstop Greg Gagne had been the Dodgers' primary concern this offseason. They found their man in free agent Jose Vizcaino, signing him to a three-year contract worth $9.5 million. Vizcaino, nearly 30, signed with the Dodgers out of the Dominican Republic in 1986. In 1990, in what proved to be an awful trade for them, they sent Vizcaino to the Chicago Cubs for outfielder Greg Smith. Smith had three at-bats for the Dodgers and was out of baseball.

Vizcaino, who made his offseason home in the Los Angeles area, said he had longed for this homecoming. "I started out as a Dodger, and I've always thought like a Dodger. I said that someday, when I'm a free agent, I would go back to the Dodgers if I had the chance. This was always my first choice, and I told my agent I would take less money to play for the Dodgers because I would be happy there." Fred Claire, who made the Vizcaino-Greg Smith trade, said: "For me, this was the key part for what we needed to do for 1998. Shortstop was our priority, and Jose fits all of our needs in a great way."[23]

Vizcaino had played for five teams in his nine-year career. After the Dodgers and Cubs, he had been with the Mets, the Indians, and this past season with the Giants. A switch-hitter, he batted .266 with five home runs and 50 RBIs in 1997. In addition, he set personal highs by playing in 151 games and scoring 77 runs for the West Division champions. But it was Vizcaino's defense that appealed most to the Dodgers. According to scouting reports, Vizcaino had good range and a better-than-average throwing arm, making him one of the league's most dependable shortstops. He committed only 16 errors this past season, and his .976 fielding percentage ranked fifth among National League shortstops.

The Dodgers liked that Vizcaino could also play second base and could bat anywhere in the order. "He's the ideal No. 2 hitter because he can do so many things for you," said manager Bill Russell. "He's a good contact hitter and he knows situations in games. I definitely think I'm going to hit him second, but we'll wait and see what happens. We're just really happy to have him back."[24]

Although they were happy with their new shortstop, the Dodgers had initially tried to trade for Montreal shortstop Mark Grudzielanek. They offered reserve second baseman Wilton Guerrero, and when the Expos asked for more, the talks broke down.

Also in 1997:

Traded: Third Baseman Eddie Williams to Pittsburgh Pirates for Minor League Pitcher Hal Garrett; Infielder-Outfielder Chad Fonville to the Chicago White Sox for Outfielder Darren Lewis

Purchased: Outfielder Matt Luke from New York Yankees; Pitcher Jim Bruske from San Diego Padres
   Chosen in Amateur Free Agent Draft: Steve Colyer
   Signed Amateur Free Agents: Victor Álvarez
   Signed Free Agents: Outfielder Eric Anthony; First Baseman Eddie Murray; Outfielder Trent Hubbard
   Chosen in Major League Draft: Pitcher Frank Lankford (returned to New York Yankees in 1998)
   Released: Infielder Chip Hale
   Left as Free Agents: Outfielder Eric Anthony; Second Baseman Nelson Liriano; Outfielder Wayne Kirby; Pitcher Mike Harkey; Shortstop Greg Gagne; Outfielder Otis Nixon; Outfielder Darren Lewis; Pitcher Tom Candiotti; Pitcher Todd Worrell; First Baseman Eddie Murray; Outfielder Brett Butler; Third Baseman Dave Hansen
   Lost in Expansion Draft: Outfielder Karim García; Pitcher Rick Gorecki

1998

In March 1998, Major League Baseball owners approved the sale of the Dodgers from the O'Malley family to Rupert Murdoch's FOX Group.

May 14, 1998: Traded Catcher Mike Piazza and Third Baseman Todd Zeile to the Florida Marlins for Outfielder Gary Sheffield, Outfielder-Third Baseman Bobby Bonilla, Outfielder Jim Eisenreich, Catcher Charles Johnson, and Pitcher Manuel Barrios

The Dodgers made the first major transaction under their new ownership over the objection of general manager Fred Claire. They traded their best and most popular player, catcher Mike Piazza, and third baseman Todd Zeile to the salary-dumping Florida Marlins. (Since their surprise World Series title in 1997, the Marlins had gotten rid of 20 players and would lose 108 games this season.) Going from Florida to Los Angeles were outfielder Gary Sheffield, outfielder-third Baseman Bobby Bonilla, outfielder Jim Eisenreich, catcher Charles Johnson, and pitcher Manuel

Barrios. Chase Carey, chairman and CEO of Fox Television, and Marlins GM Dave Dombrowski negotiated the trade. Dodgers team president Bob Graziano, said: "I think a trade of this magnitude can immediately strengthen and make us a better team." Shortstop Jose Vizcaino agreed. "This is big. We're talking about a group of big guys. It will improve the team. I'm taking nothing away from our two guys but were getting four [sic] instead of two. It'll change the whole attitude of the team. It could be good, and it could be bad. But we're talking about four guys who just won the World Series."[25]

Gary Sheffield, 29, was a three-time All-Star with a .286 career batting average. His best season was with the 1996 Marlins. He hit .314 with 42 home runs, 120 runs batted in and led the National League with a .464 on-base average and a 189 OPS+.

For Bobby Bonilla, a 35-year-old switch-hitter, the Dodgers were his sixth team. He was a six-time All-Star with a career .285 batting average and 266 home runs. Bonilla was also a better fielding third baseman than Zeile.

Charles Johnson, 26, was in his fifth season with the Marlins. Better known for his defense—he won Gold Gloves at catcher in each of the past three seasons—Johnson batted .250 in 1997, with 19 home runs and 63 RBIs.

Switch-hitter Eisenreich, 37, was in his fifteenth major league season. He had been a consistent and reliable hitter and had a career .425 batting average against the Dodgers.

Manuel Barrios, a 23-year-old right-hander, pitched in two games for Houston in 1997, without a decision and two for Florida this season, also without a decision. He would pitch in one game for the Dodgers before being sold back to the Marlins in August. The one game Barrios pitched for the Dodgers was his final game as a major leaguer.

"It won't take them very long to fit in," manager Bill Russell said of the four newcomers. "These guys are all veteran players, and we'll have positions for all of them. They're in a city that loves a winner, and I think they all want to be a winner." Dodgers outfielder Trent Hubbard emphasized that the Dodgers were getting four proven players. "We gave up a tremendous player a tremendous talent," Hubbard said of Piazza. "But then you step back and ask did we improve the team? Sure, we gave them a proven player of All-Star caliber, but I think we're a better team. We gave up one All-Star and got two or three All-Stars."[26]

Todd Zeile batted .268 with 31 home runs and a 121 OPS+ in 1997, his first season with the Dodgers. But he was mostly a one-way player with little speed and a defensive liability. Yet, after a half season in Florida, he went on to play for the Rangers, the Mets, the Yankees, the Rockies, and the Expos before retiring after the 2004 season.

Several Dodgers players said they believed the club's struggles under their new ownership (they were 19–21) was as much a factor in the trade as the team's inability to sign Mike Piazza to a long-term contract extension. Piazza, 29, reportedly had turned down a six-year $81 million offer last month and was due to become a free agent at the end of the season "Mike wanted to stay here. The people of LA wanted him to stay here," said Tom Lasorda about Piazza's pending free agency. "The ballclub made him a tremendous offer. I guess it wasn't enough." Piazza said he was shocked at being traded. "I couldn't believe it. After the game Fred Claire called me into his office and told me. For six years I have had the privilege to play for fans and with teammates who showed me a tremendous amount of appreciation and for that I will always be grateful," he said. "The business of baseball is complicated, and I try to keep the game simple. As long as I play, I'll swing hard and play hard and be grateful to have the chance to play this great game no matter where I'm playing."[27]

In his six plus season with the Dodgers, Piazza, had a .331 batting average, 177 home runs, 563 runs batted in, and a 160 OPS+. He was the Rookie of the Year in 1993, runner-up MVP twice, and an All-Star in each of his five full seasons. "I have all the respect in the world for him," said Giants GM Brian Sabean. "He's one of the most consistent and dangerous hitters we faced. We've faced those other guys with other teams, but I don't know if they'll bring the same flavor to the Dodger lineup that Piazza did."[28] Piazza would play until 2007 and be elected to the Hall of Fame in 2016.

The trade left Eric Karros and Raul Mondesi as the only regular starters that had been with the team for more than two years. "That's something you always worry about when you bring in that many new faces during the season," San Diego Padres GM Kevin Towers said. "How do they jell, how do they fit in from a chemistry standpoint?"[29]

June 4, 1998: Traded Pitcher Hideo Nomo and Pitcher Brad Clontz to the New York Mets for Pitcher Greg McMichael and Pitcher Dave Mlicki

An unhappy Hideo Nomo wanted the Dodgers to trade him. A few days after they designated the 29-year-old right-hander for assignment, the club granted his wish. They sent him, along with pitcher Brad Clontz, to the New York Mets for right-handed pitchers Greg McMichael and Dave Mlicki. (The 27-year-old Clontz, in his first season with Los Angeles, had a 2–0 record and a 5.66 ERA in 18 games.)

The Dodgers appeared to have gotten an inadequate return for Nomo, but they faced a seven-day deadline to deal him after having designated him for assignment. Fred Claire called the departure of Nomo the end of an "incredible chapter" in Dodgers history. But, Claire said, Nomo "reached the point that he thought he'd be better if he made a move, and we accommodated him." Nomo and agent Don Nomura were thrilled about the trade and the destination, Claire added. "Very frankly, I'd say the New York Mets were their No. 1 preference. That's not why this deal was made, but it so happened the deal was best for both sides."[30]

The 29-year-old Nomo was upset by the recent trade of catcher Mike Piazza. The trade to the Mets would reunite him not only with Piazza, but also with former Dodgers pitching coach Dave Wallace, now an assistant general manager with the Mets, and with his close friend, Japanese pitcher Masato Yoshii.

Nomo, only the second native of Japan to play in the major leagues, had been an immediate success. His sensational debut made him a favorite of the fans, especially among Asian fans. Nomo was the National League's Rookie of the Year in 1995 and its starting pitcher in the All-Star game. He led the league in shutouts and strikeouts and had an ERA+ of 149. He also finished fourth in voting for the Cy Young Award and repeated that fourth-place finish in 1996. Nomo was 43–29 in his first three seasons with the Dodgers but was struggling with a 2–7 record and a 5.05 earned run average this season.

Nomo pitched the rest of the 1998 season for the Mets, and then single seasons for the Milwaukee Brewers (1999), the Detroit Tigers (2000), and the Boston Red Sox (2001). He compiled a 37–35 record before resigning as a free agent with the Dodgers in January 2002.

"Dave Mlicki is a starting pitcher with outstanding ability," Claire said. "We've always liked his ability." Mlicki, 29, had a 1–4 record with a 5.68 ERA in 10 starts this season. Greg McMichael, a 31-year-old reliever, had a 1–2 record and a 3.97 ERA in 22 games this season. The Dodgers were hoping he would improve their bullpen woes. Claire called him "one of the top set-up people in the National League [with] the ability to close as well. These are two proven guys with experience and ability," he said of his new pitchers. "They'll fit in great. I think this is a very good trade for us."[31]

On June 22, 1998, Tom Lasorda replaced Fred Claire as general manager.
On June 22, 1998, Glenn Hoffman replaced Bill Russell as manager.

July 4, 1998: Traded Outfielder-First Baseman Paul Konerko and Pitcher Dennys Reyes to the Cincinnati Reds for Pitcher Jeff Shaw

In the first inning of their game in San Francisco, Dodgers manager Glenn Hoffman escorted Paul Konerko from the dugout to the clubhouse. Hoffman said he wanted to be present when interim general manager

Tom Lasorda informed Konerko, a rookie infielder-outfielder, that he and rookie pitcher Dennys Reyes had been traded to Cincinnati for All-Star closer Jeff Shaw. With the departure of Konerko and Reyes, only 14 players remained from the Dodgers' opening day roster. "You look at how many games we lost in the seventh, eighth, ninth inning," Dodgers general manager Tom Lasorda said. "You see how much I wanted to get this guy [Shaw]. I feel this Dodger club needs this relief pitcher desperately."[32] It was the team's third major trade in two months. The trades of Mike Piazza and Hideo Nomo were expected to have negative effects on the teams near future, and several players said that with the departure of Konerko and Reyes, two important pieces of the Dodgers long-range future had disappeared as well. Konerko and Reyes were the Dodgers' highest-rated prospects and were considered untouchable under the previous management regime.

Konerko, 22, was the Dodgers first-round selection in the 1994 amateur free agent draft. Playing for the Triple A Albuquerque Dukes in 1997, he was named the Minor League Player of the Year and the Pacific Coast League's Most Valuable Player. Konerko was the Dodgers' opening-day first baseman this season but also had spent time back at Albuquerque. He batted .215 with four home runs, 16 runs batted in and had a 55 OPS+ in 49 games for the Dodgers. Lasorda had denied stories in the *Los Angeles Times* that the Dodgers wanted Reds closer Jeff Shaw and were negotiating a deal that would include Paul Konerko. No way, Lasorda had said, that Konerko was being discussed or would be part of it.

Now that the deal had been made, Lasorda said it was tough to trade away Konerko, but the Reds insisted they would not make the deal for Shaw unless they got him. "I turned down seven teams asking for Konerko. The one guy I wanted I had to give up Konerko to get him."[33] Konerko had an excellent career after leaving LA. In his 18 seasons, 16 with the Chicago White Sox, he batted .279, with 439 home runs, 1,412 runs batted in, and a 118 OPS+.

Twenty-one-year-old Dennys Reyes was 2–7 with a 95 ERA+ in his season-and-a-half with the Dodgers; nevertheless, the club considered him their top pitching prospect. While Reyes's future success could not match Konerko's, he had a long and effective post–Dodgers career. Working mostly as a reliever, he pitched for 15 total seasons with a 106 ERA+.

Shaw left Cincinnati's Cinergy Field following the Reds win over St. Louis without talking to reporters or saying goodbye to most of his teammates. The 31-year-old right-hander had a 2–4 record and 1.81 ERA with 23 saves in 28 save opportunities. His 23 saves ranked third in the National League. Lasorda said the deal would allow the Dodgers to move Antonio Osuna and Scott Radinsky, who had been sharing the closer's spot, back to their normal roles as set-up men. He believed Shaw would propel the team into the National League West race by saving late-inning leads.

Shaw pitched in 235 games for the Dodgers from July 1998 to 2001, all in relief. He had a 9–17 record, a 124 ERA+, and a then club record of 129 saves. The team did not pick up Shaw's option after the 2001 season making him a free agent, but instead of continuing his career, he retired.

July 31, 1998: Traded Second Baseman Wilton Guerrero, Minor League Outfielder Peter Bergeron, Minor League Pitcher Ted Lilly, and Minor League Outfielder Jon Tucker to the Montreal Expos for Shortstop Mark Grudzielanek, Pitcher Carlos Pérez, and Minor League Outfielder Hiram Bocachica

The Dodger were five games behind the Chicago Cubs in the National League wild card race when they completed a multi-player deal with the Montreal Expos four hours before the non-waiver trading deadline. Coming to Los Angeles were shortstop Mark Grudzielanek, pitcher Carlos Pérez, and minor league outfielder Hiram Bocachica. The Expos were getting second baseman Wilton Guerrero and three minor leaguers—pitcher Ted Lilly, outfielder Peter Bergeron, and outfielder Jon Tucker. "We were on the phone all day with Montreal because we needed to get this done now," said Dodgers interim GM Tom Lasorda. "Montreal gave us some good players who can help us now, and we gave them some good prospects who can help them down the road. We've got to get this club into the playoffs," Lasorda said.[34]

One who was expected to provide immediate help was Carlos Pérez, a 27-year-old left-hander who was in his third season as a starter with the Expos. Pérez had an overall 29–31 record with 112 ERA+. He was 7–10 with a 3.75 earned run average in 23 starts this season. "He's a quality pitcher," Lasorda said. "He's a winner. I've always admired and respected him." Pérez would move into the rotation as a replacement for Ismael Valdes, who was on the 15-day disabled list. "I'm very happy to play in Los Angeles," Pérez said. "We have a lot of young players here in Montreal and the Dodgers have a lot of veterans, so I think it's going to be easier for me to win games in Los Angeles."[35]

When the Dodgers signed free agent shortstop Jose Vizcaino last winter, they had tried first to trade for the 28-year-old Grudzielanek. They offered Wilton Guerrero even-up, but the Expos wanted more, and the talks broke down. "We had discussions with the Dodgers in the off-season," Expos general manager Jim Beattie said. "They wanted Mark, and we wanted Wilton. We've had ongoing discussions." Grudzielanek had become disenchanted with the Expos as he watched an excellent team being dismantled. He had said since spring training he was not going to be back next season. "I know I said some things in the past and might have complained before, but they were very honest with me and that's what I'll remember," he said. "This is a great trade for me because I wasn't very happy in Montreal. I wanted to play for a winner, and now I'm getting that chance with the Dodgers."[36] Grudzielanek, 28, batted .306 with 201 hits in 1996 and led the major leagues with 54 doubles last season. He was batting .276 with eight homers and 41 RBIs this season. For now, he would replace Juan Castro, who was filling in for the injured Vizcaino as the Dodgers everyday shortstop.

Wilton Guerrero, 23, had a .288 batting average in 180 games for Los Angeles. He batted .291 with nine triples as a rookie last season, but he lost his job because of mental lapses and poor baserunning. The Dodgers tried to make him an outfielder this season, but that plan did not work. He was hitting .283 in 64 games and was expected to be the Expos' new second baseman. "I tell Wilton all the time that he has a chance to be a star," Lasorda said. "The last thing I wanted to do was trade Wilton, but Jim Beattie wouldn't make the deal without him." "Wilton's first choice was to play in Los Angeles," said Jeff Moorad, Guerrero's agent. "He enjoyed being here, but under the circumstances, this was the next best thing."[37] In Montreal, Guerrero became a teammate of his younger brother, star outfielder Vladimir.

On September 11, 1998, Kevin Malone replaced Tom Lasorda as general manager.

November 6, 1998: Signed Free Agent Outfielder Devon White

By signing switch-hitter Devon White, the Dodgers believed it gave them one of the best offensive outfields in the game. White, a center fielder, would be flanked by Gary Sheffield, who moved from right field to left field, and Raul Mondesi, who would return to right field after playing in center field during parts of the 1998 season. Mondesi had informed club officials he wanted to return to his former position in 1999. White, who would turn 36 in December, was a seven-time Gold Glove winner. His contract called for reported salaries of $2.5 million next season, $4 million in 2000, and $5 million in 2001.

"We needed to make a move quickly to get a player of this guy's ability," said new Dodgers GM Kevin Malone. "He's one of the best defensive center fielders in the game and he's a proven winner. He can hit 20 home runs and steal 20 bases, he's a run-producer and he can bat anywhere in the order. He can do so many things for you. There are many things we're doing to make this a championship-caliber team, and this signing White was a major piece to the puzzle."[38]

White broke in with the California Angels in 1985 and had also played with the Toronto Blue Jays, the Florida Marlins, and this past season with the Arizona Diamondbacks. He had been a member of three World Series champions—the 1992 and 1993 Blue Jays and the 1997 Marlins. The Marlins traded White to the Diamondbacks after he spent much of the 1997 season on the disabled list after surgery on his left knee. He recovered and had a strong season in 1998, batting .279 with 22 home runs and 22 stolen bases. He also had 32 doubles, 85 runs batted in, and 84 runs scored in 146 games. White was selected an All-Star for the third time and the first time as a member of the National League team. "Right out of the gate, Kevin expressed a key interest in Devon," said Eric Goldschmidt, White's agent, and "Los Angeles was his [White's] first choice. I've known Kevin for a long time," Goldschmidt said, "and we all felt good about this, so it didn't take long."[39]

November 11, 1998: Traded Third Baseman Bobby Bonilla and Cash to the New York Mets for Pitcher Mel Rojas

Looking to make room for 20-year-old Adrian Beltre to start at third base in 1999, the Dodgers sent Bobby Bonilla and $1 million to the New York Mets for relief pitcher Mel Rojas. Both Bonilla, who had had a contentious relationship with the Dodgers, and Rojas had figured prominently in trade talks at the general managers' meetings in Naples Florida. Bonilla, a six-time All-Star in his 13-year career, was happy to be going back to the Mets, for whom he played from 1992 to 1995.

Bonilla's agent, Danny Horowitz, acknowledged that the 35-year-old switch-hitter was glad to be going back to New York. "I know he's really excited because we've spoken a lot about this possibility the past couple of days. Bobby is from New York and his family is there. This is a second chance for him to finish his unfinished business there."[40] While not openly saying so, the Dodgers were eager to trade Bonilla because of their overall displeasure with him, and their confidence in Beltre.

A few days later, after returning from a Mexican vacation, Bonilla gave his side of the story. "I guess I was the reason for all of the problems the Dodgers had, so everything should be great now that they got me out of there," he said sarcastically. "I expected this because someone out there [Lasorda] doesn't like me too much. Tommy didn't want me around because he knew I wouldn't listen to all of his talk. I saw right through all of that, and he knew he better turn around when he saw me in the clubhouse. He didn't like that, he wants everyone to just sit there and listen to him, and we all know what I'm talking about." Bonilla said Lasorda was considered an unwelcome presence in the clubhouse by many players after he succeeded executive vice president Fred Claire as general manager on June 22. He said it was widely believed in the organization that Lasorda hastened the firings of Claire and manager Bill Russell by often criticizing their performances to team President Bob Graziano and former owner Peter O'Malley. "Everyone knew what he did," Bonilla said. "He would be up there in the owner's box because that's the way he is. But what's going to be interesting is the first time he tries that with [new manager] Davey [Johnson]."[41]

Mel Rojas had his best seasons with the 1990–1996 Montreal Expos, compiling 109 saves including 30 in 1995 and 36 in 1996. He had been much less effective in recent seasons, but the Dodgers believed the 32-year-old right-hander would be of help to them as a set-up man.

December 1, 1998: Traded Catcher Charles Johnson and Outfielder Roger Cedeño to the New York Mets for Catcher Todd Hundley and Minor League Pitcher Arnie Gooch

Dodgers GM Kevin Malone had declared he was not a puppet, and that he, not the Fox owners or team president Bob Graziano, was making the player personnel decisions. So, it was Malone's decision to trade catcher Charles Johnson and outfielder Roger Cedeño to the New York Mets for catcher Todd Hundley and minor league pitcher Arnie Gooch. Hundley, 29, filled the Dodgers' need for a power-hitting catcher and a left-handed bat, but they were gambling that he had completely recovered from the September 1997 reconstructive surgery on his right elbow. The year before, Hundley hit 41 home runs as a catcher, at the time a major league record for catchers. The 41 home runs were also a National League record for a switch-hitter. Hundley had 124 home runs and a 104 OPS+ in his nine years with the Mets.

Last July, when Hundley returned to the Mets after his rehabilitation, Mike Piazza had taken his position. The Mets tried Hundley in left field, but he made five errors in 34 starts. "I couldn't stand the outfield," he said. "With my personality, it was too boring." The Mets sent Hundley to their

Triple A team in Norfolk, where manager Rick Dempsey, a longtime major league catcher, put him back behind the plate. Near the end of the season the Mets brought him back to New York. Hundley said he knew he was healed, even though he played in only 53 games, hitting .161, with three home runs and 12 runs batted in. "My elbow is back to 100," he said.[42]

Mets GM Steve Phillips said, "It is a bittersweet day in Mets history with Todd Hundley leaving the organization." It was bittersweet for Hundley, as well. Yet, he knew Piazza was set as the Mets' catcher. In addition, he had never gotten along with manager Bobby Valentine. While he knew he was leaving New York, Hundley could stipulate the teams to whom he could be traded, and that list did not include the Dodgers. He changed his mind after Malone hired Davey Johnson to manage the club and Dempsey to be a Dodgers' coach. "This is an organization that I would love to finish my career with," Hundley said. "Wherever Davey goes, he doesn't accept losing." Malone took the precaution of checking with the Dodgers' physicians, with the doctor who had done the surgery, and studying the results of an MRI that showed the healing process in the elbow was complete. He also checked with Dempsey before making the deal. Dempsey had been highly impressed with Hundley when he caught for him in Norfolk. "He [Hundley] is a major piece of the puzzle," Malone said. "He is going to give us better balance in the lineup hitting between Gary Sheffield and Raul Mondesi."[43]

Roger Cedeño, a 24-year-old switch-hitter, was once thought to be the Dodgers' center fielder of the future, but he had turned out to be inconsistent at bat and had a troubling tendency to misjudge fly balls. He played in 105 games last season, batting .242 with two home runs and 17 RBIs.

When the Dodgers acquired Charles Johnson last May, in the Piazza trade, they knew they were getting a strong glove and a weak bat, and Johnson lived up to expectations. He batted .217 for them with 12 home runs and 35 RBIs in 102 games. The Mets, who were set behind the plate with Piazza, quickly traded Johnson to the Baltimore Orioles for relief pitcher Armando Benítez. Arnie Gooch was a 22-year-old righthander who had an 11–14 record and a 3.90 ERA with the Class AA Binghamton Mets of the Eastern League this past season. He would never reach the major leagues.

December 12, 1998: Signed Free Agent Pitcher Kevin Brown

A salary barrier was broken when the Dodgers and right-hander Kevin Brown's agent, Scott Boras, announced the pitcher had signed a seven-year, $105 million contract, making Brown the highest-paid player in baseball history. The no-trade contract called for a $5 million signing bonus, $10 million next year, and $15 million in each of the following six seasons. The Dodgers also agreed to charter a plane to fly Brown's family from their home in Macon, Georgia, to Los Angeles twelve times per season.

Brown, who would turn 34 in March, spent most of his 12-year career with the Texas Rangers, but had also pitched for the Orioles, the Marlins, and the Padres. He had a 139–99 record with eight seasons of double-digit wins. Brown's best season was with the 1996 Marlins, when he won 17 games and led the league with a 1.89 earned average, less than half the National League's combined ERA. Pitching for San Diego this past season, he was 18–7 with a 164 ERA+.

"From the first moment we [Brown and his wife, Candace] visited with the Dodgers in Los Angeles Wednesday, we knew that they were not only committed to us but committed to winning. It's really a relief to get the whole thing over with and to know where I'm going to be for the rest of my career," Brown said. "We feel like we logically evaluated the marketplace," said Dodgers GM Kevin Malone. "We needed the player; we wanted the player, and we made the commitment to our fans to becoming a winning team."[44]

John Moores, president of the Padres, Brown's employer in 1998, was not pleased with the amount of money the Dodgers spent on Brown. "I don't mean to criticize Kevin Brown," he said, "but it's a truly tragic day for baseball. It's extraordinary. It confirms my worst fears about what would happen if we let Rupert Murdoch buy the Dodgers and I think it represents a continuation of a very bad series of events in baseball after a spectacular season."[45] Malone defended the deal. "We weren't the only club willing to make this sort of commitment," he said. "It's been moving in that direction. It was going to be done. And I've been told it was going to be done for more than we did it for."[46]

Also in 1998:

Traded: Pitcher Greg McMichael and Cash to New York Mets for Pitcher Brian Bohanon; Pitcher Jim Bruske to San Diego Padres for Minor League Pitcher Widd Workman; Minor League Infielder Jose Pimentel to Atlanta Braves for Outfielder Damon Hollins; Pitcher Eric Weaver to Seattle Mariners for Minor League Pitcher Scott Prouty

Purchased: Outfielder Matt Luke from Cleveland Indians; Pitcher Doug Bochtler from Detroit Tigers

Sold: Outfielder Matt Luke to Cleveland Indians; Pitcher Will Brunson to Detroit Tigers

Chosen in Amateur Free Agent Draft: Bubba Crosby; David Ross

Signed Free Agents: Outfielder Thomas Howard; Outfielder Mike Devereaux; Pitcher Sean Maloney; Pitcher Alan Mills; Pitcher Pedro Borbón

Released: Outfielder Billy Ashley; Outfielder Mike Devereaux; Outfielder Thomas Howard

Left as Free Agents: Pitcher Mark Guthrie; Pitcher Brad Clontz; Pitcher Scott Radinsky; Catcher Tom Prince; Catcher Henry Blanco; Pitcher Brian Bohanon; Outfielder Jim Eisenreich; Pitcher Gary Rath; Outfielder Matt Luke; Pitcher Sean Maloney

1999

For the 1999 season, Davey Johnson replaced Glenn Hoffman as manager.

April 16, 1999: Traded Pitcher Dave Mlicki and Pitcher Mel Rojas to the Detroit Tigers for Pitcher Robinson Checo, Minor League Pitcher-Shortstop Apostol Garcia, and Minor League Pitcher Rick Roberts

The Detroit Tigers had two members of their starting rotation on the disabled list. Meanwhile, the Dodgers had a loaded five-man rotation, consisting of Kevin Brown, Chan Ho Park, Ismael Valdes, Carlos Pérez, and Darren Dreifort. That left no room for Dave Mlicki, whom manager Davey Johnson had moved to the bullpen. Except for 1996, when he was with the Mets, Mlicki had always been a starter. In 1998, his first season with Los Angeles, he was 7–3 with a league average ERA in 20 games, all starts. With the Dodgers looking to reduce their payroll and replenish their farm system, they traded Mlicki and veteran pitcher Mel Rojas to the Tigers for three minor league pitching prospects—right-handers Robinson Checo and Apostol Garcia and left-hander Richard Roberts. "My goal when I came here was two-fold," said GM Kevin Malone; "To be contenders for a championship and to improve our farm system. We needed depth and we needed prospects."[47]

Mlicki said he was pleased about the trade. "At first, I was a little shocked because I hadn't heard any trade speculation for a while, but when everything quiets down is when it happens. I'm thrilled now because this is an excellent opportunity for me. I wasn't able to start on the Dodgers, but that's nothing to be ashamed of with their rotation," said Mlicki, who was 0–1 with a 4.91 ERA in two relief appearances this season. "This was in everyone's best interest," said Malone. "Dave wasn't going to get the innings he needed here, and we needed to add some young arms. The reports on the prospects we got are good; they're their Nos. 6, 10 and 11 prospects. So, this deal helps the Dodgers, it helps Dave Mlicki, and it helps the Tigers."[48] The trade also trimmed the Dodgers' $84 million payroll, which had been second only to that of the New York Yankees.

Mel Rojas came to the Dodgers in the November 1998 trade for Bobby Bonilla. He left with a 12.60 earned run average in five appearances, in which he allowed three home runs in five innings. The Dodgers were planning to release him, but Malone mentioned him to Tigers GM Randy Smith and Rojas became part of the trade.

The Tigers released the 32-year-old Rojas in May. Montreal signed him that month and released him in July, ending his major league career. Robinson Checo, 27, was added to the Dodgers 25-man roster. He won two and lost two with a 10.34 ERA in his final major league season. Apostol Garcia, 22, and Rick Roberts, 19, were sent to the minor leagues where they remained for the rest of their careers.

November 8, 1999: Traded Outfielder Raul Mondesi and Pitcher Pedro Borbón to the Toronto Blue Jays for Outfielder Shawn Green and Minor League Second Baseman Jorge Nuñez

Over the last few seasons, the Dodgers had grown discontented with Raul Mondesi, and the feeling was mutual. The breakup seemed a certainty after Mondesi's expletive-filled tirade August 11 in Montreal. Robert Daly, the Dodgers' new chairman of the board, thought the situation could be resolved, but his meeting with Jeff Moorad, who represented Mondesi, changed his mind. The Dodgers made the breakup official when they traded Mondesi and pitcher Pedro Borbón to the Toronto Blue Jays for All-Star outfielder Shawn Green and minor league infielder Jorge Nuñez.

"Before we got into talking about Shawn, Kevin Malone and I met to talk about Mondesi," Daly said. "I was positive after that meeting that Mondesi did not want to be with the Dodgers anymore," and he was right. "I'm real happy to be a Blue Jay," was Mondesi's reaction after the trade. "I've heard a lot of good things about how they treat Latin players in Toronto. I've talked to a lot of my friends about that, and I'm looking forward to this. I'm looking to being with the Blue Jays in 2000." "Mondesi simply wanted out," Moorad said. "Raul just felt that it would be better for him to go someplace else and start over."[49]

Mondesi, who would turn 29 in March, was the NL Rookie of the Year in 1994. A consistently good hitter, he batted .288 with 163 home runs, 518 runs batted in, and had a 122 OPS+ for the Dodgers from 1993 to 1999. This past season, he hit .253 with 33 home runs, a career-high 99 RBIs, and a 109 OPS+.

Toronto's president and general manager, Gord Ash, was pleased at getting Mondesi. "We add someone who gives us power, speed, and run production. I think we got the best deal we could under the circumstances because Shawn wanted to return home." Dodgers outfielder Gary Sheffield believed Mondesi, his friend and now former teammate would do well in Toronto. "I spent a lot of time with Mondy this year, trying to help him through his bumps and bruises after what happened," Sheffield said. "Mondy is a good person, and he plays hard, and anyone who does that is going to be all right."[50]

With this trade, the Dodgers, who a year ago made pitcher Kevin Brown the highest-paid player in the game, now made Green the second highest. The 27-year-old left-handed slugger received a six-year, $84 million contract. The $14 million average annual value was second only to Brown's $15 million average. As Mondesi had done with the Dodgers, Green had spent his entire major league career with the Blue Jays. In five full seasons (1995–1999) plus six at-bats in 1993 and 33 at-bats in 1994, he batted .286 with 119 home runs, 376 runs batted in, with a 117 OPS+. This past season had been his best—a .309 batting average, with 42 home runs, 123 RBIs, and a 144 OPS+. Green led the American League in doubles (45), total bases (361), was selected for the All-Star team, and won Silver Slugger and Gold Glove Awards.

There would be a lot of pressure on the Newport Beach resident, pressure the Dodgers hoped he would handle better than residents Eric Davis and Darryl Strawberry had. Dave Stewart, the Blue Jays' assistant general manager, called it a sad day, in that "you cultivate a young player only to lose him" through baseball's ugly and unforgiving economics. The former Dodgers pitcher who was familiar with pressure and expectation said there are no maybes about Green's ability to cope with the challenge. "He is a premier player, a five-tool talent," Stewart said. "His statistics tell you what kind of player he is, but there are not a lot of kids walking the earth who are a better person than he is." Gordon Lakey, a former Toronto scout, said, "There are not many complete players, but Shawn has become one. He's made a lot of strides in all areas. He makes any team a better team."[51]

The Blue Jays had been unable to meet Green's contract demands and knew if he left as a free agent after the 2000 season, they would get only draft choices as compensation. Toronto wanted an established player, and the Dodgers' offer of Mondesi and Pedro Borbón was the best Ash received. Green, in turn, wanted the Dodgers first and foremost.

He called it an exciting opportunity to play at home, with the potentially "gratifying opportunity" to make a "big impact statistically and help elevate the performance of some of the other players." Green also said it was important to him to be traded to a community with a large Jewish population such as New York or Los Angeles. "As a Jewish athlete I think it's important to interact with the fans, and the Dodgers, of course, have a rich tradition with Sandy Koufax," he said.

Pedro Borbón went 4–3 with a 106 ERA+ in 70 relief appearances in 1999, his one season with the Dodgers. Jorge Nuñez would never reach the major leagues.

December 12, 1999: Traded Pitcher Ismael Valdez and Second Baseman Eric Young to the Chicago Cubs for Pitcher Terry Adams, Minor League Pitcher Chad Ricketts, and a Player to be Named

Dodgers GM Kevin Malone had said that every personnel decision for every team was driven by money. So, cutting costs may have been the major reason for his seemingly one-sided deal with the Chicago Cubs, a deal everyone agreed was a steal for the Cubs. Chicago was getting a proven major league starter in 26-year-old right-hander Ismael Valdes, and in 32-year-old Eric Young they were getting one of the best leadoff hitters in the National League. In return, the Dodgers were getting pitcher Terry Adams, a right-handed reliever who would turn 27 in March, Class AA right-hander Chad Ricketts, and a player to be named. That player was expected to be Class AA right-hander Brian Stephenson, and it was. Neither Ricketts nor Stephenson ever reached the major leagues.

Adams had been mostly a set-up man in Chicago, but he was thought to be an above-average reliever with the potential to be a closer. He had appeared in 276 games with a 19–26 record, 37 saves, and a 108 ERA+. He was 6–3 with a 112 ERA+ and 13 saves in 52 games last season. As Malone lamented, money was the key to this transaction. It became final only after the Cubs agreed to pay the remainder of Young's contract, which called for $9 million over the next two seasons. Valdes, who was expected to make $6 million in 2000 and would be eligible for free agency after the season was not expected to re-sign with the Dodgers. The club had been determined to move Valdes and Young before the close of the winter meetings because their 2000 payroll would have approached $100 million with them on the roster.

"If we had stayed status quo our payroll would have been too high. And, frankly, I don't know if we would have been any better," Chairman Robert Daly said. "I can understand some people might look at this and not understand it totally because we gave up two players who I like a lot," said Malone. "I like Ismael and I like E.Y., and we might not have done this in a perfect world, but the reality is this isn't a perfect world." We're committed to winning and bringing back that winning tradition to the Dodgers, and we're going through a process right now that will help us get better. "This helps give us some more payroll flexibility, which increases our options to help us improve, so it makes us better in the big picture. And the reality is we needed to do I this for a lot of reasons."[52] One of those reasons was manager Davey Johnson's opinion of Young, whom he had asked the Dodgers to trade. Johnson and members of his coaching staff considered Young a defensive liability.

Cubs manager Don Baylor had used Young as his leadoff batter when he managed him with the Rockies. "He was a very exciting player for me in Colorado," Baylor said. "He brings to us something that this club needed, which is a leadoff hitter with speed." (Young had averaged almost 37 stolen bases a season in his eight-year career.) Young was equally happy to be playing for Baylor again. "No disrespect meant for managers like Bill Russell or Glenn Hoffman, but now I can definitely appreciate a man like Don Baylor," he said. "I understand more clearly the things he was trying to do to help me improve. It's going to be good to be reunited with him." Regarding Valdez, Baylor said: "With Valdes, he has 150 starts in the major leagues, and 63 percent of the time he's gone into the seventh inning. So, getting a quality young pitcher, especially a starting pitcher, was one of our objectives this year."[53] Valdez went 61–54 with a 118 ERA+ while making 176 appearances, 150 of which were starts for the Dodgers, from 1994 to 1999. He was 9–14 with a 3.98 ERA last year while appearing in 32 games, all of them starts.

December 17, 1999: Signed Free Agent Pitcher Orel Hershiser

In 1988 Orel Hershiser won 23 games with eight shutouts and a 149 ERA+. He set the major league record by throwing 59 consecutive scoreless innings and was the unanimous winner of the National League's Cy Young Award. Hershiser followed by winning the Most Valuable Player Award in the Dodgers win over the New York Mets in the NL Championship Series and in their World Series win over the Oakland Athletics. The team had not appeared in postseason play since.

Hershiser, now 41, who left as a free agent after the 1994 season to sign with the Cleveland Indians, agreed to a one-year contract worth about $2 million. He was delighted to be returning. "I'm elated. I just can't wait. It's a sweet, sweet possible ending to my career," he said. "I've been having my last season for probably the last five years. Everyone including my wife and kids have been writing me off. I love pitching in the big leagues, I love the camaraderie in the locker room. There's no other reason to play than to win."[54]

After leaving LA, Hershiser spent three seasons with Cleveland, one with the San Francisco Giants, and one with the New York Mets. He won 69 games and lost 43 during those five seasons. Last season with the Mets, he went 13–12 with a 4.58 ERA in 32 games. All were starts but Hershiser said he would be open to being a relief pitcher. GM Kevin Malone said the Dodgers were looking at Hershiser as a reliever but said he could also start. "He's willing to do whatever," Malone said. "If we need him to start, he'll start. He's so versatile, he can help us in many areas." One of those areas, Malone stressed, was the clubhouse. "The more guys we can add like Orel, who are committed to winning, the better chance we have to win. We lacked some leadership, we lacked the right chemistry, we didn't win enough games. We've got to make the necessary changes."[55]

Hershiser was in 10 games with the 2000 Dodgers; six were starts. He had a 1–5 record with a 13.14 earned run average. He was released on June 27, ending his active career. In his 13 seasons with the Dodgers, Hershiser appeared in 353 games (309 were starts), won 135, lost 107 with an ERA+ of 116.

Also in 1999:

Traded: Pitcher Darren Hall to Chicago White Sox for Minor League Catcher Joe Sutton; Minor League Pitcher Blake Mayo to Arizona Diamondbacks for Pitcher Neil Weber; Minor League Pitcher Ryan Moskau to Florida Marlins for Infielder Craig Counsell; Minor League First Baseman Nick Leach to New York Yankees for Pitcher Dan Naulty

Purchased: Pitcher Doug Bochtler from Toronto Blue Jays

Sold: Outfielder Jacob Brumfield to Toronto Blue Jays; Pitcher Jeff Kubenka to Arizona Diamondbacks

Chosen in Amateur Free Agent Draft: Jason Repko; Joseph Thurston; Eric Junge; Shane Nance; Reggie Abercrombie

Signed Amateur Free Agents: Chin-Feng Chen; Hung-Chih Kuo; Franquelis Osoria, Francisco, Cruceta

Signed Free Agents: Pitcher Jamie Arnold; Pitcher Matt Herges; Third Baseman Dave Hansen; Outfielder Brent Cookson; Third Baseman

Chance Sanford; Outfielder Jacob Brumfield; Catcher Rick Wilkins; Pitcher Mike Maddux; Infielder-Outfielder Shawn Gilbert; Pitcher Mike Fetters; Catcher Adam Melhuse; Infielder Jeff Branson; Pitcher Kris Foster

Left as Free Agents: Pitcher Doug Bochtler; Catcher Rick Wilkins; Pitcher Mike Maddux; Third Baseman Chance Sanford; Shortstop Tripp Comer

10

2000–2004

2000

June 20, 2000: Traded Shortstop Jose Vizcaino to the New York Yankees for Catcher-Infielder Jim Leyritz

The Dodgers rewarded Jose Vizcaino for his tenth-inning hit in the Dodgers' win at Houston by trading him to the Yankees after the game ended. "This is surprising, but this is baseball, and you have to be prepared," said the 32-year-old Vizcaino. "You always want to play at home, and that's why I signed back with the Dodgers in 1998, but this is a business." The emergence of young shortstop Alex Cora, and the strong performance of second baseman Mark Grudzielanek, had limited Vizcaino's playing time this season. "Viz [Vizcaino] is a great guy and a great player," manager Davey Johnson said. "He did all I asked of him, and it's always tough when you trade one of the good guys. It's only fitting he got the key hit in the 10th."[1] Vizcaino had appeared in 40 games, batting .204 with four runs batted in and an OPS+ of 41. In two separate stints with the Dodgers, totaling five seasons, Vizcaino played 245 games, batted .250, and had a 63 OPS+.

Leyritz, 36, had been an important part of the Yankees' 1996 and 1999 World Series championship teams. He also played a key role for the pennant-winning San Diego Padres in 1998. In 24 games for the Yankees this season, Leyritz batted .218 with one home run and four runs batted in. The Dodgers expected to use him as their primary right-handed pinch-hitter and as an emergency catcher. "Leyritz brings championship experience to our bench and he's a third catcher," said Dodgers GM Kevin Malone. "Viz will get more chances to play with the Yankees, so this is a deal that will help both teams."[2]

"I have a lot of mixed emotions only because of what this organization has meant to me," Leyritz said, "but I understand the business side of the game. I talked with Dodgers general manager Kevin Malone, and he told me he knows what I did when I was with the San Diego Padres. He told me he wants me to do the same thing for the Dodgers. It's good for me because it's the National League, and I should get a chance to do more pinch-hitting. This should give me more of an opportunity to contribute."[3]

Leyritz did not contribute much. Playing in 41 games, he batted .200, with one home run, eight RBIs, and a 47 OPS+. He declared for free agency after the season, but no major league club signed him.

July 31, 2000: Traded Outfielder Todd Hollandsworth, Minor League Outfielder Kevin Gibbs, and Minor League Pitcher Randey Dorame to the Colorado Rockies for Outfielder Tom Goodwin and Cash

Board chairman Bob Daly thought the Dodgers were strong enough to win the National League West with their current roster. "We had enough to win the division before [GM] Kevin [Malone] made these trades, and what he accomplished only makes us better," Daly said. "I learned a long time ago that when you're close to the finish line, you don't sit back and do nothing."[4] Just before the trading deadline, Malone reacquired center fielder and leadoff batter Tom Goodwin (and $300,000) from the Colorado Rockies for outfielder Todd Hollandsworth, Triple A outfielder Kevin Gibbs, and Double A left-hander Randey Dorame. The Dodgers needed a leadoff batter after trading Eric Young to the Cubs last December. They tried Hollandsworth at the position, but that had been unsuccessful.

Goodwin was the Dodgers' first-round draft pick in 1989 and played in parts of three seasons with them before they released him after the 1993 season. Now 32, he had also played with the Kansas City Royals and the Texas Rangers. It was an unexpected homecoming for him. "I'm surprised, but this is the way it goes," Goodwin said. "I always kind of thought I would end my career with the Dodgers. When I signed with Colorado, I thought that was over." In 91 games with the Rockies this season, the left-handed-hitting Goodwin batted .271 with a .368 on-base average, five home runs, 65 runs scored and 47 runs batted in. From the leadoff position, he batted .281 with a .373 on-base percentage.

The speedy Goodwin was second in the major leagues with 39 stolen bases and had been caught only seven times. "He's a good player and excellent defensive outfielder," said Eric Karros, who had been Goodwin's teammate in the minor leagues and with the Dodgers. "He gets to the ball as good as anyone can and steals bases. He has slowed down a little because of injuries, but he had a really big first half of the year. Hopefully, he's ready to turn it up again."[5]

Hollandsworth, 27, was the National League's Rookie of the Year in 1996, his best season in LA. Uncomfortable batting leadoff, he was hitting just .234 this season with a 77 OPS+. He was eligible for free agency after the season, and the Dodgers did not plan to re-sign him. Hollandsworth played in 524 games with the Dodgers, batting .266 with 41 home runs and an OPS+ of 94.

Kevin Gibbs, 26, had missed much of the last three seasons with injuries, and was not in the Dodgers' plans. Twenty-three-year-old Randey Dorame, however, was the club's top left-handed pitching prospect. Dorame, was 14–3 with a 2.51 earned run average last season at Class A San Bernardino and was the California League's Pitcher of the Year. He started this season at Class A Vero Beach, going 7–1 with a 2.21 ERA. That earned him a promotion to Double A San Antonio, where he was 3–4 with a 3.86 ERA. "I spent the weekend on the phone with our player-personnel people, and we're comfortable with what we gave up," Malone said. "We feel we needed to do this to strengthen ourselves."[6] Neither Gibbs nor Dorame ever reached the major leagues.

December 6, 2000: Signed Free Agent Pitcher Andy Ashby

A day earlier the Dodgers had rescinded their offer to pitcher Andy Ashby. Ashby, a free-agent, would not agree to a three-year $22.5 million contract with a fourth-year option. Ashby's refusal surprised club chairman Bob Daly, who believed the deal had been agreed upon a week earlier. But after Ashby and his agent, Adam Katz, spoke with Daly and Dodgers GM Kevin Malone, Ashby signed. He had offers from the Cardinals and the Red Sox, as well, but Ashby said the Dodgers had been his top choice all along.

"We had been talking for a long, long time, and I'd like to thank Bob and Kevin for giving me extra time to think about everything," Ashby said. "It wasn't that I didn't want to sign with the Dodgers, I just wanted to make sure and take time to make the right decision." Katz said: "It got a little unsettling for the Dodgers because they thought it would move a little faster, and I understand that. I wanted it to move quickly too."[7] Neither Katz nor the Dodgers revealed contract terms, but sources said Ashby would receive a $1.5 million signing bonus and a $5.5 million salary in 2001. He would make $7.5 million in 2002 and $8 million in 2003. The

Atlanta Braves, Ashby's team this past season, would receive a draft pick from the Dodgers as compensation for losing him.

"We said all along that our hope was to try to sign two quality pitchers, and this is a big step in the right direction," said Malone, who was still working on retaining free agent Darren Dreifort. "Andy Ashby is a quality pitcher and a quality person. He's a hard worker and a winner, and you can't ask for any more than that." Dodgers first baseman Eric Karros said: "This is a great signing. This is a guy who, two years ago, was one of the best pitchers in the game."

Ashby, 32, had a 12–13 record with a 4.92 earned run average for the Phillies and Braves in 2000. He had pitched also for the Padres and the Rockies in his 10-year career, with an 84–87 record. "Kevin Brown [his new teammate] is a good friend of mine, and I've been watching these other guys for a long time," Ashby said. "They're all great pitchers, and I'm just really looking forward to trying to help the Dodgers get back in the playoffs again. We could have a lot of fun."[8]

Ashby pitched three seasons for the Dodgers, winning 14 and losing 23 with an ERA+ of 91. He returned to the Padres as a free agent in 2004, but appeared in only two games in what was his final season.

December 10, 2000: Free Agent Catcher Todd Hundley Signed with the Chicago Cubs

Acquired from the New York Mets in a December 1998 trade, Todd Hundley had spent the last two seasons with the Dodgers. After a poor year in 1999—a .207 batting average and an 87 OPS+—Hundley batted .284 this past season with a 143 OPS+. He had 24 home runs and 70 RBIs in only 299 at-bats. Yet it had been reported as early as September, that Hundley would not be with the Dodgers in 2001. Two days after the club did not offer him arbitration, Hundley signed with his hometown Chicago Cubs. Seth Levinson, Hundley's agent, completed the deal with Cubs' president Andy MacPhail, a four-year contract worth $23.5 million. "There was more money out there," Levinson said, "but this was just too perfect." Hundley was determined to join the Cubs once the Dodgers decided not to retain him.

"This is really like a dream come true for me," said Hundley who was reared near Chicago while his father, Randy, was a catcher for the Cubs in the 1960s and 1970s. "This is something that I've been thinking about for a long time, definitely the last couple of years. Getting a chance to go home and be with my family, and playing at Wrigley Field, it's just a great feeling to have this happen now.... Business is business and all that, and I could have gotten more money in the American League, but this is what I wanted," Hundley said.⁹

Also in 2000:

    Traded: Infielder Juan Castro to Cincinnati Reds for Minor League Pitcher Kenny Lutz; Pitcher Alan Mills to Baltimore Orioles for Pitcher Alberto Reyes; Third baseman Adam Melhuse to Colorado Rockies for Future Considerations; Pitcher Jamie Arnold, Minor League Outfielder Jorge Piedra, and Cash to Chicago Cubs for Pitcher Ismael Valdez; Future Considerations to Pittsburgh Pirates for Outfielder Bruce Aven
    Purchased: Pitcher Trever Miller from Philadelphia Phillies
    Chosen in Amateur Free Agent Draft: Koyie Hill; Ben Diggins; Víctor Díaz; Travis Ezi
    Signed Amateur Free Agents: Willy Aybar; Franklin Gutiérrez
    Signed Free Agents: Pitcher Gregg Olson; Outfielder F.P. Santangelo; Shortstop Kevin Elster; Catcher Chad Kreuter; Outfielder Geronimo Berroa; Third Baseman Chris Donnels; Outfielder-Third Baseman Phil Hiatt; Infielder Jeff Branson; Catcher Brian Johnson; Outfielder Jeff Barry
    Chosen in Major League Draft: Pitcher Jose Nunez
    Released: Second Baseman Craig Counsell; Outfielder Brent Cookson; Pitcher Orel Hershiser
    Left as Free Agents: Outfielder Trent Hubbard; Infielder-Outfielder Shawn Gilbert; Outfielder Geronimo Berroa; Shortstop Kevin Elster; Pitcher Trever Miller; Second Baseman Adam Riggs; Pitcher Ismael Valdez; Infielder-Outfielder Mike Metcalfe

2001

For the 2001 season, Jim Tracy replaced Davey Johnson as manager.

February 8, 2001: Signed Free Agent Pitcher Jesse Orosco

In December 1987 the Dodgers acquired left-handed reliever Jesse Orosco from the New York Mets in a three-team, multiplayer trade. Orosco spent the 1988 season with Los Angeles and left for Cleveland as a free agent. Now, twelve years later, after also pitching for Milwaukee, Baltimore, and St. Louis, the 21-year veteran was back. The Dodgers signed him to a one-year, $700,000 contract that guaranteed him $115,000 if he did not make the team. The Cardinals had paid him $1.1 million in 2000, although he appeared in only six games following surgery on his left elbow.

Orosco, who would turn 44 on April 21, had a lifetime record of 84–75 with 141 saves and a 3.03 earned run average. He was the major leagues' all-time leader in pitcher appearances, with 1,096. "It's a great honor to be in this situation because I had to pitch twenty seasons to get the record. I'm aware that it's not a record like Cal Ripken's consecutive games played record, but it's still a record, and just pitching a long time says a lot in itself. I know I can still pitch," Orosco said. "I still have confidence in myself, and age is not a factor to me. I don't think it's a factor for the Dodgers, or they wouldn't have signed me at age 43. I know I'm competing for a job and that's fine. I know it all depends on me."[10]

Orosco was signed after he auditioned for GM Kevin Malone and new manager Jim Tracy. "The guy knows how to get left-handed hitters out," Tracy said. "The only question is can he do it on a consistent basis." Pitcher Mike Fetters, who was Orosco's teammate in Baltimore and Milwaukee, believed his friend could still contribute. "When I first played with him in Milwaukee, and I was a lot younger, he could still outrun me," Fetters said. "That surgery he had last year was the first time he had ever been on the disabled list in 22 years. That amazes me."[11]

That Orosco was signed mainly for the purpose of retiring left-handed batters in key situations is shown in his two-year log with the Dodgers—91 games, with 43 innings pitched. He left as a free agent after the 2002 season and signed with the San Diego Padres.

February 24, 2001: Traded Outfielder Devon White to the Milwaukee Brewers for Outfielder Marquis Grissom and a Player to be Named

Devon White had asked the Dodgers to trade him last season. A few days ago, he asked again. White, 38, got his wish after the team's first full-squad workout at Dodgertown in Vero Beach. He was sent to the Milwaukee Brewers for fellow center fielder Marquis Grissom and a minor leaguer player to be named. The disgruntled seven-time Gold Glove Award-winner was excited to leave. "I think it's good for both players, for Marquis and for myself," White said. "He [Grissom] was in a situation where he was unhappy, from what I was hearing, and I was in a situation in Los Angeles where I wasn't happy with the way I was treated. It's good that we both get fresh starts," White added. "There were a lot of things that caused me to not want to be there with the Dodgers. It was a situation about how we weren't diving for balls, but throughout my career. I never dived for balls. Then, all of a sudden, I got to L.A., and they wanted me to dive. If I wasn't diving, I wasn't hustling."¹²

White had been general manager Kevin Malone's first free agent signing, a three-year, $12.4 million contract in November 1998. The Dodgers, however, had never been happy with White, who batted .268 with 14 home runs and a 92 OPS+ in 1999. Their unhappiness grew last season when a torn left rotator cuff limited him to 47 games, with four home runs and 13 runs batted in. By contrast, Grissom, who would turn 34 in April, played in 146 games despite hamstring injuries and back pain. He batted .244 with 14 home runs, 62 RBIs, and 20 stolen bases.

Also, unlike White's situation, the Dodgers wanted Grissom, and he wanted them. "Marquis Grissom wanted to be a Dodger, and Devon White did not," said Malone, who had been close to Grissom since their days in the Montreal Expos organization. "Marquis Grissom is exactly what this team needs in a lot of ways. I've known Marquis Grissom since 1988, and this is not only a championship player, he's a championship person. He's a gamer. He wants to win. He's a competitor. What he will bring to this team is tremendous attitude and tremendous makeup." Grissom, a 12-year-veteran, said: "I'm very excited about putting on the blue and white. I'm very excited about being part of history and the Dodger organization."¹³

Grissom was a four-time Gold Glove winner who had been a top center fielder in the mid–1990s, but his batting average had decreased in each of the last three seasons. Part of the decline can be attributed to injuries. But, Malone said, "This guy is going to play no matter what. That's the problem, you're not going to know when he's hurt because he's going to play all the time." In addition, Grissom was considered a positive clubhouse presence, something White had not been in his two stormy seasons in Los Angeles. Grissom was expected to be a Dodger reserve, which he said was fine with him. "At first it was kind of rough," he said of being a fourth outfielder with the Brewers. "I've been an everyday starter my whole career. It took about a week for it to sink in. The more I thought about it, I sat back and looked at the awards I've won, a World Series ring as a member of the Braves in 1995 and some Gold Gloves.... This game has been too good to me.... I'm going to focus on staying healthy, playing hard and doing the things I can do. I don't think you can gripe about being a fourth outfielder."¹⁴

On June 1, the Dodgers received Ruddy Lugo, a minor league right-hander. Lugo reached the major leagues with the 2006 Tampa Bay Devil Rays.

March 17, 2001: Traded Pitcher Antonio Osuna and Minor League Pitcher Carlos Ortega to the Chicago White Sox for Minor League Pitcher Gary Majewski, Minor League Pitcher Orlando Rodriguez, and Minor League Pitcher Andre Simpson

Right-hander Antonio Osuna had been with the Dodgers for six seasons. He pitched in 265 games, all in relief, including a high of 73 games in 1996. He had a 24–21 record, an ERA+ of 123, but despite his many relief appearances, only 10 saves. The low save total was because aside from 1998, when the Dodgers used him briefly as a closer, Osuna had mostly been a set-up man. This past season he was 3–6 with a 3.74 ERA in 46 games, after recovering from elbow surgery in 1999. Considered expendable because of a glut of relievers, the Dodgers traded Osuna and minor league left-hander Carlos Ortega to the Chicago White Sox for three minor league pitchers: Gary Majewski, Orlando Rodriguez, and Andre Simpson. The Dodgers were seeking to remedy the lack of young pitchers in their farm system.

"This eases the bullpen situation and eases the payroll a tad," said GM Kevin Malone. "We like Antonio, and he did a good job for us last year, but we have other guys in that role who we like a little better. We felt that we had enough depth, and not just depth but quality depth, to make this deal. We're trying to build for the future too, and hopefully all three of these guys will help in L.A. someday," Malone said. "When you can add three prospects, that's pretty significant to our long-term plan." White Sox general manager Kenny Williams had been after Osuna since December to fill his club's need for a hard-throwing right-handed set-up man. "Osuna is very valuable," Williams said. "Sometimes the game is on the line in the sixth or seventh inning when you need a strikeout. You may not get to the ninth without that guy doing the job in the sixth, seventh or eighth."[15]

Carlos Ortega, a 22-year-old converted outfielder, was 4–2 with a 4.55 ERA at Class A Vero Beach last season. During his three seasons as an outfielder, he batted .236 with four home runs and 42 runs batted in. Ortega never reached the major leagues.

Right-handers Gary Majewski, 21, and Andre Simpson, 20, pitched in Class A in 2000, and left-hander Orlando Rodriguez, 20, played in a rookie league. Majewski had a record of 8–11 with a 3.51 earned-run average and 161 strikeouts in 171 innings. Simpson was 5–6 with 15 saves and a 3.01 ERA. Rodriguez was 2–5 with a 4.20 ERA in rookie ball. He had 53 strikeouts in 40 innings and opponents batted .234 against him. Only Majewski would pitch in the major leagues.

On April 26, 2001, Dave Wallace replaced Kevin Malone as general manager.

July 31, 2001: Traded Mike Fetters and Minor League Pitcher Adrian Burnside to the Pittsburgh Pirates for Pitcher Terry Mulholland

Along with acquiring pitchers James Baldwin (from the White Sox) and Mike Trombley (from the Orioles), interim GM Dave Wallace and interim assistant GM Dan Evans further bolstered the Dodgers pitching for the playoff push. They traded middle reliever Mike Fetters, a right-hander, and minor league left-hander Adrian Burnside to the Pittsburgh Pirates for veteran Terry Mulholland. "Time will tell," Wallace said of the potential impact of the three pitching trades. "The other factor is you lost a guy like Mike Fetters, who has great character and is a big part of this clubhouse. But in the research we've done about the guys we're acquiring, they, as well, bring character to the clubhouse."[16]

Terry Mulholland was a 14-year veteran, with a 112–124 record for seven teams. He was a starter early in his career but had been working more out of the bullpen in recent years. Mulholland also brought postseason experience to the team. The 38-year-old lefthander had pitched in four postseasons, including the last three. He was in 22 games this season (21 in relief) with a 3.72 earned run average and no decisions. Mulholland, currently on the disabled list with a broken left index finger, saw the immediate upside of the deal. "I get traded to L.A. and I'm in first place," he said. "That's pretty good." Closer Jeff Shaw said Wallace had provided what the Dodgers needed. "I wouldn't say that we were lacking in those areas they addressed, I would just say we were a little short."[17]

The 36-year-old Fetters, who was 2–1 with a 6.07 ERA and one save in 29 innings, was not happy about leaving Los Angeles. "I was playing where I always wanted to play, had a chance to go to the playoffs for the first time in my career and they took that all away from me," he said. "I'm very, very upset and I didn't want this to happen in my wildest dreams. I always did my best out there, it might not have always been good enough, but I always gave 100 percent and I wanted to stay."

Adrian Burnside, a 24-year-old left-hander, had arthroscopic surgery on his pitching elbow last season. Now recovered, he was 4–3 with a 2.66 ERA in 13 games (12 starts) for Double A Jacksonville. Burnside never reached the major leagues.

On October 3, 2001, Dan Evans replaced Dave Wallace as general manager.

November 9, 2001: Traded Minor League Pitcher Eric Junge and Minor League Pitcher Jesus Cordero to the Philadelphia Phillies for Pitcher Omar Daal

There was a compelling reason for the Dodgers to make this trade; they needed to add a starting pitcher. Free agent Chan Ho Park seemed likely to leave, and Darren Dreifort would not be available until at least midseason. So, they sent minor league pitchers Eric Junge and Jesus Cordero to Philadelphia for left-hander Omar Daal. The Dodgers were familiar with Daal, who broke in with them as a 21-year-old in 1993. He remained for three seasons before being traded to Montreal in December 1995. New Dodgers GM Dan Evans said: "We had people that were very comfortable with him as a person and knew his makeup."[18] One of those people was Dodgers manager Jim Tracy, who was a bench coach at Montreal when Daal pitched for the Expos.

Daal was 53–58 in his career with a 4.48 earned run average. The best of his nine seasons was with the 1999 Arizona Diamondbacks, when he was 16–9 with a 125 ERA+. The following year was his worst. Pitching for Arizona and Philadelphia, he had a 4–19 record, but he showed enough this spring to be the Phillies' opening day starter. Daal won 10 of his first 12 starts but was inconsistent the rest of the season and finished with a 13–7 record and a 95 ERA+. Later in the season Phillies manager Larry Bowa dropped Daal to fifth in the pitching rotation. Daal also had criticized Bowa after he was passed over during a key series against Atlanta.

Phillies GM Ed Wade said the tension between the manager and player played a "minimal" role in the trade. "I didn't move a guy because he was sideways with the manager. I think that was something that was easily repaired," Wade said. "We have acquired two very good young pitching prospects. Both project as major league pitchers, one as a starter (Junge) and the other as a reliever (Cordero). They both have very good ceilings. We are satisfied with what we got here. This gives us a little more payroll flexibility."[19]

Right-handers Junge and Cordero had yet to pitch in the major leagues. Junge was 10–11 with a 3.46 ERA at Double A Jacksonville (FL) last season. Cordero was 8–4 with nine saves and a 2.47 ERA with Class A Wilmington (NC). Junge would pitch briefly for the Phillies in 2002 and 2003, but Cordero would never pitch in the major leagues. Daal appeared in 39 games for the 2002 Dodgers, including 23 starts. He won 11, lost 9, and had a 97 ERA+. In January 2003 he signed as a free agent with the Baltimore Orioles.

December 22, 2001: Free Agent Pitcher Chan Ho Park Signed with the Texas Rangers

South Korean-born Chan Ho Park, then 20, signed as an amateur free agent with the Dodgers in 1994 and made his major league debut that year. Park became a full-time starter in 1997 and remained a key part of the Dodgers' rotation through the 2001 season. He was 15–11 this year with a 3.50 earned run average and a career-high 218 strikeouts. Overall, Park had an 80–54 record and a 3.80 earned run average with the Dodgers. He made 33 or more starts for the last four consecutive seasons and pitched 200 or more innings for three of the past four. Park had also struck out more than 200 batters in each of the last two seasons.

If there was a negative to Park's statistics it was the disparity in his home and away splits—his ERA at spacious Dodger Stadium was 2.98, while elsewhere it was 4.77. Park, who was considered the top free-agent pitcher available this offseason, left Los Angeles to sign with the Texas Rangers. "I think the reason I pitched well at Dodger Stadium is because it was home," he said. "Now Arlington is home so I will be comfortable here. I am going to pitch better here." Park signed a five-year, $65 million contract with the Rangers, which was made possible by several Rangers players, led by shortstop Alex Rodriguez, agreeing to defer part of their salaries to future seasons. "We finally have our No 1 starter, said Rangers owner Tom Hicks."[20]

Also in 2001:

Traded: Pitcher Mike Judd to Tampa Bay Devil Rays for Future Considerations; Minor League Pitcher Wade Parrish to Chicago White Sox for Outfielder McKay Christensen; Outfielder Jeff Barry, Pitcher Osan Masaoka, and Pitcher Gary Majewski to Chicago White Sox for Pitcher James Baldwin and Cash; Pitcher Kris Foster and Catcher Geronimo Gil to Baltimore Orioles for Pitcher Mike Trombley; Pitcher Luke Prokopec and Minor League Pitcher Chad Ricketts to Toronto Blue Jays for Pitcher Paul Quantrill and Shortstop Cesar Izturis; Minor League Pitcher Nial Hughes and Minor League Pitcher Christian Bridenbaugh to Cleveland Indians for Outfielder Dave Roberts

Sold: Pitcher Jose Nunez to San Diego Padres

Chosen in Amateur Free Agent Draft: Edwin Jackson; Kole Strayhorn; Jereme Milons

Signed Amateur Free Agents: Joel Guzmán

Signed Free Agents: Pitcher Giovanni Carrara; Shortstop Tim Bogar; Infielder Jeff Reboulet; Pitcher Kevin Beirne; Pitcher Dennis Springer; Pitcher Bryan Corey; Pitcher Hideo Nomo

Released: Outfielder F.P. Santangelo; Pitcher Gregg Olson

Left as Free Agents: Pitcher Jeff Shaw; Outfielder Brent Cookson; Catcher Ángel Peña; Third Baseman Chris Donnels; Catcher Brian Johnson; Outfielder Bruce Aven; Infielder Jeff Branson; Pitcher Alberto Reyes; Pitcher James Baldwin; Pitcher Terry Adams; Shortstop Tim Bogar

2002

January 15, 2002: Traded Outfielder Gary Sheffield to the Atlanta Braves for Outfielder Brian Jordan, Pitcher Odalis Pérez, and Minor League Pitcher Andrew Brown

Gary Sheffield's combative 3½-year relationship with the Dodgers ended when they traded him to the Atlanta Braves for veteran outfielder Brian Jordan, promising young pitcher Odalis Pérez, and minor league pitcher Andrew Brown. Among his many complaints, the productive but outspoken Sheffield criticized the team for giving players he deemed of lesser ability more money than him, objected to his position in the batting order, and proclaimed his distrust of general manager Dan Evans. Still, while the 33-year-old Sheffield had caused the team many off-the-field problems, he had been a major contributor on the field. Over the last three seasons, he batted .312 with 113 home runs and 310 runs batted in, an average of 38 home runs and 103 RBIs a year. Of Sheffield's 36 home runs last season, 24 tied the game or put the Dodgers ahead.

Sheffield's complaint about the Dodgers giving "lesser" players more money was likely the result of their giving Shawn Green a six-year, $84 million contract. Although Sheffield was one of the game's highest-paid players, he often complained about his contract and a lack of respect. After Dodgers chairman Bob Daly refused to give him a "lifetime contract" last spring, Sheffield began criticizing the team on an almost daily basis. The Dodgers attempt to trade him after the season—despite Evans's claims the team was not trying to trade him—further outraged Sheffield. "It becomes frustrating to the point where you ask yourself, 'Do I really want to be with this organization?'" he said. "I don't want to be with an organization that constantly tells me one thing and then does another. I'm not going to sugarcoat that one bit. I deserve enough respect not to be told things like that." Evans defended the trade while denying they were caused by Sheffield's comments. "We didn't 'get rid' of Gary Sheffield; we were not trying to eliminate him from the Dodgers," Evans said. "We were not going to move Sheff unless a trade made sense, and we believe this one does." When Evans was asked if Sheffield's unhappiness in Los Angeles contributed to the decision to trade him, he said: "It certainly played a role, but it was not the central issue in the trade. We had been talking to [Atlanta GM John] Schuerholz for more than a month, long before [Sheffield's] comments appeared."[21]

Schuerholz described 34-year-old Brian Jordan as "a classy guy, a man of high character, a great citizen of our community and a wonderful person." Evans called him "a terrific defensive player, a solid offensive player and a leader in the clubhouse." Nevertheless, Jordan, who lived in Atlanta year-round and did not want to uproot his family, was disappointed to hear he had been traded. Moreover, his best position was right field, but that was Shawn Green's position in Los Angeles, meaning he would have to play left field or possibly center field. Jordan got the news during a workout. "I was laughing with [Atlanta manager] Bobby Cox and chuckling with [hitting instructor] Terry Pendleton and then, 'Bam!' It ruined my whole night," he said. "I couldn't even talk to [Schuerholz]. I hung up on him. He stabbed me in the back.... Even though the timing of this is not good, and I had no idea it was coming, the Dodgers are a good organization.... I have a lot of respect for them and the players they have."[22]

Jordan, a right-handed hitter, had spent ten years in the National League, seven with St. Louis and the last three with Atlanta. He had a career batting average of .287 and a career on-base average of .337, with 149 home runs and 656 runs batted in. Jordan had never hit more than 25 home runs in a season but twice had seasons with more than 100 RBIs. This past season he batted .295 with 25 home runs and 97 RBIs.

Jordan had a fine first year in Los Angeles, batting .285 with 18 home runs and 80 runs batted in. Injuries limited him to 66 games in 2003, in which he batted .299, but had only six home runs and 28 RBIs. After the season, Jordan signed with Texas for one season before returning to Atlanta to finish his career.

Odalis Pérez was a 23-year-old left-hander whom the Braves had used mostly as a starter. After missing the 2000 season because of elbow surgery, he went 7–8 with a 4.91 earned run average in 24 games (16 starts) in 2001. "He can be an elite pitcher; he just needs an opportunity to pitch every five days and not have anyone looking over his shoulder," his teammate Jordan said. "Sometimes he tries to be too perfect, but he has great stuff and great potential."[23] Right-hander Andrew Brown, 3–4 with a 3.92 ERA for the Class A Jamestown (NY) Jammers last season, would reach the big leagues with the 2006 Cleveland Indians.

March 23, 2002: Traded pitcher Matt Herges and Minor League Second Baseman Jorge Nuñez to the Montreal Expos for Pitcher Guillermo Mota and Minor League Outfielder Wilkin Ruan

In a trade of right-handed relievers, the Dodgers sent Matt Herges to the Montreal Expos for Guillermo Mota in a four-player trade that included two minor leaguers. The Expos received second baseman Jorge Nuñez and the Dodgers received outfielder Wilkin Ruan. Herges, who would turn 32 in April, had been an effective part of the Dodgers pitching staff in his three years with the team. He pitched in 151 games, with a 20–13 record and a 124 ERA+. All but four of his appearances had been in relief, but as a middle or set-up man, he had only two career saves. One came this past season, when Herges had a 9–8 record, with a 3.44 ERA in 75 games.

The Dodgers needed a closer after not re-signing Jeff Shaw, but that would not be the 28-year-old Mota, whose pitching record was similar to Herges's—three years with the Expos, 133 games, all in relief, with a 4–8 record and no saves. In 53 games for the Expos last season, part of which he missed with a shoulder injury, Mota won one, lost three, with a 5.26 ERA in 49⅔ innings. (Former starting pitcher Eric Gagne would take over the closer's role for Los Angeles in 2002.)

"We're getting a guy who's a proven commodity," said Expos general manager Omar Minaya. "I like Mota but I'm getting a guy who is better for this team right now." Dodgers GM Dan Evans was also pleased with the deal. Speaking of Mota, he said: "The scouts really liked what they saw in Mota. He's got a powerful arm and he's been throwing 94–97 mph all spring."

Evans expressed his regret at losing Herges. "I hated giving up Matty because I love Matt Herges. But this is a business." And, he added, "In Wilkin Ruan we've got a future potential Gold Glove center fielder."[24]

Baseball America ranked Ruan as the Expos' 13th-best prospect, rating his speed, outfield defense, and outfield arm ahead of any other player in their organization. His batting had been suspect though, which proved to be an accurate assessment. Ruan played in 33 games over the 2002 and 2003 seasons, with a .231 batting average and a 48 OPS+. The Dodgers released him in June 2004, and he spent the rest of his career in the minor leagues. The other player in the deal, Jorge Nuñez, would never reach the major leagues.

July 28, 2002: Traded Pitcher Terry Mulholland, Minor League Pitcher Ricardo Rodríguez, and Minor League Pitcher Francisco Cruceta to the Cleveland Indians for Pitcher Paul Shuey

This was a trade where the Dodgers gave up their highest-rated minor leaguer for a seasoned veteran who would supply an immediate boost to their pennant hopes. The minor leaguer was 24-year-old Ricardo Rodríguez, currently with the Las Vegas 51s, the Dodgers Triple A club in the Pacific Coast League. *Baseball America* ranked the 6'3", 195-pound right-hander the organization's No. 1 prospect. Before his recent promotion to Las Vegas, Rodríguez was 5–4 with a 1.99 earned run average with the Class AA Jacksonville (FL) Suns. "We like Ricardo Rodríguez a lot," said GM Dan Evans. "*Baseball America* had him as our No. 1; that may not reflect our assessments, but he's a very good prospect, no question. But at the same time, we're getting a veteran who knows how to handle the pressure of a pennant race, and we feel this guy will help us for years to come."[25]

Also going to Cleveland was minor leaguer Francisco Cruceta, a 21-year-old right-hander, and veteran left-hander Terry Mulholland. "You hate to leave a first place-caliber club, but this move may help [the Dodgers]," Mulholland said. "They're getting a very capable reliever, and let's face it, I haven't had the best year. It's been an uphill climb since I gave up all those runs to start the season. But going to Cleveland, maybe I'll have a chance to pitch more. I thought I turned the corner to where I might be a bigger part of the club after the All-Star break, but Evans is doing the best he can do—I don't fault him for trading me," said Mulholland, who had a 7.31 earned-run average in 21 games. "Had I done better earlier in the season, I would have been used more."[26] After allowing 11 earned runs and 12 hits, including five home runs, in 4⅔ innings of his first two appearances, Mulholland missed most of May because of back spasms.

Paul Shuey, 31, whose best pitch was a split-fingered fastball, was in his ninth season with the Indians. He had appeared in 361 games, all in relief, with a 34–21 record, 21 saves, and a 133 ERA+. This season he was 3–0 with a 2.41 ERA in 39 games. "He's one of the top five nastiest guys I've ever faced because of that splitter," said Shawn Green, who often faced Shuey when Green was with Toronto. "Any bullpen he's in, he's going to strengthen." The plan was for Shuey to share the set-up role with Paul Quantrill, followed by closer Eric Gagne. "This hasn't been a year where I've had a lot of butterflies in the bullpen," Shuey said of pitching with the also-ran Indians. "The climate has changed here—I don't think these guys are going to fight for it for a while. I'm looking forward to getting those butterflies back, getting back into the thick of things," he said of joining the Dodgers, leaders of the NL's wild-card race. "I'm going to a team where I can fight for it now."[27] Shuey appeared in 90 games for the Dodgers in 2002–2003, all in relief. He had a combined 11–6 record with a 116 ERA+. Injuries caused Shuey to miss the 2004 season, after which the Dodgers released him.

Ricardo Rodríguez did not live up to *Baseball America*'s high ranking. He pitched two seasons for Cleveland and two for Texas, finishing with a 10–15 record and an 88 ERA+. Class A pitcher Francisco Cruceta would reach the big leagues with Cleveland in 2004, appearing in two games. He also pitched for Seattle (2006) and Detroit (2008). Overall, he had an 0–4 record and a 7.96 ERA in 19 major league games.

December 4, 2002: Traded First Baseman Eric Karros, Shortstop-Second Baseman Mark Grudzielanek and Cash to the Chicago Cubs for Catcher Todd Hundley and Outfielder Chad Hermansen

GM Dan Evans was pleased with the roster and payroll flexibility the Dodgers now had after their four-player trade with the Chicago Cubs. Gone were first baseman Eric Karros and middle infielder Mark Grudzielanek (plus $2 million in cash) in return for catcher Todd Hundley and outfielder Chad Hermansen. "We achieved our first goal in the offseason, and now we suddenly have choices we didn't have earlier," Evans said. "This gives us some freedom, not a lot, but enough to explore some things we couldn't do prior to this. We've got a number of spots to fill on our roster, and we were very limited in our flexibility. This trade doesn't give us an unlimited amount of money, but it gives us enough to at least do some things that we think will improve our team."[28]

Still, Evans had nothing but praise for Karros. "He represents so many good things about the Dodgers," he said. According to Karros, "Dan Evans has a view and a direction and a plan. Whether you agree with the plan or don't agree with the plan, at least there is a plan. As long as he sticks to it, he'll either be the beneficiary of the results or he'll die by the results."[29]

Karros's departure seemed inevitable after he and manager Jim Tracy clashed several times during the season. "I had a very honest relationship with Jim, we were both very candid," Karros said. "But there is nobody I respected more." Karros did not deny that he and Tracy had several discussions about the way Tracy ran the club. "He was very honest with me, and I was very honest with him," Karros said. "But did I ever influence a decision or make out a lineup for him? Saying that is an insult to Tracy."[30]

In his 12 years with the team, the 35-year-old Karros had taken his place among the most productive Dodgers ever. His 270 home runs were the third most in franchise history (most in LA history) and his 976 runs batted were sixth (second in LA). He was also in the franchise's top ten in games, doubles, total bases, and extra base hits.

Mark Grudzielanek had been with the Dodgers since coming from Montreal in a July 1998 trade. His best season was 1999, when he batted .326 with a 111 OPS+. Grudzielanek's batting average was in the .270s for each of the next three seasons, though his OPS+ numbers dropped to the 80s. The Dodgers had moved him from shortstop to second base in 2000 because they felt his arm was better suited for that position. "I consider myself a good athlete and I believe I have the ability to move around," he said, adding that he even would be willing to try third base if he's asked. Going to a team that played so many day games pleased the 32-year-old Grudzielanek, "I'm looking forward to playing in the day. It brings back the kid in you."

The two veterans, Karros and Grudzielanek spoke with Dusty Baker and said they believed the new Cubs manager would give them a chance to play next season. "The way Dusty explained it was that they have some young talent, guys they expect great things from," Karros said. "I don't know if I'll be out there six out of seven days or one out of seven. Can I deal with that situation? Yes, I can." Said Grudzielanek: "All we know is that the best player is going to be out there and we're going to win."[31]

While Karros and Grudzielanek said they looked forward to playing more day games, Todd Hundley said he hated them. Calling himself a night owl, Hundley once complained that his body couldn't adjust to taking batting practice at 11 a.m. on a Tuesday. But surely Hundley knew about Chicago and day games when he left the Dodgers after the 2000 season proclaiming how happy he was to be going home. But his two-year homecoming was marked by injuries, complaints about playing time, and rough treatment from the home fans. He played in just 171 games in his two seasons with the Cubs, batting .199 with an OPS+ of 79. In 2003, in what would be the 34-year-old Hundley's final season, he batted .182 in 21 games for the Dodgers.

Chad Hermansen was a 25-year-old right-handed hitter who had played for the Pirates and Cubs in 2002. In 237 at-bats, he had a .207 batting average and a 69 OPS+. He batted .160 in 11 games for the 2003 Dodgers, who released him after the season.

December 7, 2002: Free Agent Outfielder Marquis Grissom Signed with the San Francisco Giants

A few days after trading veterans Eric Karros and Mark Grudzielanek to the Chicago Cubs, the Dodgers lost veteran outfielder Marquis Grissom.

The 35-year-old Grissom (he would turn 36 in April) signed a two-year contract for a reported $4.5 million with the San Francisco Giants. Grissom, one of the most popular players in the Dodgers' clubhouse, was a four-time Gold Glove winner with a .270 career batting average. He had played for five teams during his 13-year major league career, including several seasons in Montreal, then managed by current Giants manager Felipe Alou. In his two seasons with the Dodgers, Grissom batted .245 in 246 games, with 38 home runs and 120 runs batted in.

The Giants had lost outfielders Reggie Sanders, Kenny Lofton, and Tsuyoshi Shinjo from their 2002 club, making it likely that Grissom would be a regular in 2003. "In my 14th season, I'm kind of happy to become an everyday starter once again," Grissom said. "I think I'm in the prime of my career and healthy. My main interest in going to any team was to get out there and play every day. I think I've got a lot left. I'm nowhere near a fourth outfielder on nobody's team."[32] (Grissom did play regularly and well for the next two seasons.)

December 10, 2002: Free Agent Third Baseman–First Baseman Dave Hansen Signed with the San Diego Padres

Dave Hansen, a second-round pick in the amateur free agent draft of 1986, made his Dodgers debut in September 1990. Hansen spent 11 seasons with the club, interrupted by a one-season stint with the Chicago Cubs (1997) and one season in Japan (1998). After declaring for free agency, he left Los Angeles a second time and signed a two-year, $1.3 million contract with the San Diego Padres. The 34-year-old Hansen batted .262 in 884 games for Los Angeles, with a league average 100 OPS+. Last season he hit .292 with two home runs and 17 runs batted in over 96 games. Hansen left as the Dodgers' all-time leader with 120 pinch-hits, which at the time was the sixth best in major league history and the second-best among active players, trailing only former Dodgers teammate Lenny Harris. His seven pinch-hit home runs in 2000 is still tied for the most in a major league season.

Also in 2002:

Traded: Minor League Pitcher Lance Caraccioli to Cleveland Indians for Infielder-Outfielder Jolbert Cabrera; Minor League Pitcher Ben Diggins and Minor League Pitcher Shane Nance to Milwaukee Brewers for Third Baseman-Catcher Tyler Houston and Pitcher Brian Mallette;

Outfielder Hiram Bocachica to Detroit Tigers for Minor League Pitcher Tom Farmer and Minor League Pitcher Jason Frasor

Purchased: Minor League Pitcher Derek Thompson from Chicago Cubs

Sold: Outfielder McKay Christensen to New York Mets

Chosen in Amateur Free Agent Draft: James Loney; Jonathan Broxton; Delwyn Young; James McDonald; Eric Stults; Russell Martin; Jarod Plummer

Signed Amateur Free Agents: Eric Hull; Ramón Troncoso; Tony Abreu

Signed Free Agents: Pitcher Robert Ellis; Outfielder Mike Kincade; Pitcher Rodney Myers; Pitcher Troy Brohawn; First Baseman Fred McGriff; First Baseman Larry Barnes; Pitcher Kazuhisa Ishii

Released: Outfielder Tom Goodwin; Pitcher Mike Trombley; Pitcher Robert Ellis; Pitcher Kevin Beirne

Left as Free Agents: Outfielder-Third Baseman Phil Hiatt; Third Baseman-Catcher Tyler Houston; Pitcher Jesse Orosco; Infielder Jeff Reboulet

2003

July 14, 2003; Traded Minor League Infielder Víctor Díaz, Minor League Pitcher José Díaz, and Minor League Pitcher Kole Strayhorn to the New York Mets for Outfielder Jeromy Burnitz and Cash

On June 22 the Dodgers were tied for first place in the National League's West Division. Since then they had lost 15 of their last 20 games and at the All-Star break were in third place, 7½ games behind San Francisco. Not only did the Dodgers have the worst offense in the National League, but they had also just lost two of their starting outfielders. Left fielder Brian Jordan was out for the season after knee surgery, and center fielder Dave Roberts was out with hamstring problems. GM Dan Evans moved to alleviate the problem by acquiring veteran left-hand-hitting outfielder Jeromy Burnitz from the New York Mets for three minor leaguers—Double A infielder Víctor Díaz, Double A pitcher José Díaz, and Single A pitcher Kole Strayhorn. Evans also signed 44-year-old Rickey Henderson, who had been playing with the Newark Bears of the independent Atlantic

League, a league considered comparable to Double A. "It's certainly been no secret that the one part of our game where we felt we needed a lot of improvement was our offense," Evans said. "We felt we needed to bolster the offensive part of our program in order to have a better won-lost record in the second half of the season, and I think Jeromy and Rickey Henderson make us better."[33]

Burnitz, 34, reached the big leagues with the Mets in 1993 and played briefly for Cleveland before achieving stardom with Milwaukee. In six seasons with the Brewers, Burnitz hit 165 home runs, drove in 525 runs, and had a 123 OPS+. From 1998 to 2001 he averaged 34 home runs and 107 runs batted per season He had an off year in 2002, but had bounced back with the Mets this year, despite spending part of the season on the disabled list with a broken hand. Burnitz was batting .274 with 18 home runs, 45 RBIs, and a .581 slugging percentage while playing only 65 games. Although Burnitz's best position was right field, he agreed to play center and left to accommodate incumbent right fielder Shawn Green. He said he was getting "his biggest opportunity ever" and was "totally excited" about coming to the Dodgers.

"I played for the Brew Crew [Milwaukee Brewers] and Mets when we were struggling, so to have an opportunity to go to a club that has a shot at the playoffs … it's hard for me to explain what it means…. The ultimate goal is for me to show up, just go crazy, hope it rubs off on everyone and the team goes to the World Series," he said. Green, for one, praised the trade for Burnitz. "Jeromy is having a good year and he'll provide some more offense, which is obviously what we need," he said. "I think he'll take pressure off of everybody, because he's a guy who can hit the ball out of the park. It's definitely nice to have another guy in the lineup who can drive guys in, especially with all the injuries."[34]

Henderson was the major league's all-time leader in runs, walks, and stolen bases. With his return to the major leagues, he became the active leader in hits, with 3,040. "With Rickey, you're talking about the greatest leadoff hitter in history. At this point, we need to try to come up with something that works. Hopefully, this will," Green said. "We acquired a solid run-producer and a middle-of-our order hitter, and we also added one of the game's all-time greatest players," added Evans. "These two guys can only make us better."[35]

In what would be his final major league season, Henderson batted .208 while playing in 30 games for the Dodgers as a leftfielder and a pinch-hitter. Burnitz batted .204 with 13 home runs and 32 RBIs. After the season, he joined the Colorado Rockies as a free agent. Víctor Díaz (2004–2007) and José Díaz (2006, 2008) played in the major leagues, but Kole Strayhorn remained a minor leaguer.

July 31, 2003: Traded Outfielder Bubba Crosby and Minor League Pitcher Scott Proctor to the New York Yankees for Third Baseman Robin Ventura

Third baseman Robin Ventura was in his second season with the Yankees, but after the New Yorkers acquired All-Star third baseman Aaron Boone from Cincinnati, Ventura became suddenly expendable. The Dodgers, still searching for offensive help, traded outfielder Bubba Crosby and minor league pitcher Scott Proctor to the AL East-leading Yankees to bring the 36-year-old Ventura to LA.

"Robin is an established veteran leader who knows what it's like to play in a pennant race and in the postseason," said GM Dan Evans, whose Dodgers were still in the middle of the NL wild-card race. "He's a Gold Glove-caliber infielder whose offensive production should add a boost to our lineup." Ventura was in his fifteenth major league season, mostly with the Chicago White Sox and the New York Mets. He had 284 home runs, 1,141 RBIs, and six Gold Gloves to his credit. He was batting .251 with nine home runs and 42 RBIs this season. "If I had to get traded anywhere, I'm glad it's there," Ventura said. "I grew up in California and they're still in the race."[36]

"He's a presence in our clubhouse. He knows what it takes to participate at this time of the season," Dodgers manager Jim Tracy said. "We're getting one of the class people in the league that is a proven hitter." Tracy planned to use Ventura at first base to replace the injured Fred McGriff, although Ventura had not played first base this season and had not started a game there since September 1996. "That's fine, I've played there before," Ventura said. "I'll go and do anything they want." Yankees manager Joe Torre said first base would be no problem for Ventura. "He can play first base, he has good hands, he has good reactions," Torre said. "He's willing to play second, he's willing to play short, he's a great player to have around. He's a winner, that's the best thing I can tell you. He's got the ability to hit home runs even though he's gotten older. Even though the bottom-line numbers don't show it, he can do a lot of things." Twenty-four-year-old Adrian Beltre had been playing third base for the Dodgers, but he was struggling with a .224 batting average, eight home runs, and 40 RBIs. "We're not giving up on Adrian Beltre, let's make that clear," Tracy said. Beltre refused to talk about the deal.

Bubba Crosby, 26, was the Dodgers first-round pick in the 1998 amateur free agent draft. He played in nine games for them this season, with one hit in 12 at-bats. Crosby was currently at Las Vegas, where he was batting a Pacific Coast League-leading .361 with 12 home runs and 57 RBIs. "Maybe I'll get a call up in September and get a chance to wear the pinstripes," he said.³⁷ (Crosby did not get that call until the next season.)

Right-hander Scott Proctor, 28, had been with Las Vegas and the Double A Jacksonville (FL) Suns of the Southern League this season. He was a combined 5–4 with a 2.58 ERA in 41 relief appearances. Proctor was called up by the Yankees in 2004 and had a 2–1 record in 26 games.

December 13, 2003: Traded Pitcher Kevin Brown to the New York Yankees for Pitcher Jeff Weaver, Minor League Pitcher Yhency Brazoban, Minor League Pitcher Brandon Weeden, and Cash

With the departure of free agent Andy Pettitte looming, the Yankees came to the winter meetings in New Orleans looking for a No. 1 starter. They found him in Kevin Brown, whom the Dodgers sent to New York for pitcher Jeff Weaver, minor league pitchers Yhency Brazoban and Brandon Weeden, and a reported $2.4 million. Brown spent five seasons in Los Angeles. In four of which he had ERAs+ of 164, 143, 167, and 171. His combined innings pitched in his first two seasons was just over 480, but injuries limited him to a combined 179⅓ the next two seasons. Brown was at full strength again in 2003, throwing 211 innings with a 14–9 record and a 2.39 earned run average, second lowest in the National League.

Brown, who would turn 39 in March, was excited about joining the American League champions. He called it "a great day for myself and my family." He had a good experience in Los Angeles, Brown said, but he wanted to play for a team closer to his home in Macon, Georgia. "To come over and play for an organization with the success the Yankees have had … it's a great opportunity for me to end my career. I'm going to get a chance to be closer to home, see my kids more, and do more things in their life that I couldn't do when I was across the country. That's really what this whole thing was about for me." What the whole thing was about for Yankees GM Brian Cashman was getting a pitcher to head up their rotation. "This guy is one of the highest competitors in the game," Cashman said. "The results speak for themselves."³⁸ The Yankees reduced the cash in the deal from $3 million to $2.4 million because the cost of the chartered jet for Brown and his family was $600,000 per season.

Jeff Weaver had been a mainstay of the Detroit Tigers pitching staff from the time he broke into the major leagues, in 1999, until they traded him to the Yankees in a three-way-deal in August 2002. Much was expected of Weaver in New York, but he had been a disappointment. After a 5–3 record in 2002, he was 7–9 with a 5.99 ERA this year and had been removed from the rotation in early June. "I was hoping for big things, but it didn't work out," said the 25-year-old right-hander. "I get to start fresh in L.A. with the team that I grew up watching, so it's kind of mind-boggling. The stuff I went through in New York is only going to make me that much better for the seasons to come."[39]

Yhency Brazoban had two good seasons in Los Angeles (2004–2005), appearing in 105 games (all in relief) with 21 saves. Over the next three seasons, though, he pitched in only a combined 11 games, without a decision. The Dodgers released Brazoban in March 2009. Brandon Weeden never reached the major leagues.

Also in 2003:

Traded: Minor League Pitcher Ruddy Lugo to Houston Astros for Outfielder Daryle Ward; Outfielder Luke Allen to Colorado Rockies for Outfielder Jason Romano; Infielder Travis Dawkins to Kansas City Royals for Pitcher Scott Mullen and Minor League Infielder Victor Rodríguez; Minor League Outfielder Travis Ezi to Florida Marlins for Outfielder Juan Encarnación

Purchased: Infielder Travis Dawkins from Cincinnati Reds; Pitcher Duaner Sanchez from Pittsburgh Pirates

Chosen in Amateur Free Agent Draft: Chad Billingsley; Matt Kemp; Xavier Paul; Russ Mitchell; A.J. Ellis; Andy LaRoche; Chuck Tiffany; Lucas May

Signed Amateur Free Agents: Chin-lung Hu; Elián Herrera; Steven Schmoll; Jamie Hoffman; Julio Pimentel; Jhonny Núñez

Signed Free Agents: First Baseman-Third Baseman Ron Coomer; Pitcher Wilson Álvarez; Pitcher Masao Kida; Pitcher Tom Martin; Pitcher Brian Falkenborg

Released: Pitcher Brian Mallette; Pitcher Giovanni Carrara; Pitcher Chad Hermansen; Outfielder Mike Kinkade

Left as Free Agents: Pitcher Omar Daal; Pitcher Scott Mullen; Outfielder Daryle Ward; First Baseman Larry Barnes; Pitcher Bryan Corey; Pitcher Paul Quantrill

2004

On January 28, 2004, Major League Baseball owners approved the sale of the Dodgers from Rupert Murdoch's FOX Group's News Corporation to Frank and Jamie McCourt.

On February 6, 2004, Paul DePodesta replaced Dan Evans as general manager.

March 30, 2004: Traded Minor League Pitcher Jason Fraser to the Toronto Blue Jays for Outfielder Jayson Werth

It was the end of spring training and Paul DePodesta, the Dodgers new GM, was determined to upgrade his bench strength. DePodesta had worked previously in the Oakland A's front office under GM Billy Beane and used his Oakland connections to further his goal. A day after acquiring outfielder Jason Grabowski from his old team, he negotiated a trade with Toronto Blue Jays general manager J.P. Ricciardi, whom he also worked with at Oakland. The Dodgers sent minor league pitcher Jason Frasor to the Blue Jays for outfielder Jayson Werth. "We think there's still a lot of upside left in Jayson Werth," DePodesta said. "He's a former first-round pick, originally taken as a catcher, and he's another guy who offers us flexibility as a bat. Similar to Jason Grabowski, he has both patience and power. He's not a finished product yet, but we do think he's going to help us."[40]

The 24-year-old Werth, a 6'5" right-handed batter, was the Orioles first-round pick in 1997. He played in 701 minor league games for Baltimore and Toronto, batting .265 with 137 doubles, 71 home runs, and 364 runs batted in. Over the past two seasons, Werth played in 41 games for the Blue Jays with a .234 batting average, two home runs, and 16 RBIs.

Jason Frasor, 26, went 2–0 with a 2.51 ERA and 23 saves last season, while splitting time between the Class A Vero Beach Dodgers and the Class AA Jacksonville (FL) Suns. He had been in four exhibition games this season with a 2.08 earned-run average and one save. The 5'9" right-hander would spend the next 12 seasons in the major leagues, with four different teams. He appeared in 679 games, all in relief, with a 35–35 record and a 125 ERA+.

April 4, 2004: Traded Minor League Outfielder Franklin Gutiérrez and a Player to be Named to the Cleveland Indians for Outfielder Milton Bradley

When Frank McCourt purchased the Dodgers earlier this year, he promised the team would add a top-flight hitter before the season started. Paul DePodesta, whom he hired to replace Dan Evans as general manager, acquired that man a day before the season opener. DePodesta traded minor leaguer Franklin Gutiérrez, the Dodgers highest-rated outfield prospect, and a player to be named, to Cleveland for Milton Bradley, the Indians' talented but volatile right-handed hitting center fielder. A few days earlier, during a spring training game, the latest of Bradley's objectionable acts ended his stay in Cleveland. After he failed to run out a popup and then argued with manager Eric Wedge, the Indians announced they would trade him. "The majority of his time here he was a good teammate and a good member of our organization," general manager Mark Shapiro told reporters. "There were moments in time that he compromised the standards and expectations that we communicated to him—not one time, but a pattern of times." Bradley said: "I had a wonderful experience in Cleveland. I don't regret a minute of it."[41]

Bradley was coming off a 2003 season in which he batted .321, with 10 home runs, 34 doubles, 17 stolen bases and a .421 on-base percentage. However, he missed Cleveland's final 61 games because of a bone bruise in his lower back, an injury DePodesta said had healed. The Dodgers were gambling that they could change the 26-year-old Bradley, who, when he learned of the trade, flew immediately to Los Angeles. He batted third and played center field in that afternoon's season-opener against San Diego. "I don't think the solution lies in just one player," DePodesta said. "But if anyone is close to being that one player, he's probably the guy." Shawn Green told manager Jim Tracy he would be agreeable to play first base to open a spot for Bradley in the outfield. "I said I'd feel comfortable either way," Green said. "Obviously, it's going to be a work in progress.... Milton is going to help our team. That's the bottom line. We'll be better off than we were." Outfielder Dave Roberts, who had played with Bradley in Cleveland, said young players sometimes make mistakes and get labeled as bad guys. Roberts called Bradley "a good person and a very good player." DePodesta said Bradley had gotten "a bad rap" and said he had performed more community service than any other Cleveland player.[42]

The Dodgers believed 21-year-old Franklin Gutiérrez needed more seasoning and planned to send him back to Double A Jacksonville. "The goal here is to win major league games," DePodesta said. "We haven't won enough of them in the last 10–15 years. This organization deserves better than continually waiting for the future."[43] Gutiérrez would make his major league debut with the 2005 Indians and would play four seasons with them, seven with Seattle, and a final season with Dodgers in 2017. On May 9, the Dodgers sent minor league pitcher Andrew Brown to the Indians to complete the deal.

July 30, 2004: Traded Catcher Paul Lo Duca, Outfielder Juan Encarnación, and Pitcher Guillermo Mota to the Florida Marlins for First Baseman Hee-Seop Choi, Pitcher Brad Penny, and Minor League Pitcher Bill Murphy

That the Dodgers were leading the race in the National League West did not prevent general manager Paul DePodesta from trading three key members of the team as part of a six-player deal with the world champion Florida Marlins. Gone were catcher Paul Lo Duca, right fielder Juan Encarnación, and relief pitcher Guillermo Mota. Coming to Los Angeles from the Marlins were pitcher Brad Penny, first baseman Hee-Seop Choi, and minor league pitcher Bill Murphy. The trade stunned Lo Duca. "I've always dreamed about being a Dodger for life. This is the team that drafted me. I thought I'd be a Dodger for my whole career, for 20 years, but it didn't happen," he said. "It was a little surprising, just because we were playing so well. I could understand it if we were tailing off a little bit, but we hadn't been.… This team has a chance to go a long way. We have fallen short in the past, and the fans of L.A. were really excited this year to maybe make it to the playoffs, so it makes it difficult. I felt like I was a decent part of what's been going on. So, it makes it a little tougher."[44] The thirty-two-year-old Lo Duca, who was in his seventh season with the Dodgers, had a career .287 batting average and a 105 OPS+ in 588 games. Popular with his teammates and the fans, he was batting .301 with 10 home runs and 49 runs batted in at the time of the trade.

Guillermo Mota had a sensational season in 2003. Appearing in 76 games, he had a 6–3 record with an ERA+ of 205, twice the league average. Several teams had asked about the 6'6" right-hander in the past, but then GM Dan Evans refused to trade him. The 31-year-old Mota was having another excellent season in 2004, with an 8–4 record, a 2.14 ERA, and a 192 ERA+. The Dodgers acquired Juan Encarnación, 28, from the Marlins in a December 2003 trade. He was their regular right fielder, batting .235 with 13 home runs and 43 runs batted in.

"It's risky," Dodgers pitcher Odalis Pérez said of the trade. "Dukie [Lo Duca] is the favorite for the fans. Mota might be the best set-up man in baseball. Seriously … it's tough. Those guys have meant a lot to this team. I'm very surprised. Wow." DePodesta said parting with Lo Duca, in particular, was difficult, but it allowed him to improve the team. "He's been a big part of the Dodger organization, it's the only organization he's ever been in. It kept me up the last couple of nights thinking of us without him, even just on a personal level, it's certainly not something I relished doing," he said. "I know what they meant to us on the field, I also know what they meant to us in the clubhouse. But the guys that we're bringing in, we're adding quite a bit. At the end of the day, I felt it was something we had to do."⁴⁵

Brad Penny, a 26-year-old right-hander, had a 50–43 record and a 4.12 ERA in six seasons with the Marlins. He was 14–10 last season and had a 2–0 record with a 2.19 ERA against the Yankees in the World Series. Penny was 8–8 with a 3.15 earned-run average this season. "Our goal was, if we were going to add some guys to our team, I wanted to add some guys who have been to the World Series, who have won the World Series," DePodesta said. Penny said he was unfazed at being designated the Dodgers' new No. 1 starter. "To me, it's not about being the No. 1 guy," Penny said. "Every time you go out there, you're facing another guy who's capable of throwing a shutout. Hopefully, I can go out there and get it done."⁴⁶

He-Seop Choi, 25, was the first Korean born position player in the major leagues. The 6'5" left-handed-hitting first baseman was signed by the Chicago Cubs in 1999 and traded to the Marlins in November 2003. He was batting .270 with 15 home runs and 40 RBIs in 95 games this season. The Dodgers planned to use him at first base, allowing Shawn Green to return to right field. Choi batted .161 with no home runs in 31 games for the Dodgers after the trade. He was much better in 2005, batting .253 with 15 home runs and a 107 OPS+ in 133 games. After the season, he chose to resume his career in Korea.

Twenty-three-year-old left-hander Bill Murphy had a 6–4 record with a 4.08 ERA for the Double A Carolina Mudcats of the Southern Association. The next day the Dodgers traded Murphy to the Arizona Diamondbacks. His major league career would consist of ten games with the 2007 Diamondbacks and eight games with the 2009 Toronto Blue Jays. He had no decisions in either season.

July 31, 2004: Traded Catcher Koyie Hill, Minor League Pitcher Bill Murphy, and Minor League Outfielder Reggie Abercrombie to the Arizona Diamondbacks for Outfielder Steve Finley and Catcher Brent Mayne

A day after completing a six-player trade with the Florida Marlins, GM Paul DePodesta engineered a five-player deal with the Arizona Diamondbacks. The Dodgers sent catcher Koyie Hill, and two minor leaguers: pitcher Bill Murphy (acquired from the Marlins a day earlier) and outfielder Reggie Abercrombie to Arizona. In return, they received two veterans who were deemed more likely to help maintain the team's Western Division lead—39-year-old center fielder Steve Finley and 36-year-old catcher Brent Mayne.

Finley was in his 16th major league season, having played for Baltimore, Houston, and San Diego before joining the Diamondbacks in 1999. He was a consistent hitter, and while he had never reached the .300 mark, he almost always had an OPS+ above the league average. He had a .275 average and a 107 OPS+ in 104 games this season but had been slumping this month. Finley batted .263 in 58 games for the Dodgers, declared free agency and signed for 2005 with the Los Angeles Angels.

Finley also had earned four Gold Gloves in his career, and let the Dodgers know he preferred to remain a center fielder. Of course, the Dodgers already had a very good center fielder in Milton Bradley. DePodesta directed manager Jim Tracy to discuss the situation with Bradley. Tracy did, and the often-contentious Bradley said he would move to right field if that was best for the team. "I heard some rumblings about it a few days ago, so I was prepared," Bradley said. "Initially, my alter ego wanted to say, 'I'm a pretty damn good center fielder, I don't want to move.' But the real me, the more mature me, says it's best for the team.... Dave Roberts moved aside [from center] when I came over here. Even Adrian Beltre moved in the lineup, initially, to accommodate me," Bradley said. "So, if I've got to make somebody else feel welcomed, make them feel like part of the family, then I'm happy to do that because it's about October."[47]

With departure of Paul Lo Duca, right-hand-hitting David Ross would now share the catching duties with the newly-arrive Brent Mayne, a left-handed hitter. Mayne had played in 1,232 games for six different teams in his 15-year career, most of it with the Kansas City Royals. He had been in 36 games this season, with a .255 batting average. Mayne would bat .188 in 47 games down the stretch in what would be the final season of his career.

Catcher Koyie Hill, a 25-year-old switch-hitter, played in three games for the Dodgers in 2003. He was currently batting .286 in 91 games for Triple A Las Vegas, but the Diamondbacks added him to their roster. He would play in the major leagues in all or part of the next nine seasons.

Pitcher Bill Murphy, who came to the Dodgers as part of yesterday's six player trade, moved from the Marlins' Carolina Mudcats of the Double A Southern Association to the Diamondbacks' El Paso Diablos of the Double A Texas League. Arizona assigned outfielder Reggie Abercrombie to the Lancaster (CA) JetHawks of the Class A California League.

DePodesta's remake of the roster included two other trades this day. He traded outfielder Dave Roberts to the Boston Red Sox for minor league outfielder Henri Stanley, and pitcher Tom Martin to the Atlanta Braves for minor league pitcher Matt Merricks.

December 9, 2004: Signed Free Agent Second Baseman Jeff Kent

By signing All-Star second baseman Jeff Kent to a $17 million, two-year contract, the Dodgers added one of the game's most productive hitters. Kent, who would turn 37 in March, had 302 home runs and 1,207 RBIs in his 13-year major league career. He had seven seasons of 100+ runs batted in, including six straight with the 1997–2002 San Francisco Giants. (He was the National League's Most Valuable Player in 2000.) Kent's 27 home runs and 107 RBIs were instrumental in helping the wild-card Houston Astros reach the NL championship series last season. His 278 home runs as a second baseman were the most ever at that position, and his seven seasons with 100 RBIs tied another mark for second basemen. Kent became a free agent when the Astros declined a $9 million option and chose to give him a $700,000 buyout. His goal, Kent said, was to help the Dodgers, winners of the NL West in 2004, reach the World Series for the first time since 1988.

"I continue to want to be a winner and be on a team that has that potential," Kent said. "Paul [DePodesta] has proven to me in this offseason transition for me that this team has that mentality, and that there is more to come, so I'm impressed by that. [manager] Jim [Tracy] was able to win last year with no true—I think—franchise player, but they had a core of players that were just tremendous, full of integrity and full of enthusiasm to play the game."[48]

"To add a player of this caliber to our club is another major step in the right direction. He is a winner," Tracy said. "If you look at his resume and you look at the games played and run production columns, it tells you everything you need to know. He's a guy who lives for the big moment and loves to be at the plate when it's time to win or lose a baseball game. Adding Jeff Kent to our lineup not only gives us another major offensive force, but it provides me with flexibility in the field."[49]

Kent played four seasons with the Dodgers, retiring, at age 40, after the 2008 season. He played in 521 games, batting .291 with 75 home runs, 311 RBIs, and a 119 OPS+. His 354 home runs hit as a second baseman remain the major league record.

December 17, 2004: Free Agent Third Baseman Adrian Beltre Signed with the Seattle Mariners

Two days after free agent first baseman Richie Sexson agreed to a four-year, $50 million deal with the Seattle Mariners, the Mariners signed

Adrian Beltre to a $64 million, five-year contract. The addition of the two sluggers were part of the Mariners promise to improve the American League's most anemic offense in 2004. They finished last in the league in home runs (136) and runs scored (698) and had their worst record since 1983. "Actions speak louder than words," said Mariners chairman Howard Lincoln. "We've just demonstrated that we were dead serious about turning things around as quickly as possible. I don't think there was any hesitation to make these large financial commitments."[50]

Beltre, a 25-year-old right-handed-hitter, spent the first seven years of his career with the Dodgers. The first six were up-and-down, but this past season Beltre reached the potential the Dodgers envisioned for him. He batted .334 with 121 RBIs, a 163 OPS+, and led the major leagues with 48 home runs, while finishing second to Barry Bonds in the vote for the National League's Most Valuable Player. Beltre said it was tough to leave the Dodgers, but felt Seattle was a better fit for his family. "It's a great opportunity," he said. "It's a great baseball city and a great organization. They're going to have a great team. They want to be competitive here sooner rather than later."[51]

The Dodgers wanted to keep Beltre and made him a generous offer. "He turned down a great deal of guaranteed money to come to Seattle" said his agent, Scott Boras. Beltre said he was not concerned about switching to the American League, nor was he worried his numbers could drop at pitcher-friendly Safeco Field. He pointed out he had already been playing in a pitchers' ballpark at Dodger Stadium. "We've played in some American League parks," he said. "I didn't really keep stats on it, but I don't really think it will be hard to adjust."[52]

Beltre adjusted well enough to play 14 seasons in the AL for Seattle, Boston, and Texas. He retired after the 2018 season, having accumulated 3,166 hits, 477 home runs, and 1,707 RBIs. Beltre was elected to baseball's Hall of Fame in 2024.

Also in 2004:

Traded: Pitcher Steve Colyer to Detroit Tigers for Outfielder Cody Ross; Outfielder Jason Romano to Tampa Bay Devil Rays for Infielder Antonio Pérez; Infielder-Outfielder Jolbert Cabrera to Seattle Mariners for Pitcher Aaron Looper and Minor League Pitcher Ryan Ketchner; Pitcher Tanyon Sturtze to New York Yankees for First Baseman Brian Myrow; Minor League Pitcher Elvin Nina to Kansas City Royals for Pitcher Mike Venafro; Minor League Catcher Tony Socarras to New York Mets for Catcher Tom Wilson; Future Considerations to Cleveland Indians for Pitcher Scott Stewart; Minor League Outfielder Jereme Milons to Arizona Diamondbacks for Pitcher Elmer Dessens

Purchased: Infielder José Flores from Oakland Athletics; Outfielder Jason Grabowski from Oakland Athletics
Sold: Pitcher Masao Kida to Seattle Mariners
Chosen in Amateur Free Agent Draft: Scott Elbert; Blake DeWitt; Javy Guerra; Cory Wade; Justin Ruggiano; Blake Johnson
Signed Amateur Free Agents: Kenley Jansen; Luis Garcia
Signed Free Agents: Third Baseman-First Baseman Olmedo Saenz; Pitcher José Lima; Infielder José Hernández; Minor League Pitcher Derek Thompson; Pitcher Giovanni Carrara; Outfielder Mike Edwards; Pitcher Buddy Carlyle; Catcher Mike Rose; Outfielder Ricky Ledee; Pitcher Kelly Wunsch; Shortstop José Valentin; Outfielder J.D. Drew; Pitcher Tanyon Sturtze
Chosen in Minor League Draft: Pitcher D.J. Houlton
Released: Pitcher Giovanni Carrara; Outfielder Wilkin Ruan; Pitcher Rodney Myers
Left as Free Agents: Outfielder Jeromy Burnitz; Outfielder Brian Jordan; First Baseman Fred McGriff; Pitcher Andy Ashby; Pitcher Brian Falkenborg; Infielder José Flores; Pitcher Mike Venafro; Infielder José Hernández; Pitcher José Lima; Third Baseman Robin Ventura

11

2005–2009

2005

January 11, 2005: Traded Outfielder Shawn Green to the Arizona Diamondbacks for Catcher Dioner Navarro, Minor League Pitcher Beltran Perez, Minor League Pitcher Danny Muegge, and Minor League Pitcher William Juarez

Since becoming the general manager in February 2004, Paul DePodesta had set about remaking the Dodgers to conform with his vision of what constitutes a successful team. Traded away from the 2004 National League West champions were Paul Lo Duca, Guillermo Mota, and Juan Encarnación. Gone via free agency were Alex Cora; Steve Finley; and Adrian Beltre, the reigning NL home-run king. The latest to go was Shawn Green, who was traded to the Arizona Diamondbacks for catching prospect Dioner Navarro and three minor league pitchers.

In his five seasons with Los Angeles, Green batted .280 with 162 home runs, including 49 in 2001 and 42 in 2002. He had 509 runs batted in and a 130 OPS+. While he was only 31, Green did not fit into DePodesta's plans. The analytically minded DePodesta particularly wanted the 20-year-old switch-hitting Navarro to replace the departed Lo Duca behind the plate. But he had to wait until Arizona acquired Navarro from the Yankees, which they did earlier in the day in a trade that sent pitcher Randy Johnson to New York.

The Diamondbacks had also added third baseman Troy Glaus and pitcher Russ Ortiz this offseason, which Green found encouraging. He said he believed Arizona was building a team that can contend for a pennant. He called Bank One Ballpark his favorite, and he had the numbers that showed his success there—a .314 batting average and 14 home runs against the Diamondbacks in Phoenix. "I knew how great it would be to play in Arizona, just to talk about guys that are added to the ballclub and the coaching staff," he said. "From my perspective, you just kind of sit there and start salivating a little bit and think of the opportunity that's ahead."[1]

Of the three minor league pitchers coming to Los Angeles—Beltran Perez, Danny Muegge, and William Juarez—only Perez would pitch in the major leagues. He had a 2–1 record in eight games for the 2006 Washington Nationals.

January 11, 2005: Signed Free Agent Pitcher Derek Lowe

On the day the Dodgers traded Shawn Green to Arizona, they signed Derek Lowe, a 31-year-old right-hander, to a $36 million, four-year contract. Lowe began his career with the 1997 Seattle Mariners. He was traded during that '97 season to the Boston Red Sox, along with minor league catcher and future team captain Jason Varitek. In return, the Mariners received Heathcliff Slocumb, a journeyman relief pitcher. It was among the best trades the Red Sox ever made.

Lowe had a 72–59 career record with a 3.88 earned run average and 85 saves. The Red Sox originally had used him as a relief pitcher, before making him a starter in 2002, two years after he led the American League with 42 saves. Lowe had the best season of his career that year, a 21–8 record and a 177 ERA+. His 52 wins over the past three seasons were tied with Curt Schilling for second most in the major leagues, one behind Bartolo Colón. Lowe was 14–12 with a 5.42 ERA in 33 starts with the Red Sox in 2004, then went 3–0 with a 1.86 ERA in the postseason. He was the winning pitcher in the final game of all three postseason series, against the Angels, the Yankees, and the Cardinals.

"Derek is a front-line starter with a history of success in the regular season and in the postseason," said Dodgers general manager Paul DePodesta. "He adds great depth to our rotation and will help anchor our pitching staff for years to come. We're ecstatic that we were able to add a pitcher of his caliber to our team." Manager Jim Tracy said: "When you look at the four guys at the top [Brad] Penny, Lowe, [Odalis] Perez and [Jeff] Weaver, those are four awfully good guys."[2]

Lowe had expected to remain in Boston. "The Red Sox made it perfectly clear right after the World Series that nothing was going to happen with me," he said. "I had offers for more money from other teams (Baltimore and Detroit), but once the Dodgers stepped forth and showed interest, I told [agent] Scott Boras it would be a perfect fit." The idea of changing leagues and playing for a team he believed was committed to winning appealed to him. "There is something to be said for tradition," Lowe said.³

January 19, 2005: Free Agent Infielder Alex Cora Signed with the Cleveland Indians

Alex Cora played in 684 games for Los Angeles, primarily a shortstop early in his career and a second baseman in recent seasons. Cora was better known for his defense than his offense. In his seven seasons with the club, he batted .246 with a 77 OPS+, including a .264 average last season with 10 home runs and 47 RBIs in 138 games. His fielding percentage, however, was .987, fifth best among National League second basemen. The Dodgers chose not to offer Cora a contract for the 2005 season, allowing him to become a free agent. The Cleveland Indians signed him to a two-year contract, reportedly worth $2.7 million.

Although the 29-year-old Cora started 122 games at second base last season, he knew the Indians planned to use him in a utility role. They already had Ronnie Belliard at that position and an up-and-coming Jhonny Peralta at shortstop. Indians GM Mark Shapiro thought Cora had more to contribute than the typical utility player. "Alex is overqualified to be called a utility player and has the upside to be a starter," Shapiro said. "He should get a chance to start 50, 60 games." Meanwhile, Cora accepted his new role willingly. "I'm comfortable at either position and I understand this is a different situation than I had in Los Angeles" he said. "I know Ronnie had a great season last year and that Jhonny is one of the top prospects in baseball. I'll just help the best way I can."⁴

January 27, 2005: Free Agent Pitcher Hideo Nomo Signed with the Tampa Bay Devil Rays

Following his trade from the Dodgers to the New York Mets in June 1998, Hideo Nomo had also pitched for the Milwaukee Brewers (1999), the Detroit Tigers (2000), and the Boston Red Sox (2001). In his season with the Red Sox, he won 13 games and led the American League with 220 strikeouts. Boston offered him a three-year contract worth $19 million, which Nomo turned down and signed for a second stint with the Dodgers. He won 16 games in each of his first two seasons in Los Angeles, but shoulder problems limited him to just 18 starts and a 4–11 record in 2004. In his combined seven seasons with the Dodgers, Nomo had a record of 81–66 with 1,200 strikeouts and a 104 ERA+. When the Dodgers released him at the end of the 2004 season, the Tampa Bay Devil Rays signed him to a minor league contract with an invitation to spring training. The 36-year-old right-hander would get a contract for $800,000 if he was added to Tampa Bay's roster, with the chance to make an additional $700,000 in performance bonuses.

Devil Rays manager Lou Piniella already had six pitchers competing for the five-man rotation—Dewon Brazelton, Scott Kazmir, Doug Waechter, Rob Bell, Mark Hendrickson, and Seth McClung—but said he would give Nomo every opportunity to join the competition. "We do need experience, and this guy's had success," Piniella said. "So, let's hope that he bounces back from a down year, and we'll give him an opportunity to make our ballclub." (Nomo had 118 major league wins in his career, while the other six had a combined 72.) "I'm happy to have reached an agreement with Tampa Bay," Nomo said. "I will continue to work hard and try my best to be in the starting rotation when the season starts."[5] But Nomo was finished. He had a 5–8 record with a 7.24 ERA when Tampa released him in mid-July.

On November 16, 2005, Ned Colletti replaced Paul DePodesta as general manager.

On December 8, 2005, Grady Little replaced Jim Tracy as manager.

December 13, 2005: Traded Outfielder Milton Bradley and Infielder Antonio Pérez to the Oakland Athletics for Minor League Outfielder Andre Ethier

The Dodgers ended their rocky relationship with Milton Bradley by trading him, with infielder Antonio Pérez, to the Oakland Athletics for Double A outfielder Andre Ethier. New general manager Ned Colletti said he had tried everything to resolve the differences between Bradley and those connected with the team who disapproved of him. Among those in that group was second baseman Jeff Kent. Bradley had accused Kent of racism and lack of leadership skills in late August. "I don't know how they expected to keep me in center field if nobody even spoke to me," Bradley said. "They weren't trying to reconcile anything. They made up their minds to go with Jeff Kent. They wanted the old man instead of the young man."[6] (Bradley would be 28 in 2006, while Kent would be 38.) Bradley's feud with Kent occurred around the time Bradley injured his left knee, ending his season. He underwent surgery and said he was recovering and expected to play right field for the A's.

"According to the people that are close to him," Colletti said, "they thought another club and another place was the only way it was going to work." He said he spoke to players on the roster and others in the organization, including owner Frank McCourt, and concluded that Bradley would no longer be accepted among them. "I was looking for a way to mediate it, I was looking for a way to reconcile it," Colletti said. "At every turn, I just got stopped. I'd ask once, I'd ask twice, I'd ask three times, and it was clear there was no way to make this work.... I got no glimmer of hope at all that it would work."[7] Despite the turmoil around him, Bradley played well in his season and a half with the Dodgers. He batted .275 with 32 home runs, 105 RBIs, and a 111 OPS+, while playing a strong center field.

Antonio Pérez, who accompanied Bradley to Oakland, was a versatile 25-year-old infielder, who batted .297 in 98 games last season. He batted .102 for the A's in 2006, his final big-league season.

Left-handed-hitting Andre Ethier, who would turn 24 in April, batted .319 with 18 home runs, 80 runs batted in, and 104 runs scored for the Midland (TX) RockHounds, and was the Texas League player of the year. This would turn out to be a wonderful trade for the Dodgers. Ethier played for them from 2006 until he retired after the 2017 season. Appearing in 1,455 games, he had a .285 batting average, with 162 home runs and a 122 OPS+.

December 19, 2005: Signed Free Agent Shortstop Rafael Furcal

At age 22, Atlanta Braves shortstop Rafael Furcal was the National League's Rookie of the year in 2000. Now, after six solid seasons with the Braves—a .284 batting average and 189 stolen bases—Furcal was a free agent. The Chicago Cubs made a strong bid for him, and he seemed ready to sign when he had a call from Paul Kinzer, his agent. Kinzer told him the Dodgers were interested and he should fly to Atlanta to meet with Dodgers owner Frank McCourt. The three met over dinner and, according to Kinzer, McCourt impressed Furcal with his passion and his plan for turning the Dodgers around. "He and Raffy really hit it off," Kinzer said. "Frank did a good job of selling the team. Raffy got all the answers he needed."[8]

McCourt scheduled another dinner that included longtime Dodgers coach Manny Mota to further woo Furcal. Like many players who grew up in the Dominican Republic, Furcal attended Mota's clinics as a youngster and regarded him as a father figure. "They flew Manny in to go out to dinner with us," Kinzer said. "He and Raffy sat together and talked all night."[9] Furcal signed a three-year, $39 million contract that included a signing bonus.

December 19, 2005: Signed Free Agent Shortstop Nomar Garciaparra

Ned Colletti replaced fired general manager Paul DePodesta following the Dodgers' disappointing fourth-place finish in the NL West. In preparation for the 2006 season, Colletti continued to stock the team with veterans. Some were clearly past their prime, like today's addition of former Red Sox star shortstop Nomar Garciaparra. Garciaparra was the American League's Rookie of the Year in 1997 and won back-to-back batting championships in 1999 (.357) and 2000 (.372). In his nine years with the Red Sox, he had a .323 batting average with a 133 OPS+. But Garciaparra's fielding had become suspect, and he was unhappy in Boston.

In July 2004 the Red Sox traded him to the Chicago Cubs as part of a four-player deal. Injuries had limited his playing time these past two seasons, and the Cubs did not seem interested in re-signing him. As a free agent Garciaparra considered offers from the New York Yankees, the Cleveland Indians, and the Houston Astros, in addition to the Dodgers. But after conversations with Dodgers' executives; with his agent, Arn Tellem; and with his wife, soccer star Mia Hamm, he signed a one-year $6 million contract with Los Angeles.

The 32-year-old Garciaparra played mostly third base after returning to the Cubs last August and would likely play first base or the outfield with the Dodgers. "As of today, he's a first baseman," Colletti said. Garciaparra understood he was no longer a shortstop. "I'm not here looking to achieve what I did (in Boston)," he said. "The biggest thing I can achieve is being part of a World Series team. That's what I want to achieve here. I've never set personal goals for myself. It doesn't matter whether you hit .370 or .250 or .210 if you have a ring on your finger." The Whittier, California, native admitted that coming home was a major factor in his decision. "The first big league game I've ever seen was at Dodger Stadium," he recalled. "I grew up cheering for all the L.A. teams. I remember the World Series games (in 1988). I can tell you the lineup as well.... To come home and put on this uniform is a great feeling."[10]

Garciaparra had two solid seasons with the Dodgers—as a first baseman in 2006 and a third baseman in 2007. Injuries limited him to 55 games in 2008. Overall, he appeared in 298 games with a .289 batting average and a 102 OPS+. After strongly considering retirement following the 2008 season, the 35-year-old Garciaparra signed to play for the Oakland Athletics in 2009. It would be his final season.

December 20, 2005: Signed Free Agent Outfielder Kenny Lofton

In signing free agent Kenny Lofton, the Dodgers filled the opening in center field created by the previous week's trade of Milton Bradley to Oakland. The 38-year-old Lofton signed a one-year contract for $3.85 million. In addition he received a $350,000 signing bonus and the chance to earn $150,000 in performance bonuses. The left-handed-hitting Lofton, a four-time Gold Glove winner, had a .299 batting average in his 15-year career, and his 567 stolen bases were the most of any current major leaguer. Lofton led the American League in steals for five consecutive seasons (1992–1996) and was an All-Star from 1994 to 1999. This past season he batted .335 with a .392 on-base average in 110 games for the Philadelphia Phillies.

"His ability to get on base and score runs, combined with his speed and defense, are great additions to our club," said general manager Ned Colletti. "His skills are very similar to earlier in his career. He knows how to play, how to win." Lofton agreed with that assessment. "I've always been a guy who can impact the team in so many aspects: defensively, offensively, on the base paths, in the dugout. As long as I'm out there I feel good about it," he said. "I understand what I can and can't do and just go out and play the game my way." Lofton approved of the additions made by Colletti this offseason. "I know they're looking to win, and that's what I'm all about. At this point, I see that the Dodgers are making their move forward, putting guys on the field who have been there, done that."[11]

Lofton batted .301 and stole 32 bases in 129 games for a much-improved Dodgers club in 2006. After the season, he signed to play for the Texas Rangers in 2007.

Also in 2005:

Traded: Pitcher Kazuhisa Ishii to New York Mets for Catcher Jason Phillips; Infielder Joseph Thurston to New York Yankees for Future Considerations

Purchased: Outfielder José Cruz from Boston Red Sox

Sold: Catcher David Ross to Pittsburgh Pirates; Catcher Mike Rose to Tampa Bay Devil Rays

Chosen in Amateur Free Agent Draft: Ivan De Jesus, Jr.; Josh Bell; Josh Wall; Steve Johnson; Jon Meloan; Brent Leach; Scott Van Slyke; Sergio Pedroza; Trayvon Robinson

Signed Amateur Free Agents: Norihiro Nakamura

Signed Free Agents: Catcher Paul Bako; Pitcher Scott Erickson;

Infielder Oscar Robles; Catcher Sandy Alomar, Jr.; Third Baseman Bill Mueller

Released: Pitcher Buddy Carlyle; Pitcher Scott Erickson; Third Baseman Norihiro Nakamura; Outfielder Jason Grabowski; Outfielder-Third Baseman Mike Edwards; Pitcher Wilson Álvarez (retired)

Left as Free Agents: Outfielder Chin-Feng Chen; Pitcher Kelly Wunsch; Shortstop José Valentin; Catcher Paul Bako; Pitcher Elmer Dessens; Catcher Jason Phillips; First Baseman Brian Myrow

2006

February 15, 2006: Free Agent Pitcher Jeff Weaver Signed with the Los Angeles Angels

Pitcher Jeff Weaver, the last available major free agent of the offseason, signed a one-year contract with the Los Angeles Angels worth $8,325,000. Weaver's contract included $600,000 worth of performance bonuses: $300,000 each for 32 starts and 200 innings pitched. Weaver had surpassed both those goals in each of his two seasons with the Dodgers, while winning 27 and losing 24. The 29-year-old right-hander had a 14–11 record last season, with three complete games, two shutouts, and a 4.22 ERA in 34 starts. Weaver was eighth in the National League in starts and innings pitched and sixth in complete games. He also set career highs in wins, strikeouts, fewest walks, and tied his best mark for starts.

Weaver told the Dodgers he would be willing to sign a three-year, $27 million deal, but the Dodgers never made a firm offer. "I think all of the teams in baseball thought Jeff would be with the Dodgers," Scott Boras, his agent, said. "Once they [pulled out] a lot of teams had already made some decisions. Jeff wanted to go to the right place. He wanted to go to a winning team," said Boras.[12]

"It's another quality arm that we're getting in here," said Angels pitcher John Lackey. "You never can have too much pitching."[13] (The Angels had lost two of their starters from last year, Jarrod Washburn and Paul Byrd.)

June 27, 2006: Traded Catcher Dioner Navarro, Pitcher Jae Weong Seo, and a Player to be Named to the Tampa Bay Devil Rays for Catcher Toby Hall, Pitcher Mark Hendrickson, and Cash

With Derek Lowe and Brad Penny as the only starters able to pitch deep into games, the Dodgers were leading the major leagues in losses by relievers. "Our bullpen is holding together right now," GM Ned Colletti said, "but it's been tested over and over by five-inning starts and six-inning starts."[14] In a move designed to lessen the burden on the overworked bullpen, Colletti acquired 32-year-old left-hander Mark Hendrickson in a multi-player trade with the Tampa Bay Devil Rays. In addition to Hendrickson the Dodgers would receive catcher Toby Hall and $1 million. Going to Tampa Bay were catcher Dioner Navarro, pitcher Jae Weong Seo, and a minor leaguer to be named.

The 6'9" Hendrickson had played four seasons in the National Basketball Association before becoming a full-time baseball player in 2001. "I'm excited," he said. "In 10 years of professional sports, this is the first time I've really been on a team that had a chance to win it all." In his five-year major league career, with Toronto and Tampa Bay, Hendrickson had a record of 37–40 with a 5.01 earned-run average. He was s 4–8 with a 3.81 ERA as a starter this season. "I feel like I'm starting to come into my own as a pitcher," he said.[15] Dodgers scouts had noted improvements in his curve ball, changeup, and command this month. And he had pitched into the seventh inning in his last five starts.

Toby Hall, a 30-year-old right-handed-hitter, broke in with Tampa Bay in 2000 and had been the Devil Rays starting catcher for the last four years. He was a lifetime .262-hitter with an 81 OPS+. Hall was batting .231 with eight home runs in 64 games this season. With rookie Russell Martin having taken over as the Dodgers everyday catcher, Hall would share backup duties with Sandy Alomar, Jr. Martin had won the job from 22-year-old Dioner Navarro, who had opened the season in that role. Navarro batted .280 in 25 games but was unable to throw out any of the 16 runners attempting to steal a base. A badly bruised wrist put him on the disabled list in May and Martin won the job in his absence.

Jae Weong Seo, 29, had a 2–4 record with a 5.78 ERA and had been moved from the rotation to the bullpen. To complete the trade, the Dodgers sent minor league outfielder Justin Ruggiano to Tampa Bay on July 19.

Hendrickson would pitch in 57 games in his two seasons in LA, with only 27 as starts. He had a 6–15 record with an 89 ERA+ and signed as a free agent with the Florida Marlins for 2008.

Hall batted .368 in 21 games over the second half of the season and signed with the Chicago White Sox for 2007.

July 26, 2006: Traded Pitcher Odalis Pérez, Minor League Pitcher Blake Johnson, Minor League Pitcher Julio Pimentel, and Cash to the Kansas City Royals for Pitcher Elmer Dessens

Odalis Pérez came to the Dodgers with outfielder Brian Jordan in the January 2002 trade that sent Gary Sheffield to Atlanta. Pérez was very effective in his first season in LA, winning 15 games with a 127 ERA+ and earning his first all-star selection. He won 12 in 2003 and had a 126 ERA+ in 2004, but injuries limited him to 19 starts in 2005. Used mostly in relief this season, he reached a low point on July 13 in St. Louis. After yielding a game-winning home run to Albert Pujols, Pérez accused the Dodgers of treating him like "trash." The Dodgers claimed they had no plans to trade the disgruntled left-hander, but obviously they did have such plans. They sent him to the Kansas City Royals, along with two minor league pitchers and cash, for right-hander Elmer Dessens, a former Dodger.

"Moving him [Pérez] was something we really needed to do for all concerned, including him," said general manager Ned Colletti. "He lost his starting job. It's probably best to cut ties and move on. We were not getting much productivity out of that roster spot." Colletti said the Royals would not accept a straight-up trade for Pérez, and demanded prospects and cash, too. "It hasn't been easy." he said. "If it was easy, it would've happened a while ago."[16]

Being traded away from Los Angeles did not make Pérez any less disgruntled. "I'm mad because I'm leaving this town. My best years have been here," he said. "Sometimes people judge you because they think your work habits haven't been the same. But that's not true. As a professional, you have your ups and downs. But I don't think I have any mechanical problems. This year has been tough," Pérez said. "But at the same time, I really appreciate what the people in the front office and the fans have done for me since I've been here. I had a great time here. I didn't want to leave, but it's a business. It's time to move on. It's time to go to a different franchise and show I still have the skill to pitch and the stuff to do it."[17]

Dayton Moore, the Royals GM who came to them from the Atlanta Braves, said he had known Pérez since he was a young prospect with that organization. "Whatever has happened in the past is very manageable," Moore said. "We feel very, very secure in our belief that he is going to come here and do a good job on the field certainly and off the field as well."

Neither of the two pitchers the Royals received, Blake Johnson and Julio Pimentel, would ever reach the major leagues.

Right-hander Elmer Dessens, 35, had pitched for the Dodgers in 2004 and 2005. He pitched in in 28 games in 2005, including seven starts, with a 116 ERA+ in 65⅔ innings. This season Dessens had a 5–7 record in 43 games for the Royals, all in relief. He made 19 appearances for the Dodgers, losing his only decision.

July 31, 2006: Traded Shortstop César Izturis to the Chicago Cubs for Pitcher Greg Maddux

On the day of the trading deadline the Dodgers were in last place, but only five games behind first place San Diego in the tightly packed National League West. To better position themselves for the stretch drive, they traded shortstop César Izturis and $2 million to the Chicago Cubs in exchange for pitcher Greg Maddux. The 40-year-old Maddux, winner of 327 games and four Cy Young Awards, waived his no-trade clause to go to Los Angeles. After winning his first five decisions with the Cubs, Maddux had lost 11 of his next 15. "I haven't pitched as well as I would've liked the past month," he said, "but my health is still good and I look forward to pitching for the Dodgers," Maddux said he gave the Cubs a "short list" of places he was willing to go, with Los Angeles on top. "They're only five games out right now and there's plenty of baseball left. I grew up going to Dodger games. It was the first ballpark I ever went to," Maddux said.[18]

GM Ned Colletti said the club had been scouting Maddux most of the season. For the past month, Colletti added, he had been in talks with Cubs general manager Jim Hendry about acquiring the future Hall of Famer. "He's not what he was when he was winning Cy Young Awards, but we still think he has the ability to pitch and win games. He's probably one of the smartest players I've ever been around. I think he'll find a way." Colletti said.[19] The Dodgers also expected Maddux to provide veteran leadership in a clubhouse filled with rookies who have become starters, like pitcher Chad Billingsley, catcher Russell Martin, and outfielder Andre Ethier.

Maddux started 12 games for the Dodgers with a 6–3 record and a 137 ERA+. He helped them reach the playoffs, where they were swept by the New York Mets. At the time of the trade, he had said: "I would think I would play next year, but I haven't 100 percent decided."[20] Maddux turned out to be a two-month rental for the Dodgers as he did "play next year" (2007) after signing as a free agent with the San Diego Padres.

Shortstop César Izturis had been with the Dodgers since 2002. He played in 590 games with a .260 batting average and an OPS+ of 68. Newcomer Rafael Furcal had replaced him this season, and Izturis had been in only 32 games.

November 22, 2006: Signed Free Agent Outfielder Juan Pierre

The Dodgers' total of 153 home runs in 2006 placed them fifteenth in the sixteen-team National League. But unable to sign a power hitter among the available free agents, general manager Ned Colletti shifted to adding speed. He signed left-handed-hitting center fielder Juan Pierre, one of the most prolific base stealers in the game. The 29-year-old Pierre, who batted .292 with 204 hits and 58 stolen bases for the Chicago Cubs this past season, signed a $44 million, five-year contract. "Juan's ability to hit combined with his speed make him a perfect catalyst for our lineup," Colletti said. "I've long admired how he plays the game. We're thrilled he's here, he's a good man, he's going to be a great player for us a great addition.... Juan Pierre brings us a dimension of offense and speed to high degree. He gets on base a lot, a lot of hits. Stolen bases are obvious."[21] Pierre had 325 stolen bases in his career and had finished first or second in the NL in stolen bases in each of the past six seasons.

Prior to his one year with the Cubs, Pierre played two full seasons and part of another with the Colorado Rockies and three years with the Florida Marlins. He had a .303 career batting average, and his 1,182 hits since 2001 were the second-highest total in the major leagues, trailing only the Seattle Mariners' Ichiro Suzuki. Pierre also had been the most difficult player in the National League to strike out in five of the last six seasons.

"I'm just happy to be part of a storied franchise, a playoff-caliber team," Pierre said. "Hopefully I can be another piece of the puzzle to help them win the World Series. They're a winning team, and most of the guys they had last year are coming back. I think there's a good mixture as far as the young and old. I felt that it was the right spot for me." Pierre was expected to bat first, with Rafael Furcal batting second. Or they could be switched. "It doesn't matter, wherever I can fit in," Pierre said. "I'd probably be most comfortable hitting leadoff because that's all I've ever done." Regarding where Pierre and Furcal hit in the lineup, Colletti said: "However that works out gives the middle of our lineup extra opportunities to produce."[22]

December 19, 2006: Free Agent Pitcher Eric Gagne Signed with the Texas Rangers

Eric Gagne's eight-year career with the Dodgers ended when he signed a $6 million, one-year contract to pitch for the Texas Rangers in 2007. Included in the deal was an opportunity for him to earn about $5 million in performance bonuses. Gagne was a starter when he came up in 1999, but in 2002 then manager Jim Tracy converted him to a reliever. He left as the Dodgers all-time leader in saves, 161 (later surpassed by Kenley Jansen), and his 96 percent career save percentage (161-of-167) was the highest in major league history for pitchers with at least 100 saves. From August 2002 to July 2004, Gagne converted a major league-record 84 consecutive save opportunities.

The 31-year-old right-hander had 152 saves in those three seasons, including all 55 chances in 2003, when he had a 1.20 earned run average and won the National League's Cy Young Award. Injuries had limited him to 14 appearances in 2005 and just two this past season. Yet Gagne was confident he would return to form with the Rangers in 2007. "I have no doubt in my mind I'll be healthy on the mound all year. I haven't felt this good for 2 or 2½ years," he said. "I know I haven't lost anything. I still know how to pitch. It's just a matter of getting back on the mound."[23]

Texas GM Jon Daniels acknowledged he was taking a chance in signing Gagne. "There is some risk there," he said. "If you get past that and he's healthy, which we think he is, and he maximizes his ability, you didn't just add another piece, you added a premium part. It's a risk well worth taking."[24]

Gagne had 16 saves and a 2.16 ERA in 34 games with the 2007 Rangers before they traded him to the Red Sox at the July 31 deadline. He finished his career making 50 appearances with 10 saves for the 2008 Milwaukee Brewers.

Also in 2006:

Traded: Pitcher Duaner Sanchez and Pitcher Steve Schmoll to New York Mets for Pitcher Jae Weong Seo and Pitcher Tim Hamulak; Pitcher Edwin Jackson and Minor League Pitcher Chuck Tiffany to Tampa Bay Devil Rays for Pitcher Danys Baez and Pitcher Lance Carter; Minor League Pitcher Jarod Plummer to Kansas City Royals for Pitcher Wilson Valdez; Outfielder Cody Ross to Cincinnati Reds for Pitcher Ben Kozlowski; Catcher Sandy Alomar, Jr., to Chicago White Sox for Minor League Pitcher B.J. LaMura; Pitcher Danys Baez and Third Baseman Willy Aybar to Atlanta Braves for Third Baseman Wilson Betemit; Third Baseman Joel

Guzmán and Minor League Outfielder Sergio Pedroza to Tampa Bay Devil Rays for Shortstop Julio Lugo; Minor League Pitcher Jhonny Núñez to Washington Nationals for Infielder-Outfielder Marlon Anderson

Purchased: Catcher Einar Díaz from Cleveland Indians

Sold: First Baseman Hee-Seop Choi to Boston Red Sox; Outfielder Ricky Ledee to New York Mets; Pitcher Franquelis Osoria to Pittsburgh Pirates

Chosen in Amateur Free Agent Draft: Clayton Kershaw; Bryan Morris; Justin Fuller; Kyle Smit

Signed Amateur Free Agents: Takashi Saito; Elisaul Pimentel

Signed Free Agents: Pitcher Brett Tomko; Pitcher Aaron Sele; Pitcher Joe Beimel; Infielder Ramón Martínez; Pitcher Randy Wolf; Catcher Mike Lieberthal; Pitcher Jason Schmidt; Outfielder Luis Gonzalez

Released: Outfielder José Cruz

Left as Free Agents: Outfielder J.D. Drew; Pitcher Aaron Sele; Pitcher Derek Thompson; Catcher Einar Díaz; Pitcher Giovanni Carrara; Pitcher Lance Carter; Shortstop Julio Lugo; Outfielder Jayson Werth

2007

August 9, 2007: Traded a Player to be Named to the San Francisco Giants for Outfielder–First Baseman Mark Sweeney

Perhaps the major significance of this minor deal was that it was the first between Los Angeles and San Francisco since December 1985, when the Dodgers traded outfielder Candy Maldonado to the Giants for catcher Alex Trevino. In this one the Dodgers acquired 37-year-old Outfielder-First Baseman Mark Sweeney for a player to be named. Sweeney, a left-handed hitter, was in his thirteenth big league season, but only in two of those seasons did he have more than 200 at-bats. His greatest value for the six National League teams he had played with was as a pinch-hitter. A pinch-single in his final at-bat as a Giant was his major league-leading sixteenth of the season and 155th of his career, second only to Lenny Harris. Sweeney was 16-for-49 (.327) as a pinch-hitter for the Giants this season and had 11 hits in his last 23 at-bats in that role. (Dodgers pinch-hitters were batting just .235 [36-for-153]).

"To be frank, we're not a good enough team to have somebody

like Mark on it as a premium pinch-hitter," Giants general manager Brian Sabean said. "He was playing sparingly, and we do need to look at some of these other guys." The Dodgers were five games behind Arizona in the NL West and had been struggling offensively. In addition to his value as a pinch hitter, Sweeney could also play first base and the outfield. "Baseball-wise it's a better opportunity for me," Sweeney said. "Being with a contender and doing the utility job, it's a lot more important and has more relevance with what you do when the team is winning, rather than building." Giants manager Bruce Bochy said: "He's been around this game for a long time. You've got a club that is contending that wants one of the best pinch-hitters in the game. He should be flattered."[25]

On August 25 the Dodgers sent minor league second baseman Travis Denker to San Francisco to complete the deal. Denker would play in 24 games for the Giants in 2008.

Also in 2007:

Traded: Pitcher Elmer Dessens to Milwaukee Brewers for Outfielder Brady Clark and Cash; Third Baseman Wilson Betemit to New York Yankees for Pitcher Scott Proctor

Purchased: Catcher Chad Moeller from Cincinnati Reds; Pitcher Esteban Loaiza from Oakland Athletics

Chosen in Amateur Free Agent Draft: Chris Withrow; Mike Watt; Andrew Lambo

Signed Amateur Free Agents: Carlos Frías; Pedro Baez; Rubby De La Rosa; José Domínguez

Signed Free Agents: Pitcher Rudy Seanez; Pitcher Chin-hui Tsao; Second Baseman Luis Maza; Pitcher Roberto Hernández; First Baseman-Third Baseman Shea Hillenbrand; Pitcher David Wells; Pitcher Travis Schlichting; Third Baseman Terry Tiffee; Pitcher Hiroki Kuroda; Outfielder Andruw Jones; Pitcher Tanyon Sturtze; Pitcher Brian Falkenborg; Catcher Gary Bennett; Catcher Danny Ardoin

Chosen in Minor League Draft: Pitcher Victor Garate

Released: Infielder Oscar Robles; Outfielder Brady Clark; Infielder-Outfielder Marlon Anderson; Pitcher Brett Tomko

Left as Free Agents: Pitcher Roberto Hernández; Third Baseman-First Baseman Olmedo Saenz; First Baseman-Third Baseman Shea Hillenbrand; Pitcher Tim Hamulak; Catcher Chad Moeller; Pitcher Rudy Seanez; Pitcher David Wells (retired); Catcher Mike Lieberthal (retired); Pitcher Randy Wolf; Pitcher Chin-hui Tsao; Pitcher Mark Hendrickson

On November 1, 2007, Joe Torre replaced Grady Little as manager.

2008

July 26, 2008: Traded Pitcher Jon Meloan and Minor League Catcher-First Baseman Carlos Santana to the Cleveland Indians for Third Baseman Casey Blake and Cash

As they had been so often in recent years, the Dodgers were struggling to score runs. With the July 31 non-waiver trade deadline nearing, they acquired third baseman Casey Blake from the Cleveland Indians for a pair of minor leaguers—right-handed pitcher Jon Meloan, who was at Triple A Las Vegas, and Class A catcher-first baseman Carlos Santana. To make room for Blake the Dodgers sent rookie third baseman Blake DeWitt to Las Vegas. New manager Joe Torre denied the trade meant the Dodgers had given up on DeWitt and Andy LaRoche, the two youngsters who were platooning at third. Casey Blake, nearly 35, would be a free agent at the end of the season. He almost became a Dodger earlier in the month; the teams were discussing a multiplayer trade that would also have brought ace pitcher CC Sabathia and infielder Jamey Carroll to Los Angeles.

While Blake was also capable of playing the outfield, Torre designated him as his everyday third baseman. "He's the type of player who doesn't take an at-bat off," GM Ned Colletti said of Blake. "He's a great character guy." The right-handed-hitting Blake was in his tenth major league season, with previous stops in Toronto, Minnesota, and Baltimore. His best season was with the 2004 Indians, when he set career highs in home runs (28) and runs batted in (88). Blake had 18 home runs and 78 RBIs in 2007 and was batting .289 with 11 home runs and 58 RBIs this season. "If you follow my career, you'll know I'm a blue-collar guy," Blake said. "I might not hit 40 home runs or drive in 100 runs, but I'd like to think I'm a consistent performer."[26]

Jon Meloan, 24, made five relief appearances, without a decision, for the Dodgers in September 2007. They moved him from their bullpen to Las Vegas's rotation this spring, where he was 5–10 with a 4.97 earned-run average in 21 games.

Carlos Santana, 22, was hitting .323 with 14 home runs for Class A Inland Empire, where his 96 runs batted in were the most in the California League. For the 15 seasons (2010–2024) Santana played for seven different teams. He had 1,789 hits, 324 home runs, 1,082 RBIs, and a 114 OPS+. (He was still an active player, with the Minnesota Twins, in 2024.) Meanwhile,

Casey Blake would play for the Cleveland Guardians from 2003–08 and play for the Dodgers from 2008 through the 2011 season before leaving as a free agent. In 406 games, he had a .260 batting average, 49 home runs, 192 RBIs, and a 108 OPS+.

July 31, 2008: Traded Third Baseman Andy LaRoche and Minor League Pitcher Bryan Morris to the Pittsburgh Pirates in a Three-Way Deal that brought them Outfielder Manny Ramírez from the Boston Red Sox

Hours before the trading deadline, the Florida Marlins were working to put together a deal that would bring them slugging Boston Red Sox outfielder Manny Ramírez. When that failed, the Dodgers jumped in to get Ramírez as part of a three-team, six-player trade. It was one of the most significant deadline deals in their history, and it came cheap. They sent third baseman Andy LaRoche, currently at Triple A Las Vegas, and Class A right-hander Bryan Morris, a former first-round draft choice, to the Pittsburgh Pirates. The Pirates sent outfielder Jason Bay to the Red Sox to replace Ramirez, and the Red Sox sent outfielder Brandon Moss and right-hander Craig Hansen to Pittsburgh.

In his eight seasons with Cleveland, followed by the last eight in Boston, the 36-year-old Ramírez had established himself as one of the greatest right-hand hitters ever. The 12-time All-Star (including the last 11 seasons) had a combined total of 510 home runs, 1,672 runs batted in, and was considered a sure bet for the Hall of Fame. In addition to winning a batting title, a home run title, and an RBI title, he also had led the league in on-base average, slugging percentage, and OPS three times each.

And while Ramírez was having another fine season, a .299 batting average, 20 home runs, 68 RBIs, and a 137 OPS+, management and fans in Boston had tired of his antics, on and off the field. Despite the "baggage" Ramírez carried, Dodgers manager Joe Torre said the deal had no downside. General manager Ned Colletti said he felt it was a deal that had to be made. "We figured we had to do it," Colletti said. "Why would we not do it?"[27] The Dodgers already had four outfielders (Matt Kemp, Andre Ethier, Juan Pierre, and Andruw Jones) competing for three spots, but with the arrival of Ramírez to play left field, it now would be four outfielders competing for two spots. "That makes you yearn for the DH," said Torre, the former manager of the American League's New York Yankees. "In the big picture, you're helping your team and that has to take precedence over playing time. We're going to have to, as we go along, try to figure it out," he said.[28]

"I really don't know who's going to get impacted the most on this thing," said Andruw Jones, while acknowledging that it could result in less playing time for him. "It's just bringing a big bat in the lineup, and I think if we stay healthy, we've got a good chance to win the National League West." (The Dodgers were trailing the Arizona Diamondbacks by two games.) Matt Kemp said that adding "one of the best hitters in baseball" could only be a positive, regardless of who was in the starting lineup each day. "Whoever gets to get in the game at that time has to go out there and help the team win any chance they can, even if they're not starting," Kemp said.[29]

Ramírez, of course, had his say about Boston's treatment of him. "The Red Sox don't deserve a player like me," Ramírez told ESPN. "During my years here, I've seen how they have mistreated other great players when they didn't want them, to try to turn the fans against them. The Red Sox did the same with guys like Nomar Garciaparra and Pedro Martinez, and now they do the same with me. Their goal is to paint me as the bad guy."[30]

December 28, 2008: Free Agent Pitcher Brad Penny Signed with the Boston Red Sox

Brad Penny came to the Dodgers in a July 2004 six-player trade with the Florida Marlins. An arm injury limited him to just three starts the rest of that season. Penny, a right-hander, was 7–9 in 2005 and followed with the two best seasons of his career. He had 16 wins (16–9) in 2006, tied for most in the National League, with a 104 ERA+. He again won 16 in 2007, which along with only four losses gave him a league-leading .800 winning percentage. His ERA+ for the season was a career-high 147.

After Penny's struggle with a sore shoulder, a 6–9 record, and a 67 ERA+ in 2008, the Dodgers chose to exercise a $2 million buyout rather than pay him $9.25 million in 2009. The Red Sox, needing a mid- to back-end of the rotation starter, signed the 30-year-old free agent to a one-year contract worth $5 million. The contract gave Penny the opportunity to earn an additional $3 million in performance bonuses.

Also in 2008:

Traded: Pitcher Eric Hull to Boston Red Sox for Minor League Shortstop Christian Lara and Cash; Minor League Shortstop Juan Rivera to Kansas City Royals for Shortstop Ángel Berroa; Minor League Pitcher Eduardo Pérez and Minor League Pitcher Mike Watt to San Diego Padres for Pitcher Greg Maddux

Sold: Pitcher Wilson Valdez to Kia Tigers of Korea; Pitcher D.J.

Houlton to Fukuoka Daiei Hawks of Japan Pacific League; Pitcher Brian Falkenborg to San Diego Padres

Chosen in Amateur Free Agent Draft: Josh Lindblom; Ethan Martin; Dee Gordon; Nick Buss; Nathan Eovaldi; Jerry Sands; Matt Magill; Allen Webster

Signed Free Agents: Pitcher Chan Ho Park; Pitcher Jason Johnson; Outfielder Mitch Jones; Infielder-Outfielder Pablo Ozuna; Infielder Mark Loretta

Released: Infielder Ramón Martínez; Pitcher Esteban Loaiza; Pitcher Tanyon Sturtze

Left as Free Agents: Third Baseman Terry Tiffee; Pitcher Joe Beimel; Pitcher Greg Maddux (retired); Pitcher Jason Johnson (retired); Pitcher Chan Ho Park; Outfielder-First Baseman Mark Sweeney (retired); Catcher Gary Bennett; Second baseman Jeff Kent (retired); Infielder-Outfielder Pablo Ozuna; Shortstop Ángel Berroa; Pitcher Scott Proctor; Pitcher Takashi Saito

2009

January 13, 2009: Free Agent Pitcher Derek Lowe Signed with the Atlanta Braves

The Dodgers had already lost pitchers Brad Penny and Greg Maddux this winter, yet they made no attempt to re-sign Derek Lowe, a 14-game winner with a 129 ERA+ this past season. Instead, Lowe signed a four-year, $60 million contract with the Atlanta Braves. According to Dodgers GM Ned Colletti, Lowe made it clear he intended to sign elsewhere. Lowe's agent, Scott Boras, denied Colletti's claim, saying the 35-year-old Lowe had never expressed that intention to him. "Derek told me he enjoyed pitching for [manager] Joe [Torre] and would have considered L.A. But early in the process when I was collecting information from teams, I spoke to the Dodgers, and they indicated they were going in a different direction."[31]

Torre and his coaches did want to retain Lowe, but owners Frank and Jamie McCourt, who paid the salaries and with whom the pitcher had personality conflicts, did not. Lowe's affair with a woman from Fox Sports West who covered the team, which led them each to divorce their spouses, upset the McCourts for the negative publicity it brought to the team.

Adding to the animosity was Lowe's feeling the club favored Penny over him. He was particularly upset when he had to pitch on three days' rest in a May 18 game at Anaheim when Penny said he could not take his turn in the rotation. In his four seasons with the Dodgers, Lowe was 54–48 with a 3.59 earned run average and a 120 ERA+.

"This is a great day," Lowe said. "When you think about the Atlanta Braves, you think about starting pitching. That's what the organization has always been about. I left here [after his January 8 visit] feeling very comfortable that this is a place I'd love to play. The division is very competitive. [But] we feel like we have every right to win this division. It's going to be a lot of fun."[32]

In March 2009, Dennis Mannion assumed the club presidency.

December 15, 2009: Traded Outfielder Juan Pierre to the Chicago White Sox for Two Minor League Pitchers to be Named

In Juan Pierre's first season with the Dodgers, 2007, he played in 162 games, the fifth consecutive season Pierre had appeared in all his team's games. He had 196 hits and 64 stolen bases, but hit no home runs, which contributed to a subpar OPS+ of 77. Pierre's streak of playing in 162 games ended in 2008 when the Dodgers signed Andruw Jones and then traded for Manny Ramírez. (Ramírez's 50-game suspension for PED use in 2009 did afford Pierre more playing time.) Pierre played in 426 games in his three seasons in Los Angeles, with a .294 batting average and 134 stolen bases. But he hit only one home run and his combined OPS+ was 84. Wanting more playing time for younger and more productive outfielders Andre Ethier and Matt Kemp, the Dodgers traded Pierre to the Chicago White Sox, where manager Ozzie Guillen was more comfortable with Pierre's offensive contributions. The 32-year-old Pierre appeared relieved when he learned of the trade. "I've been in the witness protection program for the last two years," he said.[33]

The White Sox agreed to pay $8 million of the $18.5 million Pierre was owed over the next two seasons, providing the Dodgers with some financial flexibility. GM Ned Colletti said the trade was not simply a salary dump: the $8 million saved would be spent on player acquisitions. On December 18 the Dodgers received the two minor league pitchers. Jon Link, a 25-year-old reliever, was closer to being major-league-ready, Colletti said. "He has a chance to be on our club this year."[34] Link, a right-hander, saved 13 games and had a 3.99 earned-run average in 48 relief appearances for the Triple A Charlotte Knights of the International League last season.

His major league career would consist of nine relief appearances with a 4.15 earned run average for the 2010 Dodgers.

John Ely, a 23-year-old right-handed starter, had a 14–2 record with a 2.82 earned run average for the Double A Birmingham Barons of the Southern League in 2009. The Dodgers considered him a candidate to earn a spot in their 2010 rotation. Ely won that slot and started 18 games in 2010, with a 4–10 record and a 5.49 ERA. He spent most of 2011 and 2012 with Triple A Albuquerque and was traded to Houston in December 2012.

December 16, 2009: Signed Free Agent Infielder Jamey Carroll

A day earlier GM Ned Colletti said he would use the $8 million saved by trading Juan Pierre to the White Sox on player acquisitions. He took the first step when he signed veteran infielder Jamey Carroll to a two-year contract worth $3.85 million. Jonathan Maurer, Carroll's agent, said the deal included incentives up to $525,000 a year, which Carroll would earn by making at least 275 plate appearances. Carroll, who would turn 36 in February, was an eight-year veteran with a .273 career batting average, 12 home runs, and 174 runs batted in. In 93 games for the Cleveland Indians last season, the right-handed-hitting Carroll batted .276 with two home runs and 26 RBIs. His best season was in 2006, when he hit .300 with five home runs and 36 RBIs for the Colorado Rockies. The Dodgers expected Carroll to share second base with Blake DeWitt in 2010, as well as backing up Casey Blake at third base and Rafael Furcal at shortstop.

Maurer said Carroll had turned down two-year offers from Cleveland and the Oakland Athletics. Oakland offered more money and more playing time, said Maurer, but Carroll wanted to play for Dodgers manager Joe Torre and coach Don Mattingly, who was from Carroll's hometown of Evansville, Indiana. Maurer also commented on the Dodgers expectation that DeWitt would be their starting second baseman. "Jamey has said he looks to partner with Blake DeWitt and form a tremendous 1–2 punch at second base to help this team get back to the playoffs," he said.[35]

With the Dodgers Carroll played in 279 games over the 2010 and 2011 seasons, mostly at second base and shortstop. He batted .290 with a league-average OPS. In November 2011 he signed as a free agent with the Minnesota Twins.

Also in 2009:

Traded: Outfielder Delwyn Young to Pittsburgh Pirates for Pitcher Harvey García and Minor League Pitcher Eric Krebs; Minor League

Pitcher Josh Bell and Minor League Pitcher Steve Johnson to Baltimore Orioles for Pitcher George Sherrill; Pitcher Claudio Vargas to Milwaukee Brewers for Outfielder Vinny Rottino; Minor League Infielder Justin Fuller to Chicago White Sox for First Baseman Jim Thome and Cash; Minor League Pitcher Luis Garcia and Minor League Pitcher Victor Garate to Washington Nationals for Second Baseman Ronnie Belliard; Infielder Tony Abreu to Arizona Diamondbacks for Pitcher Jon Garland

Purchased: Minor League Infielder Justin Sellers from Chicago Cubs; Minor League Pitcher Carlos Monasterios from New York Mets

Chosen in Amateur Free Agent Draft: Steve Ames; Blake Smith; Brett Wallach

Signed Amateur Free Agents: Yimi García

Signed Free Agents: Pitcher Claudio Vargas; Infielder Juan Castro; Pitcher Guillermo Mota; Pitcher Ronald Belisario; Catcher Brad Ausmus; Pitcher Randy Wolf; Pitcher Jeff Weaver; Pitcher Charlie Haeger; Pitcher Eric Milton; Second Baseman Orlando Hudson; First Baseman Doug Mientkiewicz; Pitcher Will Ohman; Pitcher Vicente Padilla; Pitcher Justin Miller; First Baseman John Lindsey

Lost in Major League Draft: Outfielder Jamie Hoffman (Returned to Dodgers from New York Yankees in 2010)

Released: Outfielder Andruw Jones; Pitcher Yhency Brazoban

Left as Free Agents: First Baseman Nomar Garciaparra; Outfielder Mitch Jones; Pitcher Jon Garland; Second Baseman Orlando Hudson; Pitcher Eric Milton; Pitcher Randy Wolf; Pitcher Guillermo Mota; First Baseman Jim Thome; Catcher Danny Ardoin; Infielder Juan Castro; Pitcher Harvey García; Infielder Mark Loretta; Second Baseman Luis Maza; Pitcher Will Ohman; Outfielder Vinny Rottino; Pitcher Jason Schmidt (retired)

12

2010–2014

2010

July 31, 2010: Traded Infielder Blake DeWitt, Minor League Pitcher Brett Wallach, and Minor League Pitcher Kyle Smit to the Chicago Cubs for Pitcher Ted Lilly, Shortstop Ryan Theriot, and Cash

Fourteen years after the Los Angeles Dodgers chose him in the amateur draft, left-hander Ted Lilly would finally get the chance to pitch for them. The Dodgers sent infielder Blake DeWitt and minor league pitchers Brett Wallach and Kyle Smit to the Chicago Cubs in exchange for Lilly and shortstop Ryan Theriot. Los Angeles also received $2.5 million to cover about half of what remained of Lilly's and Theriot's salaries this year. There was some disagreement on the Dodgers part over what it took to get Lilly. Manager Joe Torre said they had to give up the left-handed-hitting DeWitt to get him, while general manager Ned Colletti said they could have obtained Lilly without including him.

The 24-year-old DeWitt was well-liked by the front office and the coaching staff for his willingness to do whatever was asked of him. When Nomar Garciaparra and Andy LaRoche were hurt in spring training in 2008, DeWitt, a rookie, was the Dodgers' opening day third baseman. In the postseason he played second base, a position he had never played as a professional. Last season he was their full-time second baseman.

"I'm definitely a little surprised," said DeWitt, the Dodgers first-round pick in the 2004 amateur draft. "It's the first time anything like this has happened to me. It's definitely not easy. I haven't had time to gather my thoughts yet."[1] DeWitt played in 230 games in his three seasons in Los Angeles. He batted .262 with a 94 OPS+. The two minor league pitchers traded to Chicago—Kyle Smit and Brett Wallach remained career minor leaguers.

Since leaving the Dodgers organization, Lilly, now 34, had pitched, in addition to the Cubs, for the Expos, the Yankees, the Athletics, and the Blue Jays. His overall record was 106–92, with double-digit wins in each of the last seven years. In 18 starts this season, he had a 3–8 record, but a creditable 115 ERA+. Torre, who managed Lilly with the Yankees, was not worried about his numbers. "What he has inside him is one of his real plusses. He competes."[2] Torre inserted Lilly into the team's pitching rotation as their fifth starter.

"Really cool," was Lilly's reaction to the trade. "I'm clearly excited. They've been playing good baseball. Not scoring a lot of runs, but hopefully that will change, and we'll find ways to win games." He acknowledged it was difficult to leave Chicago. "It's always shocking, even though I kind of was aware something would be happening before the deadline," Lilly said. "I was really lucky to play in the city of Chicago and I had a great experience there. On the same token I consider myself pretty fortunate to come back and play for the Dodgers. My dreams since I signed was to come up and pitch for the Dodgers. It took me 14 years but I'm getting my chance. It's an opportunity to get into the postseason and hopefully win a World Series. The Cubs weren't going in that direction this year and I'm fortunate to have a chance to do that over here."[3]

Ryan Theriot, a 30-year-old right-handed batter, was hitting .284 with one home run and 21 runs batted in. He had a .287 batting average in 609 games in his six seasons in Chicago. Theriot had been the Cubs' full-time shortstop in 2008 and 2009 but was switched to second base this season to make room for rookie Starlin Castro. The Dodgers would keep him at second as a replacement for DeWitt.

August 30, 2010: Sold Outfielder Manny Ramírez to the Chicago White Sox

In the summer of 2008 Manny Ramírez was looking to leave the Boston Red Sox. Meanwhile, the Dodgers, lacking offense and color, were looking to boost their club in both departments. In what was a perfect fit at the time, they acquired Ramírez from the Red Sox at the end of July. "We knew that if Manny performed at the level that we thought he could perform, he would be a long-term investment for us," Dodgers president Dennis Mannion said. And over the last two months of that season Ramírez performed significantly better than expected. In 53 games, he batted .396 with 17 home runs and 53 runs batted in; his OPS+ was a spectacular 221. Los Angeles reached the National League Championship Series for the first time in 20 years. Ramírez played with great enthusiasm and the fans loved him. "He was really critical to the psyche of the team and really critical to the psyche of our fan base too," Mannion said. "He was our Pete Rose for that window of time."[4]

The Dodgers re-signed Ramirez for 2009, but a month into the season he received a 50-game suspension for violating baseball's drug policy. Ramirez played in only 104 games in 2009, batting .290 with 19 home runs, 63 RBIs, and a 155 OPS+. His demeanor was noticeably less pleasant this season, and he was uncooperative with the press, often refusing to speak to reporters. Ramirez was now 38 and he had been on the disabled list three times this season. After being benched for two games in Colorado, manager Torre told him if he stayed with the Dodgers, he would play only three or four times a week. The club chose to put Ramirez on waivers, and the Chicago White Sox claimed him. Ramirez said he would rather play every day as a designated hitter for the White Sox than be a part-time player with the Dodgers.

"It was probably time for both of us," general manager Ned Colletti said. When Mannion was asked if the entirety of Ramirez's tenure with the Dodgers had been worth the cost and trouble, he said, "Oh my gosh, absolutely. He was a plus for the club on the field and on the ticket-sales front." Colletti agreed. "He helped the franchise get back to the playoffs and helped us win a couple of series, in '08 and '09. He accomplished a lot here. He showed a lot of our younger players how to win and how to play."[5]

In October 2010, owner Frank McCourt replaced Dennis Mannion as club president.

December 15, 2010: Free Agent Catcher Russell Martin Signed with the New York Yankees

Russell Martin had been the Dodgers' catcher for the past five seasons. In the first four he appeared in 121, 151, 155, and 143 games. Martin had managed to stay off the disabled list until August 4, 2010, after he tore a hip muscle the previous day. The injury ended the season for Martin, his first poor one. He played in only 97 games, with a .248 batting average, five home runs, and 26 runs batted in. The Dodgers were unsure about the 28-year-old Martin's ability to make a full recovery from his injury and chose not to offer him arbitration, making him a free agent. Shortly thereafter, Martin's agent, Matt Colleran, said six teams had contacted him. Martin chose the New York Yankees. He received a one-year, $4 million contract that included performance-based incentives that could make the contract worth as much as $5.375 million. The Yankees expected him to replace 40-year-old Jorge Posada as their starting catcher in 2011.

Martin said it was hard to believe he was no longer a Dodger. "I think it's going to hit more once I'm in a different uniform. They're still my boys over there. I wish them the best of luck." Martin came up to the Dodgers around the same time as Matt Kemp, Andre Ethier, James Loney, and Chad Billingsley, a group known collectively as "The Kids." He said he felt the group fell short of what it set out to do. "We got to the playoffs, we had some good seasons," he said. "But the goal is to win the whole thing, so it's a little disappointing." Martin was, however, happy to be with the Yankees. "If you want a chance to win, I don't think there's any better place to play than in New York with the Yankees."[6]

Also in 2010:

Traded: Minor League Catcher Lucas May and Minor League Pitcher Elisaul Pimentel to Kansas City Royals for Outfielder Scott Podsednik; Pitcher James McDonald and Minor League Outfielder Andrew Lambo to Pittsburgh Pirates for Pitcher Octavio Dotel and Cash; Pitcher Octavio Dotel to Colorado Rockies for Minor League Outfielder Anthony Jackson; Shortstop Ryan Theriot to St. Louis Cardinals for Pitcher Blake Hawksworth; Infielder Chin-lung Hu to New York Mets for Minor League Pitcher Mike Antonini

Purchased: Catcher Rod Barajas from New York Mets

Sold: Pitcher Eric Stults to Hiroshima Toyo Carp of Japan Central League

Chosen in Amateur Free Agent Draft: Zach Lee; Joc Pederson; Scott Schebler; Leon Landry; Shawn Tolleson; Red Patterson; Noel Cuevas; Logan Bawcom; Jake Lemmerman

Signed Amateur Free Agents: Angel Sánchez

Signed Free Agents: Outfielder Jay Gibbons; Pitcher Nick Green; Pitcher Russ Ortiz; Outfielder Reed Johnson; Pitcher Ramón Ortiz; Outfielder Garret Anderson; Pitcher Jack Taschner; Outfielder Trent Oeltjen; Infielder Juan Castro (retired in 2011); Catcher Héctor Giménez; Infielder Juan Uribe; Outfielder Tony Gwynn, Jr.; Outfielder-Second Baseman Eugenio Vélez; Pitcher Jon Garland; Catcher Dioner Navarro; Pitcher Matt Guerrier; Pitcher Dana Eveland

Released: Pitcher Jason Repko; First Baseman Doug Mientkiewicz; Pitcher Russ Ortiz; Pitcher Ramon Ortiz; Pitcher Nick Green; Pitcher Claudio Vargas; Second Baseman Ronnie Belliard; Pitcher Brent Leach

Left as Free Agents: Outfielder Garret Anderson; Pitcher Jack Taschner; Pitcher Justin Miller; Catcher Brad Ausmus (retired); Outfielder Reed Johnson; Pitcher Jeff Weaver; Outfielder Scott Podsednik; Pitcher Charlie Haeger; Pitcher Cory Wade; Pitcher George Sherrill

2011

For the 2011 season, Don Mattingly replaced Joe Torre as manager.

July 31, 2011: Traded Shortstop Rafael Furcal to the St. Louis Cardinals for Minor League Outfielder Alex Castellanos

The rumored trade that would send Dodgers shortstop Rafael Furcal to the St. Louis Cardinals for minor league outfielder Alex Castellanos was completed just before the trading deadline. The 33-year-old Furcal waived his no-trade rights to move to the contending Cardinals. He had played six seasons with Los Angeles, compiling a .283 batting average with 109 stolen bases. The Dodgers made the deal to open a spot in their infield for rookie Dee Gordon. After opening the season with the club, Gordon was sent to Triple A Albuquerque but was recalled after batting .333 in 70 games. Gordon would take over the shortstop position while Jamey Carroll, who had been playing there, would move to second base.

"I'm going to come in and do the same thing I did the first time I was here," said the 23-year-old Gordon. "I'm the same person, the same player. I just want to help the Dodgers win games." GM Ned Colletti said of the departing Furcal: "Now he gets an opportunity to play, we get financial savings on it and most importantly, we get to watch Dee Gordon and not have a situation where you have a veteran watching a kid play every day."[7]

Outfielder Alex Castellanos was a Texas League All-Star who was batting .319 with 19 home runs and 62 runs batted in for the Springfield (MO) Cardinals. Colletti described him as possessing power and speed. The Dodgers sent Castellanos to the Chattanooga Lookouts of the Southern League, where he continued to impress, batting .322 with a 1.009 OPS in 32 games. But Castellanos could not duplicate that success in the major leagues. His big-league career consisted of 24 games and a .171 batting average with a .576 OPS over the 2012 and 2013 seasons.

November 15, 2011: Signed Free Agent Second Baseman Mark Ellis

Second baseman Mark Ellis was in his ninth season with the Oakland Athletics when they traded him to the Colorado Rockies on June 30, 2011.

Ellis, 34, batted a combined .248 for the year. That was below the .265 average he had in 1,056 games with the A's and the .274 average he had with the Rockies in the second half of 2011. But the Dodgers wanted Ellis more for his defense and signed him to a two-year contract that would pay him $2.5 million in 2012 and $5.25 million in 2013.

When GM Ned Colletti was asked why he would pay that much for Ellis, he explained that a run on middle infielders had raised their asking price. He said defense was a priority at second base. More and more, clubs were taking advantage of analytical methods of judging what players could contribute to a team's success. An analysis of advanced defensive metrics by new front-office executive Alex Tamin indicated that overall, Ellis would be a significant upgrade at second base.

November 29, 2011: Free Agent Pitcher Jonathan Broxton Signed with the Kansas City Royals

Jonathan Broxton, the Dodgers' second-round pick in the 2002 draft, made his major league debut in 2005. Used originally as setup man, he replaced Takashi Saito as the closer in 2008. Broxton thrived in that role, twice being selected to the 2009 and 2010 National League All-Star teams. Broxton was at his peak in the first half of the 2010 season, with an 0.83 earned run average through his first 33 games. But he was never the same after a 48-pitch appearance against the New York Yankees on June 27 of that year. He had trouble with his control, and when he threw strikes, batters were getting hits against him more often. This past season was the 27-year-old Broxton's worst. In 12⅔ innings over 14 games, he allowed 15 hits and issued nine walks. Broxton's poor 2011 season was due in part to recurring right elbow problems. The Dodgers put him on the disabled list in early May and on September 19 he underwent arthroscopic surgery on the elbow. For his seven seasons in Los Angeles, he won 25, lost 20, had 84 saves, and had an ERA+ of 132.

Broxton signed a one-year contract believed to be worth $4 million with an added $1 million in incentives. Kansas City GM Dayton Moore said the Royals would use Broxton in a setup role for closer Joakim Soria. "We felt it was important for us to be in a position to shorten games as best we can," Moore said. "You don't know," Moore said when asked about Broxton's health. "But our medical team feels like there's no doubt in their mind that he'll come back to his accustomed level. Obviously, he has to go out and perform."[8]

Also in 2011

Traded: Minor League Outfielder Trayvon Robinson to Seattle Mariners in a three-team trade and received Minor League Catcher Tim Federowicz, Minor League Pitcher Stephen Fife, and Minor League Pitcher Juan Rodriguez from the Boston Red Sox; Pitcher Dana Eveland to Baltimore Orioles for Minor League Pitcher Jarret Martin and Minor League Infielder-Outfielder Tyler Henson

Purchased: Outfielder Juan Rivera from Toronto Blue Jays

Sold: Outfielder Xavier Paul to Pittsburgh Pirates; Sold Outfielder Jamie Hoffman to Colorado Rockies

Chosen in Amateur Free Agent Draft: Scott McGough; Stefan Jarrin; Ryan O'Sullivan; Chris Reed

Signed Amateur Free Agents: O'Koyea Dickson

Signed Free Agents: Outfielder Marcus Thames; Pitcher Mike MacDougal; Infielder Aaron Miles; Pitcher Lance Cormier; Catcher Matt Treanor; Infielder Luis Cruz; Second Baseman Adam Kennedy; Pitcher Chris Capuano; Infielder-Outfielder Jerry Hairston; Pitcher Aaron Harang

Released: Pitcher Lance Cormier; Outfielder Marcus Thames; Catcher Dioner Navarro

Left as Free Agents: Outfielder Jay Gibbons; Catcher Héctor Giménez; Catcher Rod Barajas; Third Baseman Casey Blake; Infielder Jamey Carroll; Pitcher Hiroki Kuroda; Infielder Aaron Miles; Pitcher Vicente Padilla; Pitcher Jon Link; First Baseman John Lindsey; Pitcher Travis Schlichting; Outfielder-Second Baseman Eugenio Vélez; Pitcher Hong-Chih Kuo

2012

In Early 2012, Major League Baseball owners approved the sale of the Dodgers from Frank McCourt to the Guggenheim Partners. Mark Walter was the principal owner and Stan Kasten was named president.

June 28, 2012: Signed Outfielder Yasiel Puig as a Non-Drafted Free Agent

In its first big move the Baseball Management division of the Guggenheim Partners, the Dodgers' new owners, signed outfielder Yasiel Puig to a

$42 million, seven-year contract. Puig, a 21-year-old Cuban defector, had not played organized baseball in more than a year. Yet he was paid more than two other recent Cuban defectors, Yoenis Cespedes of the Oakland Athletics (four years, $36 million) and Jorge Soler of the Chicago Cubs (nine years, $30 million). The contract was the most lucrative ever given to a Cuban amateur, a statement that the Dodgers would again be active in an international market that was neglected under Frank McCourt's ownership.

The 6'2" right-handed-hitting Puig was a major star in Cuba but was suspended from the country's top league for the 2011–12 season for attempting to leave the country. Because he was unable to practice while suspended, Puig fell out of shape, said his agent, Jaime Torres. When he worked out for major league teams on arriving in Mexico City the previous weekend, Puig had not held a bat in five months. The Dodgers had scouted him before his suspension but did not think he would be ready to play for them this season.

New team president Stan Kasten promised the Dodgers would spend money at all venues where they saw a chance to improve. "I promise you we'll explore everything. Look, as candid as we can be, we're the Dodgers. We're supposed to be big. We intend to be big. Will we look at big things? You bet." Reminded of the shortage of top-tier prospects in their farm system, what other teams would want in return for established players, Kasten said, "I wish we were deeper in that regard. But if the resources involve money, we'll be very flexible."[9]

July 5, 2012: Traded Pitcher Nathan Eovaldi and Minor League Pitcher Scott McGough to the Miami Marlins for Shortstop Hanley Ramírez and Pitcher Randy Choate

In July 2008 the Dodgers traded for 36-year-old Manny Ramírez, a star player but one with a well-deserved reputation for being temperamental, failing to hustle, and making bad decisions. In July 2012, they traded for another Ramírez, Hanley, who was eight years younger but was usually described in the same way. The Dodgers acquired Ramírez, a right-handed-hitting shortstop, and pitcher Randy Choate from the Miami Marlins in exchange for second-year pitcher Nathan Eovaldi and minor league pitcher Scott McGough.

Ramírez was in his seventh season with the Marlins. He had a .300 batting average with a 129 OPS+. His 148 home runs and 230 stolen bases were reflective of his power and speed. Ramírez was the National League's

Rookie of the Year in 2006 and its batting champion (.342) in 2009. Albert Pujols was the league's unanimous MVP that year, with Ramírez finishing second. Injuries and disciplinary action limited him to 92 games and a .243 batting average in 2011. So far this season, he was batting .246 with 14 home runs and 48 runs batted in.

"I never thought I was going to be traded," Ramírez said. "It happens. It's a business. The only thing I can control is just going out there and playing hard every day." He said, "it's kind of hard" leaving Florida, but he viewed the Dodgers as a new beginning. "I'll do whatever for the ballclub to help them win." Ramírez had been a shortstop throughout his career, but manager Ozzie Guillen moved him to third base this season after the Marlins signed free agent shortstop José Reyes. Dodgers manager Don Mattingly said Ramírez would play shortstop for now, pending the return of the injured Dee Gordon. "I'm excited that he's here," said outfielder Matt Kemp. "Hanley has been one of the top hitters in the league in the last four years, and if we can get him on track to where he's been hitting in the past and get him going again, [he] will help us win a lot of baseball games."[10]

Randy Choate, 36, a left-handed relief pitcher in his twelfth major league season, had appeared in 440 games, all in relief, for five different teams. He had always been a middle-innings man, with only six saves in his career. Choate was having a fine season with Miami. He had a 2.49 earned run average in 44 games and had held opposing hitters to a .178 batting average, with left-handers batting only .150.

Nathan Eovaldi, a 22-year-old right-hander, had a 1–6 record and a 4.15 ERA this season, but the Dodgers had hoped to keep him. Veteran pitcher Ted Lilly said, "I really liked Nathan Eovaldi. I think they got a pretty special pitcher and a really good, hard-working, talented young man." General manager Ned Colletti said, "I hate to give up Nathan Eovaldi, somebody who's got a great future. You have to give up talent to acquire talent.... We're not going to let money stand in the way of a true baseball deal. We're not going to be reckless, do things just to do things, but when it comes down to strictly a baseball deal, we're going to have the right to do whatever we need to do. That's a tremendous position to be in."[11]

Scott McGough, a 22-year-old right-handed reliever, was 3–5 in 35 games for the Class A Rancho Cucamonga Quakes of the California League. The Marlins kept him in Class A, sending him to the Jupiter Hammerheads of the Florida State League. McGough made it to Miami for six games in 2015 and was 2–7 for the 2023 Arizona Diamondbacks.

August 25, 2012: Traded First Baseman James Loney; Second Baseman Ivan De Jesus, Jr.; Minor League Pitcher Allen Webster; and Two Players to be Named to the Boston Red Sox for Pitcher Josh Beckett, First Baseman Adrián González, Outfielder Carl Crawford, Infielder Nick Punto, and Cash

Los Angeles began the day in second place in the National League West, three games behind the San Francisco Giants. Before the day was over, they put together a major trade with the Boston Red Sox involving nine players and included an innovative financial component. The Dodgers acquired three former All-Stars, first baseman Adrián González, pitcher Josh Beckett, and outfielder Carl Crawford, along with infielder Nick Punto. Going to the Red Sox were first baseman James Loney; infielder Ivan De Jesus, Jr.; minor league pitcher Allen Webster; and two players to be named. After the season Boston received outfielder Jerry Sands and minor league pitcher Rubby De La Rosa. As part of the agreement the Dodgers would assume more than $260 million in salary obligations, despite Crawford's recent elbow surgery and Beckett's declining effectiveness.

González was the man the Dodgers wanted. They had asked about him before the July 31 non-waiver trade deadline and were turned down. They tried again after the Minnesota Twins declined their attempt to trade for their first baseman, Justin Morneau. In González's nine seasons with Texas, San Diego, and Boston, the 30-year-old left-handed slugger accumulated 210 home runs and 728 runs batted in while also earning three Gold Gloves. Pitcher Heath Bell of the Miami Marlins was González's teammate with the Padres. "You're going to get a class act," Bell said. "He definitely doesn't have Derek Jeter's name, but everybody says Derek Jeter is a class act, and Adrian is right up there. He's a hard worker. He's great in the community. He tries to help out the Hispanic community—but not just the Hispanic community, every community. He runs a lot of fundraisers. The community will love him."[12]

Carl Crawford joined the Tampa Bay Devil Rays as a 20-year-old in 2002 and had an outstanding nine-year career with them. He batted above .300 five times and led the American League in triples and stolen bases four times each. His composite batting average was .296, with 409 stolen bases and a 107 OPS+. In 2011, his first year with the Red Sox after signing as a free agent, Crawford batted just .255 and stole only 18 bases. His elbow injury limited him to 31 games this past season. Crawford batted .278 with 48 stolen bases and a 102 OPS+ in 320 games in his four years with the Dodgers. They released him in June 2016.

Josh Beckett began his career with the Florida Marlins in September

2001. He had a 41–34 record and a 118 ERA+ in five years with the Marlins. The highlight of his career with Florida was being named the Most Valuable Player in the Marlins 2003 World Series win over the New York Yankees. The Marlins traded Becket to the Red Sox following the 2005 season. He quickly became one of the top pitchers in the American League, helping lead Boston to the postseason in 2007, 2008, and 2009. Beckett had a 5–1 record in the various playoffs and the 2007 World Series and was named the Most Valuable Player of the 2007 American League Championship Series. During the regular season that year, he led the AL with 20 wins and finished second in the voting for the Cy Young Award. Overall, Beckett was 89–58 for Boston with a 109 ERA+. This season had been the worst of his career, a 5–11 record with an 81 ERA+. Injuries limited Beckett's effectiveness in his three years in LA. He made only 35 starts and had an 8–14 record. He was 6–6 in 2014, a season cut short by a recurring hip injury and chose to retire at age thirty-four.

Nick Punto, a 34-year-old utility infielder, appeared in 952 games in his career. Before joining the Red Sox this season, he played for Philadelphia (three years), Minnesota (seven years), and St. Louis (one year). At the time of the trade, he was batting .200 in 125 at-bats.

Left-handed-hitting James Loney, 28, was in his seventh season with the Dodgers and his fifth as their everyday first baseman. Loney left with a career batting average of .284 and an OPS+ of 105. This had been his worst season, a .254 average, four home run, and 33 RBIs, and a 79 OPS+; and he would be a free agent after the season. With the Dodgers looking for more power from the first base position, González was clearly an upgrade. "It's a little frustrating because you just think there's so much more there," said Dodgers manager Don Mattingly. "And I know James thinks there's more there. It's hard to have anything really negative to say about James because he's a great kid and he works really hard. He's giving us everything that he's got. It's not a matter of not wanting to or not trying to or not doing the work. It's just not coming out."[13]

Ivan De Jesus, Jr., was a 25-year-old middle infielder who made brief appearances with the Dodgers in 2011 and in 2012, batting .231 in 40 games. Right-hander Allen Webster, 22, was 6–8 with a 3.55 ERA for the Dodgers Double A affiliate in the Southern League, the Chattanooga Lookouts. He would make his Boston debut in April 2013.

December 9, 2012: Purchased Pitcher Hyun-Jin Ryu from Hanwha Eagles of the Korean Baseball Organization

Hyun-Jin Ryu became the first player to go directly from a Korean league to the major leagues after the Dodgers paid the Hanwha Eagles

$25.7 million for the rights to the 26-year-old left-hander. Confident that Ryu could be their No. 3 or No. 4 starter, they signed him to a six-year contract worth $36 million. Scott Boras, his agent, believed Ryu's transition to the majors would be easier than it would be for a pitcher from the Japanese leagues. "They have more power hitters," Boras said of the Korean league. "Pitching in Korea is a lot like pitching here."

The 6'3" Ryu, a seven-time All-Star with the Eagles, had a career record of 98–52 with a 2.80 earned run average. He expected he would continue to be an effective pitcher in the major leagues. "Obviously, there's pressure in all levels of baseball," he said through an interpreter. "But from my experiences in Korea, I have no doubt I could succeed in the United States."[14] Dodger Stadium would not be completely new to Ryu. He pitched there twice in relief in the 2009 World Baseball Classic.

December 10, 2012: Signed Free Agent Pitcher Zack Greinke

When Guggenheim Partners bought the Dodgers last spring, they announced a willingness to spend money to bring a championship to Los Angeles. This week they had demonstrated that willingness twice. Yesterday they spent more than $61 million to obtain the rights to and to sign pitcher Hyun-Jin Ryu, the first player ever to go directly from a Korean league to the major leagues. Today they signed 29-year-old right-hander Zack Greinke, the most sought-after pitcher in this year's free agent market, to a six-year, $147 million contract.

Greinke was the Kansas City Royals first pick in the 2002 amateur player draft. He spent seven years with the Royals (2004–2010); the best was 2009, when he won the Cy Young Award based on his 2.16 earned run average that was half the league total. (In other words, he allowed two fewer earned runs per games than the league average for pitchers.) The Royals traded Greinke to the Milwaukee Brewers after the 2010 season, who then traded him to the Anaheim Angels in July 2012. In those two seasons (2011–2012), Greinke won 31 games and lost 11. He finished the 2012 season with Anaheim going 5–0 with a 2.04 ERA in his last eight starts.

"We were definitely hoping for Zack," said Magic Johnson, a former player for the Los Angeles Lakers of the NBA and now a partner in Guggenheim Baseball Management. "When you put him together with Clayton [Kershaw], man, we feel really good. When we took over the team, we said we were going to spend money and I guess you guys are seeing that we're trying to do that," Johnson said.[15]

Newcomers Ryu and Greinke, added to holdovers Kershaw, Chad

Billingsley, Josh Beckett, Ted Lilly, Chris Capuano, and Aaron Harang, gave the Dodgers eight starting pitchers under contract for the 2013 season. "Feeling more fortunate than gluttonous" said general manager Ned Colletti. "It's better to be sitting where we're sitting than where we've been. It's rare you need just five [starting] pitchers." Colletti called Greinke the main addition. "We believe he brings a lot to this team and to a pitching staff that was already very good."[16]

People who knew Greinke called him highly intelligent but at times aloof. Ron Roenicke, his manager with Milwaukee, said: "Zack was one of the most interesting players that I've had and one of the most enjoyable players that I've had. He's brutally honest and he's going to make some comments at times that you're not going to be happy about. Then he turns around a couple days later and you talk and all of a sudden, you're laughing and really enjoying the guy."[17]

Also in 2012

Traded: Minor League Outfielder Leon Landry and Minor League Pitcher Logan Bawcom to Seattle Mariners for Pitcher Brandon League; Pitcher Josh Lindblom, Minor League Pitcher Ethan Martin, and Minor League Outfielder Stefan Jarrin to Philadelphia Phillies for Outfielder Shane Victorino; Minor League Pitcher Ryan O'Sullivan to Philadelphia Phillies for Pitcher Joe Blanton; Minor League Infielder Jake Lemmerman to St. Louis Cardinals for Infielder-Outfielder Skip Schumaker; Pitcher John Ely to Houston Astros for Minor League Pitcher Rob Rasmussen

Chosen in Amateur Free Agent Draft: Corey Seager; Paco Rodríguez; Onelki García; Ross Stripling; Daniel Coulombe; Jharel Cotton; Dalton Von Schamann; Zachary Bird; Darnell Sweeney; Joey Curletta

Signed Amateur Free Agents: Victor González; Julio Urias; Miguel Rojas; Jesmuel Valentin

Signed Free Agents: Pitcher Todd Coffey; Pitcher Jamey Wright; Outfielder Bobby Abreu

Released: Pitcher Carlos Monasterios; Pitcher Mike MacDougal

Left as Free Agents: Outfielder Trent Oeltjen; Pitcher Blake Hawksworth; Outfielder Bobby Abreu; Pitcher Joe Blanton; Pitcher Randy Choate; Pitcher Todd Coffey; Second Baseman Adam Kennedy; Catcher Matt Treanor; Outfielder Shane Victorino; Pitcher Ramón Troncoso; Third Baseman Russ Mitchell

2013

November 25, 2013: Signed Free Agent Pitcher Dan Haren

Free-agent pitchers had done particularly well this offseason. Tim Lincecum re-signed with the San Francisco Giants for $35 million over two seasons, and Jason Vargas, despite a career earned run average of 4.30, signed a four-year, $32 million deal with the Kansas City Royals. Teams seemed willing to sign even those pitchers recovering from injuries. The Giants signed Tim Hudson, who fractured his ankle in July, to a two-year, $23-million contract, and the San Diego Padres signed Josh Johnson, who was coming back from elbow surgery to a one-year contract worth $8 million.

The biggest prize on the market, right-hander Masahiro Tanaka of the Japan Pacific League, remained unsigned. The Dodgers were one of several teams seriously pursuing Tanaka, who would later sign with the New York Yankees. While the pursuit continued, they signed veteran pitcher Dan Haren to a one-year, $10 million deal, plus an opportunity to raise the value of the contract. If Haren pitched 180 innings, he would have an option for 2015 worth another $10 million. He could also earn an additional $3 million each season in performance-based incentives.

GM Ned Colletti was pleased to have signed one of the few starting pitchers on the free agent market who would agree to a one-year deal. And, he would not have to forfeit a draft pick to do so. The Dodgers now had five starting pitchers under contract for 2014, including Chad Billingsley and Josh Beckett who were recovering from major operations. Haren said he was not concerned about his place in the rotation. He said Colletti told him the team intended for him to be one of its five starters. "I'm not going to be looking over my shoulder," said the 33-year-old right-hander. Haren acknowledged he was surprised by the health of the market. "The numbers out there, the millions of dollars getting paid is ridiculous," he said, while pointing out television revenue was increasing and pitching was always in short supply.[18]

Haren had pitched for the Cardinals, Athletics, Diamondbacks, Angels, and Nationals in his 11-year career. A three-time all-star, he had a 129–111 record with double-digit win totals in nine of those eleven seasons. His record with Washington in 2013 was 10–14 with a 4.67 ERA.

Also in 2013:

Traded: Pitcher Aaron Harang to Colorado Rockies for Catcher Ramón Hernández; Pitcher Matt Guerrier to Chicago Cubs for Pitcher Carlos Marmol; Pitcher Josh Wall, Minor League Pitcher Steve Ames, and Minor League Pitcher Angel Sánchez to Miami Marlins for Pitcher Ricky Nolasco and Cash; Minor League Pitcher Miguel Sulbaran to Minnesota Twins for Catcher Drew Butera; Minor League Pitcher Rob Rasmussen to Philadelphia Phillies for Infielder Michael Young and Cash; Outfielder Alex Castellanos to Boston Red Sox for Minor League Outfielder Jeremy Hazelbaker

Purchased: Outfielder Mike Baxter from New York Mets

Sold: Outfielder Elián Herrera to Milwaukee Brewers; Pitcher Shawn Tolleson to Texas Rangers

Chosen in Amateur Free Agent Draft: Cody Bellinger; Kyle Farmer; Tom Windle; Greg Harris; Brandon Dixon; José De León; Jacob Rhame

Signed Amateur Free Agents: Dennis Santana; Alex Guerrero, Victor Arano

Signed Free Agents: Pitcher J.P. Howell; Pitcher Peter Moylan; Pitcher Brian Wilson; Pitcher Edinson Volquez; Outfielder Clint Robinson; Outfielder Jamie Romak; Pitcher Josh Ravin; Pitcher Chris Pérez

Released: Catcher Ramon Hernandez; Pitcher Ted Lilly

Left as Free Agents: Infielder Louis Cruz; Pitcher Chris Capuano; Outfielder Tony Gwynn, Jr.; Pitcher Ronald Belisario; Infielder-Outfielder Skip Schumaker; Infielder Nick Punto; Infielder-Outfielder Jerry Hairston; Infielder Luis Cruz; Pitcher Edinson Volquez; Pitcher Carlos Marmol; Outfielder Juan Rivera

2014

February 6, 2014: Signed Free Agent Third Baseman Justin Turner

The Dodgers signed free agent Justin Turner, 29, to a minor league contract with an invitation to their major league spring training camp. The versatile right-handed-hitting Turner could play any infield position, which gave him a strong chance to break camp with the parent club. Turner debuted with the 2009 Baltimore Orioles and was sold to the New York Mets in May 2010. In 301 games for the Mets, he batted .265, but showed little power—eight home runs and 86 runs batted in. Turner hit .280 last season with two home runs and 16 RBIs in 86 games.

On October 14, 2014, Andrew Friedman was hired to be the president of Baseball Operations.

On November 6, Farhan Zaidi was named general manager under president of baseball operations Andrew Friedman.

December 11, 2014: Traded Second Baseman Dee Gordon, Pitcher Dan Haren, Shortstop Miguel Rojas, and Cash to the Miami Marlins for Pitcher Andrew Heaney, Pitcher Chris Hatcher, Infielder-Outfielder Enrique "Kiké" Hernández, and Minor League Catcher Austin Barnes

New president of baseball operations Andrew Friedman began a flurry of personnel changes by completing a seven-player trade with the Miami Marlins. The Dodgers sent second baseman Dee Gordon, shortstop Miguel Rojas, pitcher Dan Haren, and cash to Miami in exchange for pitchers Andrew Heaney and Chris Hatcher, Infielder-Outfielder Enrique "Kiké" Hernández and minor league catcher Austin Barnes.

Gordon, who would turn 27 in April, was coming off an excellent 2014 season. Playing a full season for the first time in his four years with the club, he batted .289 in 148 games, led the major leagues with 64 steals and 12 triples, and made the All-Star team. However, Friedman was a great believer in the more analytical approach to player evaluations that was taking place across baseball. He had used analytics to build strong teams in Tampa Bay, a franchise with limited financial resources. The Dodgers' analysts were alarmed at Gordon's performance in the season's second half. He drew only four walks in 57 games after the All-Star break, a major factor in a disappointing .300 on-base percentage during that stretch. They believed Gordon had peaked, but his 2015 season with the Marlins would be the best of his career. He led the league in batting (.333), hits (205), and again in stolen bases (58). Gordon would have several more successful years with the Marlins and the Seattle Mariners.

In his one season with the Dodgers, Dan Haren won 13, lost 11, and had a subpar 87 ERA+. The 34-year old Haren, who lived in Orange County, had said he would retire if traded to a team other than the Los Angeles Angels. "My strong desire to remain in southern California has been well-documented. I will have to evaluate my options carefully before making any decisions."[19] His decision was to go to Miami. In what would be his final season, Haren had a 7–7 record with the Marlins before being traded to the Chicago Cubs on July 31. He won four of six decisions with the Cubs.

Twenty-five-year-old Miguel Rojas was primarily a shortstop but played second base and third base when needed. Rojas was batting .302 at Triple A Albuquerque when the Dodgers called him up in June. He was not nearly as successful against major league pitching, appearing in 85 games with a .181 batting average and a 34 OPS+. Rojas would play eight years for the Marlins before they traded him back to the Dodgers in 2023.

Andrew Heaney, a 23-year-old left-hander, was considered one of the game's top pitching prospects entering the 2014 season. But he had not lived up to expectations. Heaney was 0–3 in seven games for Miami in 2014. Later in the day the Dodgers traded him to the Los Angeles Angels for 31-year-old infielder-outfielder Howie Kendrick.

Chris Hatcher, a 30-year-old-right-handed reliever, pitched briefly for the Marlins from 2011 to 2013 and fulltime in 2014. He lost his only three decisions in 2014 but had a respectable 110 ERA+. Hatcher made 112 relief appearances for the Dodgers from 2015 until he was traded to Oakland on August 15, 2017. He had an 8–10 record with an 86 ERA+.

Enrique "Kiké" Hernández, 23, played second base, third base, and left field for the Houston Astros and Marlins as a rookie in 2014. He batted a combined .248 with 3 home runs, 14 RBIs, and a 108 OPS+ in 42 games.

Austin Barnes, a 25-year-old catcher who could also play the infield, split the 2014 season between two of the Marlins farm teams located in Florida: The Class A Jupiter Hammerheads of the Florida State League and the Class AA Jacksonville Suns of the Southern League. Barnes batted a combined .304 with 13 home runs and 57 RBIs.

Barnes made his Dodgers debut in 2015 and has been with the club ever since. Primarily a weak-hitting backup catcher, he played in just 599 games through 2024, with a .223 batting average and an 81 OPS+. Barnes's best year was in 2017, his first full season as a Dodger. Appearing in a career-high 102 games, he batted .289 with 38 runs batted in and an OPS+ of 138. Each of those offensive measurements were career highs that Barnes has yet to come close to again.

December 11, 2014: Traded Pitcher Andrew Heaney to the Los Angeles Angels for Infielder-Outfielder Howie Kendrick

The Dodgers needed a second baseman to replace Dee Gordon, whom they traded to Miami earlier in the day. They used left-hander Andrew Heaney, acquired in that trade, to secure Howie Kendrick to replace

Gordon. Kendrick, 31, had been with the Angels for nine seasons. Over that time, he had a .292 batting average, 78 home runs, 501 runs batted, and a 108 OPS+. Kendrick was instrumental in the Angels winning the American League West this past season, with a .293 average, 85 runs, and 75 RBIs.

"It will be difficult to replace Howie, he's been one of the more productive offensive players in the league at his position," said Angels GM Jerry Dipoto. "We just felt like with one year of control of Howie as a pending free agent, compared to six years of control with Andrew Heaney, it was impossible to walk away from a left-handed starter who has a top-of-the-rotation upside.... Andrew is a premium prospect who is just starting to cut his teeth in the major leagues. He's a really polished left-hander who we feel has a chance to pitch up in our rotation."[20]

Kendrick played second base for the Dodgers in 2015 but moved to left field in 2016 to make room for Chase Utley. He batted a combined .274 in 263 games, with 16 home runs and 94 runs batted in. In November 2016 the Dodgers traded him to Philadelphia.

December 16, 2014: Signed Free Agent Pitcher Brandon McCarthy

By trading Dan Haren to Miami earlier in the week, the Dodgers were left without a fourth starter to follow Clayton Kershaw, Zack Greinke, and Hyun-Jin Ryu. Hoping that man would be Brandon McCarthy, they signed the 6'8" right-hander to a four-year, $48 million contract. They made roster room by designating reliever Brian Wilson for assignment. McCarthy grew up rooting for the Dodgers and was grateful for the opportunity to join the NL West champions.

"There was nothing that didn't intrigue me about the Dodgers," he said. "I grew up 10 miles from the stadium. The Dodgers were what I knew, who I looked up to as a kid."[21] The 31-year-old McCarthy had idolized former Dodgers pitcher Orel Hershiser and remembered getting Hershiser's autograph at Disneyland as a high point of his youth. Having played for five teams in his first nine years, McCarthy was thrilled by the Dodgers' four-year commitment. "It was a very big thing for me, because having that stop-start identity with each organization, it weighs on you," McCarthy said. He added that he wanted "to have a chance to actually make a name for myself and actually leave an identity and a long-term reputation with a team."[22]

McCarthy had a career record of 52–65 and 4.09 earned run average pitching for the White Sox, the Rangers, the Athletics, the Diamondbacks, and the Yankees. He split the 2014 season between the Diamondbacks and the Yankees, going 3–10 with a 5.01 ERA for Arizona and 7–5 with a 2.89 ERA for the Yankees.

December 18, 2014: Traded Outfielder Matt Kemp and Catcher Tim Federowicz to San Diego Padres for Catcher Yasmani Grandal, Pitcher Joe Wieland, and Minor League Pitcher Zach Eflin

A deal the Dodgers had been negotiating with their division rival San Diego Padres for a while became final just before each team's self-imposed deadline. The five-player trade sent centerfielder Matt Kemp and catcher Tim Federowicz to San Diego for catcher Yasmani Grandal, pitcher Joe Wieland, and minor league pitcher Zach Eflin. (The Dodgers would cover $32 million of the $107 million Kemp was guaranteed over the next five seasons.) An agreement had been reached at last week's winter meetings, but because the Padres had concerns about the 30-year-old Kemp's health, it could not be completed until Kemp underwent a physical examination. The Padres requested the examination because of Kemp's major shoulder surgery after the 2012 season and his career-threatening ankle surgery the following winter. In addition, the Padres were worried enough about Kemp's arthritic hips to have come close to canceling the deal.

Matt Kemp had been one of the Dodgers most popular players since joining them in 2006. In his 10 seasons in Los Angeles, the 6'4" right-handed hitter batted .292 with 203 home runs and 733 runs batted in and won the Gold Glove and Silver Slugger Awards twice each. A two-time All-Star, he had one of the franchise's best all-around offensive seasons in 2011 and was the runner-up to Milwaukee's Ryan Braun in the MVP voting. Kemp hit .324 with a league-leading 172 OPS+. He also led the league in home runs (39), RBIs (126), runs (115), and total bases (353). He also had 40 stolen bases. Barring further moves, Kemp's departure indicated the Dodgers 2015 starting outfield would likely be Yasiel Puig in right field, Carl Crawford in left field, and top prospect Joc Pederson in center field.

When he was asked about trading a player as popular as Kemp, president of baseball operations Andrew Friedman replied: "Sure. He was a really popular player because of how gifted he is offensively. We get it. I have a lot of respect for what he can do in the batter's box. You have to give up talent to get talent, and we felt this put us in a position to be a better baseball team."[23]

Tim Federowicz, a backup catcher to A.J. Ellis the past two seasons, had a .194 batting average and a 54 OPS+ in 89 games spread over four seasons. He would miss the 2015 season but play for five different teams from 2016 to 2019.

The Dodgers were looking to upgrade the catching position and chose Yasmani Grandal for the role. Grandal, a 26-year-old switch-hitter, batted .225 with a 111 OPS+ as the Padres No. 1 catcher in 2014. But Grandal came with baggage. After batting .297 with a 143 OPS+ in 60 games as a rookie in 2012, he was suspended for 50 games in 2013 for using PEDs. Along with his disappointing .225 average this season, Padres pitchers had voiced a preference to pitch to Rene Rivera, the team's other catcher.

Twenty-five-year-old right-hander Joe Wieland had a 1–4 record with a 5.31 earned run average in nine games (seven starts) in brief stays with San Diego in 2012 and 2014. He was 0–1 in two starts for the 2015 Dodgers and was traded to Seattle after the season. Zach Eflin's career as a Dodger would be a short one; a day later the Dodgers traded him to the Philadelphia Phillies for shortstop Jimmy Rollins.

December 19, 2014: Traded Minor League Pitcher Zach Eflin and Minor League Pitcher Tom Windle to the Philadelphia Phillies for Shortstop Jimmy Rollins

A day after the Matt Kemp to San Diego trade was completed, the Dodgers traded newly acquired 21-year-old Zach Eflin, a 6'6" right-hander, to Philadelphia for veteran shortstop Jimmy Rollins. Also going to the Phillies was minor league pitcher Tom Windle, a 23-year-old left-hander who would never reach the major leagues.

Rollins would replace departed free agent Hanley Ramírez at shortstop, and along with the change from Dee Gordon to Howie Kendrick, the Dodgers would have a new double play combination for 2015. The thirty-six-year-old Rollins, a former National League MVP (2007), played in 2,090 games over his 15-year career with Phillies. A speedy switch-hitter—he led the league in triples four times—Rollins had a .267 batting average, 453 stolen bases, and a 97 OPS+. In his one season in LA, he hit .224, his career-low average (to that point), stole only 12 bases, and had a 79 OPS+. He signed as a free agent with the Chicago White for 2016, which would be his final season.

Also in 2014:

Traded: Minor League Pitcher Dalton Von Schamann to Cleveland Indians for Pitcher Colt Hynes; Minor League Pitcher Jonathan Martinez to Chicago Cubs for Second Baseman Darwin Barney and Cash; Minor

League Infielder Jesmuel Valentin and Minor League Pitcher Victor Arano to Philadelphia Phillies for Pitcher Fausto Carmona; A Player to be Named or Cash to Minnesota Twins for Pitcher Kevin Correia; Pitcher José Domínguez and Minor League Pitcher Greg Harris to Tampa Bay Rays for Pitcher Joel Peralta and Minor League Pitcher Adam Liberatore; Outfielder Noel Cuevas to Colorado Rockies for Pitcher Juan Nicasio; Pitcher Matt Magill to Cincinnati Reds for Outfielder Chris Heisey; Catcher Drew Butera to Anaheim Angels for Minor League Outfielder Matt Long

Purchased: Shortstop Carlos Triunfel from Seattle Mariners; Pitcher Mike Bolsinger from Arizona Diamondbacks

Sold: Infielder Justin Sellers to Cleveland Indians; Pitcher Javy Guerra to Chicago White Sox; Outfielder Nick Buss to Oakland Athletics; Pitcher Colt Hynes to Toronto Blue Jays; Pitcher Onelki García to Chicago White Sox

Chosen in Amateur Free Agent Draft: Alex Verdugo; Brock Stewart; Caleb Ferguson; Trevor Oaks; Jeff Brigham; John Richy; Grant Holmes

Signed Amateur Free Agents: Erisbel Arruebarrena; Keibert Ruiz

Signed Free Agents: Catcher Miguel Olivo; Infielder-Outfielder Chone Figgins; First Baseman Aaron Bates; Pitcher Paul Maholm; Outfielder Roger Bernadina; Pitcher Brett Anderson

Released: Catcher Miguel Olivo; Infielder-Outfielder Chone Figgins; Pitcher Brian Wilson

Left as Free Agents: Outfielder Clint Robinson; Outfielder Roger Bernadina; Pitcher Scott Elbert; Outfielder Jamie Romak; Shortstop Carlos Triunfel; Outfielder Mike Baxter; Pitcher Kevin Correia; Pitcher Carlos Marmol

13

2015–2019

2015

July 30, 2015: Traded Pitcher Paco Rodríguez, Minor League Third Baseman Héctor Olivera, and Minor League Pitcher Zachary Bird to the Atlanta Braves, and Minor League Pitcher Jeff Brigham, Minor League Pitcher Kevin Guzman, and Minor League Pitcher Victor Araujo to the Miami Marlins in a Three-Way Deal that brought them Infielder-Outfielder José Peraza, Pitcher Alex Wood, Pitcher Bronson Arroyo, Pitcher Jim Johnson, Pitcher Luis Avilán, and Cash from Atlanta, and Pitcher Matt Latos and Infielder-Outfielder Michael Morse from Miami

The Dodgers were in a close race with the Giants for the lead in the National League West. They hoped to boost their chances by acquiring one of the three top pitchers available at the trading deadline: Cincinnati's Johnny Cueto, Detroit's David Price, or Philadelphia's Cole Hamels. They missed out on all three. Cueto was traded to Kansas City, Hamels to Texas, and Price to Toronto. Instead, the club traded for two pitchers a cut below those three—right-hander Mat Latos and left-hander Alex Wood—as part of a three-team trade with Atlanta and Miami. The trade of 13 players was a franchise record.

Seven players came to the Dodgers, including Latos from the Marlins and Wood from the Braves, and six left, none of whom were on their 25-man roster. Infielder-outfielder Michael Morse came from Miami with Latos, while infielder-outfielder José Peraza, pitcher Bronson Arroyo, pitcher Jim Johnson, pitcher Luis Avilán, and an undisclosed amount of money accompanied Wood from Atlanta.

Before coming to Miami this season, the 6'6", 27-year-old Latos spent three years with the San Diego Padres and three with the Cincinnati Reds. He had a combined 64–52 record that included three 14-win seasons. In his half-season with the Marlins, Latos had a 4–7 record with a 4.48 earned run average. Wood, 24, was 7–6 with a 3.54 ERA for the Braves this season, his third with the club. He had an overall 21–20 record with a 119 ERA+. President of baseball operations Andrew Friedman said he was happy to have a pitching rotation of Clayton Kershaw, Zack Greinke, Brett Anderson, Latos, and Wood. "We feel like every day with our rotation, we have a chance to win."[1]

After designating veteran Michael Morse for assignment, Los Angeles traded him the next day. Morse and cash went to Pittsburgh for outfielder Jose Tabata, currently at Triple A Indianapolis. The Dodgers kept Tabata at Triple A, shifting him to Oklahoma City where he remained until they released him in June 2016. He never returned to the major leagues.

Infielder José Peraza was the most highly regarded of the other players coming from Atlanta. Peraza had hit well in each of his five seasons in the Braves farm system, but the Dodgers had no room for him and sent him to their Triple A club in Oklahoma City. Peraza got into seven big-league games for Los Angeles during the season before being traded to Cincinnati in December.

Thirty-eight-year-old pitcher Bronson Arroyo had undergone Tommy John surgery in June and was placed on the 60-day disabled list. He would never get into a game with the Dodgers and left as a free agent in December.

Jim Johnson, 32, was a 6'6" right-hander in his tenth big league season, mostly with Baltimore, where he led the American League in saves in 2012 and 2013. Johnson was ineffective with Oakland and Detroit in 2014, but had regained his form this year with Atlanta, with nine saves and an ERA+ of 172. Whatever Johnson found in Atlanta, he lost in Los Angeles, going 0–3 with a 37 ERA+ in 23 games. The Dodgers released him after the season.

Left-hander Luis Avilán, 26, was in his fourth season as a successful middle-innings reliever with the Braves—a combined 12–5 record with a 137 ERA+ in 218 games.

Right-handed reliever Paco Rodríguez pitched in 124 games over four seasons with the Dodgers. Despite a mediocre 4–5 record and two saves, he had a sparkling 144 ERA+. His major league career was now ended.

Friedman felt that the Dodgers' biggest loss was minor league infielder Héctor Olivera, whom he had signed to a $62.5 million contract in May. The Braves brought Olivera up immediately, but he played in just 30 games over the next two seasons, batting .245 with an 85 OPS+.

The other Dodgers dealt to Atlanta, pitchers Kevin Guzman, Victor Araujo, and Jeff Bingham, were minor league pitchers. Only Bingham would reach the major leagues.

"We feel we've solidified our bullpen; we lengthened our starting pitching options and think we're in better position than we were a couple of days ago," Friedman said. "We feel good about what we've done to date, but we're by no means sitting back and kicking our feet up and exhaling. We're still going and having conversations and working through things."[2]

Mat Latos pitched well in his first start as a Dodger, but in his next five appearances he went 0–3 with an 8.35 ERA. On September 17 the Dodgers designated him for assignment and released him a week later. The club was unhappy with Latos, and Latos was unhappy with being removed from the rotation. Overall, he pitched in six games with an 0–3 record and an ERA of 6.66.

August 19, 2015: Traded Outfielder Darnell Sweeney and Minor League Pitcher John Richy to the Philadelphia Phillies for Second Baseman Chase Utley and Cash

Philadelphia Phillies second baseman Chase Utley was struggling through the worst year of his career when Los Angeles acquired him, along with $4 million, for two minor leaguers. The Dodgers wanted the 36-year-old Utley to fill the void at second base until Howie Kendrick recovered from a strained left hamstring. Kiké Hernández had filled that role, but the Dodgers wanted to move Hernández to the outfield, where he would give them a right-handed-hitting alternative to slumping rookie Joc Pederson. The left-handed-hitting Utley, a six-time All-Star and four-time Silver Slugger, was one of the most beloved players in Phillies history. He had a .282 batting average and a 122 OPS+ in his 13 seasons with Philadelphia. But he had slipped sharply this year—a .217 average with five home runs, 30 runs batted in, and a 71 OPS in 73 games. Philadelphia was ready to replace him with 25-year-old César Hernández.

No one connected to the Dodgers was more pleased with the addition of Utley than shortstop Jimmy Rollins, his longtime double-play partner with Philadelphia. "He has a chance to play some meaningful baseball late in the year again," Rollins said. "That's what we all want." With Rollins at shortstop and Utley at second base, the Phillies won a World Series in 2008. "With me and Chase, we've done it for a long time together. I don't have to worry about him, I don't have to think about him. It's an unspoken language that middle infielders have. We have that trust and comfort."

When he was asked whether Utley had spoken to him about what it was like to play for the Dodgers, Rollins said, "We may have had a conversation or something. Those things remain between us."³ Recently acquired third baseman Alberto Callaspo was designated for assignment to clear a place for Utley on the 40-man roster.

The two minor league players sent to Philadelphia were outfielder Darnell Sweeney and pitcher John Richy. Sweeney, 24, was ranked among the top 20 players in the Dodgers farm system. He was currently with Oklahoma City of the Pacific Coast League, where he was batting .271. The Phillies called him up immediately. Richy, a 23-year-old right-hander, was 10–5 with a 4.20 earned-run average at Class A Rancho Cucamonga. He would never play in the major leagues.

Chase Utley played for the Dodgers through the 2018 season, in each of those four years the team reached the postseason. He batted .236 with an 88 OPS+ in 386 regular-season games. The Dodgers released the 39-year-old Utley following the 2018 season, the last of his career.

On November 23, 2015, Dave Roberts replaced Don Mattingly as manager.

December 16, 2015: Traded Infielder-Outfielder José Peraza, Outfielder Scott Schebler, and Minor League Outfielder-First Baseman Brandon Dixon to the Cincinnati Reds in a Three-Way Deal that brought them Pitcher Frankie Montas, Outfielder Trayce Thompson, and Second Baseman Micah Johnson from the Chicago White Sox

Although four of the players involved in the Dodgers second three-way trade of the year had limited major league experience, this deal was primarily the exchanging of three prospects for three other prospects. Leaving the Dodgers for the Cincinnati Reds were infielder-outfielder José Peraza, outfielder Scott Schebler, and minor league outfielder-first baseman Brandon Dixon, while coming from the Chicago White Sox were pitcher Frankie Montas, outfielder Trayce Thompson, and second baseman Micah Johnson.

President of baseball operations Andrew Friedman believed Montas, a 22-year-old right-hander, was the best of the three coming to Los Angeles. "Our scouts feel like his fastball-slider combination is one of the best in the minor leagues," Friedman said. "We feel like he has a chance to develop into a really good starting pitcher."⁴ Called up by the White Sox in September of this past season, Montas appeared in seven games, with an 0–2 record and a 4.80 earned run average.

Right-handed-hitting Trayce Thompson, Chicago's pick in the second round of the 2009 amateur free agent draft, made his big-league debut this past August. He batted .295 with five home runs and a 147 OPS+ in 44 games. Friedman was impressed with the 6'3", 25-year-old's athleticism and his ability to play center field. Thompson was essentially replacing Scott Schebler who could play only the corner outfield positions. He said he was not concerned with the speculation that the Dodgers would make him part of another trade. "I try not to pay attention to what's going on in the baseball world until something like that actually happens," Thompson said. "Wherever I end up, I'm going to play as hard as I can. Right now, I'm a Los Angeles Dodger."[5]

Second baseman Micah Johnson, 24, batted .230 in 36 games for the White Sox early in the season. They sent him to their Triple A team, the International League's Charlotte Knights, where the speedy Johnson had a .315 batting average and 28 stolen bases. Johnson would play seven games for the Dodgers in 2016, with one hit in six at-bats. In January 2017, they traded him to Atlanta.

Scott Schebler, a 25-year-old left-handed hitter, batted .250 in 19 games for the Dodgers this past season. He would play four seasons with the Reds and one season with the Braves and one with the Angels.

José Peraza, a 21-year-old utility player, batted .182 in seven games this past season. He, too, would play four seasons with the Reds and one season with two other teams: the Red Sox, and the Mets.

Brandon Dixon would not reach Cincinnati until 2018. After his one season with the Reds, he played two with the Tigers and two with the Padres.

Also in 2015:

Traded: Minor League Pitcher Blake Smith to Chicago White Sox for Pitcher Eric Surkamp; Third Baseman Juan Uribe and Pitcher Chris Withrow to Atlanta Braves for Third Baseman Alberto Callaspo, Pitcher Eric Stults, Pitcher Ian Thomas, and Pitcher Juan Jaime; Two International Bonus Slots to Toronto Blue Jays for Minor League Pitcher Chase De Jong and Minor League Outfielder Tim Locastro; Pitcher Chris Reed to Miami Marlins for Minor League Pitcher Grant Dayton; International Slot Money to Atlanta Braves for Pitcher Caleb Dirks; A Player to be Named or Cash to Seattle Mariners for Outfielder Justin Ruggiano and Cash; Second Baseman Darwin Barney to Toronto Blue Jays for Minor League Catcher Jack Murphy; A Player to be Named or Cash to Seattle Mariners for Pitcher Tyler Olson

Purchased: Pitcher Daniel Corcino from Cincinnati Reds; Pitcher

Matt West from Toronto Blue Jays; Minor League Infielder Ronald Torreyes from Toronto Blue Jays

Sold: Pitcher Daniel Coulombe to Oakland Athletics

Chosen in Amateur Free Agent Draft: Walker Buehler; Josh Sborcz; Edwin Rios; Matt Beaty; Kyle Garlick; Phil Pfeifer; Willie Calhoun; Brendon Davis; Tommy Bergjans; Jordan Tarsovich; Corey Copping; Andrew Sopko

Signed Amateur Free Agents: Héctor Olivera; Andrew Istler; Oneil Cruz; Jair Camargo

Signed Free Agents: Pitcher Chin-hui Tsao; Pitcher Sergio Santos; Pitcher David Huff; Pitcher Brandon Beachy; Pitcher Scott Baker; Outfielder Andrew Toles; Infielder Charlie Culberson; Outfielder Yusniel Díaz; Pitcher Scott Kazmir

Released: Pitcher Brandon League; Outfielder Chris Heisey; Third Baseman Alberto Callaspo; Pitcher Jim Johnson; Pitcher Scott Kazmir

Left as Free Agents: Pitcher Sergio Santos; Pitcher Brandon Beachy; Pitcher Bronson Arroyo; Pitcher Juan Nicasio; Outfielder Justin Ruggiano; Pitcher Eric Surkamp; Pitcher Joel Peralta; Pitcher Paul Maholm; Pitcher Jamey Wright

2016

January 7, 2016: Signed Free Agent Pitcher Kenta Maeda

Japanese born Kenta Maeda signed the longest contract ever offered by the Dodgers to a pitcher, eight years. This despite the results of his physical examination, which was deemed "irregular." Maeda, a 27-year-old right-hander, did not say what the problem was, but it was said to be in his pitching elbow. Maeda said he never had been out of action for an extended period in his eight seasons with the Hiroshima Carp of the Japan Western League. "I have absolutely no uncertainty," he said. "Zero."[6] Still, the Dodgers had structured his contract to be incentive-based. In addition to a $1 million signing bonus, Maeda was guaranteed $25 million over the next eight seasons; but if he remained healthy, he could earn more than $10 million a year in bonuses based on games started and innings pitched. The Dodgers also had to pay $20 million to the Hiroshima team.

Maeda, listed at 6'1" and 185 pounds, had missed no time this past season, when he had a record of 15–8 with a 2.09 earned run average and won the Japanese equivalent of the Cy Young Award. He said he hoped to pitch 200 innings in 2016. "The fact that he's totally asymptomatic, the fact that he pitched as recently as roughly six weeks ago, gives us as much confidence as we could have at this point that he will be a meaningful part of our team in 2016," said Andrew Friedman, the Dodgers president of baseball operations. "We're optimistic that he is going to help us win a lot of games over a lot of years."[7]

In eight seasons with Hiroshima, Maeda had a 100–68 record with a 2.42 earned run average. According to scouting reports, his strength was off-speed pitches, particularly a curve ball and a changeup. He was seen as a mid-level starter in the major leagues, rather than an ace.

August 1, 2016: Traded Pitcher Frankie Montas, Minor League Pitcher Jharel Cotton, and Minor League Pitcher Grant Holmes to the Oakland Athletics for Outfielder Josh Reddick and Pitcher Rich Hill

A trade with the Oakland Athletics that brought outfielder Josh Reddick and starting pitcher Rich Hill to the Dodgers strengthened the team at a seemingly cheap price. Going to Oakland were minor league pitchers Frankie Montas, Jharel Cotton, and Grant Holmes, all right-handers.

Reddick, a 29-year-old left-handed hitter, spent his first three major league seasons with Boston. He played in 143 games with a .243 batting average and 10 home runs. The Red Sox traded him to Oakland after the 2011 season. In his first season with the Athletics, Reddick hit 32 home runs, won a Gold Glove, and even got some votes for the American League's Most Valuable Player. In 68 games this season he was batting .296 with a 124 OPS+. "As far as our outfield picture, this is a team that is not unfamiliar to having healthy depth in the outfield," said Dodgers GM Farhan Zaidi. "We're just going to take it day by day and put out the lineup that gives us the best chance to win."[8] Reddick appeared in 47 games for the Dodgers, batting .258 with only two home runs and a 74 OPS+. He left as a free agent after the season.

Oakland was the seventh team left-hander Rich Hill had pitched for in his twelve-year major league career. Hill was a starter in his early years, with the Cubs and Orioles, before the Red Sox turned him into a full-time reliever in 2010. After Hill signed with the Athletics as a free agent this season, A's manager Bob Melvin returned him to a starting role. The change resulted in Hill being on the way to the best season of his career. In 14 starts, he had a 9–3 record and a 182 ERA+. The 36-year-old Hill was currently on the disabled list because of a blister on the middle finger of his pitching hand. He last pitched on July 17, when the blister ripped open during a start. "I can't wait to get back out there," Hill said. "To miss a couple weeks because of a blister is something else. But it's a big part of it. It's like the steering wheel of a car. You need it."[9] Zaidi said the Dodgers were unsure when Hill would be available. "We don't have an exact timetable on that, but obviously his availability in the short term was an important part of us moving ahead on this deal. So, we feel pretty good about it, but we don't have an exact date for when he'd be out there for us."[10] Hill returned to start six games, winning three and losing two with a 1.83 earned run average for the NL West champions.

Grant Holmes, 20, was the Dodgers' first-round pick in the 2014 amateur free agent draft. He would reach the major leagues with the Atlanta Braves in 2024. The Dodgers thought highly enough of 24-year-old Jharel Cotton to choose him to represent them at last month's Futures Game. Cotton pitched for the A's, Rangers, Twins, and Giant over the next four seasons, winning 17 and losing 12. He left after the 2022 season to pitch in Japan.

While the additions of Reddick and Hill helped the Dodgers win the NL West this season, they lost a fine young pitcher in 23-year-old Frankie Montas. Injuries and drug violations have prevented Montas from reaching his potential. Cincinnati's opening day starter in 2024, he was 4–8 with the Reds when they traded him to Milwaukee on July 30. His 3–3 record with the Brewers (his fifth team in nine seasons) gave Montas a career record of 44–46

Also in 2016:

Traded: Pitcher Joe Wieland to Seattle Mariners for Minor League Outfielder Erick Mejia; Pitcher Tyler Olson and Infielder Ronald Torreyes to New York Yankees for Minor League Outfielder-First Baseman Rob Segedin and a Player to be Named or Cash; Pitcher Zach Lee to Seattle Mariners for Shortstop Chris Taylor; Minor League Pitcher Phil Pfeifer and Minor League Pitcher Caleb Dirks to Atlanta Braves for Pitcher Bud Norris, Minor League Outfielder Dian Toscano, and Minor League Pitcher Alec Grosser; Minor League Outfielder Yordan Alvarez to Houston Astros for Pitcher Josh Fields; Pitcher Mike Bolsinger to Toronto Blue Jays for Pitcher Jesse Chavez; Catcher A.J. Ellis, Minor League Pitcher Tommy Bergjans, Minor League Outfielder Joey Curletta to Philadelphia Phillies for Catcher Carlos Ruiz and Cash; Catcher Carlos Ruiz to Seattle Mariners for Pitcher Vidal Nuno; Second Baseman Howie Kendrick to Philadelphia Phillies for Outfielder-First Baseman Darin Ruf and Outfielder Darnell Sweeney

Purchased: Infielder-Outfielder Zach Walters from Cleveland Indians; Pitcher Casey Fien from Minnesota Twins

Sold: Pitcher Nick Tepesch to Oakland Athletics

Chosen in Amateur Free Agent Draft: Gavin Lux, Will Smith; Dustin May; DJ Peters; Luke Raley; Tony Gonsolin; Dean Kremer; A.J. Alexy; Cody Thomas; Zach McKinstry; Andre Scrubb; Stevie Berman; Mitch White

Signed Amateur Free Agents: Yordan Alvarez; Pitcher Edwin Uceta; Devin Smeltzer

Signed Free Agents: Pitcher Joe Blanton; Pitcher Louis Coleman; Pitcher Nick Tepesch; Outfielder Will Venable; Pitcher Wilmer Font; Pitcher Fabio Castillo; Pitcher Jamey Wright

Chosen in Major League Rule 5 Draft: Pitcher Edward Paredes

Released: Pitcher Red Patterson; Outfielder Alex Guerrero; Outfielder Carl Crawford; Pitcher Ian Thomas; Pitcher Matt West; Pitcher Bud Norris; Pitcher Alec Grosser

Left as Free Agents: Pitcher Brett Anderson; Pitcher Joe Blanton; Pitcher Jesse Chavez; Pitcher J.P. Howell; Outfielder Will Venable; Pitcher Casey Fien; Pitcher David Huff

2017

April 28, 2017: Signed Free Agent
Infielder Max Muncy

In a little-noted transaction, the Dodgers signed left-handed-hitting Max Muncy, a utility player, to a minor league contract. Muncy, 26, was a true utility man, having played first, second, and third bases, and both corner outfield positions for Oakland over the past two seasons. His poor hitting—a .195 batting average and a 70 OPS+ in 245 at-bats—led the A's to release him this spring. The Dodgers assigned him to the Oklahoma City Dodgers, their Triple A team in the Pacific Coast League, where manager Bill Haselman continued to make use of Muncy's versatility, using him at all five of his infield and outfield positions. His hitting, a .309 average and 12 home runs in 110 games, led the Dodgers to bring him back to the major leagues in 2018.

Muncy has been with the Dodgers ever since, although it was not until 2023 that he played one defensive position—third base—for an entire season. The two-time All-Star has developed into one of the top power hitters in the National League. Muncy hit 35 home runs in a season twice and 36 in a season twice. An oblique injury in May 2024 limited him to just 73 games this past season. Through 2024, Muncy had hit 190 home runs, driven in 520 runs, and had a 127 OPS+ for the Dodgers. His four postseason home runs is tied for the most in franchise history.

July 31, 2017: Traded Minor League Outfielder Willie Calhoun, Minor League Infielder Brendon Davis, and Minor League Pitcher A.J. Alexy to the Texas Rangers for Pitcher Yu Darvish

The Dodgers had finished first in the National League West in each of the past four seasons. However, a division championship was not enough to satisfy the team or its fans. The goal was to win a World Series, something the Dodgers had not done since 1988. So, despite going 20–3 in July, and owning the best record in baseball, and leading the second-place Arizona Diamondbacks by 14 games, the Dodgers were looking ahead to the World Series. They wanted to add a proven right-handed starter to a rotation led by left-handers Clayton Kershaw, Alex Wood, and Rich Hill. They found their man fifteen minutes before the non-waiver deadline and sent three pitching prospects to the Texas Rangers to get 30-year-old Yu Darvish. "I think it will definitely be an emotional boost for the team," said general manager Farhan Zaidi. "It's hard to say they needed it, the way we've been playing. Every team wants to load up with as many starting pitchers they feel good about starting playoff games as possible. Having four is certainly better than having three."[11]

Since coming to the Rangers from the Japan Pacific League's Nippon Ham Fighters in 2012, Darvish had won 52, lost 39, and had an impressive 127 ERA+. He missed the 2015 season after undergoing elbow surgery and pitched in just 17 games in 2016. He was 6–9 this season, including his last start, the worst start of his career. The 10 runs Darvish allowed against the Miami Marlins did not deter Zaidi from pursuing him. "The quality of his stuff has been there, the velocity, the breaking ball," he said. "His health has been good. We're not concerned. It's certainly fortunate we got it done," Zaidi continued. "It did come down closer to the wire, from a quality of life and stress standpoint, then I think anybody had hoped." The Dodgers had announced they would not include their top two minor leaguers, Triple A pitcher Walker Buehler and Triple A outfielder Alex Verdugo, in any trade. They held that stance as they negotiated with Texas for Darvish. "There were certain guys that we were really reluctant to talk about in trades," Zaidi said.[12]

The three prospects going to Texas were Triple A outfielder Willie Calhoun, Class A pitcher A.J. Alexy, and Class A infielder Brendon Davis. Texas called up Calhoun later that summer, while Alexy reached the major leagues with the 2021 Rangers, and Davis did so with the 2022 Detroit Tigers.

Darvish had a 4–3 record and a 3.44 ERA in nine starts over the last two months of the season. He won a game against Arizona in the 2017 NL Division Series and one against the Chicago Cubs in the NL Championship. But he was 0–2 against Houston in the World Series, including Game Seven and the Dodgers fell short yet again. Darvish left as a free agent and signed with the Cubs for 2018.

December 16, 2017: Traded First Baseman Adrián González, Pitcher Scott Kazmir, Pitcher Brandon McCarthy, Infielder Charlie Culberson, and Cash to the Atlanta Braves for Outfielder Matt Kemp

The reason the Dodgers made this trade was less about the talent involved than it was about money. The club had been penalized for the past five seasons for luxury tax violations and were seeking financial relief and positioning itself to be active in the free-agent market following the 2018 season. The upcoming class of free agents was likely to have several of the game's biggest stars, each of whom would be demanding lucrative contracts. In addition to their own Clayton Kershaw, other possible free agents included outfielder Bryce Harper, third baseman Manny Machado, and pitchers Andrew Miller and Craig Kimbrel. The trade allowed them to move first baseman Adrián González, pitchers Brandon McCarthy and Scott Kazmir, and infielder Charlie Culberson to the Atlanta Braves and bring popular outfielder Matt Kemp back to Los Angeles. (They also sent some money to Atlanta.) It was a first step in the Dodgers plan to reduce their luxury-tax below the $197-million threshold for 2018. Kemp was owed $43 million through 2019, while the Dodgers owed González, Kazmir, and McCarthy a total of $47.5 million. As a result, the Dodgers had reduced their luxury tax number by about $23 million.

"This deal is a little more subtle than most," said the Dodgers president of baseball operations Andrew Friedman. "Obviously one of the main considerations in this deal was economic. But they're part of the bigger picture, the longer-term plan. It's a necessary, strategic part of moves yet to come."[13] Alex Anthopoulos, who had spent the last two seasons as a vice president in the Dodgers organization, was now the general manager in Atlanta. The two teams had begun discussing this trade last month, shortly after Anthopoulos left. One potential problem was the 35-year-old González, who was coming off the worst season of his career and had a no-trade clause in his contract. Friedman told him there might not be place on the roster for him in 2018, and González accepted the trade. The Braves released González the next day, allowing him to reach free agency. He signed with the Mets for the 2018 season, his final one.

"My final decision was not based on playing time, as I had agreed to a limited bench role," González wrote in a statement. "It is a way to test the free-agent market and see what opportunities are out there for me so I can make the best decision moving forward for me and my family. Lifting the no-trade clause is the hardest decision I have ever made in my career due to the fact that I loved every single second being a Dodger." González averaged 24 home runs and 99 RBIs during his first four full seasons as a Dodger, but back and elbow injuries this past season resulted in Rookie of the Year Cody Bellinger replacing him at first base. "The entire Dodger nation welcomed me with open arms and took me in right away," González said. "Thank you for everything to the fans and the city of L.A. You will always be in my heart. This closes a chapter for me, but not the book."[14]

Neither McCarthy nor Kazmir gave the Dodgers what they expected when they signed as free agents. McCarthy underwent Tommy John surgery in 2015, his first season with the club after pitching in just four games. In his three seasons in LA, he made 29 starts with an 11–7 record and a 4.51 earned run average. Kazmir was 10–6 with a 4.56 ERA in 2016, his first year as a Dodger. It would be his only year with the club as he missed the 2017 season due to what the *Los Angeles Times* called a mysterious hip condition. Culberson played in 49 games over two seasons with a .275 batting average.

Kemp batted .276 with 19 home runs and 64 RBIs for the 2017 Braves. But because the Dodgers had a surplus of outfielders, Friedman told Kemp that there might not be room for him. "I was very open and honest with him about what the future might hold," Friedman said. "It's just too difficult to say, definitively, at this point."[15] Kemp exceeded expectations. He played in 146 games, batted .290, hit 21 home runs, and drove in 85 runs.

Also in 2017:

Traded: Infielder-Outfielder Micah Johnson to Atlanta Braves for a Player to be Named or Cash; Pitcher José De León to Tampa Bay Rays for Infielder Logan Forsythe; Minor League Infielder Jordan Tarsovich to Oakland Athletics for Outfielder Brett Eibner; Pitcher Carlos Frías to Cleveland Indians for a Player to be Named or Cash; Pitcher Sergio Romo to Cleveland Indians for a Player to be Named or Cash; Minor League

Infielder Oneil Cruz and Minor League Pitcher Angel German to Pittsburgh Pirates for Pitcher Tony Watson; Outfielder Scott Van Slyke and Minor League Catcher Hendrick Clementina to Cincinnati Reds for Pitcher Tony Cingrani; Pitcher Chris Hatcher to Oakland Athletics for International Bonus Slot Money; Minor League Pitcher Jacob Rhame to New York Mets for Outfielder Curtis Granderson

Purchased: Infielder Mike Freeman from Seattle Mariners; Pitcher Dylan Floro from Chicago Cubs

Sold: Outfielder Darnell Sweeney to Cincinnati Reds; Pitcher Grant Dayton to Atlanta Braves; Pitcher Josh Ravin to Atlanta Braves

Chosen in Amateur Free Agent Draft: Connor Wong; Zach Pop; Zach Reks; Rylan Bannon; Andre Jackson; Jacob Amaya; James Marinan; Nathan Witt; Donovan Casey

Signed Amateur Free Agents: Justin Bruihl; Miguel Vargas

Signed Free Agents: Pitcher Brandon Morrow; Pitcher Sergio Romo; Pitcher Daniel Corcino; Pitcher Manny Bañuelos; Pitcher Pat Venditte

Released: Outfielder-First Baseman Darin Ruf; Outfielder Brett Eibner

Left as Free Agents: Infielder Mike Freeman; Pitcher Dylan Floro; Outfielder Curtis Granderson; Outfielder Franklin Gutiérrez; Pitcher Brandon Morrow; Outfielder Andre Ethier (retired); Pitcher Louis Coleman; Pitcher Fabio Castillo; Outfielder O'Koyea Dickson; Infielder-Outfielder Zach Walters

2018

July 18, 2018: Traded Infielder Breyvic Valera, Minor League Pitcher Zach Pop, Minor League Pitcher Dean Kremer, Minor League Outfielder Yusniel Díaz, and Minor League Infielder Rylan Bannon to the Baltimore Orioles for Third Baseman Manny Machado

Two days earlier, shortstop Manny Machado represented the Baltimore Orioles at the All-Star Game played at Washington's Nationals Park. It was his last game in an Orioles' uniform. Machado had played in three previous All-Star Games, but this was his first as a shortstop. The previous three had been at third base, but the departure of J. J Hardy from Baltimore opened the position for Machado, who had been drafted as a shortstop. Machado was in his seventh season with Baltimore and had been open in his plan to become a free agent. Knowing the Orioles were ready to trade him and get some prospects in return, several teams were making offers, including the Dodgers, the Brewers, the Phillies, the Diamondbacks, and the Yankees. The Dodgers, whose GM Farhan Zaidi had been discussing a trade for Machado for a month, won out by sending five young players to the Orioles: infielder Breyvic Valera and four minor leaguers—pitchers Zach Pop and Dean Kremer, outfielder Yusniel Díaz, and infielder Rylan Bannon.

The Dodgers held on to three of their best prospects, pitcher Walker Buehler, outfielder Alex Verdugo, and catcher Keibert Ruiz, but lost the highly regarded Díaz. The 21-year-old Díaz defected from Cuba when he was 17 and signed as an international free agent with the Dodgers in 2015, receiving a signing bonus of $15.5 million. To date, his major league career has consisted of one at-bat for the 2022 Orioles.

Dean Kremer, 22, would prove to the best of those leaving LA. Kremer reached the Orioles in 2020, and through the 2024 season had a 30–30 record with 94 ERA+ in 95 games, 94 of which were starts. Pop reached the majors with Miami in 2021 and was traded to Toronto in 2022. His combined record through 2024 was 8–5 with a 93 ERA+ in 100 games.

Pop has been strictly a relief pitcher, with no starts and one save. Rylan Bannon had played in seven major league games through 2023, with Baltimore, Atlanta, and Houston. He had two hits in 20 at-bats.

Valera, in the minor leagues at the time of the trade, played 20 games for LA this season, with a .172 batting average and a 26 OPS+. His departure opened a place on the 40-man roster for Manny Machado.

The Orioles picked Machado first (third overall) in the 2010 amateur free agent draft. He made his debut with the Orioles in August 2012 and had been a standout player ever since. He left Baltimore with a .283 batting average, 162 home runs, 471 runs batted in, and a 121 OPS+. He was batting .315 this season with 24 home runs and a career-high 162 OPS+. But Machado's flashiness and showboating had never captured the hearts of the fans in blue-collar Baltimore. He was expected to feel more at home in Hollywood.

Machado had struggled in adjusting to shortstop this year, which led manager Dave Roberts to speak to him about the team's preference for flexibility. Machado said he was willing to shift between third base and shortstop when needed. "Everybody is on the same page about that," Zaidi said. "He understands the way we manage the roster and the options that Doc [Roberts] likes to have moving guys around. He's told us he wants to do whatever he can to succeed and win." Zaidi claimed he was not concerned about Machado's impending free agency. "This is about 2018 for us," Zaidi said. "We hope he plays well and creates a good market for himself. We're not worried about what happens beyond 2018 right now."[16]

Machado did play well, helping the Dodgers to another National League pennant. He appeared in 66 games after the All-Star break, batted .273 with 13 home runs, 42 RBIs, and a 122 OPS+. Shortly after the team's loss to the Red Sox in the World Series, he filed for free agency. In February 2019, Machado signed to play for the San Diego Padres.

December 21, 2018: Signed Free Agent Pitcher Joe Kelly

Pitcher Joe Kelly was yet another Southern California kid who grew up rooting for the Dodgers and now would get to play for them. After helping the Boston Red Sox defeat the Dodgers in the World Series, he left Boston via free agency. Kelly's contract with Los Angeles included a $1 million signing bonus, a salary of $3 million in 2019 and $8.5 million in 2020 and 2021. At that time, there would be a $12 million team option or a $4-million buyout for 2022.

"I still feel young," Kelly said. "I'm 30 years old. But I wanted to be local. I've missed so much with baseball. Family. Birthdays. Summers. Weddings. And I just wanted to be able to stay at home and enjoy all those things while being able to win every single day and be ready to win a World Series."[17]

Kelly, a right-hander, began his major league career with the St. Louis Cardinals in 2012. The Cardinals traded him to the Red Sox in the July 2014 deal that sent John Lackey to St. Louis. Kelly was mostly a starter then; he remained so until the Red Sox moved him to the bullpen full-time in 2017. While his contract included incentives for games finished each season, finishing games was not the role that was planned for him. The Dodgers already had a successful closer in Kenley Jansen.

"When I moved to the bullpen, there was no role for me, so I just went out there and pitched. And that was when I performed my best," Kelly said. "During the playoffs, I think, that's huge. It can be the first inning or the third inning. And that's something me and the Dodgers spoke about. I'm not dedicated to any role. I think if you wanted to name a role, I think it's me being able to pitch whenever the big outs are. And that's when I perform the best and that's when I feel the most comfortable."[18]

After a 4–2 record with two saves and a 4.39 ERA in 73 appearances for the 2018 Red Sox during the regular season, Kelly had a spectacular postseason. In nine games he allowed just one earned run in 11⅓ innings. Called on by Red Sox manager Alex Cora in all five World Series games,

Kelly pitched six scoreless innings and struck out 10 of the 22 Dodgers batters he faced. President of baseball operations Andrew Friedman was expecting that Kelly would be close to the pitcher they saw in October. "It's not often in free agency," Friedman said, "where you can get real upside."[19]

December 21, 2018: Traded Outfielder Yasiel Puig, Outfielder Matt Kemp, Pitcher Alex Wood, Infielder Kyle Farmer, and Cash to the Cincinnati Reds for Pitcher Homer Bailey, Pitcher Josiah Gray, and Minor League Infielder Jeter Downs

The Dodgers made a seven-player trade with the Cincinnati Reds that on the surface seemed puzzling. They sent the Reds four established major leaguers plus cash in exchange for two minor leaguers and a veteran pitcher they had no intention of keeping. Going to Cincinnati were outfielders Yasiel Puig and Matt Kemp, pitcher Alex Wood, infielder Kyle Farmer, and $7 million in exchange for pitcher Homer Bailey, minor-league infielder Jeter Downs and minor-league pitcher Josiah Gray. But the Dodgers had their reasons. They were trading surpluses in their outfield and starting rotation to obtain assets and more flexibility. Overall, it would give them an extra $14 million to pursue talent in the free agent and trade markets without exceeding baseball's $206 million competitive-balance tax limit.

"We are in position right now where we still feel like we have a really good team but feel like we want to continue to add to it before we get to spring training," Andrew Friedman said. "What exactly that looks like, I'm not sure yet.... If you look at our rotation and outfield four hours ago, it was a situation that I think was not a functional roster with the depth that we had all concentrated at the major-league level," Friedman added. "We had a lot of different conversations involving a lot of different guys, and this was the deal we feel made the most sense."[20]

For 34-year-old Matt Kemp this was the second time Andrew Friedman had traded him. In his one year back in Los Angeles, Kemp batted .290 with 21 home runs, 85 RBIs, and a 121 OPS+. He made the All-Star team with an excellent first half, but tailed off after the break and became a platoon player. In Kemp's 10 years as a Dodger, he batted .292, with 203 home runs (seventh most in franchise history), 733 RBIs, and a 127 OPS+.

Puig made his major league debut in June 2012 and was an immediate sensation. In 104 games, he batted .319 with 19 home runs, 42 RBIs, and a 159 OPS+. In the NL Rookie of the Year voting, he received the only four first-place votes (out of thirty) that did not go to Miami Marlins pitcher José Fernández. During his six years with the Dodgers, Puig batted .279

with a 127 OPS+ and led the team with 108 home runs and 256 extra-base hits. The 28-year-old Puig's exuberance delighted the fans, but his troublesome behavior, personality, and demeanor often offended teammates, opponents, and the front office. The club had been looking to trade him for the past two years. When Friedman was asked how he would characterize Puig's time in Los Angeles, he chuckled and said, "That is a very deep question."[21]

Alex Wood was a 28-year-old left-hander, who like Kemp and Puig, would be a free agent after the 2019 season. Wood had a 6–10 record in his first two seasons in LA, 2015 and 2016, but had the best season of his career in 2017. He was an All-Star, his .842 winning percentage (16–3) led the National League, and he finished ninth in voting for the Cy Young Award. In 2020, Wood returned to the Dodgers as a free agent for one season. He was still active, with Oakland, in 2024, but he has never again been an All-Star or received any Cy Young Award votes.

Kyle Farmer, who played part of the 2017 and 2018 seasons for LA, was a versatile infielder for the Reds from 2019 through 2022 and the Minnesota Twins in 2023 and 2024.

Twenty-year-old infielder Jeter Downs was Cincinnati's first-round pick in the 2017 amateur free agent draft. Downs, a right-handed hitter, batted .257 with 13 home runs and a .753 OPS for the Dayton Dragons, the Reds' Class A affiliate in the Midwestern League this past season.

Cincinnati drafted Josiah Gray, a 21-year-old right-hander, in the second round of this year's amateur free agent draft. The Reds sent him to their rookie-league affiliate in Greenville, Tennessee, where he had a 2–2 record with a 2.58 earned run average.

The Dodgers released Homer Bailey the next day. The 12-year-veteran right-hander eventually signed to play for the Kansas City Royals in 2019.

Also in 2018:

Traded: As part of a three-way trade, sent Minor League Pitcher Trevor Oaks and Minor League Outfielder Erick Mejia to Kansas City Royals and Pitcher Luis Avilán and Cash to the Chicago White Sox and received Pitcher Scott Alexander from the Royals and Minor League Infielder Jake Peter from the White Sox; Minor League Outfielder Johan Mieses to St. Louis Cardinals for Infielder Breyvic Valera; Pitcher Zach Neal and Minor League Outfielder-First Baseman Ibandel Isabel to Cincinnati Reds for Pitcher Ariel Hernández; Pitcher Wilmer Font to Oakland Athletics for Minor League Pitcher Logan Salow; Minor League Pitcher Aneurys Zabala and Minor League Pitcher James Marinan to Cincinnati Reds for Pitcher Zach Neal, Pitcher Dylan Floro, and International

Bonus Slot Money; Second Baseman Logan Forsythe, Minor League Outfielder Luke Raley, and Minor League Pitcher Devin Smeltzer to Minnesota Twins for Second Baseman Brian Dozier; Minor League Pitcher Corey Copping to Toronto Blue Jays for Pitcher John Axford; Minor League Pitcher Andrew Istler to Washington Nationals for Pitcher Ryan Madson; Minor League Infielder Jesus Valdez to Pittsburgh Pirates for Third Baseman David Freese; outfielder Tim Locastro to New York Yankees for Minor League Pitcher Drew Finley; Pitcher Manny Bañuelos to Chicago White Sox for Minor League First Baseman Justin Yurchak

Purchased: Pitcher J.T. Chargois from Minnesota Twins; Pitcher Erik Goeddel from Seattle Mariners; Pitcher Zac Rosscup from Colorado Rockies

Sold: Outfielder Trayce Thompson to New York Yankees

Chosen in Amateur Free Agent Draft: Michael Grove; James Outman; Caleb Sampen; Niko Hulsizer; Justin Hagenman; Hunter Feduccia

Signed Amateur Free Agents: Darien Núñez; Jeff Belge; Andy Pages; Dillon Paulson; Benony Robles; Edgardo Henriquez

Signed Free Agents: Pitcher Zach Neal; Catcher Rocky Gale; Pitcher Daniel Hudson; Pitcher Kevin Quackenbush; Infielder Daniel Castro

Released: Shortstop Erisbel Arruebarrena; Pitcher Adam Liberatore; Second Baseman Chase Utley; Pitcher Zac Rosscup; Pitcher Erik Goeddel

Left as Free Agents: Pitcher Edward Paredes; Pitcher Pat Venditte; Pitcher John Axford; Pitcher Tony Watson

2019

Also in 2019:

Traded: Minor League Pitcher Caleb Sampen to Tampa Bay Rays for Pitcher Jaime Schultz; Minor League Pitcher Andrew Sopko and Minor League Infielder Ronny Brito to Toronto Blue Jays for Catcher Russell Martin; Minor League Pitcher Nathan Witt to Tampa Bay Rays for Pitcher Casey Sadler; Minor League Pitcher Andre Scrubb to Houston Astros for First Baseman Tyler White; Infielder Daniel Castro to Seattle Mariners for Infielder-Outfielder Kristopher Negron; Minor League Outfielder Niko Hulsizer to Tampa Bay Rays for Pitcher Adam Kolarek; Pitcher Tony Cingrani and Minor League Pitcher Jeffry Abreu to St. Louis Cardinals for Infielder Jedd Gyorko, International Bonus Slot Money and Cash

Sold: Catcher Travis d'Arnaud to Tampa Bay Rays; Pitcher Zac Rosscup to St. Louis Cardinals; Pitcher Brock Stewart to Toronto Blue Jays; Catcher Rocky Gale to Tampa Bay Rays

Chosen in Amateur Free Agent Draft: Ryan Pepiot; Jonny Deluca; Michael Busch; Nick Robertson

Signed Free Agents: Outfielder AJ Pollock; Catcher Travis d'Arnaud; Pitcher Zac Rosscup; Pitcher Blake Treinin

Released: Pitcher Josh Fields; Infielder-Outfielder Kristopher Negron; Pitcher J.T. Chargois

Left as Free Agents: Third Baseman David Freese; Pitcher Rich Hill; Catcher Russell Martin; Pitcher Hyun-Jin Ryu; Pitcher Yimi Garcia; Infielder Jedd Gyorko

14

2020–2024

2020

February 10, 2020: Traded Pitcher Kenta Maeda and Minor League Catcher Jair Camargo to the Minnesota Twins for Pitcher Brusdar Graterol, Minor League Outfielder Luke Raley, and Future Considerations

The Dodgers had been negotiating a three-team trade with the Red Sox and the Twins that would bring them Mookie Betts and David Price from Boston. The deal fell apart when the Red Sox expressed concern about the condition of pitcher Brusdar Graterol's right arm. Graterol had undergone Tommy John surgery in 2016 and missed that entire season. In 2019, his rookie season with Minnesota, he missed two months with a shoulder injury. If the deal had gone through, Graterol would have gone from the Twins to the Red Sox. Instead, the Dodgers made separate deals with Boston and Minnesota. The Minnesota portion involved sending pitcher Kenta Maeda and minor league catcher Jair Camargo to the Twins for Graterol, minor league outfielder Luke Raley, and future considerations. The future considerations would be the Dodgers sixty-seventh pick in the 2020 amateur free agent draft.

The 21-year-old Graterol made his major league debut on September 1, 2019, after going 7–0 with a 1.92 earned run average at three levels of the Twins farm system. He made 12 relief appearances for Minnesota, splitting two decisions with 10 strikeouts in 9⅔ innings. The Dodgers were also concerned about Graterol's pitching arm; however, they were willing to take the gamble for a highly rated prospect whose fastball reached triple digits. "A guy with his stuff, it's just a different look for our bullpen," said Dodgers pitching coach Mark Prior. "The ability to bring that kind of raw power, impact into the game is only a good thing for us."

To keep Graterol healthy, the Dodgers planned to pay close attention to his workload. "From what I hear, the medical is sort of benign and it's asymptomatic," said Dodgers manager Dave Roberts. "And you see 100 [mph] in the postseason, and you talk to the player, and he says he feels good, and he looks great." Graterol was happy that the uncertainty of where he would play in 2020 was behind him. "I'm really grateful for my new family here," he said. "And I'm here to give it my all."[1]

Right-hander Kenta Maeda won 16 games (16–11) in 2016 and finished third in the Rookie of the Year voting. Maeda, who would turn 32 in April, won 47 games, lost 35 and had a 3.87 earned run average in his career with the Dodgers. He was 10–8 with a 4.04 ERA this past season. Maeda was guaranteed an annual salary of $3 million for the 2021 season and an additional $150,000 for being on the Twins Opening Day roster. Jair Camargo would make his major league debut with Minnesota in 2024.

Graterol was a regular in the Dodgers' bullpen from 2020 to 2023. Appearing in 171 games (173⅔ innings pitched), he had a 10–8 record, 11 saves, and an excellent 158 ERA+. Graterol began the 2024 season on the injured list with a sore shoulder and appeared in just seven games for the Dodgers. Luke Raley batted .182 in 33 games for the Dodgers in 2021. In March 2022 he was traded to the Tampa Bay Rays.

February 10, 2020: Traded Outfielder Alex Verdugo, Minor League Infielder Jeter Downs, and Minor League Catcher Connor Wong to the Boston Red Sox for Outfielder Mookie Betts and Pitcher David Price

When the Dodgers attempt to land Boston's Mookie Betts via a three-team trade with Minnesota fell apart, they made a separate deal with Boston. Los Angeles sent promising young outfielder Alex Verdugo and two minor leaguers, infielder Jeter Downs and catcher Connor Wong, to the Red Sox for the right-hand-hitting Betts and left-handed pitcher David Price. The apparent one-sidedness of the deal had the press and the fans in Boston comparing it to the Red Sox's sale of Babe Ruth to the Yankees in December 1919. Red Sox general manager Chaim Bloom defended the trade. "You can't be afraid to do something that you think is right in the big picture," Bloom said. "Knowing how great a player Mookie is, how important he's been to us, it had to be a high bar for us to consider moving him. This return met that bar."[2]

Mookie Betts was only 21 when he made his major league debut with the Red Sox in June 2014. In the five years since, the unimposing 5'9" Betts had established himself as one of the best players in the game. He left Boston with a .301 batting average, 139 home runs, 470 runs batted in, and a

134 OPS+. Betts's best season was 2018, when he won the American League batting title and its Most Valuable Player Award. In five full seasons, he was an All-Star four times and won four Gold Glove awards and three Silver Slugger awards.

"He embodies everything we really value about a position player," said Dodgers president of baseball operation Andrew Friedman. "The impact he has on defense, the instincts on the bases … in the batters' box, guys who are aggressive in the strike zone …, he embodies all of that. When I talked to him the other day, I told him that in all the digging that we do on players that we're looking to acquire, all the feedback we got from teammates and clubhouse guys and different guys that he's come across in his career … he'd blush if he heard all the nice things that were said about him," Friedman said.[3]

Betts was in the final year of his contract and had asked the Red Sox for a $420 million extension. The Red Sox chose not to extend Betts, deciding instead to trade him and get what they could. Meeting Betts's salary demands to keep him in Los Angeles was now the Dodgers problem. "We're hoping he falls in love with the team, the city, the fans, and he wants to be here for a long time," said Friedman.[4]

Beginning with the second of his twelve years in the American League, David Price had consistently posted earned run averages below the league average. He won the Cy Young Award with the 2012 Tampa Bay Rays and had been on five All-Star teams. In addition to the Rays, Price had pitched for Detroit, Toronto, and for the last four seasons, Boston. He had a 150–80 record, but he was now 34 and had lost velocity on his fastball. In addition, arm injuries had reduced his innings pitched in two of the last three seasons. The Dodgers were not sure how they would use him. "Right now, I see him in the middle of our starting rotation, and we'll go from there," said manager Dave Roberts.[5]

Friedman was Tampa Bay's general manager when they selected Price as the first overall pick in the 2007 amateur free agent draft. "Obviously, the success he's had is evident and everybody knows about that, but he was as good of a teammate as I've ever seen," Friedman said. "Just the impact he has in the clubhouse was as significant as I've seen."[6]

Price sat out the 2020 season because of the COVID pandemic. He appeared in 79 games for Los Angeles over the next two seasons, mostly in relief. He was 5–2 in 2021 and 2–0 in 2022, his final major league season.

The best of the Dodgers leaving for Boston was left-handed-hitting Alex Verdugo, whom LA picked in the second round of the 2014 amateur free agent draft. This past season, the 23-year-old Verdugo batted .294 in 106 games. He batted .281 with a 105 OPS+ in four seasons with the Red Sox before being traded to the Yankees in December 2023.

In 2023, Connor Wong's first full season with Boston, he batted .235 with an 80 OPS+ in 126 games. Playing in the same number of games in 2024, his batting average rose to .280, with 13 home runs, 52 runs batted in, and a 110 OPS+. Jeter Downs played in fourteen games for Boston in 2022 and six games for the Washington Nationals in 2023. He began the 2024 season with the Yankees Triple A Scranton/Wilkes-Barre RailRiders of the International League but left after 69 games to play in Japan.

In Mookie Betts' first season with the Dodgers, the COVID-shortened 2020 season, he was a major factor in them winning their first World Series since 1988. Betts batted .292, had a 147 OPS+, won Gold Glove and Silver Slugger awards, and finished second in Most Valuable Player voting. Moving between the infield and outfield, he continued to rank among the top players ever since. Betts has a .284 batting average for his five seasons in LA, with 132 home runs, 361 RBIs, and a combined OPS+ of 145.

Also in 2020:

Traded: Pitcher Casey Sadler to Chicago Cubs for Minor League Infielder Clayton Daniel; Outfielder Kyle Garlick to Philadelphia Phillies for Minor League Pitcher Tyler Gilbert; Pitcher Ross Stripling to Toronto Blue Jays for Minor League Pitcher Kendall Williams and Minor League First Baseman Ryan Noda; Minor League Pitcher Leo Crawford to Milwaukee Brewers for Pitcher Corey Knebel; Received Pitcher Garrett Cleavinger from Philadelphia Phillies in three-team trade and sent Minor League First Baseman Dillon Paulson and a Player to be Named to Tampa Bay Rays

Chosen in Amateur Free Agent Draft: Bobby Miller; Clayton Beeter; Landon Knack; Gavin Stone

Signed Free Agents: Pitcher Jimmy Nelson; Pitcher Alex Wood; Outfielder Terrance Gore; Pitcher Jake McGee; Pitcher Tommy Kahnle

Released: First Baseman Tyler White

Left as Free Agents: Pitcher Pedro Baez

2021

February 5, 2021: Signed Free Agent Pitcher Trevor Bauer

In his six years as president of baseball operations, Andrew Friedman's personnel moves had helped the Dodgers win six division titles and make three World Series appearances, winning one. Friedman took what appeared to be a major step in defending that World Series title, won in the COVID-shortened 2020 season, by signing pitcher Trevor Bauer. Bauer, who won that year's Cy Young Award while pitching for Cincinnati, signed a three-year deal worth $102 million that included opt-outs after the first and second seasons.

Friedman acknowledged that signing a pitcher of Bauer's caliber and age to a contract that short was unusual. Bauer, however, welcomed it. "I'm looking for a partnership, for a chance to win, and I don't want to be a player who signs a long-term deal and toward the end is resented either by the fan base, by the organization, for having my performance slip below what my contract dictates," he said. "I wanted something with flexibility. I wanted something that works for me and the organization. And as far as security goes, I'm very aware of the fact that I'm well-compensated, plenty secure in my life, family's life, future kids' life. It wasn't about the money for me."[7]

The 30-year-old right-hander, consider the prize pitcher in this year's free agent market, had narrowed his decision to the Dodgers and the New York Mets before choosing the Dodgers. He joined an already strong rotation, led by Clayton Kershaw and Walker Buehler.

Bauer had a 75–64 record in his nine major league seasons, including a 52–35 record with the Cleveland Indians from 2015 to 2018. His best season was for Cleveland in 2018, when he had a 2.21 earned run average over 175 1/3 innings and made his only All-Star team. However, a history of bad behavior, on and off the field, led to Bauer being a controversial figure. Cleveland traded him to the Reds in 2019 after he threw a baseball from the mound over the center field wall after Indians manager Terry Francona removed him from a game in Kansas City. Bauer did not deny he had a history of upsetting people. "I'm good at two things in this world: throwing baseballs and pissing people off," he was quoted as saying in a *Sports Illustrated* story published in February 2019.[8]

Bauer's social media activity had also been troubling. Two women—a college student and a reporter—had accused him of harassment and encouraging others to harass them. "I don't shy away from confrontation and am often quick to defend myself, but I am by no means a bully and I take great offense to my character being called into question"[9]

But when more such charges by women emerged in June and July 2021, it led Major League Baseball (MLB) to place Bauer on administrative leave. He had appeared in 17 games with an 8–5 record and a 163 ERA+. On April 29, 2022, MLB suspended him for the 2022 and 2023 seasons. The Dodgers released Bauer in January 2023, and to date no major league club has signed him.

At the time of his signing, *Los Angeles Times* columnist Dylan Hernandez was among those who were uneasy with the Dodgers acquiring someone with Bauer's history. "More than wins and losses are at stake," Hernandez wrote. "This is about what the franchise stands for, the values it represents."[10]

May 17, 2021: Signed Free Agent First Baseman Albert Pujols

Albert Pujols joined Rickey Henderson, Jim Thome, Frank Robinson, Greg Maddux, Juan Marichal, and Gary Carter as future Hall of Famers who played briefly for the Los Angeles Dodgers at the end of their careers. This surprise signing was set in motion four days earlier when the Los Angeles Angels unexpectedly gave Pujols his release. Pujols was in this tenth season with the Angels after having spent eleven seasons with the St. Louis Cardinals. Over those twenty-one years the right-handed hitting slugger had won a Rookie of the Year Award and three Most Valuable Player Awards. His 667 home runs and 2,112 runs batted in earned him a place among baseball's all-time power hitters. However, his production had fallen off since 2016. The 41-year-old Pujols was batting just .198 in 24 games this season, leading Angels manager Joe Maddon to let him go.

He "did not want to be a bench player of any kind," Maddon said of Pujols in defense of his decision. Pujols saw it differently. While acknowledging he was "shocked, like everybody," and that he did not hold "hard feelings" toward the Angels, he said, "I think there were a lot of things said out there, that I wanted more playing time, that I wanted to play every day. That never came out of my mouth. You guys asked me that question over and over, so many times, and I always told you, however the team needs me, I'm here for that." When asked about Pujols's statement, Maddon said: "I wish Albert nothing but the best. I mean that sincerely."[11]

"We believe he can help us win a championship," manager Dave Roberts said; he proved it the next day when he started Pujols at first base and batted him fourth, making Pujols the oldest clean-up hitter in Dodgers history. "I feel like I still have some gasoline left in my tank," Pujols said.[12] He played in 85 games for the 2021c Dodgers, batting .254 with 12 home runs and 38 runs batted in. He left as a free agent and played a final season with his original team, the Cardinals, and then retired. Pujols's 24 home runs in 2022 gave him a final total of 703, putting him in fourth place all-time.

July 30, 2021: Traded Catcher Keibert Ruiz, Minor League Pitcher Josiah Gray, Minor League Pitcher Gerardo Carrillo, and Minor League Outfielder Donovan Casey to the Washington Nationals for Pitcher Max Scherzer and Shortstop Trea Turner

For the fourth time in six years, Andrew Friedman used the trading deadline to acquire at very little cost an established player for the stretch drive. He had added Rich Hill in 2016, Yu Darvish in 2017, and Manny Machado in 2018; all had helped lead the Dodgers to three consecutive division titles and two National League pennants. This time Friedman added two established players, both from the Washington Nationals: ace pitcher Max Scherzer and sensational young shortstop Trea Turner. In return, Washington received rookie catcher Keibert Ruiz; pitcher Josiah Gray, who had made his major league debut ten days earlier; minor league pitcher Gerardo Carrillo; and minor league outfielder Donovan Casey. Through the 2024 season, Carrillo and Casey have remained in the minor leagues. The trade made the Dodgers the overwhelming favorites to win another pennant.

Scherzer, a 37-year-old right-hander, was in his fourteenth major league season. He was a three-time Cy Young Award winner who had led his league in wins four times and in strikeouts three times. Scherzer had a lifetime record of 183–97 with a 3.19 earned run average. He was 8–4 with a 2.76 ERA with Washington this season. Friedman's failure to sign Scherzer when he was a free agent after the 2014 season was likely his biggest blunder in his seven seasons as the president of baseball operations. The Nationals signed him and Scherzer won two of his Cy Young awards with them. (The first was with Detroit in 2013.)

"Max has done it all in this game," said Friedman. "He's on the Mt. Rushmore of pitchers in terms of what he's done in the regular season, and what he's done in the playoffs, and adding him to our rotation creates lot of depth and options."[13] The Dodgers had lost three of their starting pitchers since the start of the season. Dustin May had season-ending elbow surgery in early May, Trevor Bauer was lost as the result of a domestic violence investigation in late June, and Clayton Kershaw had suffered an elbow injury in early July. Kershaw was due to return next week and would join Scherzer and Walker Buehler at the top of the rotation, with Julio Urías and either David Price or Tony Gonsolin occupying the other two spots.

Twenty-eight-year-old shortstop Trea Turner was in his seventh season with Washington. He had a .300 batting average with 93 home runs and 192 stolen bases. The speedy Turner was batting .322 this season, with

18 home runs, 49 RBIs and a 142 OPS+ in 96 games. "He's very dynamic," manager Dave Roberts said. "There's nothing on a baseball field he can't do. He can beat you in so many ways. He's on a short list of guys who can beat you with all the different tools—the arm, the glove, the power, the speed. There's not many guys who play a premium position who can do that."[14] Turner was under club control through 2022, and the Dodgers felt he would be a more than adequate replacement at shortstop if the incumbent, Corey Seager, left as a free agent.

Also in 2021:

Traded: Pitcher Dylan Floro to Miami Marlins for Pitcher Alex Vesia and Minor League Pitcher Kyle Hurt; Pitcher Adam Kolarek and Minor League Outfielder Cody Thomas to Oakland Athletics for Infielder Sheldon Neuse and Minor League Pitcher Gus Varland; Pitcher Josh Sborz to Texas Rangers for Minor League Pitcher Jhan Zambrano; A Player to be Named to Tampa Bay Rays for Outfielder Yoshi Tsutsugo; Pitcher Dennis Santana to Texas Rangers for Minor League Pitcher Kelvin Bautista; Minor League Outfielder Carlos Rincon to New York Mets for Pitcher Billy McKinney; Minor League Catcher Stevie Berman to Minnesota Twins for Pitcher Andrew Vasquez

Purchased: Pitcher Phil Bickford from Milwaukee Brewers; Pitcher James Sherfy from San Francisco Giants; Pitcher Connor Greene from Baltimore Orioles; Pitcher Evan Phillips from Tampa Bay Rays

Sold: Pitcher Jake Reed to Tampa Bay Rays; Outfielder DJ Peters to Texas Rangers; Pitcher Connor Greene to Baltimore Orioles; Pitcher Edwin Uceta to Arizona Diamondbacks; Outfielder Zach Reks to Texas Rangers

Chosen in Amateur Free Agent Draft: Emmett Sheehan, Nick Nastrini, Jordan Leasure; Justin Wrobleski; Ben Casparius

Signed Amateur Free Agents: Thayron Liranzo; Rayne Doncon

Signed Free Agents: Infielder Andy Burns; Pitcher Mike Kickham; Pitcher Yefry Ramírez; Outfielder Steven Souza, Jr.; Pitcher Kevin Quackenbush; Pitcher Nate Jones; Pitcher Jake Reed; Pitcher Neftali Feliz; Catcher Tony Wolters; Pitcher Shane Greene; Pitcher Andrew Heaney; Pitcher Daniel Hudson

Released: Infielder Eddy Alvarez; Outfielder Yoshi Tsutsugo; Infielder Andy Burns; Pitcher James Sherfy

Left as Free Agents: Outfielder Steven Souza, Jr.; Outfielder Terrance Gore; Pitcher Nate Jones; Pitcher Scott Alexander; Pitcher Joe Kelly; Pitcher Andrew Vasquez; Infielder-Outfielder Kiké Hernández; Pitcher Neftali Feliz; Pitcher Mike Kickham; Pitcher Kevin Quackenbush; Pitcher James Sherfy; Pitcher Jake McGee; Pitcher Pedro Baez

2022

On January 18, 2022: Dodgers promoted Brandon Gomes to General Manager.

March 18, 2022: Signed Free Agent First Baseman Freddie Freeman

First baseman Freddie Freeman had spent his entire 12-year career with the Atlanta Braves. He had a .295 batting average with 271 home runs, 941 runs batted in, and a 138 OPS+. The 32-year-old, left-handed-hitting Freeman was a five-time All-Star and the National League's Most Valuable Player in 2020. He was a major factor in the Braves' World Series championship season in 2021, with a .300 batting average, a 136 OPS+, and a league-leading 120 runs scored. Freeman batted .300 or higher in six of the last nine seasons and had missed only a combined seven games over the last four years. Yet the Braves seemed willing to let him go.

"I've been trying to think of how this was going to go in my head with these questions," Freeman said. "You spend fifteen years in an organization, twelve in the big leagues, a lot of memories are made.... I didn't get any calls last offseason, didn't really get any calls last spring training either," he said. "So, I was pretty sure I was going to be a free agent. You still think you're going to come back at that point. But the doubts started to go when the phone didn't ring. I can't control someone wanting to call. I got one call before the lockout, a checking-in call. And that was it. Then after the lockout, a checking-in call again."[15]

Freeman said he was surprised when the Braves traded for Oakland A's first baseman Matt Olson earlier in the week. "To be honest, I was blind-sided," said Freeman, who still believed a return to Atlanta was possible. "I think every emotion came across. I was hurt. It's really hard to put into words still."[16]

The Southern California native said he was delighted to return home, where his 67-year-old father and 86-year-old grandfather could see him play. His contract with the Dodgers was for six years and $162 million. "What he does on the field is obvious to everyone," said Andrew Friedman. "We've competed against them three of the last four years in the playoffs and the stress, [even in] the innings before he comes up, the lineup kind of orbits around him."[17]

Freeman was everything the Dodgers had expected of him, and more.

In his first season, 2022, he played in 159 games, batted .325 and led the National League in runs (117), hits (199), doubles (47) and on-base average (.407). He played in 161 games in 2023, with a .331 batting average and had a league-leading, franchise record 59 doubles. Although Freeman's production declined slightly in 2024, he was the offensive star of the Dodgers' five-game World Series win over the Yankees. His four home runs and World Series record-tying 12 runs batted in earned him the Series' Most Valuable Player Award. Freeman's batting average for his three years as a Dodgers was .314, with 291 runs batted in and an OPS+ of 155. The 15-year veteran ended the 2024 season as MLB's active leader in runs, hits, doubles, RBIs, and total bases.

March 19, 2022: Free Agent Pitcher Kenley Jansen Signed with the Atlanta Braves

In what was the equivalent of a trade, a day after Freddie Freeman left the Braves to sign with the Dodgers, pitcher Kenley Jansen left the Dodgers to sign with the Braves. Even the circumstances were alike. Jansen had enjoyed a stellar career with the Dodgers, who chose not to retain him. Like Freeman, Jansen had spent his entire 12-year career with one club. The 34-year-old right-hander had been the Dodgers closer since 2012. He left as the club's all-time leader in games pitched (701) and saves (350). In the 705 innings Jansen pitched, he struck out 1,022 batters. His ERA+ for his years as a Dodger was an impressive 164. Jansen was asking for a three-year contract, but the Dodgers wanted a shorter deal. Although the Braves offered just a one-year deal, worth $16 million, Jansen accepted it.

Several Dodgers paid tribute to their now former teammate. "He has dominated for a long time, and he was always there, every year," said pitcher Clayton Kershaw, a teammate of Jansen's going back to their minor league days. "He went out there and did what he was asked to do. We're going to miss him. I'm going to miss him." Catcher Austin Barnes said: "It'll be weird not having him. But I'm happy for him, going to Atlanta, got a good contract and I'm sure he'll be good over there." Manager Dave Roberts said of Jansen: "He would do it naturally. I understood him, he understood me. He made my job much easier."[18]

April 1, 2022: Traded Outfielder AJ Pollock to the Chicago White Sox for Pitcher Craig Kimbrel

Two weeks after cutting ties with 34-year-old All-Star closer Kenley Jansen, the Dodgers replaced him with 34-year-old All-Star closer Craig

Kimbrel. To get Kimbrel, the Dodgers sent outfielder AJ Pollock, also 34, to the Chicago White Sox. The right-handed-batting Pollock, signed by Los Angeles as a free agent in 2019, had become one of the team's best hitters. He batted .297 with 21 home runs, 69 RBIs, and an .892 OPS in 2021. Appearing in 258 games over three seasons, he batted .282 with 52 home runs, 150 runs batted in, and a 124 OPS+. But the Dodgers felt their offense was strong enough to sacrifice Pollock's bat to get a proven closer. "As much as the players, clubhouse, manager, staff, the front office loves AJ," general manager Brandon Gomes said, "we felt like it was a way to balance up the roster, add to our pitching depth. It was an opportunity for us to strengthen our pitching and take from an area that we felt had a little bit more depth."[19]

Kimbrel, a right-hander, was the Rookie of the Year with the Atlanta Braves in 2011 when he led the National League with 46 saves. He was also the saves leader in each of the next three years, with 42, 50, and 47. Since then Kimbrel had pitched for the Padres, the Red Sox, and the Cubs before joining the White Sox. Overall, the eight-time All-Star had 372 saves and a 2.18 earned run average for his 12-year career. "I don't think I could be any happier," said Kimbrel, who had lost his closer's job in Chicago to Liam Hendricks. "I mean, you come over to a team like this that already expects to win, and I'm being asked to come in and just do my job. It feels really nice…. I'm going to be able to put some shoes on that I know that fit. Hopefully it turns into good results."[20]

Kimbrel appeared in 63 games for the 2022 Dodgers, with a 6–7 record, 22 saves, and a 108 ERA+. In January 2023, he signed as a free agent with the Philadelphia Phillies.

December 8, 2022: Free Agent Shortstop Trea Turner Signed with the Philadelphia Phillies

Several teams had bid for 29-year-old shortstop Trea Turner. The Philadelphia Phillies won out by offering him an 11-year contract worth $300 million. (Reportedly, the San Diego Padres had offered him $342 million.) Turner came to the Dodgers with pitcher Max Scherzer in a July 30, 2021, trade with Washington. He played in 52 games over the final two months of the season, mostly at second base, batting .338 with a 149 OPS+. When shortstop Corey Seager left to play for the Texas Rangers in 2022, manager Dave Roberts moved Turner back to shortstop. The speedy right-handed hitter batted .298, with 21 home runs, 100 RBIs and 27 stolen bases. In both his seasons in Los Angeles, Turner was instrumental in the Dodgers reaching the playoffs. He was voted MLB's best shortstop, and his departure left a big hole for the Dodgers to fill.

Turner and the Dodgers had been working on a contract extension ever since he arrived. "We had a lot of different conversations over the last year with his camp," Andrew Friedman said. "We had a pretty good feel for what they were looking for. They had a pretty good feel for where we were." Meanwhile, Friedman would have to look for a replacement, via free agency or a trade. "There's still a lot of really good players on the market," he said, while not ruling out 25-year-old Gavin Lux, who played second base this past season.[21]

December 14, 2022: Free Agent Outfielder Cody Bellinger Signed with the Chicago Cubs

In 2017 Cody Bellinger was the National League's Rookie of the Year. Two years later he was the league's Most Valuable Player. For his first four seasons, the left-handed slugger had a .911 OPS, 123 home runs, and was twice selected to the All-Star team. The Dodgers expected to build around him for years to come. They won a World Series in the COVID-shortened 2020 season, but during the postseason Bellinger injured his shoulder during a celebration with Kiké Hernández. The injury required him to get labrum surgery during the offseason. He had never been the same hitter since, batting just .193 with 29 home runs over the last two years.

After the Dodgers chose not to offer him a contract for 2023, Bellinger signed a one-year deal with the Chicago Cubs worth $17.5 million. His salary would be $12 million next season, with a $5.5 million buyout if a mutual option for 2024 did not materialize. "Obviously, when we made the decision with Cody a few weeks ago," president of baseball operations Andrew Friedman said, "we knew that this was a possibility."[22] Bellinger's agent, Scott Boras, claimed the 27-year-old outfielder garnered interest from 11 or 12 teams. Some were multiyear offers, but Bellinger wanted a one-year deal that could allow him to increase his desirability and allow him to test free agency again next winter. Boras said his client was rebuilding strength in his shoulder and predicted he would do well in Chicago. It was a good prediction. Bellinger batted .307 for the 2023 Cubs, with 26 home runs, 97 runs batted in, and a 139 OPS+. He did not do as well in 2024, batting .266, with 18 home runs, 78 runs batted in, and a 111 OPS+.

December 16, 2022: Signed Free Agent Pitcher Noah Syndergaard

Noah Syndergaard caught everyone's attention when he broke in with the New York Mets in 2015. The 22-year-old right-hander struck out 166 batters in 150 innings, while going 9–7 with a 117 ERA+. Syndergaard was even better in 2016 when his blazing fastball and flowing blond hair earned him the nickname "Thor." He had a 14–9 record with an ERA+ of 155 and struck out 218 batters in 183⅔ innings. Over the next four years Syndergaard had mixed results as he struggled with injuries. He missed all of 2020 and most of 2021 because of Tommy John surgery. This past season, pitching for the Los Angeles Angels and the Philadelphia Phillies, he had 10–10 record with a 102 ERA+.

Syndergaard's early brilliance and his injury-free 2022 season induced several teams to attempt to sign him. He had offers for more years and money from other teams, but the Dodgers won out with a one-year deal worth $13 million, with the opportunity to earn $1.5 million in performance bonuses. Syndergaard, now 30, said he was impressed with the Dodgers' recent track record of helping veteran pitchers improve and wanted another chance to bet on himself before re-entering free agency next winter.

"I feel like everything that they touch turns to gold," Syndergaard said. "This is a pretty surreal moment. It's been my dream ever since I was first introduced to Dodger Stadium…. I just feel really fortunate and blessed to play for such a great organization."[23]

Signing Noah Syndergaard turned out to be among the most unfortunate moves ever for the Dodgers. He had a 1–4 record and a 7.16 ERA in 12 starts before a blister problem put him on the injured list. He was sent to Triple A Oklahoma City, where he started twice, with one loss and a 5.40 ERA. On July 26, the Dodgers sent him, plus cash, to the Cleveland Indians for infielder Amed Rosario.

December 29, 2022: Signed Free Agent Designated Hitter J.D. Martinez

At this year's July 31 trading deadline, the Dodgers attempt to buy right-handed-hitting J.D. Martinez from the Boston Red Sox failed when the teams could not agree on a price. Four months later they signed the 35-year-old free agent to a $10 million, one-year contract. Martinez was expected to replace Justin Turner as the team's primary designated hitter. Turner had filled that role in 2022, the first year the DH was used in the National League, but he was a free agent whom the Dodgers were not expected to re-sign.

In his 12-year career, with Houston, Detroit, Arizona, and Boston, Martinez had a .288 batting average with 282 home run and 899 RBIs in 1,409 games. His best season was with the 2018 Red Sox, when he batted .330 with 43 home runs and 130 RBIs. Martinez, a five-time All-Star, hit .274 this past season with 16 home runs, 43 doubles, and 62 RBIs.

Used almost exclusively as a designated hitter, Martinez batted .271 for the 2023 Dodgers, with 33 home runs, 103 RBIs, and a 135 OPS+. In March 2024, he signed as a free agent with the New York Mets.

Also in 2022:

Traded: Outfielder Luke Raley to Tampa Bay Rays for Minor League Pitcher Tanner Dodson; Outfielder First Baseman Matt Beaty to San Diego Padres for Minor League Pitcher River Ryan; Infielder-Outfielder Zach McKinstry to Chicago Cubs for Pitcher Chris Martin; Pitcher Garrett Cleavinger to Tampa Bay Rays for Minor League Outfielder German Tapia; Pitcher Mitch White and Minor League Shortstop-Third Baseman Alex De Jesus to Toronto Blue Jays for Minor League Pitcher Moises Brito and Minor League Pitcher Nick Frasso; Pitcher Jake Lamb to Seattle Mariners for a Player to Be Named; Pitcher Clayton Beeter to New York Yankees for Outfielder Joey Gallo; Minor League Pitcher Jeff Belge to Tampa Bay Rays for Pitcher J.P. Feyereisen

Purchased: Outfielder Trayce Thompson from Detroit Tigers; Pitcher Jake Reed from New York Mets; Outfielder Luke Williams from Miami Marlins; Pitcher Jake Reed from Boston Red Sox; Infielder Yonny Hernández from the Oakland Athletics

Sold: Infielder Sheldon Neuse to Oakland Athletics; Pitcher Darien Núñez to San Francisco Giants; Pitcher Reyes Moronta to Arizona Diamondbacks; Pitcher Jake Reed to Baltimore Orioles; Minor League Pitcher Gus Varland to Milwaukee Brewers

Signed Free Agents: Pitcher Yency Almonte; Pitcher Tyler Anderson; Third Baseman Jake Lamb; Infielder Hanser Alberto; Outfielder Kevin Pillar; Pitcher Heath Hembree; Pitcher Reyes Moronta; Pitcher Shelby Miller; Outfielder Jason Heyward; Pitcher Bryan Hudson; Infielder Eddy Alvarez

Released: Pitcher Yefry Ramírez; Catcher Tony Wolters; Infielder Eddy Alvarez

Left as Free Agents: Pitcher Shane Greene; Pitcher Tyler Anderson; Outfielder Joey Gallo; Pitcher Andrew Heaney; Pitcher Tommy Kahnle; Pitcher Craig Kimbrel; Pitcher Chris Martin; Outfielder Kevin Pillar; Pitcher David Price; Pitcher Jimmy Nelson

2023

January 6, 2023: Free Agent Third Baseman Justin Turner Signed with the Boston Red Sox

When the Dodgers signed free agent J.D. Martinez to be their designated hitter in 2023, it became apparent that they were unlikely to re-sign Justin Turner, their 2022 DH. Both were right-handed-hitters, and Martinez was three years younger than the 38-year-old Turner. The club had already declined a $16 million option on Turner at the start of the offseason. After batting .260 with eight home runs in his first five major league seasons, with the Orioles and the Mets, Turner signed a minor league contract with the Dodgers in 2014. He made the club out of spring training, and in his nine years with Los Angeles, Turner batted .296 with 156 home runs and a combined OPS+ of 133.

Moreover, he was active in local charities, earning him the prestigious Roberto Clemente Award this past season. "It's crazy looking back and seeing how everything, on all fronts, took off for me... since the day I put the Dodger uniform on," he said after hosting one of his charitable events. At the Clemente award ceremony, Turner repeated how important playing for the Dodgers had been for him. "Obviously it's very special to me, growing up in Southern California and getting to wear that jersey," he said.[24]

January 11, 2023: Traded Minor League Infielder Jacob Amaya to the Miami Marlins for Shortstop Miguel Rojas

The Dodgers filled the hole at shortstop created by free agent Trea Turner's departure to the Phillies by trading minor league infielder Jacob Amaya to the Miami Marlins for veteran Miguel Rojas. After Rojas's rookie season with the Dodgers in 2014, he was traded to Miami, where he had been for eight years. He was the longest-tenured member of the Marlins and the team's unofficial leader. Don Mattingly, the Marlins manager for the last seven seasons, often commented on what Rojas's presence in the clubhouse meant to the club.

The right-handed-hitting Rojas batted .265 with an OPS+ of 87 in his years in Miami. This past October he had surgery on an injured right wrist, which may have been partly responsible for his low .236 batting average and an OPS+ of 71. But the Dodgers were more interested in Rojas's defense than his offense. In 2022, he made only seven errors in 531 chances at shortstop and was a National League Gold Glove finalist. While primarily a shortstop, Rojas, who would turn 34 in a month, could play all the infield positions and play them well.

Rojas played in 103 games in 2024, mostly at shortstop. He batted better than the Dodgers expected, a .283 average with a 113 OPS+, but was replaced at shortstop late in the season (and in four of the five World Series games) by newcomer Tommy Edman.

Twenty-four-year-old Jacob Amaya was the Dodgers eleventh-round pick in the 2017 amateur draft. He was rated strong defensively at both middle infield positions. Amaya, a right-handed batter, hit a combined .261 with 17 home runs and 71 RBIs in 133 games for Double A Tulsa and Triple A Oklahoma City in 2022. He played in four games for Miami in 2023 and was traded to Houston in April 2024.

February 16, 2023: Signed Free Agent Outfielder David Peralta

Among those gone from the 2022 Dodgers, a team that won 111 games, was outfielder Cody Bellinger. Aside from Mookie Betts, who would again be the right fielder, the two other outfield positions would be determined in the spring. By signing free agent David Peralta to a one-year, $6.5 million deal, with incentives that could add up to $2 million, the team added one more name to the mix. Rookie James Outman was expected to replace Bellinger in center field, while manager Dave Roberts planned to platoon Peralta, Trayce Thompson, and Chris Taylor in left field. The left-handed-hitting Peralta would face the right-handers, and Thompson or Taylor the left-handers

"I still believe that the talent in the room and how we can put it together is going to make us a very good ballclub," Roberts said. "But compared to last year's team, where I don't think we really had questions.... I'm not going to sit here and say that we have as much depth." Attempting to put a positive spin on the situation, Roberts suggested the increased competition for playing time could provide its own benefits during the season. "I don't think that we've really had that in years past," he said. "A little competition, earning playing opportunities, I think it's a good thing."[25]

The 35-year-old Peralta had spent eight and a half years of his nine-year career with the Arizona Diamondbacks, before Arizona traded him to Tampa Bay at the trading deadline last July. He had a career .796

OPS and twice led the National League in triples. Peralta won a Silver Slugger Award in 2018, after batting .293 with a career-high 30 home runs. In his one season in Los Angeles, he batted .259 with an 82 OPS+ in 133 games. Peralta, a free agent, signed to play for San Diego in 2024, his fourth team in the last four seasons.

July 25, 2023: Traded Pitcher Nick Robertson and Minor League Pitcher Justin Hagenman to the Boston Red Sox for Infielder-Outfielder Kiké Hernández

In six seasons with the Dodgers (2015 to 2020), Kiké Hernández was a fan favorite and a valuable utility man who could play the infield and the outfield. Now he was coming back to Los Angeles. In return for Hernández, Boston was getting rookie pitcher Nick Robertson, 24, and minor league pitcher Justin Hagenman, 26. "We're excited to get Kiké back here," manager Dave Roberts said. "He obviously helped us win a championship. And he had his best years here in a Dodgers uniform."[26]

Hernández signed a two-year, $14 million contract as a free agent with Boston in 2021, following the Dodgers' 2020 World Series win. He did well in his first season with the Red Sox, batting .250, with 20 home runs, and he had 20 hits in 11 games in the postseason. But his offense had slipped sharply since then. Now in his third season in Boston, the 31-year-old Hernández was having the worst season of his career, a .222 batting average with six home runs and a 62 OPS+. His overall average in his three years with the Red Sox was .234 with an 86 OPS+.

"He hasn't had the best of seasons," Roberts said. "But for us, the bet is being back home, with familiarity, we can tap back into him being the player we know he can be and that we've seen. I still stand by he's one of the most talented baseball players I've been around," Roberts added. "So, I'm excited to see him blend in with this ballclub."[27]

Hernández batted .262 with 5 homers and 30 RBIs in 54 games, while playing wherever needed in the second half of 2023. His versatility continued in 2024, though his offense fell off. Hernández rebounded by batting .294 in 14 postseason games helping the Dodgers to a five-game defeat of the Yankees in the World Series. Following the 2024 season, he became a free agent and was still unsigned when the year ended.

Nick Robertson pitched in nine games for Boston in 2023. In December he was traded to St. Louis for outfielder Tyler O'Neill, who had 31 home runs and an OPS+ of 132 for the 2024 Red Sox. Justin Hagenman, a 2018 draft choice, has yet to pitch in the major leagues.

July 28, 2023: Traded Outfielder Trayce Thompson, Minor League Pitcher Jordan Leasure, and Minor League Pitcher Nick Nastrini to the Chicago White Sox for Pitcher Lance Lynn and Pitcher Joe Kelly

The Dodgers were in first place with slim leads over San Francisco and Arizona—three and four games respectively—but they worried about their pitching. As they should have. The staff's collective earned run average of 4.47 ranked twentieth in the major leagues. With the trading deadline three days away, and unsure if they could trade for a top-flight pitcher, they swung a deal with the Chicago White Sox. In acquiring Lance Lynn and Joe Kelly, they added two veteran right-handers, neither of whom were having good seasons. Leaving Los Angeles for Chicago were outfielder Trayce Thompson and two minor-league pitchers: Jordan Leasure and Nick Nastrini.

Thirty-six-year-old Lance Lynn, now in his 12th season, had spent the best part of his career with his original team, the St. Louis Cardinals. Lynn, who had also spent time with the Twins, the Yankees, and the Rangers, was a two-time All-Star. He had a career record of 129–93, including eight seasons with double digit wins. But in 21 starts this season, Lynn had a 6–9 record and a 6.47 ERA, highest among qualified MLB starters. He had also given up the most hits in the American League, and his 28 home runs allowed were the most in either league. Lynn did have one highlight performance this season. In a June game against Seattle, he struck out 16 batters, the most strikeouts ever in a game by a pitcher with an ERA above 6.00.

One big-league scout damned him with faint praise: "His results have been trash. But he's still not terrible." General manager Brandon Gomes believed Lynn could be a big help to the Dodgers staff, not just someone to help raise its floor. "His under-the-hood [numbers] aren't that different than they've been in the past," Gomes said. "We feel like there are some suggestions that we'll have on pitch selection that should be helpful."[28] Lynn pitched well for the Dodgers down the stretch. He made 11 starts with a 7–2 record and signed as a free agent with the Cardinals after the season.

Thirty-five-year-old reliever Joe Kelly had been a fan favorite when he pitched for the Dodgers from 2019 to 2021. As a member of their 2020 World Series championship team, Kelly gave up one earned run in 3 2/3 innings of five high-pressure playoff games that postseason. His subpar season with Chicago included a 1–5 record and a 4.97 ERA in 31 games. He had, however, struck out 41 in 29 innings. "Obviously, the people of Los Angeles know Joe," manager Dave Roberts said. "And I would argue that his stuff is even better than it was then when he was with us."[29]

Kelly had a 1.74 ERA in 11 games for the 2023 Dodgers but was limited for much of the 2024 season with a shoulder injury. His 2024 record was 1–1 with a 4.78 ERA in 35 games. The injured shoulder caused him to miss the World Series. Kelly declared for free agency after the season.

Trayce Thompson, 32, batted .268 with 13 home runs and a 149 OPS+ in 2022. But he, too, was having a poor season, a .155 batting average and an 83 OPS+ in 36 games. Thompson incurred an oblique strain in June, and only recently had begun a rehabilitation assignment with the Triple A Oklahoma City Dodgers. He returned to bat .171 in 36 games for the White Sox. After the season Thompson signed as a free agent with the New York Mets, who kept him in the minor leagues in 2024.

Right-handers Nick Nastrini and Jordan Leasure, both chosen in the 2021 amateur free agent draft, were teammates on the Tulsa Drillers, the Dodgers Double A team in the Texas League. Chicago promoted them to the Triple A Charlotte Knights of the International League to finish the rest of the 2023 season. Both pitchers made their major-league debuts with the 2024 White Sox.

December 11, 2023: Signed Free Agent Outfielder-Pitcher Shohei Ohtani

The Dodgers years-long pursuit of Shohei Ohtani finally came to fruition. They had tried to sign him out of high school, in 2013, but the 18-year-old Ohtani chose to stay home and play for the Nippon Ham Fighters of the Japan Pacific League. They tried again in 2018, when Ohtani chose to play in the United States, but missed out because the National League had not yet adopted the designated hitter rule. Ohtani, who wanted to continue as both a pitcher and an outfielder/DH, chose the American League's Los Angeles Angels. As a left-handed-hitter and right-handed-pitcher he won the AL's Rookie of the Year Award in 2018 and began drawing comparisons to Babe Ruth. He was the unanimous winner of the league's MVP Award in 2021 and 2023 and finished second in 2022.

Over those three seasons, Ohtani hit 124 home runs and had 290 RBIs, while also going 34–16 with a 2.84 ERA and 542 strikeouts as a pitcher. In 2023, his second MVP season, he led the AL with 44 home runs and led both leagues with a .654 slugging percentage and a 1.066 OPS. As a starting pitcher, Ohtani went 10–5 with a 3.14 ERA in 23 starts. However, elbow surgery this past September would preclude his pitching in 2024. His free agency was the major topic of discussion among baseball fans this offseason. The Red Sox, the Braves, the Rangers, and the Cubs were each rumored as having the inside track. But at the winter meetings, the finalists were said to be the Angels, the Cubs, the Giants and, most of all, the Blue Jays.

Then came the stunning announcement that Ohtani had agreed to a 10-year, $700 million contract with the Dodgers. Ohtani broke the news on his Instagram account a day after reports suggested he was on the verge of signing with Toronto. "To all the fans and everyone involved in the baseball world, I apologize for taking so long to come to a decision," Ohtani said. "I have decided to choose the Dodgers as my next team."[30]

According to the *Los Angeles Times*, the deal was believed to be the largest in sports history, surpassing even the reported totals of soccer superstars Lionel Messi and Kylian Mbappe. Furthermore, the Times reported, the majority of Ohtani's contract would be paid out in "unprecedented" deferrals, which were Ohtani's idea. Most of the money would be paid out after the 10 seasons, which would provide Ohtani some tax benefits. More importantly for the Dodgers, it would ease potential year-to-year payroll and luxury tax complications of having a single player making $70 million annually. Ohtani's primary reason for the deferrals, according to the Times's source, was to help the team be successful on the field.

"This is a unique, historic contract for a unique, historic player," said Nez Balelo of CAA Sports, Ohtani's agent. "Shohei is thrilled to be a part of the Dodgers organization. He is excited to begin this partnership, and he structured his contract to reflect a true commitment from both sides to long-term success." Ohtani said in a post on Instagram: "First of all, I would like to express my sincere gratitude to everyone involved with the Angels organization and the fans who have supported me over the past six years, as well as to everyone involved with each team that was part of this negotiation process. Especially to the Angels fans who supported me through all the ups and downs, your guys' support and cheers meant the world to me. The six years I spent with the Angels will remain etched in my heart forever."[31]

Manager Dave Roberts discussed the Dodgers meeting with Ohtani before the signing.

"I think it was more [about] just getting more familiar with him," Roberts said of the three-hour session, which included a lunch at Dodger Stadium with members of the Dodgers front office and ownership group. Ohtani was taken on a tour of the ballpark and the team's clubhouse facilities. "He had questions for us, just trying to get more of the landscape," Roberts added. "But being in this league for six years he's got a pretty good idea of the Dodgers, what we're about, the city itself. So, for me, and speaking for our guys, it was just a pleasure to get to spend some time with him."[32]

Ohtani proved his worth by winning his record third unanimous Most Valuable Player Award in 2024. He batted .310 with a league-leading 54 home runs, 130 RBIs, and a league-leading 1.036 OPS. His 59 stolen bases made him the first player to have 50 or more home runs and 50 or more stolen bases in the same season. Ohtani also led the NL in runs (134), on-base average (.390), slugging percentage (.646), and total bases (411).

December 16, 2023: Traded Pitcher Ryan Pepiot and Outfielder Jonny DeLuca to the Tampa Bay Rays for Pitcher Tyler Glasnow, Outfielder Manuel Margot, and Cash

Five days after signing Shohei Ohtani, the Dodgers began their efforts to upgrade their starting pitching. They began by announcing the completion of a four-player trade that had been under discussion for several days. The deal brought them highly coveted pitcher Tyler Glasnow, outfielder Manuel Margot, and $4 million, in exchange for pitcher Ryan Pepiot and outfielder Jonny DeLuca.

Glasnow, a 30-year-old, 6'8" right-hander, signed a five-year, $135 million contract with the Dodgers that included both a club and a player option for the 2028 season. Glasnow had a 30–27 record with a 3.89 earned run average in his eight-year career, the first two with Pittsburgh and the last six with Tampa Bay. Injuries had been a problem for him throughout his career, including a Tommy John surgery in 2021.

But the Dodgers were encouraged by his performance this past season, when he went 10–7 with a 3.53 ERA. His 21 starts and 120 innings pitched in 2023 were his most in any major-league season. The Rays said they received interest in Glasnow from more than a dozen teams before making the deal with the Dodgers.

"This is somewhere I've wanted to be my entire life," said Glasnow, a native Californian. "They were very bullish on trying to get me, and I appreciate the fact they thought so highly of me. I get to go home. It's like the best possible scenario."[33]

Injuries continued to prevent Glasnow from playing a full season. An inflammation in his right elbow in August that kept him out for the rest of the season and the entire postseason. When healthy, Glasnow was effective, compiling an 9–6 record, with 168 strikeouts in 134 innings, and a 111 ERA+ in 22 starts. He was selected to the All-Star team for the first time, though he did not appear in the game.

For the small-market Rays, this deal was the kind that had helped them become a power in the AL East. It saved them about $33 million and rid them of older, more expensive players, replacing them with younger, cheaper ones who were under team control for a longer time. Twenty-six-year-old Ryan Pepiot would not be eligible for free agency until 2029; Johnny DeLuca, not until 2030.

Pepiot, whose fastball was clocked in the high 90s, had been ranked among *Baseball America*'s top 100 prospects the last two years. He had a 5–1 record with a 2.76 ERA in 17 games for the Dodgers over those two seasons. Pepiot started 26 games for the 2024 Rays, with an 8–8 record and a 111 ERA+.

Jonny DeLuca, 25, was a speedy right-handed hitter with a strong arm who could play anywhere in the outfield. He was ranked 17th among Dodgers prospects going into 2023, a season in which he moved from Double A to Triple A to Los Angeles. Playing in 107 games for the Rays in 2024, he batted a disappointing .217 with an OPS+ of 75.

Manuel Margot, 29, had also been hampered with injuries over recent seasons, including right elbow surgery in 2023 and a right knee sprain in 2022. In February 2024, the Dodgers traded him to the Minnesota Twins.

December 27, 2023: Signed Free Agent Pitcher Yoshinobu Yamamoto

Manager Dave Roberts called it a "monumental offseason," after the Dodgers completed their third transaction this month. Following the signing of free agent outfielder-pitcher Shohei Ohtani and trading for pitcher Tyler Glasnow, they signed pitcher Yoshinobu Yamamoto, a free agent from Japan. Yamamoto, a 25-year-old right-hander, agreed to a 12-year, $325 million deal. Added to Ohtani's $700-million contract, it raised the money spent on the two former Japan Pacific League players to $1.025 billion. The Dodgers also paid a $50.6 million posting fee to Japan's Orix Buffaloes, Yamamoto's former team.

The 5'10", 176-pound Yamamoto was the Dodgers' twelfth Japanese-born player. In his seven seasons in Japan, primarily for the Buffaloes, he had a 70–29 record with a 1.82 earned run average in 897 innings. He struck out 922, walked 206 and allowed only 36 home runs.

Yamamoto's dominance was reflected in his winning the last three Pacific League Most Valuable Player Awards and Sawamura Awards. (The Sawamura Award is the Japanese equivalent of the Cy Young Award.)

"You can never have enough starting pitching—all of us in baseball realize that—but certainly, the landscape of our starting staff has changed considerably over the last few weeks," Roberts said. "It's hard to compare year to year, players to players, staffs to staffs, but this is a pretty good staff we got."[34]

The Dodgers beat out more than a dozen teams that aggressively pursued Yamamoto, including both New York teams, the San Francisco Giants, and the Boston Red Sox. Ohtani, who deferred $680 million of his deal until after it expires, freed up the money for the Dodgers to pursue more players. "The fact that Shohei was willing to do that signaled that it wasn't just the front office, it was also the players that have bought into this winning atmosphere," Yamamoto said through his interpreter, Mako Allbee. "That really resonated with me. I wouldn't say [Ohtani] was the sole reason I decided to come here—even if he went somewhere else, I probably would have ended up in L.A. as a Dodger," Yamamoto added. "But on top of that, Shohei is not only one of the best Japanese players, but he's one of the best players, period, in all of MLB. It was very important to be with a team that wants to win, not only now but in the future as well. And I really felt throughout this process that the Dodgers provided that opportunity the most."[35]

"Being able to watch Yoshinobu pitch, his stuff is special," Dodgers general manager Brandon Gomes said. "The command is up there with the upper echelon of guys I've seen his command the baseball…. That command not only allows him to go deep into games, but when needed, he can feature swing-and-miss stuff that is elite."

Unlike the past, when there were often questions as to whether players from Japan could succeed in the major leagues, Yamamoto was expected to make the transition easily. "I think he will be dominant for a long time," said St. Louis Cardinals outfielder Lars Nootbaar, who was a teammate of Yamamoto's with Japan's World Baseball Classic team last spring. "From today moving forward, I promise to all the fans of L.A. that I will focus my everything to become a better player and become a world champion as a member of the Dodgers," Yamamoto said. "I will stop simply admiring the players I looked up to, but rather strive to become the player that others want to become."[36]

Despite suffering a rotator cuff injury in June that kept him out for close to three months, Yamamoto had a successful first season. He won seven and lost two with a 129 ERA+ and had winning starts against the Padres in the National League Championship Series and the Yankees in the World Series.

Also in 2023:

Traded: Minor League Pitcher Luis Valdez to Texas Rangers for Minor League Pitcher Ricky Vanasco; Pitcher Victor González and Minor League Infielder Jorbit Vivas to New York Yankees for Minor League

Infielder Trey Sweeney; Pitcher Noah Syndergaard and cash to the Cleveland Guardians for Infielder Amed Rosario; Minor League First Baseman Derlin Figueroa and Minor League Infielder Devin Mann to Kansas City Royals for Pitcher Ryan Yarbrough

Purchased: Pitcher Tyson Miller from the Milwaukee Brewers; Pitcher Tyson Miller from the New York Mets; Pitcher Gus Varland returned from Milwaukee Brewers

Sold: Pitcher Tayler Scott to Boston Red Sox; Pitcher Andre Jackson to Pittsburgh Pirates; Pitcher Tyson Miller to New York Mets; Outfielder Luke Williams to Atlanta Braves; Pitcher Dylan Covey to Philadelphia Phillies; Catcher Austin Wynns to Colorado Rockies; Pitcher Justin Bruihl to Colorado Rockies; Pitcher Adam Kolarek to New York Mets; Pitcher Phil Bickford to New York Mets

Signed Free Agents: Pitcher Nabil Crismatt; Pitcher Tayler Scott; Pitcher Ryan Brasier; Pitcher Eduardo Salazar; Outfielder Jake Marisnick; Catcher Austin Wynns; Pitcher Wander Suero; Pitcher Tyler Cyr; Pitcher Dylan Covey

Released: Pitcher Trevor Bauer

Left as Free Agents: Pitcher Tyson Miller; Infielder Hanser Alberto; Pitcher Heath Hembree; Third Baseman Edwin Rios; Infielder Amed Rosario; Infielder Yonny Hernández; Outfielder Jake Marisnick; Pitcher Dylan Covey; Pitcher Wander Suero; Pitcher Tyler Cyr; Pitcher Shelby Miller

2024

January 16, 2024: Signed Free Agent Outfielder Teoscar Hernández

The Dodgers had already acquired Shohei Ohtani, Yoshinobu Yamamoto, and Tyler Glasnow but continued spending money to strengthen their team for the 2024 season. In their first deal of the new year, they signed free agent outfielder Teoscar Hernández to a one-year deal worth $23.5 million. The club had been interested in signing him since the November 2023 general manager meetings. Hernández, 31, who played for Seattle in 2023, was a career American Leaguer who began his eight-year career with Houston in 2016 and played for Toronto from 2017 to 2022. In those eight years, the right-handed slugger had a .261 batting average with 159 home runs, 473 runs batted in, and a 118 OPS+.

"We're planning on Teo being an everyday guy," said general manager Brandon Gomes. "We feel like his power and ability to really handle left-handed pitching was an exceptional fit for how our lineup is constructed. What was very intriguing with Teo is that he crushes velocity, and crushes velocity up in the zone," Gomes added. "He's not susceptible to any one pitch type. He can hit all pitch types. And when he's getting those pitches in the zone, he can do real damage."[37]

"I wanted to go to a team that can compete and be in the playoffs and … make me a better player," Hernández said. "That's the biggest reason I signed with the Dodgers. I wanted to sign a multi-year deal, like every free agent," Hernández said. "But everyone knows how hard it's been this winter.… It's not like I had a lot of choices."[38]

Hernández wanted to go to a team that would go to the postseason. His contributions to the 2024 Dodgers helped that happen. He played in 154 games, starting 104 in left field and 50 in right field. Offensively, Hernández batted .272 with a 137 OPS+, while leading all National League outfielders in home runs 33 and RBIs (99). He played in all 16 of the postseason games, getting 15 hits, including two home runs in the National League Division Series and one in the World Series. With his one-year contract at an end, Hernández became a free agent but re-signed with the Dodgers.

January 29, 2024: Signed Free Agent Pitcher James Paxton

Uncertain if Clayton Kershaw would be available, and certain that Julio Urias was lost forever, the Dodgers continued to reconstruct their 2024 pitching rotation. After several weeks of negotiation, they officially signed 6'4" free-agent James Paxton to a one-year, $11 million deal. The 35-year-old left-hander had a 7–5 record with a 4.50 earned run average in 19 starts for the Boston Red Sox in 2023. Paxton had pitched in the American League for 10 seasons—seven with Seattle, two with the Yankees, and one with Boston—with a 64–38 record. His best seasons were 2017 to 2019 when he won 38 and lost 17. But injuries limited Paxton to only a combined six games the next two seasons, and Tommy John surgery caused him to miss the entire 2022 season.

Paxton won eight and lost two with a 4.43 earned run average in 18 starts for the Dodgers in 2023. But on July 22, when pitchers Kershaw and Tyler Glasnow returned from their injuries, the club designated Paxton for assignment. Four days later they traded him back to the Red Sox for Moises Bolivar, a 17-year-old minor league shortstop.

June 12, 2024: Traded Minor League Pitcher Braydon Fisher and Cash to the Toronto Blue Jays for Second Baseman Cavan Biggio

The Dodgers added a versatile infielder by acquiring Cavan Biggio from the Toronto Blue Jays for minor league pitcher Braydon Fisher. Biggio, a 29-year-old left-handed hitter, had been designated for assignment a week earlier. Called up to Toronto in May 2019, Biggio played in 100 games with 16 home runs, 48 runs batted in and a fifth-place finish in Rookie of the Year voting. After a strong COVID-shortened 2020, he had struggled offensively the last four seasons. His six-year totals for the Blue Jays were a .227 batting average, with 48 home runs and 176 RBIs in 490 games. In 44 games this season, he was batting .200 with just six extra-base hits and nine RBIs in 110 at-bats. Nevertheless, the Dodgers expected him to add strength to their defense. Although primarily a second baseman, Biggio could also play first base, third base, and right field.

"To have a team like the Dodgers come and pick me up after my time in Toronto, where I spent so many years with so many relationships there and playing against this team about a month and a half ago. Obviously very special and very fortunate and grateful to be here," Biggio said. "I know the player that I can be. I know what I'm capable of, I know that I can reach it and I'm hoping to do so with the Dodgers."[39]

On August 8, the Dodgers released Biggio. He had played in 30 games, batting .192 in 88 plate appearances, with a double, three home runs, and 10 runs batted in. Through the 2024 season right-hander Braydon Fisher had yet to reach the major leagues.

July 29, 2024: Traded Infielder-Outfielder Miguel Vargas, Minor League Infielder Jeral Perez, Minor League Infielder Alexander Albertus and a Player to be Named or Cash to the Chicago White Sox, and a Player to be Named or Cash to the St. Louis Cardinals in a Three-Way Deal that brought them Pitcher Michael Kopech from Chicago and Infielder Tommy Edman and Minor League Pitcher Oliver Gonzalez from St. Louis

First-place Los Angeles used prospects and money to acquire relief pitcher Michael Kopech and infielder Tommy Edman in a three-team trade with the Chicago White Sox and the St. Louis Cardinals. The Dodgers expected the new additions to strengthen their roster—Kopech by providing added depth in the bullpen and Edman, a switch-hitter, to bolster the bottom of the batting order. Both would be under team control through the end of the 2025 season.

Kopech, 28, had an excellent fastball but spotty control. He pitched in four games in 2018 and then missed the 2019 season with an injury and opted out of the 2020 season because of COVID-19 precautions. He returned as a reliever in 2021, was a starter the next two seasons, and moved back to the bullpen in 2024. Kopech had a 2–8 record, with a 4.74 ERA and nine saves for the woeful White Sox this season. Of his 14 save opportunities for Chicago, he had blown five.

Going from the worst team in baseball to one that would that win the World Series did wonders for Kopech. Appearing in 24 games for LA, all in relief, he had a 4–0 record, six saves, and a 1.13 earned run average that was three times better than the league average ERA.

Edman, whom the Dodgers had long seen as a player they wanted, was considered the more valuable of the two new acquisitions. The 29-year-old utility man had experience at second base, shortstop, third base and all three outfield positions. In 2021 he won a Gold Glove as a second baseman. Edman had been with the Cardinals since 2019, with a combined batting average of .265. His one downside was his health. Erdman's 2023 season was adversely affected by wrist problems, resulting in a career-low .248 batting average. Surgery on the wrist last October forced him to miss the start of this season. A sprained ankle he suffered in late June while fielding ground balls delayed his return. Edman spent most of July on a rehabilitation assignment with the Cardinals' Double-A affiliate, batting .207 in eight games. But he had not appeared in the field in that stretch, serving as a designated hitter in each game.

Upon joining the Dodgers Edman justified the team's hopes for him. He played in 37 games, splitting his time between shortstop and center field, baseball's two most skilled positions. He batted just .237, but had six home runs, twenty runs batted in, and six stolen bases. Edman was a key part of the Dodgers' offense in the postseason, batting a combined .328, including a .407 average and 11 RBIs in the National League Championship Series and a .294 mark in the World Series. His play in the NLCS earned him the MVP Award for that series. In December, the Dodgers re-signed Edman to a five-year contract

The Dodgers also acquired 17-year-old, right-handed pitcher Oliver Gonzalez from St. Louis in the deal. They kept Gonzalez in the Dominican Summer League, moving him from the Cardinals team in that league to theirs.

Leaving for the White Sox were spare outfielder Miguel Vargas and minor league infielders Jeral Perez and Alexander Albertus. In addition, the Dodgers were sending a player to be named or cash to the White Sox and to the Cardinals. The 24-year-old Vargas was the player the White Sox wanted most. A one-time top prospect, he had struggled to find a place in the Dodgers' lineup the last two years. Vargas batted .104 in 42 games for Chicago over the remainder of the season. Perez and Albertus remained in the minor leagues.

July 30, 2024: Traded Minor League Catcher Thayron Liranzo and Minor League Shortstop Trey Sweeney to the Detroit Tigers for Pitcher Jack Flaherty

Clayton Kershaw had just returned to the club, but Yoshinobu Yamamoto and Walker Buehler were on the injured list and Bobby Miller was struggling. In need of a starting pitcher, the Dodgers acquired right-hander Jack Flaherty from the Detroit Tigers minutes before the trading deadline. The Tigers received two minor leaguers, catcher Thayron Liranzo and shortstop Trey Sweeney. Liranzo, a 21-year-old switch-hitter, was the better of the two prospects. Playing in the Low A California League in 2023, Liranzo had a .962 OPS with 24 home runs in 94 games.

Flaherty was a 28-year-old Burbank native who grew up rooting for the Dodgers. "Jack, he's a guy that's been wanting to be a Dodger, being from the Valley, for so long," said Dodgers manager Dave Roberts. "So, to get that done, I'm really excited."[40]

Flaherty had a 41–31 record in seven seasons with the Cardinals. His best year was 2019, when he won 11 and lost 8, with a 152 ERA+ and a fourth-place finish in voting for the Cy Young Award. He was traded to Baltimore last August, declared for free agency, and signed with Detroit. Flaherty said he made a pair of mechanical adjustments coming into the season, which worked out well. He had a 7–5 record and a 2.95 ERA for the Tigers with 133 strikeouts in 106⅔ innings.

"We had a ton of conversations with a lot of teams over this last week," general manager Brandon Gomes said. "We felt like getting an impact starter was a very high priority for us, and Jack is definitely that. His command, his stuff, the swing-and-miss, we feel like that's a real power option come October, so he fits into this rotation really well."[41]

Flaherty was an excellent pickup for the Dodgers injury-ridden pitching staff. He made 10 starts with a 6–2 record and a 3.58 earned run average. In 10 postseason appearances, all starts, he won one game and lost two. Flaherty declared for free agency after the season and was unsigned when the year ended.

November 26, 2024: Signed Free Agent Pitcher Blake Snell

The Dodgers made their first move in defense of their world championship by signing highly sought after free agent Blake Snell to a five-year contract worth $182 million. The organization felt a need to add at least one new starter to their already strong rotation and found their man in Snell. They had bid for Snell, a left-hander a week shy of his thirty-second birthday, following his 2023 season with San Diego, in which he won the second of his two Cy Young Awards, but lost out to the Giants. They tried again, unsuccessfully, at the 2024 trading deadline. When declarations of free agency began the Dodgers made their wishes known to Snell's agent, Scott Boras. The final agreement included a $52 million signing bonus, as well as deferred money.

"If you can't beat him, just have him join us," said Dodgers president of baseball operations Andrew Friedman. "What's really difficult is to win. What's even harder to do is to repeat. Our players, coaching staff, everyone is of the mind, let's run it back, let's do everything we can to win, so everything for us was, what puts us in the best position to do that?"[42]

Snell's first Cy Young Award came in 2018, as a member of the Tampa Bay Rays, when he led the American League with 21 wins (21–5) and a 1.89 earned run average. He was 14–9 with a league-best 2.25 ERA 234 strikeouts over 180 innings in his award-winning 2023 season. Snell's 11.2 career strikeouts per nine innings is the highest in in major league history.

Snell's signing as a free agent with the Giants did not come until March. That resulted in a slow start to the season before he regained his form. Over his final 14 starts, he had a 1.23 ERA and 114 strikeouts, while limiting his opponents to a .123 batting average. One of those starts was an August 2 no-hitter against the Cincinnati Reds, his first-ever complete game. Over his nine-year career—five with the Ray, three with the Padres, and one with the Giants—Snell had won 76, lost 58, with an ERA+ of 128.

"It's fun to know you're joining a team with that experience," Snell said. "Being able to learn from that, I'm excited. I've been there. I failed. They've been there. They've succeeded. Want to do what I can do to help get them to World Series."[43]

December 8, 2024: Signed Free Agent Outfielder Michael Conforto

The New York Mets signing Juan Soto to the most lucrative baseball contract ever overshadowed everything on the day before the start of the 2024 winter meetings in Dallas. Little noticed was the Dodgers signing free agent Giants outfielder Michael Conforto to a one-year, $17 million contract. Conforto became the second free agent this offseason to leave San Francisco for Los Angeles. (Blake Snell was the first.)

Conforto, who would turn 32 the following March, was the Mets first-round draft choice in 2014 and played for them from 2015 to 2021. Over the three seasons 2017–2019, he hit 88 home runs and drove in 242 runs. In all, the left-handed-hitting Conforto batted .255 for the Mets with 132 home runs, 396 runs batted in, and an OPS+ of 124.

After missing the 2022 season because of a shoulder injury, Conforto joined the Giants in 2023. He played in 255 games over the past two seasons, batting .238 with 35 home runs, 124 RBIs and a 108 OPS+. With the Dodgers planning to move Mookie Betts from the outfield to shortstop and the re-signing of free agent Teoscar Hernández their starting outfield in 2025 figured to be Conforto in right field, Hernández in left, and Tommy Edman in center.

Also in 2024:

Traded: Pitcher Bryan Hudson to Milwaukee Brewers for Minor League Pitcher Justin Chambers; Third Baseman Michael Busch and Pitcher Yencey Almonte to Chicago Cubs for Minor League Pitcher Jackson Ferris and Minor League Outfielder Zyhir Hope; Outfielder Manuel Margot and Minor League Infielder Rayne Doncon to Minnesota Twins for Minor League Infielder Noah Miller; Minor League Pitcher Benony Robles to Philadelphia Phillies for Pitcher Connor Brogdon; Minor League Pitcher Michael Flynn to Tampa Bay Rays for Infielder Amed Rosario; Pitcher Ryan Yarbrough to Toronto Blue Jays for Outfielder Kevin Kiermaier; Pitcher Caleb Ferguson to New York Yankees for Pitcher Matt Gage and Minor League Pitcher Christian Zazueta

Purchased: Pitcher Nick Ramirez from New York Yankees; Outfielder Taylor Trammell from Seattle Mariners; Pitcher Brent Honeywell, Jr., from Pittsburgh Pirates; Pitcher Anthony Banda from Cleveland Guardians; Pitcher Yohan Ramírez from New York Mets

Sold: Pitcher Ricky Vanasco to Detroit Tigers; Outfielder Taylor Trammell to New York Yankees; Pitcher Matt Gage to New York Mets; Pitcher Eduardo Salazar to Seattle Mariners; Pitcher Yohan Ramírez to Boston Red Sox; Infielder Amed Rosario to Cincinnati Reds

Signed Free Agents: Pitcher Robbie Erlin; Pitcher Elieser Hernández;

Pitcher Dinelson Lamet; Pitcher Michael Petersen; Shortstop Nick Ahmed; Pitcher Zach Logue

Left as Free Agents: Designated Hitter J.D. Martinez; Pitcher Elieser Hernández; Pitcher Dinelson Lamet; Outfielder David Peralta; Pitcher Nabil Crismatt; Pitcher Walker Buehler

Chapter Notes

Chapter 1

1. Ben Gould, "Dodgers Sign 2 Negro Aces for Nashua Farm," *Brooklyn Eagle*, April 4, 1946.
2. "Newk Ready to Report to Redlegs," *Los Angeles Mirror*, June 16, 1958.
3. "Dodgers Get Steve Bilko," *Los Angeles Mirror*, June 16, 1958.
4. George Lederer, "Jackson Glad to be Traded," *Press-Telegram* (Long Beach, CA), August 5, 1958.
5. Charlie Park, "Out of the Park," *Los Angeles Mirror*, August 5, 1958.
6. Art Rosenbaum, "Gino Cimoli Not Surprised at Being Traded to St. Louis," *Los Angeles Times*, December 9, 1958.
7. Jack Herman, "Cardinals Send Wally Moon to Dodgers," *St. Louis Globe-Democrat*, December 5, 1958.

Chapter 2

1. George Lederer, "Zimmer Goes to Cubs For 3 Minor Leaguers," *Independent* (Long Beach, CA), April 8, 1960.
2. Wells A. Twombley, "Clem Pens Sorrowful Farewell," *Valley Times* (North Hollywood, CA), June 17, 1960.
3. "Pignatano, Essegian Peddled by Dodgers," *Los Angeles Times*, February 2, 1961.
4. Lou Hatter, "Orioles Buy Essegian from Dodgers' Spokane Farm," *Baltimore Sun*, February 2, 1961.
5. "Dodgers Obtain Farrell for Smith, Demeter," *Daily News-Post* (Monrovia, CA), May 5, 1961.
6. "Dodgers Obtain Farrell."
7. "Spencer Obtained in 2-for-1 Trade," *Los Angeles Times*, May 31, 1961.
8. "Spencer Obtained."
9. George Lederer, "Spencer at Third; Tommy to Outfield," *Independent* (Long Beach, CA), May 31, 1961.
10. Don Johnson, "Hodges, Larker Go in Draft," *Pasadena Independent*, October 11, 1961.
11. Johnson, "Hodges, Larker Go."
12. "Stengel Waits Six Years for Neal," *News-Pilot* (San Pedro, CA), December 16, 1961.
13. "Stengel Waits Six Years."
14. Wells A. Twombley, *Valley Times* (North Hollywood, CA), December 16, 1961.
15. "Dodgers Swap Williams for Skowron," *Progress-Bulletin* (Sonoma, CA), November 27, 1962.
16. "Dodgers Shed Williams to Get Yanks' Skowron," *Pasadena Independent*, November 27, 1962.
17. "Dodgers Swap Williams."
18. Frank Finch, "Burright, Harkness Swapped for Miller," *Los Angeles Times*, December 2, 1962.
19. George Lederer, "Buzzie Balks but Snider Urges Trade," *Press-Telegram* (Long Beach, CA), April 1, 1963.
20. "Ed Roebuck Mad at Alston," *Progress-Bulletin* (Sonoma, CA), July 30, 1963.
21. George Lederer, "Winter—Dodgers Deal Only in Snow," *Independent* (Long Beach, CA), December 7, 1963.
22. Frank Finch, "Dodgers May Add Brewer to Roster," *Los Angeles Times*, April 10, 1964.
23. Finch, "Dodgers May Add Brewer."
24. "Sherry Moves to Detroit Tigers," *News-Pilot* (San Pedro, CA), April 9, 1964.
25. Finch, "Dodgers May Add Brewer."

26. "Dodgers Recall Frank Howard," *Daily News-Post* (Monrovia, CA), June 15, 1959.
27. "Hodges Happy He'll Have Frank Howard," *Los Angeles Times*, December 18, 1964.
28. "Howard, 'Bo' Both Gone in a Day," *Evening Vanguard* (Venice, CA), December 5, 1964.
29. "Howard, 'Bo' Both Gone."

Chapter 3

1. "Dodgers Get Hurler for Tracewski," *Press-Telegram* (Long Beach, CA), December 16, 1965.
2. George Lederer, "4 Brooklyns Left as Podres Goes," *Press-Telegram* (Long Beach, CA), May 10, 1966.
3. Lederer, "4 Brooklyns Left."
4. Lederer, "4 Brooklyns Left."
5. "Tommy Davis Sent 'Home,'" *Ventura County [CA] Star*, November 30, 1966.
6. Dick Young, "Mets get a Batting Champ: Hunt, Hick Go for T. Davis," *New York Daily News*, November 30, 1966.
7. "Tommy Davis Sent to Mets for Ron Hunt," *Los Angeles Times*, November 30, 1966.
8. "Hunt Liked Mets, But L.A.'s Okay," *Ventura County [CA] Star*, November 30, 1966.
9. Charles Maher, "Wills Goes to Bucs for Bailey, Michael," *Los Angeles Times*, December 2, 1966.
10. "Wills Traded to Pirates," *Los Angeles Times*, December 2, 1966.
11. Paul Zimmerman, "'I'm Thrilled to Death,' Says Bailey of Trade," *Los Angeles Times*, December 2, 1966.
12. Charles Maher, "Dodgers Trade Kennedy to Yankees," *Los Angeles Times*, April 4, 1967.
13. Charles Maher, "Versalles, Grant Traded by Minnesota," *Los Angeles Times*, November 29, 1967.
14. Maher, "Versalles, Grant Traded."
15. Marshall Klein, "Roseboro Sorry to Leave Dodgers but Trade Came as No Surprise," *Los Angeles Times*, November 29, 1967.
16. Charles Maher, "Dodgers Deal Sweet Lou to Chicago Cubs," *Los Angeles Times*, December 1, 1967.
17. Frank Finch, "Traded for Personal Reasons—Lou," *Los Angeles Times*, December 1, 1967.
18. Maher, "Dodgers Deal Sweet Lou."
19. "Dodgers Trade Oliver and Hunt for Tom Haller," *News-Pilot* (San Pedro, CA), February 14, 1968.
20. George Lederer, "Bavasi Trades 'Vulture,'" *Independent* (Long Beach, CA), April 24, 1968.
21. Robert Markus, "Who Is the First Met Who, and Who?" *Chicago Tribune*, July 4, 1968
22. George Lederer, "Dodgers Don't 'K'—Kosco for Kekich,'" *Independent* (Long Beach, CA), December 5, 1968.
23. "Wills Happy to Be Home," *Daily News Post* (Monrovia, CA), June 12, 1969.

Chapter 4

1. John Wiebusch, "Dodgers Obtain Clout—Richie Allen." *Los Angeles Times*, October 6, 1970.
2. Wiebusch, "Dodgers Obtain Clout."
3. Gordon Verrell, "Bye-Bye, Teddy—Hello Richie!" *Independent* (Long Beach, CA), October 6, 1970.
4. John Wiebusch, "Dodgers Get Catcher Duke Sims in Trade," *Los Angeles Times*, December 12, 1970.
5. "Dodgers Trade for Duke Sims," *Progress Bulletin* (Pomona, CA), December 11, 1970.
6. Ross Newhan, "Brewers' Downing Comes to Dodgers in Swap for Kosco," *Los Angeles Times*, February 11, 1971.
7. Gordon Verrell, "'New Dodgers Like Old Yankees,' Says Downing," *Independent* (Long Beach, CA), February 25, 1971.
8. Don Merry, "Angels Go Fishing, Come Up Big Catch in Jeff Torborg," *Independent* (Long Beach, CA), March 15, 1971
9. Merry, "Angels Go Fishing."
10. Ross Newhan, "L.A. Dumps Allen, Adds F. Robinson," *Los Angeles Times*, December 3, 1971.
11. "Dodgers Ship Allen to White Sox, Trade for Orioles' Frank Robinson," *Daily News-Post* (Monrovia, CA), December 3, 1971.
12. "Robby, 36, Sure He Has One Good Year Left, Then...," *Los Angeles Times*, December 3, 1971.
13. "Dodgers Ship Allen to White Sox."
14. Ross Newhan, "L.A. Dumps Allen,

Adds F. Robinson," *Los Angeles Times*, December 3, 1971.
15. Ron Rapoport, "Dodgers Trade Robinson to Angels," *Los Angeles Times*, November 29, 1971.
16. Don Merry, "'Dodgers Gave Up Too Much'—Singer," *Press-Telegram* (Long Beach, CA), November 29, 1972.
17. Rapoport, "Dodgers Trade Robinson."
18. Merry, "'Dodgers Gave Up Too Much.'"
19. Don Merry, "Willie D. Traded for Montreal Ace," *Press-Telegram* (Long Beach, CA), December 6, 1973.
20. Merry, "Willie D. Traded."
21. "Mike Marshall Not Sure He'll Join Dodgers," *Los Angeles Times*, December 7, 1973.
22. Gordon Verrell, "Marshall: Winning Isn't Everything," *Independent* (Long Beach, CA), March 20, 1974.
23. Ross Newhan, "Wynn No Longer Has a Roof Over His Head ... He's Happy," *Los Angeles Times*, December 7, 1973.
24. Newhan, "Wynn No Longer Has a Roof Over His Head."
25. Newhan, "Wynn No Longer Has a Roof Over His Head."

Chapter 5

1. Ross Newhan, "Giants Buy Joshua for Waiver Price," *Los Angeles Times*, January 30, 1975.
2. Bob Verdi, "Hooton Gets Way—Traded to Dodgers for 2 Hurlers," *Chicago Tribune*, May 3, 1975.
3. "Dodgers Obtain Cubs' Hooton," *Los Angeles Times*, May 3, 1975.
4. Ross Newhan, "L.A. Gets Dusty Baker for Wynn, Lacy, Others," *Los Angeles Times*, November 18, 1975.
5. Newhan, "L.A. Gets Dusty Baker."
6. "Sizemore Back with Dodgers," *Progress Bulletin* (Pomona, CA), March 3, 1976.
7. "Messersmith Finds a Home—in Atlanta," *Los Angeles Times*, April 11, 1975.
8. "Messersmith Finds a Home."
9. Gordon Verrell, "Dodgers Acquire Reggie Smith in Ferguson Trade," *Press-Telegram* (Long Beach, CA), June 16, 1976.
10. Verrell, "Dodgers Acquire Reggie Smith."
11. Warren Corbett, "Mike Marshall," SABRBioProject.
12. Ross Newhan, "Dodgers Trade Ferguson for Cards' Reggie Smith," *Los Angeles Times*, June 16, 1976.
13. Ross Newhan, "Marshall Marked Down and Sold to the Braves," *Los Angeles Times*, June 24, 1976.
14. "Marshall Sold to Braves at a Discount," *News-Pilot* (San Pedro, CA), June 24, 1976.
15. "L.A. Deals Sizemore to Phillies for Oates," *Progress Bulletin* (Pomona, CA) December 21, 1976.
16. Ross Newhan, "Monday: The 4-year Pitch," *Los Angeles Times*, January 12, 1977.
17. Ross Newhan, "Buckner on Trade: 'I Feel Like a Piece of Meat,'" *Los Angeles Times*, January 13, 1977.
18. Newhan, "Buckner on Trade."
19. Ross Newhan, "Dodgers Add Some Insurance, Then Win,'" *Los Angeles Times*, September 1, 1977.
20. Frank Mazzeo, "Dodgers Bolster 'Pen with Forster," *Valley News* (Van Nuys, CA) November 19, 1977.
21. Mazzeo, "Dodgers Bolster 'Pen."
22. Ross Newhan, "A Clean Start...," *Los Angeles Times*, May 18, 1978.
23. Newhan, "A Clean Start."
24. Ross Newhan, "Ferguson Is Back as Backup Man for Dodgers," *Los Angeles Times*, July 2, 1978.
25. Newhan, "Ferguson Is Back."
26. Ross Newhan, "Dodgers Get Thomas, but All is Not Well," *Los Angeles Times*, November 15, 1978.
27. Newhan, "Dodgers Get Thomas."
28. Newhan, "Dodgers Get Thomas."
29. "John Joins the Rolls-Royce Staff," *Los Angeles Times*, November 23, 1978.
30. Chris Mortensen, "Dodgers Get Outfielder in Trade," *News-Pilot* (San Pedro, CA), February 15, 1979.
31. "Rhoden Happy About Trade to Pirates," *News-Pilot* (San Pedro, CA), April 9, 1979.
32. "Reuss Comes to Dodgers in 'a Dream Come True,'" *Los Angeles Times*, April 9, 1979.
33. Mike Littwin, "The Dodgers Say It with Dollars," *Los Angeles Times*, November 16, 1979.
34. Littwin, "The Dodgers Say It with Dollars."

Chapter 6

1. "Dodgers Sell Hough to Texas," *Los Angeles Times*, July 12, 1980.
2. Dodger Notes, *Los Angeles Times*, July 12, 1980.
3. Ross Newhan, "Sutton Moves Up a Notch, Signs with the Astros," *Los Angeles Times*, December 4, 1980.
4. Newhan, "Sutton Moves Up a Notch."
5. Mark Heisler, "Landreaux to Dodgers; Hatcher is Now a Twin," *Los Angeles Times*, March 31, 1980.
6. Heisler, "Landreaux to Dodgers."
7. Heisler, "Landreaux to Dodgers."
8. Heisler, "Landreaux to Dodgers."
9. Mark Heisler, "Sutcliffe and Perconte Get their Wish," *Los Angeles Times*, December 10, 1981.
10. Heisler, "Sutcliffe and Perconte Get their Wish."
11. Mark Heisler, "Lopes is Traded; Nine-Year Career as a Dodger Ends," *Los Angeles Times*, February 9, 1982.
12. Heisler, "Lopes is Traded."
13. Mark Heisler, "Lopes Goes with Head Up," *Los Angeles Times*, February 10, 1982.
14. Chris Mortensen, "Dodgers send Law to Chisox for 2 players," *News-Pilot* (San Pedro, CA), March 31, 1982.
15. Tim Tucker, "Braves Sign Lefty Reliever Forster," *Atlanta Constitution*, December 2, 1982.
16. Tim Tucker, "Forster is Happy to Join Strong Bullpen of Braves," *Atlanta Constitution*, December 3, 1982.
17. Maxwell Kates, "Steve Garvey," SABR BioProject.
18. Mark Heisler, "For Dodgers and Garvey it Ended Badly," *Los Angeles Times*, December 22, 1982.
19. Heisler, "For Dodgers and Garvey."
20. Mark Heisler, "Cey Dealt to the Cubs for 2 Minor Leaguers," *Los Angeles Times*, January 20, 1983.
21. "It's Official: Cey Goes to Cubs," *News-Pilot* (San Pedro, CA), January 20, 1983.
22. Terry Johnson, "Dodgers Sweeten Pennant Chances with Honeycutt," *News-Pilot* (San Pedro, CA), August 20, 1983.
23. Johnson, "Dodgers Sweeten Pennant Chances."
24. Gordon Edes, "Dodgers Trade Fernandez and Beckwith," *Los Angeles Times*, December 9, 1983.
25. Gordon Edes, "Former Giants Outfielder Leaves Japan, Signs with Dodgers," *Los Angeles Times*, January 13, 1984.
26. Gordon Edes, "Hooton Goes to Rangers for Work," *Los Angeles Times*, December 21, 1984.

Chapter 7

1. Terry Johnson, "Finally, Campanis Gets His Man: Enos Cabell," *News-Pilot* (San Pedro, CA), July 11, 1985.
2. Johnson, "Finally, Campanis Gets His Man."
3. Dan Hafner, "Madlock Joins Dodgers; Pirates get 3 Players," *Los Angeles Times*, September 1, 1985.
4. Hafner, Madlock Joins Dodgers."
5. Ross Newhan, "Yeager Traded to Mariners," *Los Angeles Times*, December 12, 1985.
6. Newhan, "Yeager Traded to Mariners."
7. Newhan, "Yeager Traded to Mariners."
8. Terry Johnson, "Dodgers Show Off Their Christmas Gifts Early," *News-Pilot* (San Pedro, CA), December 18, 1985.
9. Terry Johnson, "Dodgers Deal Brock, Powell," *News-Pilot* (San Pedro, CA), December 11, 1986.
10. Johnson, "Dodgers Deal Brock."
11. Ross Newhan, "New Dodger Matt Young Says His Arthritic Condition is Under Control," *Los Angeles Times*, December 14, 1986.
12. Johnson, "Dodgers Deal Brock."
13. Terry Johnson, "Brock Leaves Dodgers Happy, But Confused," *News-Pilot* (San Pedro, CA), December 11, 1986.
14. Johnson, "Dodgers Deal Brock."
15. Sam McManis, "Dodgers Trade Niedenfuer to Orioles for Shelby," *Los Angeles Times*, May 23, 1987.
16. McManis, "Dodgers Trade Niedenfuer."
17. McManis, "Dodgers Trade Niedenfuer."
18. Sam McManis, "Dodgers Trade for a Center Fielder … But it Doesn't Help," *Los Angeles Times*, May 23, 1987.
19. Sam McManis, "Honeycutt Traded to Oakland," *Los Angeles Times*, August 30, 1987.
20. McManis, "Honeycutt Traded."

21. Ross Newhan, "Dodgers Pay a Big Price (Welch) to Improve," *Los Angeles Times*, December 12, 1987.
22. Newhan, "Dodgers Pay a Big Price."
23. Sam McManis, "Dodgers Pay a Big Price (Welch) to Improve," *Los Angeles Times*, December 12, 1987.
24. McManis, "Dodgers Pay a Big Price."
25. McManis, "Dodgers Pay a Big Price."
26. Ross Newhan, "Kirk Gibson Agrees to Dodger Green," *Los Angeles Times*, January 30, 1988.
27. Newhan, "Kirk Gibson Agrees."
28. Ross Newhan, "Claire Proves Himself with Bold Moves," *Los Angeles Times*, August 17, 1988.
29. Sam McManis, "He Won't Look Back," *Los Angeles Times*, August 17, 1988.
30. McManis, "He Won't Look Back."
31. Ross Newhan, "Sax Goes to Yankees for 3 Years, $4 Million," *Los Angeles Times*, November 24, 1988.
32. Newhan, "Sax Goes to Yankees."
33. Newhan, "Sax Goes to Yankees."
34. Gordon Edes, "Finally, Deal is Done, Dodgers Get Murray," *Los Angeles Times*, December 5, 1988.
35. Edes, "Finally, Deal is Done."
36. Edes, "Finally, Deal is Done."
37. Gordon Edes, "Dodgers Sign Randolph for 2 Years," *Los Angeles Times*, December 11, 1988.
38. Edes, "Dodgers Sign Randolph."
39. Bob Wolf, "Devereaux is Traded to Orioles in Exchange for Pitcher Morgan," *Los Angeles Times*, March 12, 1989.
40. Wolf, "Devereaux is Traded."
41. Chris Long, "Dodgers Find Offensive Help in Trade," *News-Pilot* (San Pedro, CA), July 19, 1989.
42. Long, "Dodgers Find Offensive Help."
43. Long, "Dodgers Find Offensive Help."
44. Long, "Dodgers Find Offensive Help."
45. Terry Johnson, "Dodgers Anderson Goes to SF," *News-Pilot* (San Pedro, CA), November 29, 1989.
46. Bill Plaschke, "Dodgers Trade Marshall, Pena to Mets," *Los Angeles Times*, December 21, 1989.
47. Terry Johnson, "Dodgers, Mets Exchange Problems," *News-Pilot* (San Pedro, CA), December 21, 1989.

Chapter 8

1. Bill Plaschke, "Stubbs' Wish Comes True with Deal," *Los Angeles Times*, April 2, 1990.
2. Plaschke, "Stubbs' Wish Comes True."
3. Bill Plaschke, "Dodgers Send A's Randolph," *Los Angeles Times*, May 13, 1990.
4. Plaschke, "Dodgers Send A's Randolph."
5. Plaschke, "Dodgers Send A's Randolph."
6. "Strawberry: 'Mets Just Let Me Walk Away,'" *Los Angeles Times*, November 8, 1990.
7. Marty Noble, "Former Teammates Can't Believe the Mets Let Straw Slip Away," *Los Angeles Times* (from *Newsday*), November 9, 1990.
8. "Teufel: Darryl Isn't a Team Player," *Los Angeles Times*, November 9, 1990.
9. "Teufel: Darryl Isn't a Team Player."
10. "Gibson Gets Royal Treatment," *Daily Breeze* (Torrance, CA), December 2, 1990.
11. Ross Newhan, "$6.4 Million Gets Gross to Dodgers for Three Years," *Los Angeles Times*, December 4, 1990.
12. Newhan, "$6.4 Million Gets Gross to Dodgers."
13. Terry Johnson, "Butler Did It: He's a Dodger" *News-Pilot* (San Pedro, CA), December 15, 1990.
14. Bill Plaschke, "Odd Man Out is Dealt for Ojeda," *Los Angeles Times*, December 16, 1990.
15. Plaschke, "Odd Man Out."
16. Plaschke, "Odd Man Out."
17. Bill Plaschke, "Candelaria Signed; Carter Must Wait a Day," *Los Angeles Times*, March 26, 1991.
18. Plaschke, "Candelaria Signed."
19. Plaschke, "Candelaria Signed."
20. "Carter Catches on with Dodgers," *San Francisco Examiner*, March 27, 1991.
21. "Fernandomania Moves to Orange County," *The Signal* (Santa Clarita, CA), May 21, 1991.
22. Bill Plaschke, "Gonzalez Gets Wish, Dodgers Trade Him for Webster," *Los Angeles Times*, July 4, 1991.
23. "Dodgers, A's Just Beat Deadline in Arms Race," *Fresno Bee*, August 1, 1991.
24. Bill Plaschke, "Dodgers Bring Davis

Home," *Los Angeles Times*, November 28, 1991.
25. Bill Plaschke, "Dodgers Bring Davis Home."
26. Plaschke, "Dodgers Bring Davis Home."
27. Plaschke, "Dodgers Bring Davis Home."
28. Bill Plaschke, "Dodgers Lose One, Keep One, Get One," *Los Angeles Times*, December 4, 1991.
29. Plaschke, "Dodgers Lose One."
30. Bill Plaschke, "Dodgers Put Benzinger on First," *Los Angeles Times*, December 12, 1991.
31. Plaschke, "Dodgers Put Benzinger on First."
32. Plaschke, "Dodgers Put Benzinger on First."
33. "Daniels Goes to Cubs for Real Unknown," *Los Angeles Times*, June 28, 1992.
34. "Daniels Goes to Cubs."
35. MaryAnn Hudson and Helene Elliott, "Dodgers Sign Cory Snyder, Re-Sign Pitcher McDowell," *Los Angeles Times*, December 6, 1992.
36. Hudson and Elliott, "Dodgers Sign Cory Snyder."
37. MaryAnn Hudson, "Dodgers Get Relief in Worrell," *Los Angeles Times*, December 10, 1992.
38. Hudson, "Dodgers Get Relief."
39. "Dodgers Trade for Expos' Wallach," *The Signal* (Santa Clarita, CA), December 25, 1992.
40. "Dodgers Trade for Expos' Wallach."
41. John Maffei, "Padres Pick Up Scioscia," *North County Times* (Ontario, CA), February 12, 1993.
42. "Davis' Career with Dodgers Ends," *The Signal* (Santa Clarita, CA), September 1, 1993.
43. "Davis' Career with Dodgers Ends."
44. Mark Langill, "Weight Program Saves Career for Giants' Beck," *Pasadena [CA] Star-News*, September 5, 1993.
45. Tim Kawakami, "Dodgers Deal for DeShields Costs Them Pedro Martinez," *Los Angeles Times*, November 20, 1993.
46. Kawakami, "Dodgers Deal for DeShields."
47. "Gross Signs $6 Million Deal with Rangers," *Los Angeles Times*, December 14, 1995.

Chapter 9

1. Bob Nightengale, "East Meets West for New Dodger," *Los Angeles Times*, February 14, 1995.
2. Nightengale, "East Meets West."
3. "Lasorda Salutes Hershiser," *Daily Breeze* (Torrance, CA), April 9, 1995.
4. "Hershiser Takes Cleveland Deal," *Daily Breeze* (Torrance, CA), April 9, 1995.
5. "Hershiser Takes Cleveland Deal."
6. "Less is More for Free Agents," *News-Pilot* (San Pedro CA), April 12, 1995.
7. "Less is More."
8. Bob Nightengale, "Dodgers Pull Off a Big One: Rodriguez for Expos' Kelly," *Los Angeles Times*, May 24, 1995.
9. Nightengale, "Dodgers Pull Off a Big One."
10. Bob Nightengale, "Dodgers React, Grab Tapani from Twins," *Los Angeles Times*, August 1, 1995.
11. Jim Souhan, "Tapani, Guthrie, Dealt to Dodgers," *Star Tribune* (Minneapolis, MN), August 1, 1995.
12. Ross Newhan, "Dodgers Get Blowers for 2 Minor Leaguers," *Los Angeles Times*, November 30, 1995.
13. Newhan, "Dodgers Get Blowers."
14. Ross Newhan, "First It's Blowers, Now Gagne," *Los Angeles Times*, December 1, 1995.
15. Newhan, "First It's Blowers."
16. Newhan, "First It's Blowers."
17. Terry Johnson, "Dodgers Get 1 Player for 2 Needs," *News-Pilot* (San Pedro, CA), August 1, 1996.
18. Johnson, "Dodgers Get 1 Player."
19. Johnson, "Dodgers Get 1 Player."
20. "Cardinals Sign Delino DeShields," *The Signal* (Santa Clarita, CA), November 21, 1996.
21. "It's Official: Dodgers Sign Zeile," *Los Angeles Times*, December 9, 1996.
22. "Dodgers Acquire Young," *News-Pilot* (San Pedro, CA), August 19, 1997.
23. Jason Reid, "Dodgers Bring Back Vizcaino," *Los Angeles Times*, December 9, 1997.
24. Reid, "Dodgers Bring Back Vizcaino."
25. Bill Cizek, "Piazza to Go," *Daily Breeze* (Torrance, CA), May 16, 1998.
26. Cizek, "Piazza to Go."
27. Cizek, "Piazza to Go."

28. Ross Newhan, "They'll Wait to See How Fantasy Ends," *Los Angeles Times*, May 16, 1998.
29. Cizek, "Piazza to Go."
30. Robyn Norwood, "Mets Become Dodger Ex-Files," *Los Angeles Times*, June 5, 1998.
31. Norwood, "Mets Become Dodger Ex-Files."
32. Rob Gloster, "Dodgers Continue Shakeup," *Daily Breeze* (Torrance, CA), July 5, 1998.
33. Gloster, "Dodgers Continue Shakeup."
34. "Wheeling Becomes Dealing," *Los Angeles Times*, August 1, 1998.
35. "Wheeling Becomes Dealing."
36. "Wheeling Becomes Dealing."
37. "Expos Wanted Guerrero or There was No Deal," *Los Angeles Times*, August 1, 1998.
38. Jason Reid, "White Takes Center Stage," *Los Angeles Times*, November 7, 1998.
39. Reid, "White Takes Center Stage."
40. Jason Reid, "It's a Relief as Dodgers Say Goodbye to Bonilla," *Los Angeles Times*, November 12, 1998.
41. Jason Reid, "Bonilla Lashes Out at Lasorda, Dodgers," *Los Angeles Times*, November 16, 1998.
42. Steve Springer, "L.A. Motto: Todd Help Us," *Los Angeles Times*, December 2, 1998.
43. Springer, "L.A. Motto."
44. Jason Reid, "Dodgers Tip Brown Derby," *Los Angeles Times*, November 7, 1998.
45. Reid, "Dodgers Tip Brown Derby."
46. Michael Knisely, "A 105 Million Headache," *Sporting News*, December 13, 1998.
47. "Mlicki, Rojas Traded to Tigers," *Los Angeles Times*, April 17, 1999.
48. "Mlicki, Rojas Traded."
49. Jason Reid, "In the End, Mondesi's Departure Was Mutual," *Los Angeles Times*, November 8, 1999.
50. Reid, "Mondesi's Departure Was Mutual."
51. Ross Newhan, "Mondesi-for-Green a Big Deal in More ways Than One," *Los Angeles Times*, November 9, 1999.
52. *Los Angeles Times*, December 13, 1999.
53. *Los Angeles Times*, December 13, 1999.
54. John Nadel, "Dodgers Bring Back Orel," *The Signal* (Santa Clarita, CA), December 18, 1999.
55. Nadel, "Dodgers Bring Back Orel."

Chapter 10

1. Jason Reid, "Vizcaino Gives Team a Going-Away Present," *Los Angeles Times*, June 21, 2000.
2. Reid, "Vizcaino Gives Team."
3. "Loose Ends Tied Up in Leyritz Deal," *Los Angeles Times*, June 22, 2000
4. Jason Reid, "Swap Meets," *Los Angeles Times*, August 1, 2000.
5. Reid, "Swap Meets."
6. Reid, "Swap Meets."
7. Jason Reid, "After a Balk, Pitcher Ashby is Brought In," *Los Angeles Times*, December 7, 2000.
8. Reid, "After a Balk."
9. Jason Reid, "Hundley Agrees to Cub Contract," *Los Angeles Times*, December 10, 2000.
10. Jason Reid, "At 43, Reliever Orosco Says Time on His Side," *Los Angeles Times*, February 18, 2001.
11. Reid, "At 43, Reliever Orosco Says.
12. Jason Reid, "Dodgers Send White to Brewers," *Los Angeles Times*, February 26, 2001.
13. Reid, "Dodgers Send White to Brewers."
14. Reid, "Dodgers Send White to Brewers."
15. Jason Reid, "Osuna Trade Eases Logjam in Bullpen," *Los Angeles Times*, March 19, 2001.
16. Jason Reid, "Dodgers Add Relievers," *Los Angeles Times*, August 1, 2001.
17. Reid, "Dodgers Add Relievers."
18. "Phillies Trade Daal to Dodgers for 2 Major Leaguers," *Los Angeles Times*, November 10, 2001.
19. "Phillies Trade Daal to Dodgers."
20. Mac Engel, "Rangers Pin Hopes on Park," *Fort Worth Star-Telegram*, December 23, 2001.
21. Mike DiGiovanna and Jason Reid, "Sheffield Goes South," *Los Angeles Times*, January 16, 2002.
22. DiGiovanna and Reid, "Sheffield Goes South."

23. DiGiovanna and Reid, "Sheffield Goes South."
24. "Herges Sent to Montreal," *Ventura County Star*, March 24, 2002.
25. Mike DiGiovanna, "Dodgers Get Shuey to Fill Out Bullpen," *Los Angeles Times*, July 28, 2002.
26. Mike DiGiovanna, "Mulholland: Trade Will Help," *Los Angeles Times*, July 28, 2002.
27. DiGiovanna, "Dodgers Get Shuey."
28. Jason Reid, "Deal Gives Dodgers Flex Factor," *Los Angeles Times*, December 5, 2002.
29. Bill Plaschke, "It's Clearly Tracy's Team," *Los Angeles Times*, December 5, 2002.
30. Plaschke, "It's Clearly Tracy's Team."
31. Teddy Greenstein, "Deal Like Night and Day," *Chicago Tribune*, December 5, 2002.
32. "SF Inks Durham, Grissom, to Deals," *Modesto Bee*, December 8, 2002.
33. Jason Reid, "Dodgers Add Some Offense," *Los Angeles Times*, July 15, 2003.
34. Reid, "Dodgers Add Some Offense."
35. Reid, "Dodgers Add Some Offense."
36. Rob Maadl, "Ventura Heads South to L.A.," *The Signal* (Santa Clarita, CA), August 1, 2003.
37. Maadl, "Ventura Heads South."
38. Jason Reid and Ross Newhan, "Dodgers Trade Could Be a Hit," *Los Angeles Times*, December 14, 2003.
39. Reid and Newhan, "Dodgers Trade."
40. Jason Reid, "DePodesta Alters Look of the Bench," *Los Angeles Times*, March 31, 2004.
41. Bill Shaikin, "Dodgers Acquire Bradley," *Los Angeles Times*, April 5, 2004.
42. Shaikin, "Dodgers Acquire Bradley."
43. Shaikin, "Dodgers Acquire Bradley."
44. Mike DiGiovanna and Jason Reid, "Dodgers Get a Move On," *Los Angeles Times*, July 31, 2004.
45. DiGiovanna and Reid, "Dodgers Get a Move On."
46. Jason Reid, "Bradley Agrees to Yield Center Stage to Finley," *Los Angeles Times*, August 1, 2004.
47. Reid, "Bradley Agrees."
48. "Kent Signs $17 Million Deal with Dodgers," *The Signal* (Santa Clarita, CA), December 10, 2004.
49. "Kent Signs $17 Million Deal."
50. Tim Korte, "Beltre Makes Move from L.A. Official," *The Signal* (Santa Clarita, CA), December 18, 2004.
51. Korte, "Beltre Makes Move."
52. Korte, "Beltre Makes Move."

Chapter 11

1. Mel Reisner, "Finally, D-backs Acquire Green," *Arizona Daily Sun*, January 12, 2005.
2. John Nadel, "Lowe Finalizes Deal to Join Dodgers," *The Signal* (Santa Clarita, CA), January 12, 2005.
3. Steve Henson, "Lowe Happy His Number is Up," *Los Angeles Times*, January 13, 2005.
4. "Cleveland and Cora Reach Deal," *Los Angeles Times*, January 19, 2005.
5. Carter Gaddis, "Rays Give Nomo Shot to Make Rotation," *Tampa Tribune*, January 28, 2005.
6. Tim Brown, "Dodgers Solve Bradley Problem," *Los Angeles Times*, December 14, 2005.
7. Brown, "Dodgers Solve Bradley Problem."
8. Steve Henson, "Dodgers' Frank Discussion Sold Furcal," *Los Angeles Times*, December 18, 2005.
9. Henson, "Dodgers' Frank Discussion."
10. John Nadel, "Nomar Embraces Challenge of Playing First Base," *The Signal* (Santa Clarita, CA), December 20, 2005.
11. Ken Peters, "Lofton Adds New Element to Dodgers," *The Signal* (Santa Clarita, CA), December 21, 2005.
12. Mike DiGiovanna, "Weaver Goes to Other L.A.," *Los Angeles Times*, February 16, 2006.
13. "Angels Sign Weaver to One-Year Contract," *The Signal* (Santa Clarita, CA), February 16, 2006.
14. Bill Shaiken, "Dodgers Trade for a Ray of Hope," *Los Angeles Times*, June 28, 2006.
15. Shaiken, "Dodgers Trade."
16. Beth Harris, "Dodgers Ship Perez off to Royals," *The Signal* (Santa Clarita, CA), July 26, 2006.
17. Harris, "Dodgers Ship Perez."
18. Beth Harris, "Dodgers Busy at

Deadline," *The Signal* (Santa Clarita, CA), August 1, 2006.
    19. Harris, "Dodgers Busy."
    20. Harris, "Dodgers Busy."
    21. John Nadel, "L.A. Gets Speed Fiend for $44 Million," *The Signal* (Santa Clarita, CA), November 23, 2006.
    22. Nadel, "L.A. Gets Speed Fiend."
    23. "Gagne Finalizes Contract," *The Signal* (Santa Clarita, CA), December 20, 2006.
    24. "Gagne Finalizes Contract."
    25. Josh Dubow, "Dodgers, Giants Strike Rare Deal," *The Signal* (Santa Clarita, CA), August 1, 2007.
    26. Dylan Hernandez, "Dodgers Get Blake, Put Him at Third," *Los Angeles Times*, July 27, 2008.
    27. Dylan Hernandez, "Odd Manny In," *Los Angeles Times*, August 1, 2008.
    28. Ben Bolch, "Overflow Crowd Fills Up the Outfield," *Los Angeles Times*, August 1, 2008.
    29. Bolch, "Overflow Crowd."
    30. Bill Shaiken, On Baseball, *Los Angeles Times*, August 1, 2008.
    31. Dylan Hernandez, "Lowe Makes Brave Career Choice," *Los Angeles Times*, January 14, 2009.
    32. David O'Brien, "Lowe Has Ability to Anchor Rotation," *Atlanta Journal-Constitution*, January 17, 2009.
    33. Dylan Hernandez, "Dodgers and Angels Stick to Little Ball," *Los Angeles Times*, December 16, 2009.
    34. "Dodgers Talks About Harang 'All but Dead,'" *Los Angeles Times*, December 19, 2009.
    35. "Dodgers Make Minor Moves," *The Signal* (Santa Clarita, CA), December 18, 2009.

Chapter 12

    1. Dylan Hernandez, "Colletti, Torre Like Deals," *Los Angeles Times*, August 1, 2010.
    2. "Lilly Happy to Be Back," *The Signal* (Santa Clarita, CA), August 2, 2010.
    3. "Lilly Happy to Be Back."
    4. Dylan Hernandez, "Cutting Their Losses," *Los Angeles Times*, August 31, 2010.
    5. Hernandez, "Cutting Their Losses."
    6. Dylan Hernandez, "Martin Acts on the Dodgers' Inaction," *Los Angeles Times*, December 17, 2010.
    7. Ben Bolch, "Dodgers Go to Market," *Los Angeles Times*, August 1, 2011.
    8. Rustin Dodd, "Royals Pick Up Broxton," *Kansas City Star*, November 30, 2011.
    9. Dylan Hernandez, "Dodgers Give Puig Big Deal," *Los Angeles Times*, June 29, 2012.
    10. Dylan Hernandez, "Dodgers Take Another Gamble," *Los Angeles Times*, July 26, 2012.
    11. Bill Plaschke, "Dodgers Do Well to Get Ramirez," *Los Angeles Times*, July 26, 2012.
    12. Dylan Hernandez, "Flashing the Cash," *Los Angeles Times*, August 25, 2012.
    13. "Dodgers Try to Add Sock," *The Signal* (Santa Clarita, CA), August 25, 2012.
    14. Dylan Hernandez, "They Bleed Dodger Green Now," December 10, 2012.
    15. "Dodgers Strike Deal with Greinke, Welcome Ryu," *The Signal* (Santa Clarita, CA), December 11, 2012.
    16. "Dodgers Strike Deal with Greinke."
    17. Dylan Hernandez, "Addition of Greinke to Rotation Would Complement Ace Kershaw," *Los Angeles Times*, December 9, 2012.
    18. Dylan Hernandez, "Dodgers to Stay Up in Arms," *Los Angeles Times*, November 26, 2013.
    19. Dylan Hernandez, "Infield in Play," *Los Angeles Times*, December 11, 2014.
    20. Mike DiGiovanna, "Kendrick Trade Gets Angels a Young Arm," *Los Angeles Times*, December 11, 2014.
    21. "L.A. Makes McCarthy Move Official," *The Signal* (Santa Clarita, CA), December 11, 2014.
    22. "L.A. Makes McCarthy Move Official."
    23. Dylan Hernandez, "He Won't Be Flip if Kemp deal Flops," *Los Angeles Times*, December 20, 2014.

Chapter 13

    1. Steve Dilbeck, "Dodgers Stock Their Cart," *Los Angeles Times*, July 31, 2015.
    2. Dilbeck, "Dodgers Stock Their Cart."
    3. Dylan Hernandez, "Utley Eases Day for Dodgers," *Los Angeles Times*, August 20, 2015.

4. Dylan Hernandez, "Dodgers Trade for Prospects," *Los Angeles Times*, December 17, 2015.
5. Hernandez, "Dodgers Trade for Prospects."
6. Dylan Hernandez, "Dodgers Introduce Pitcher Maeda," *Los Angeles Times*, January 18, 2016.
7. Hernandez, "Dodgers Introduce Pitcher Maeda."
8. Andy McCullough, "A Line in The Sand," *Los Angeles Times*, August 2, 2016.
9. Andy McCullough, "It's a Slow Start for the New Dodgers," *Los Angeles Times*, August 3, 2016.
10. McCullough, "A Line in The Sand."
11. Andy McCullough, "Daring Deal Delivers Ace," *Los Angeles Times*, August 1, 2017.
12. McCullough, "Daring Deal."
13. Andy McCullough, "Kemp Deal is About Money," *Los Angeles Times*, December 16, 2017.
14. McCullough, "Kemp Deal."
15. McCullough, "Kemp Deal."
16. Andy McCullough, "Dodgers Man Up," *Los Angeles Times*, July 19, 2018.
17. Jorge Castillo, "Ready to Do it Again, This Time for Dodgers," *Los Angeles Times*, December 22, 2018.
18. Castillo, "Ready to Do it Again."
19. Castillo, "Ready to Do it Again."
20. Jorge Castillo, "Time for Holiday Spending Spree," *Los Angeles Times*, December 22, 2018.
21. Castillo, "Time for Holiday Spending Spree."

Chapter 14

1. Jorge Castillo, "'Raw Power' Ready for Its Refinement," *Los Angeles Times*, February 21, 2020.
2. Peter Abraham, "For Bloom, a Risk Worth Taking," *Boston Globe*, February 11, 2020.
3. Bill Plaschke, "Betts Could Be the Missing Piece to Ending Drought," *Los Angeles Times*, February 13, 2018.
4. Plaschke, "Betts Could Be the Missing Piece."
5. Dylan Hernandez, "Determined Not to Be the 'Other Guy,'" *Los Angeles Times*, February 13, 2020.
6. Hernandez, "Determined Not to Be."
7. Jorge Castillo, "Deal Should Throw Them Off," *Los Angeles Times*, February 12, 2021.
8. Jorge Castillo and Jack Harris, "With Bauer, the Cup Runneth Over," *Los Angeles Times*, February 6, 2021.
9. Castillo and Harris, "With Bauer."
10. Dylan Hernandez, "Bauer's Presence Compromises Dodgers' Values" *Los Angeles Times*, February 12, 2021.
11. Jorge Castillo, "Pujols Disputes Angels' Take on His Release," *Los Angeles Times*, May 18, 2021.
12. Castillo, "Pujols Disputes Angels' Take."
13. Mike DiGiovanna, "Two Stars at the Cost of One," *Los Angeles Times*, July 31, 2021.
14. DiGiovanna, "Two Stars."
15. Dylan Hernandez, "Jansen Must Know Freeman's Feelings," *Los Angeles Times*, March 19, 2022.
16. Jack Harris, "Freeman Feels Glad to Be Wanted," *Los Angeles Times*, March 19, 2022.
17. Harris, "Freeman Feels Glad."
18. Jack Harris, "As Jansen Era Ends, His Legacy Starts to Sink In," *Los Angeles Times*, March 20, 2022.
19. Jack Harris, "New Star of the Ninth," *Los Angeles Times*, April 2, 2022.
20. Harris, "New Star of the Ninth."
21. Jack Harris, "They Win One, Lose Some," *Los Angeles Times*, December 6, 2022.
22. Jack Harris, "The Winds of Change Have Hit Dodgers," *Los Angeles Times*, December 7, 2022.
23. Juan Toribio, "Why Thor Picked Dodgers," MLB.com, December 19, 2022.
24. Jack Harris, "Turner, Red Sox Agree to a Deal, Ending His Tenure with Dodgers," *Los Angeles Times*, December 19, 2022.
25. Jack Harris, "Dodgers Quiet Winter Might Bring Some Cold, Hard Truths," *Los Angeles Times*, February 14, 2023.
26. Jack Harris, "Fan Favorite Hernandez is Returning for Playoff Push," *Los Angeles Times*, July 26, 2023.
27. Harris, "Fan Favorite Hernandez is Returning."
28. Jack Harris and Mike DiGiovanna, "Dodgers Fortify Their Pitching Staff with Kelly, Lynn," *Los Angeles Times*, July 29, 2023.

Notes—Chapter 14

29. Harris and DiGiovanna, "Dodgers Fortify Their Pitching Staff."

30. Jack Harris and Mike DiGiovanna, "Two-way Superstar Shohei Ohtani Joining Dodgers on Record $700 Million Deal," *Los Angeles Times*, December 10, 2023.

31. Harris and DiGiovanna, "Two-way Superstar Shohei Ohtani Joining Dodgers."

32. Harris and DiGiovanna, "Two-way Superstar Shohei Ohtani Joining Dodgers."

33. Mike DiGiovanna, "Coming Home Attraction," *Los Angeles Times*, December 19, 2023.

34. Mike DiGiovanna, "Another Sleek Import Arrives," *Los Angeles Times*, December 28, 2023.

35. DiGiovanna, "Another Sleek Import Arrives."

36. DiGiovanna, "Another Sleek Import Arrives."

37. Jack Harris, "After Signing a One-Year Deal, Newest Dodger Knows His Role," *Los Angeles Times*, January 16, 2024.

38. Harris, "After Signing a One-Year Deal."

39. Juan Toribio, "Dodgers Add Cavan Biggio in Trade with Blue Jays," MLB.com, June 13, 2024.

40. Juan Toribio, "LA Adds Flaherty, Kiermaier at Deadline," MLB.com, July 30, 2024.

41. Toribio, "LA Adds Flaherty, Kiermaier."

42. Tom Ruminski, "Dodgers Introduce Snell," theScore, December 3, 2024.

43. Ruminski, "Dodgers Introduce Snell."

Selected Bibliography

Alexander, Charles C. *Our Game: An American Baseball History.* New York: Henry Holt, 1991.
Alston, Walter, and Jack Tobin. *A Year at a Time.* Waco: World Books, 1976.
Anderson, Dave. *Pennant Races: Baseball at Its Best.* New York: Doubleday, 1994.
Armour, Mark L., and Daniel R. Levit. *In Pursuit of Pennants: Baseball Operations from Deadball to Moneyball.* Lincoln: University of Nebraska Press, 2015.
Bjarkman, Peter C., editor. *Encyclopedia of Major League Baseball Team Histories: National League.* Westport, CT: Meckler, 1991.
Cohen, Stanley. *Dodgers! The First 100 Years.* New York: Carrol Publishing Group, 1990.
D'Antonio, Michael. *Forever Blue: The True Story of Walter O'Malley, Baseball's Most Controversial Owner, and the Dodgers of Brooklyn and Los Angeles.* New York: Riverhead Books, 2009.
Dewey, Donald, and Nicholas Acocella. *The Ball Clubs.* New York: HarperCollins, 1996.
Dewey, Donald, and Nicholas Acocella. *The Biographical History of Baseball.* New York: Carroll & Graf, 1995.
Endsley, Brian M. *Bums No More: The 1959 Los Angeles Dodgers, World Champions of Baseball.* Jefferson, NC: McFarland, 2009.
Goldblatt, Andrew. *The Giants and the Dodgers: Four Cities, Two Teams, One Rivalry.* Jefferson, NC: McFarland, 2003.
Helyar, John. *Lords of the Realm: The Real History of Baseball.* New York: Ballantine Books, 1994.
James, Bill. *The New Bill James Historical Baseball Abstract.* New York: Free Press, 2001.
Knorr, Charles P. *The End of Baseball as We Knew It: The Players Union, 1960–81.* Urbana: University of Illinois Press, 2002.
Lasorda, Tommy, and David Fisher. *The Artful Dodger.* New York: Avon Books, 1986.
Leahy, Michael. *The Last Innocents. The Collision of the Turbulent Sixties and the Los Angeles Dodgers.* New York: Harper Paperbacks, 2017.
Leavy, Jane. *Sandy Koufax: A Lefty's Legacy.* New York: HarperCollins, 2002.
Light, Jonathan F. *The Cultural Encyclopedia of Baseball.* Jefferson, NC: McFarland, 1997.
Lowenfish, Lee. *Baseball's Endangered Species: Inside the Craft of Scouting by Those Who Lived It.* Lincoln: University of Nebraska Press, 2023.
Lowenfish, Lee. *The Imperfect Diamond: A History of Baseball's Labor Wars.* New York: Da Capo Press, 1991.
Lowry, Philip J. *Green Cathedrals: The Ultimate Celebration of Major League and Negro League Ballparks.* New York: Walker & Company, 2006.
McCue, Andy. *Mover & Shaker: Walter O'Malley, the Dodgers, & Baseball's Westward Expansion.* Lincoln: University of Nebraska Press, 2014.
McKelvey, G. Richard. *The MacPhails: Baseball's First Family of the Front Office.* Jefferson, NC: McFarland, 2005.
McNeil, William F. *The Dodger Encyclopedia.* Champaign, IL: Sports Publishing, 1997.
Miller, Patrick B., and David K. Wiggins, editors. *Sport and the Color Line: Black Athletes and Race Relations in Twentieth Century America.* New York: Routledge, 2004.

Moss, Robert A. "The Fireman." *NINE: A Journal of Baseball History and Culture*, University of Nebraska Press, Volume 21, Number 2, Spring 2013, pages 125–134.
Pietrusza, David, Matthew Silverman, and Michael Gershman, editors. *Baseball: The Biographical Encyclopedia*. Kingston, NY: Total/Sports Illustrated, 2000.
Porter, David L., editor. *Biographical Dictionary of American Sports: Baseball, Revised and Expanded Edition*. Westport, CT: Greenwood, 2000.
Reed, Ted. *Carl Furillo: Brooklyn Dodgers All-Star*. Jefferson, NC: McFarland, 2011.
Schiavone, Michael. *The Dodgers: 60 Years in Los Angeles*. New York: Sports Publishing, 2020.
Shatzkin, Mike. *The Ballplayers*. New York: William Morrow, 1990.
Snider, Duke, with Phil Pepe. *Few and Chosen: Defining Dodger Greatness Across the Eras*. Chicago: Triumph Books, 2006.
Stout, Glenn, and Richard A. Johnson. *The Dodgers: 120 Years of Dodgers Baseball*. Boston: Houghton Mifflin, 2004.
Wiebusch, John. "The New Willie Davis," *Baseball Digest*, May 1969, p. 15.

Newspapers

Arizona Daily Sun
Atlanta Constitution
Atlanta Journal-Constitution
Baltimore Sun
Boston Globe
Chicago Tribune
Daily Breeze (Torrance, CA)
Daily News-Post (Monrovia, CA)
Evening Vanguard (Venice, CA)
Fort Worth Star-Telegram
Fresno Bee
Independent (Long Beach, CA)
Independent Star-News (Pasadena, CA)
Kansas City Star
Los Angeles Mirror
Los Angeles Times
Milwaukee Journal
Modesto Bee
New York Times
News-Pilot (San Pedro, CA)
North County [CA] *Times*
Pasadena Independent
Pasadena [CA] *Star-News*
Philadelphia Inquirer
Pittsburgh Post-Gazette
Press-Telegram (Long Beach, CA)
Progress-Bulletin (Sonoma, CA)
St. Louis Globe-Democrat
St. Louis Post-Dispatch
San Francisco Examiner
The Signal (Santa Clarita, CA)
Sporting News
Star Tribune (Minneapolis, MN)
Tampa Tribune
Valley News (Van Nuys, CA)
Valley Times (North Hollywood, CA)
Ventura County [CA] *Star*
Washington Post

Index

Aaron, Hank 47, 59
Aase, Don 122
Abercrombie, Reggie 169, 197–98
Abreu, Bobby 236
Abreu, Jeffry 262
Abreu, Tony 189, 223
Adams, Terry 167, 182
Adcock, Joe 17
Agee, Tommie 55–56
Aguire, Hank 41–42
Ahmed, Nick 294
Albert, Jeff 66–67
Alberto, Hanser 277, 287
Albertus, Alexander 289–90
Alcaraz, Luis 42
Alderson, Sandy 100
Alexander, Doyle 42, 49–50
Alexander, Scott 261, 271
Alexy, A.J. 253–55
Allbee, Mako 286
Allen, Dick 44–48, 50–51, 61, 73
Allen, Luke 150, 193
Allen, Steve 122
Almonte, Yency 277, 293
Alomar, Sandy, Jr. 209–10, 214
Alou, Felipe 144, 188
Alston, Walter 5, 7, 14–15, 17–18, 23, 25, 27, 32, 35, 37–40, 43, 45, 48, 53–54, 57–59, 64, 66, 79
Altobelli, Joe 21
Alvarez, Eddy 271, 277
Álvarez, Orlando 46, 66
Álvarez, Victor 153
Álvarez, Wilson 193, 209
Alvarez, Yordan 252–53
Amaro, Ruben 34–35
Amaya, Jacob 257, 278–279
Amelung, Ed 79
Ames, Steve 223, 238
Amorós, Sandy 13
Anderson, Brett 244, 246, 253
Anderson, Dave 82, 93, 112, 113, 136

Anderson, Garret 227
Anderson, Marlon 215–16
Anderson, Sparky 9
Anderson, Tyler 277
Andrews, Fred 65
Anthony, Eric 115, 153
Anthopoulos, Alex 255–56
Antonini, Mike 227
Aparicio, Luis 38
Arano, Victor 244
Araujo, Victor 238, 245, 247
Ardoin, Randy 223
Arnold, Jamie 169, 175
Arroyo, Bronson 245–46, 250
Arruebarrena, Erisbel 244, 262
Ash, Gord 66–67
Ashby, Andy 173–74, 201
Ashley, Billy 109, 164
Aspromonte, Bob 19–20
Astacio, Pedro 103, 121, 151
Attanasio, Tony 78, 105
Auerbach, Rick 55, 69
Ausmus, Brad 223, 227
Aven, Bruce 175, 182
Avilán, Luis 245–46, 261
Axford, John 262
Aybar, Willy 175, 214

Backman, Wally 108
Baez, Danys 214
Baez, Pedro 216, 267, 271
Bailey, Bob 33–34, 42, 53
Bailey, Homer 260–61
Bailor, Bob 89, 93, 98
Baker, Dusty 59–60, 72, 87, 187
Baker, Scott 250
Bako, Paul 208–09
Baldwin, James 179, 182
Balelo, Nez 283
Banda, Anthony 293
Banks, Willie 147
Bannister, Floyd 85

Index

Bannon, Rylan 257–58
Bañuelos, Manny 257, 262
Barajas, Rod 227, 230
Barber, Steve 16
Barbieri, Jim 15
Barker, Tim 135–36
Barnes, Austin 239–40, 273
Barnes, Brian 140
Barnes, Larry 189, 193
Barney, Darwin 243, 249
Barragan, Cuno 26–27
Barrios, Manuel 153–54
Barry, Jeff 175, 181
Bartels, Billy 98, 103
Bates, Aaron 244
Bauer, Trevor 267–70, 287
Bautista, Kelvin 271
Bavasi, Buzzie 8, 16, 18, 21–25, 29, 31–33, 36, 40
Bawcom, Logan 227, 236
Baxes, Jim 11
Baxter, Mike 238, 244
Bay, Jason 218
Baylor, Don 49–50, 151, 168
Beachy, Brandon 250
Bean, Billy 114, 132
Beane, Billy 194
Beattie, Jim 158–59
Beaty, Matt 250, 277
Beckert, Glenn 38, 43
Beckett, Josh 233–34, 236–37
Beckman, Bernie 50–51
Beckwith, Joe 69, 90, 98
Beeter, Clayton 267, 277
Beimel, Joe 215, 220
Beirne, Kevin 181, 189
Belanger, Mark 82
Belcher, Tim 100–01, 127–29
Belge, Jeff 262, 277
Belisario, Ronald 223, 238
Bell, George 108
Bell, Heath 233
Bell, Josh 208, 223
Bell, Juan 107–08
Bell, Rob 205
Belliard, Ronnie 204, 223, 227
Bellinger, Cody 238, 256, 275, 279
Beltre, Adrian 140, 160 191, 198–200, 202
Benítez, Armando 162
Bennett, Gary 216, 220
Benzinger, Todd 130–31, 136
Bergeron, Peter 158
Bergjans, Tommy 250, 252
Berman, Stevie 253, 271
Bernadina, Roger 244
Berroa, Ángel 219–20

Berroa, Geronimo 175
Bessent, Don 5
Betemit, Wilson 214, 216
Betts, Mookie 264–67, 279, 293
Bickford, Phil 271, 287
Biggio, Cavan 289
Bilko, Steve 5–7
Billingham, Jack 21, 40–41
Billingsley, Chad 193, 212, 227, 236–37
Bird, Zachary 236, 245
Bittiger, Jeff 114
Black, Bud 142
Blake, Casey 217, 222, 230
Blanco, Henry 114, 164
Blanton, Joe 236, 250
Bloom, Chaim 265
Blowers, Mike 135, 145–46
Blue, Vida 75
Bocachica, Hiram 158, 189
Bochtler, Doug 163, 169–70
Bochy, Bruce 71, 216
Bogar, Tim 181–82
Boggs, Wade 96
Bohanon, Brian 163–64
Bolivar, Moises 288
Bolsinger, Mike 244, 252
Bonds, Barry 200
Bonilla, Bobby 153–54, 160–61, 165
Boone, Aaron 191
Boone, Bob 147
Boras, Scott 162, 200, 203, 209, 220, 235, 275, 292
Borbón, Pedro 164–65, 167
Bosio, Chris 146
Bournigal, Rafael 103, 147
Bowa, Larry 180
Boyd, Bob 10
Boyer, Ken 32, 42–43
Bradley, Mark 61, 90
Bradley, Milton 194–95, 198, 205, 208
Branson, Jeff 170, 175, 182
Brasier, Ryan 287
Braun, Ryan 242
Brazleton, Dewon 205
Brazoban, Yhency 192–93, 223
Bream, Sid 82, 92, 93
Breeden, Scott 26
Breeding, Marv 24–25, 29
Brennan, Tom 91, 96
Brennan, William 91
Brett, Ken 77, 79
Brewer, Billy 147, 150
Brewer, Jim 26–27, 58–59
Brewer, Tony 77
Bridenbaugh, Christian 181
Brigham, Jeff 244–45, 247
Bristol, Dave 60

Index

Brito, Moises 277
Brito, Ronny 262
Brock, Greg 77, 97
Brogdon, Connor 293
Brohawn, Troy 189
Brooks, Hubie 114, 12021
Brooks, Jerry 109, 140
Brown, Andrew 182–83, 195
Brown, Joe L. 33, 93
Brown, Kevin 162–64, 166, 174, 192
Brown, Richard 125
Broxton, Jonathan 189, 229
Brubaker, Bruce 34, 46
Bruihl, Justin 257, 287
Brumfield, Jacob 169–70
Brumley, Mike 25
Brunson, Will 140, 163
Bruske, Jim 150, 153, 163
Buckner, Bill 42, 47–48, 66–67, 80–81
Buehler, Walker 250, 254, 268, 270, 291, 294
Buhner, Jay 146
Bunning, Jim 43
Burke, Glenn 52, 70
Burnitz, Jeromy 189–90, 201
Burns, Andy 271
Burnside, Adrian 179
Burright, Larry 20, 23
Busch, Michael 263, 293
Busch, Mike 122, 150
Buss, Nick 220, 244
Butera, Drew 238, 244
Butler, Bill 69
Butler, Brett 120–21, 126–27, 138, 142–43, 147–49
Byrd, Paul 209

Cabell, Enos 92–93, 98
Cabrera, Jolbert 188, 200
Cairo, Miguel 145
Calhoun, Willie 250, 254–55
Callaspo, Alberto 248–50
Calmus, Dick 23, 39
Camargo, Jair 250, 264–65
Camilli, Doug 29
Campanella, Roy 5
Campanis, Al 42, 44–47, 54, 57, 59–61, 63, 65–71, 76, 80, 82–85, 87–89, 92–98
Campanis, Jim 23, 42
Candelaria, John 94, 122, 136
Candiotti, Tom 129–30, 153
Cannizzaro, Chris 51, 55
Canseco, José 117
Capuano, Chris 230, 236, 238
Caraccioli, Lance 188
Carew, Rod 63, 81
Carey, Andy 23

Carey, Chase 154
Carlyle, Buddy 201, 209
Carmel, Duke 17
Carmona, Fausto 244
Carrara, Giovanni 181, 193, 201, 215
Carrillo, Gerardo 270
Carroll, Jamey 217, 222, 228, 230
Carter, Gary 123, 132, 269
Carter, Joe 87
Carter, Lance 214–15
Casey, Donovan 257, 270
Cash, Dave 65
Cashen, Frank 89
Cashman, Brian 192
Casparius, Ben 271
Castellanos, Alex 228
Castillo, Bobby 69, 86, 96, 98
Castillo, Braulio 126–27
Castillo, Fabio 253, 257
Castro, Daniel 262
Castro, Juan 132, 159, 175, 223, 227
Castro, Starlin 225
Cataline, Dan 86–87
Caughey, Wayne 79
Cedeño, César 98
Cedeño, Roger 132, 161–62
Cespedes, Yoenis 230
Cey, Ron 42, 60, 72, 86–88, 94
Chambers, Justin 293
Chance, Bob 28
Chargois, J.T. 262–63
Chavez, Jesse 252–53
Checo, Robinson 164–65
Chen, Chin-Feng 169, 209
Chittum, Nelson 15
Choate, Randy 231–32, 236
Choi, Hee-Seop 196–97, 215
Christensen, McKay 181, 189
Christopher, Mike 114, 132
Churn, Chuck 11
Cimoli, Gino 5, 8
Cingrani, Tony 257, 262
Claire, Fred 98–102, 104–13, 116–19, 121–23, 126–28, 130–32, 134–35, 138–39, 143–45, 147–53, 155–56, 160–61
Clark, Brady 216
Clark, Dave 150
Cleavinger, Garrett 267, 277
Clelland, Rick 147
Clemens, Roger 96, 103
Clementina, Hendrik 257
Clontz, Brad 155, 164
Cobb, Ty 33
Coffee, Todd 236
Colavito, Rocky 42
Coleman, Louis 251, 257

Index

Colleran, Matt 226
Colletti, Ned 205–08, 210–13, 217–18, 220–22, 224, 226, 228–29, 232, 236–37
Collum, Jackie 5
Colón, Bartolo 203
Colyer, Steve 153, 200
Conde, Ramón 9, 23
Conforto, Michael 92
Cook, Dennis 122, 132
Cookson, Brent 169, 175, 182
Coomer, Ron 144–45, 193
Cooper, Cecil 97
Copping, Corey 250, 262
Cora, Alex 150, 171, 202, 204, 259
Corcino, Daniel 257
Cordero, Jesus 180
Corey, Bryan 181, 193
Cormier, Lance 230
Correia, Kevin 244
Cotton, Jharel 236, 251–52
Coulombe, Daniel 237, 250
Counsell, Craig 169, 175
Covey, Dylan 287
Covington, Wes 34
Cox, Bobby 183
Craig, Roger 5, 14, 19–20, 24
Crawford, Carl 233, 242, 253
Crawford, Leo 267
Crawford, Willie 29, 41, 47, 61
Crews, Tim 97–98, 107, 131, 136
Cripps, Bobby 151
Crismatt, Nabil 287, 294
Cristante, Leo 11
Cromer, Tripp 150–51, 169–70
Crosby, Bubba 163, 191–92
Crow, Don 77
Crowley, Terry 49
Cruceta, Francisco 169, 185–86
Cruz, Henry 51, 69
Cruz, José 208, 215
Cruz, Luis 230, 238
Cruz, Oneil 250, 257
Cuccinello, Tony 20
Cueto, Bert 23
Cueto, Johnny 245
Cuevas, Noel 227, 244
Culberson, Charlie 250, 255–56
Cullen, Blake 58
Cullen, Jack 34–35
Culpepper, David 54–55
Culver, George 55
Cummings, John 147–49
Cunningham, Joe 8
Curletta, Joey 236, 252
Curtis, Chad 148–49
Cyr, Tyler 287

Daal, Omar 122, 147, 180, 183
Dalton, Harry 51–52, 79
Daly, Robert 165, 168, 172–73
Daniel, Clayton 267
Daniels, Jon 214
Daniels, Kal 111–12, 120–21, 132–33
Dark, Al 45
D'Arnaud, Travis 263
Darvish, Yu 254–55, 270
Darwin, Bobby 42, 51
Daspit, Jimmy 140
Davalillo, Vic 69, 77, 79
Davis, Brendon 250, 254–55
Davis, Butch 122
Davis, Eric 112, 127–29, 131–32, 137–38, 166
Davis, Glenn 115
Davis, Mike 103, 110, 114
Davis, Ron 103, 110
Davis, Tommy 18, 32, 93
Davis, Willie 9, 32, 47, 53, 55, 64
Dawkins, Travis 193
Dawson, Andre 133
Dayton, Grant 249, 257
Dean, Tommy 29, 43
Decker, Steve 124
Dedeaux, Rod 35
De Jesus, Alex 277
De Jesus, Ivan 43, 66–67
De Jesus, Ivan, Jr. 208, 233–34
De Jong, Chase 249
De La Rosa, Rubby 216, 233
De León, José 238, 256
Deluca, Jonny 263, 284–85
DeMarco, Tony 124–25
Demeter, Don 5, 17
Dempsey, Rick 105, 109, 122, 162
Denker, Travis 216
DePodesta, Paul 194–99, 203, 205, 207
DeShields, Delino 138–39, 149
DeSilva, John 137, 140
Dessens, Elmer 200, 209, 211–12, 216
Detherage, Bob 63–64, 69, 74
Devereaux, Mike 96, 107, 110, 164
Devine, Bing 8, 18, 61
DeWitt, Blake 201, 217, 222, 224–25
Diaz, Carlos 89, 95, 98, 102
Díaz, Einar 215
Díaz, José 150, 189–90
Díaz, Víctor 175, 189–90
Díaz, Yusniel 250, 257–58
Dickson, O'Koyea 230, 257
Didier, Mel 145
Dietz, Dick 52, 55
Diggins, Ben 175, 188
Dipoto, Jerry 241
Dirks, Caleb 249, 252
Dixon, Brandon 238, 248–49

Index

Dodson, Tanner 277
Dombrowski, Dave 154
Domínguez, José 216, 244
Doncon, Rayne 271, 293
Donnels, Chris 175, 182
Dorame, Randey 172–73
Dotel, Octavio 227
Downing, Al 46–47, 69
Downs, Jeter 260–61, 265, 267
Dozier, Brian 262
Drake, Solly 9, 11
Dreifort, Darren 139, 164, 174, 180
Dressen, Chuck 27, 31
Drew, J.D. 201, 215
Drysdale, Don 5, 25, 29–31, 40, 54
Duffie, John 34
Duncan, Mariano 86, 102, 111, 132
Duquette, Dan 138
Durocher, Leo 20, 38, 43, 55
Dwyer, Jim 99

Eastwick, Rawly 69
Eckersley, Dennis 88, 119
Edman, Tommy 279, 289–90, 293
Edwards, Jeff 91, 103
Edwards, Mike 201, 209
Eflin, Zach 242–43
Egan, Richard Wallis "Dick" 34
Eibner, Brett 256–57
Eischen, Joey 143–44, 148–49
Eisenreich, Jim 153–54, 164
Elbert, Scott 201, 244
Ellingsen, Bruce 55, 105
Ellis, A.J. 193, 242, 252
Ellis, Jim 40–41
Ellis, Mark 228–29
Ellis, Robert 189
Elster, Kevin 139, 175
Ely, Jon 222, 236
Encarnación, Juan 193, 196, 202
Eovaldi, Nathan 220, 231–32
Erickson, Scott 208–09
Erlin, Robbie 293
Ermer, Cal 36
Erskine, Carl 5
Espy, Cecil 84, 93
Essegian, Chuck 10, 16
Estrada, Chuck 16
Ethier, Andre 205–06, 212, 218, 221, 227, 257
Evans, Dan 179–80, 182–86, 189–191, 194, 196
Evans, Darrell 60
Eveland, Dana 227, 230
Everitt, Leon 30, 43
Ezell, Glenn 55
Ezi, Travis 175, 193

Fairey, Jim 30, 41, 55
Fairly, Ron 9, 22–23, 42–43
Falkenborg, Brian 193, 201, 216, 220 216, 220
Fanning, Jim 42, 53
Farmer, Kyle 238, 260–61
Farmer, Tom 189
Farrell, Turk 17, 19
Federowicz, Tim 230, 242
Feduccia, Hunter 262
Feeney, Chub 40
Feliz, Neftali 271
Ferguson, Caleb 244, 293
Ferguson, Joe 42, 48, 63, 71, 82, 87
Fernández, José 260
Fernandez, Sid 82, 89
Ferrara, Al 11, 41
Ferris, Jackson 293
Fetters, Mike 170, 176, 179
Feyereisen, J.P. 277
Fielder, Cecil 148
Fields, Josh 252, 263
Fien, Casey 253
Fife, Stephen 230
Figgins, Chone 244
Figueroa, Derlin 287
Fimple, Jack 81–82, 98
Finch, Bob 6
Finley, Charles 67, 70
Finley, Drew 262
Finley, Steve 197–98, 202
Fischer, Jeff 114
Fisher, Braydon 289
Flaherty, Jack 291
Fletcher, Darrin 103, 116, 122
Flood, Curt 8, 19, 44
Flores, José 201
Floro, Dylan 257, 261, 271
Floyd, Cliff 144
Floyd, Mike 55
Flynn, Michael 293
Foley, Tom 109
Font, Wilmer 253, 261
Fonville, Chad 147, 152
Forster, Terry 68–69, 84–85
Forsythe, Logan 256, 262
Fosnow, Jerry 39
Fosse, Ray 45
Foster, Alan 30, 42, 45, 46
Foster, Kris 147, 170, 181
Fowler, Art 7, 21
Franco, John 82, 90
Francona, Terry 268
Frasor, Jason 189
Frasso, Nick 277
Frazier, Joe 11
Freehan, Bill 50

Freeman, Freddie 272–73
Freeman, Mike 257
Freese, David 262–63
Frías, Carlos 216, 256
Frías, Pepe 79, 82
Friedman, Andrew 239, 242, 246–49, 251, 255–56, 260–61, 266–68, 270, 272, 275, 292
Fuentes, Tito 39
Fuller, Justin 215, 223
Furcal, Rafael 206, 213, 222, 228
Furillo, Carl 5, 14–15

Gabrielson, Len 35–36
Gage, Matt 293
Gagne, Eric 147, 184–85, 214
Gagne, Greg 146–47, 152–53
Gale, Rocky 262–63
Gallo, Joey 277
Galvez, Balvino 82, 103
Garate, Victor 216, 223
Garcia, Apostol 164–65
Garcia, Dave 82
García, Harvey 222–23
García, Karim 136, 153
Garcia, Luis 201, 223
García, Onelki 236, 244
García, Yimi 223
Garciaparra, Nomar 207, 219, 223–24
Garland, Jon 223, 227
Garlick, Kyle 250, 267
Garman, Mike 66–67, 74
Garner, Phil 103
Garr, Ralph 60
Garrett, Hal 152
Garvey, Steve 42, 64, 72, 81, 85–87, 94, 97, 107
Geiger, Bert 84
Genovese, George 75
Gentile, Jim 10
German, Angel 257
Gibbons, Jay 227, 230
Gibbons, John 109
Gibbs, Kevin 172–73
Gibson, Kirk 104, 110, 116, 118–19
Gil, Geronimo 150, 181
Gilbert, Shawn 170, 175
Gilbert, Tyler 267
Gilliam, Jim 5, 9, 20, 31, 34
Giménez, Héctor 227, 230
Glasnow, Tyler 284–85, 287–88
Glaus, Troy 202
Gleason, Roy 21
Goeddel, Erik 262
Goggin, Chuck 29, 43
Golden, Jim 9, 17, 19–20
Goldschmidt, Eric 160

Goliat, Mike 11
Goltz, Dave 76, 86
Gomes, Brandon 272, 274, 281, 286, 288, 291
Gomez, Preston 40, 54
Gómez, Rubén 8
Gonsolin, Tony 253, 270
González, Adrián 233–34, 255–56
Gonzalez, Jose 79, 125–26
Gonzalez, Luis 215
Gonzalez, Oliver 289–90
González, Victor 236, 286
Gooch, Arnie 161–62
Gooden, Dwight 97, 105, 118
Goodson, Ed 59, 74
Goodwin, Tom 114, 140, 172, 189
Gordon, Dee 220, 228, 232, 239–41, 243
Gore, Terrance 267, 271
Gorecki, Rick 132, 153
Goryl, Johnny 12–13
Gossage, Goose 69
Gott, Jim 114, 140
Grabarkewitz, Billy 34, 51
Grabowski, Jason 194, 201, 209
Grandal, Yasmani 242–43
Granderson, Curtis 257
Grant, Jim "Mudcat" 36–37, 41
Graterol, Brusdar 264–65
Gray, Dick 5, 9–10
Gray, Josiah 260–61, 270
Graziano, Bob 164–65
Grba, Eli 14
Green, Dallas 87, 107, 143
Green, Nick 227
Green, Shawn 165–67, 182–83, 185, 190, 195, 197, 202–03
Green, Steve 103, 114
Greenberg, Hank 28
Greene, Conner 271
Greene, Shane 271, 277
Greinke, Zack 235–36, 241, 246
Grieve, Tom 91
Griffey, Ken, Jr. 146
Griffin, Alfredo 101–03, 136
Griffith, Calvin 36
Griffith, Derrell 23, 32
Grissom, Marquis 176–77, 187–88
Gross, Kevin 119–20, 127–29, 139–40
Gross, Kip 140
Grosser, Alec 252–53
Grote, Jerry 68, 71–72, 74, 82
Grove, Michael 262
Grudzielanek, Mark 152, 158–59, 171, 186–87
Guerra, Javy 201, 244
Guerrero, Alex 238, 253
Guerrero, Pedro 55, 80, 93, 104–06

Guerrero, Vladimir 159
Guerrero, Wilton 132, 151–52, 158–59
Guerrier, Matt 227, 238
Guillen, Ozzie 221, 232
Gulden, Brad 61, 74
Guthrie, Mark 144, 164
Gutiérrez, Franklin 175, 194–95, 257
Guzmán, Joel 181, 215
Guzmán, Juan 96, 103
Guzman, Kevin 245, 247
Gwynn, Chris 96, 120–21, 130, 140, 148
Gwynn, Tony, Jr. 227, 238
Gyorko, Jedd 262

Haeger, Charlie 223, 227
Hagenman, Justin 262, 280
Hairston, Jerry 230, 238
Hale, Chip 150, 153
Hale, John 51, 69
Hall, Darren 147, 169
Hall, Toby 210–11
Haller, Tom 39–40, 45–47, 50
Hamels, Cole 245
Hamey, Roy 22
Hamilton, Jeff 86, 131
Hamulak, Tim 214, 216
Handley, Lee 12–13
Hanlon, Dick 11
Hannahs, Gerry 74
Hansell, Gregg 120–122, 144–45
Hansen, Craig 218
Hansen, Dave 98, 131, 169, 188
Harang, Aaron 230, 236, 238
Harcourt, Larue 76, 79
Hardy, J.J. 257
Haren, Dan 237, 239, 241
Harkey, Mike 150, 153
Harkness, Tim 20, 23
Harmon, Terry 65
Harper, Bryce 255
Harris, Gail 13
Harris, Greg 238, 244
Harris, Lenny 111–12, 131–32, 139, 188, 215
Hart, John 142
Hartley, Mike 98, 126–27
Hartsock, Jeff 132
Haselman, Bill 253
Hatcher, Chris 239–40, 257
Hatcher, Mickey 69, 80, 103
Hatfield, Fred 11
Havens, Brad 98–99, 110
Hawksworth, Blake 227, 237
Hazelbaker, Jeremy 238
Heaney, Andrew 239, 241, 271, 277
Heep, Danny 103, 110
Heffernan, Bert 122
Heisey, Chris 244, 250

Held, Woodie 28
Hembree, Heath 277, 287
Hemond, Roland 107
Hemus, Solly 18
Henderson, Rickey 107, 189–90, 269
Hendrick, George 94
Hendricks, Liam 274
Hendrickson, Mark 205, 210, 216
Hendry, Jim 212
Henriquez, Edgardo 262
Henson, Tyler 230
Herges, Matt 136, 169, 184
Herman, Billy 20
Hermansen, Chad 186–87, 193
Hernández, Ariel 261
Hernández, Carlos 91, 150
Hernández, César 247
Hernández, Elieser 293–94
Hernández, Enrique "Kiké" 239–40, 247, 271, 275, 280
Hernández, Enzo 74
Hernandez, Jackie 36
Hernández, José 201
Hernández, Leo 74, 86
Hernández, Ramón 238
Hernández, Roberto 216
Hernández, Teoscar 287–88, 293
Hernández, Yonny 277–78
Herr, Tommy 108
Herrera, Elián 193, 238
Hershiser, Orel 77, 91, 101, 128–29, 134, 142, 168–69, 175, 241
Heydeman, Greg 51
Heyward, Jason 277
Hiatt, Phil 175, 189
Hibbard, Greg 146
Hickman, Jim 32–33, 40
Hicks, Tom 181
Hill, Koyie 175, 197–98
Hill, Quency 66
Hill, Rich 251–52, 254, 263, 270
Hillegas, Shawn 91, 101, 109
Hillenbrand, Shea 216
Hilsizer, Niko 262
Himes, Larry 132
Hinton, Chuck 28
Hisle, Larry 51
Hodges, Gil 5, 7, 10, 19–20, 24–25, 27–28
Hoffman, Glenn 103, 156, 164, 168
Hoffman, Jamie 193 223, 230
Holland, John 38
Hollandsworth, Todd 172–73
Hollins, Damon 163
Holmes, Darren 90, 122
Holmes, Grant 244, 251–52
Holton, Brian 74, 107–08
Honeycutt, Rick 88–89, 100

316 Index

Honeywell, Brett, Jr. 293
Hooton, Burt 58, 76, 88, 91
Hope, Zyhir 293
Hopkins, Gail 56
Horowitz, Danny 160
Horton, Ricky 109, 114
Horwitz, Jay 117
Hough, Charlie 34, 64–65, 78
Houk, Ralph 22, 34–35, 41
Houlton, D.J. 201, 219
Houston, Tyler 188–89
Howard, Frank 9, 27–29
Howard, Thomas 164
Howe, Steve 77, 89, 96, 101–02
Howell, Jay 101–03, 126, 134
Howell, J.P. 238, 253
Howell, Ken 86, 95
Howser, Dick 34–35
Hu, Chin-lung 193, 227
Hubbard, Trent 153–54, 175
Hudson, Bryan 277, 293
Hudson, Daniel 262, 271
Hudson, Lance 83–84
Hudson, Orlando 223
Hudson, Rex 51, 69
Hudson, Tim 237
Huff, David 250, 253
Huff, Mike 96, 122
Hughes, Nial 181
Hull, Eric 189, 219
Hundley, Randy 174
Hundley, Todd 161–62, 174–75, 186–87
Hunt, Ron 32–33, 39, 53
Hunter, Scott 147
Hunter, Willard 21
Huntz, Steve 48–49
Hurt, Kyle 271
Hutchinson, Fred 8
Hutton, Tom 29, 51
Hynes, Colt 243–44

Ingram, Garey 109, 114
Isabel, Ibandel 261
Ishii, Kazuhisa 189, 208
Istler, Andrew 250, 262
Izturis, César 181, 212–13

Jackson, Andre 257, 287
Jackson, Anthony 227
Jackson, Edwin 181, 214
Jackson, Randy 5, 7
Jaime, Juan 249
James, Cleo 21
James, Mike 98, 139
Jansen, Kenley 201, 214, 259, 273
Jarrin, Stefan 230, 236
Javier, Julian 45

Javier, Stan 116, 136
Jenkins, Jack 43
Jeter, Derek 233
Jobe, Dr. Frank 73, 101, 111–12, 134
John, Tommy 48–49, 73–74
Johnson, Blake 201, 211–12
Johnson, Brian 175, 182
Johnson, Charles 153–54, 161–62
Johnson, Cliff 74
Johnson, Davey 121, 161–62, 164, 168, 171, 175
Johnson, Earvin "Magic" 235
Johnson, Jason 220
Johnson, Jim 245–46, 250
Johnson, Josh 237
Johnson, Lou 26, 32, 37–38
Johnson, Micah 248–49, 256
Johnson, Randy 146, 202
Johnson, Reed 227
Johnson, Stan 21
Johnson, Steve 208, 223
Johnson, Tim 39, 55
Johnston, Jody 90
Johnstone, Jay 77, 80, 86, 96
Jones, Andruw 216, 218–19, 221, 223
Jones, Mitch 220, 223
Jones, Nate 271
Jones, Ross 89
Jordan, Brian 182–83, 189, 201, 211
Jordan, Jimmy 20
Joshua, Von 39, 57, 77
Joyner, Wally 131
Juarez, William 203
Judd, Mike 150, 181
Junge, Eric 169, 180
Justice, David 123

Kahnle, Tommy 267, 277
Kapstein, Jerry 85, 106
Karros, Eric 109, 127, 131, 145, 150, 155, 172, 174, 186–87
Kasten, Stan 230–31
Katz, Adam 173
Kazmir, Scott 205, 250, 255–56
Kearney, Bob 94
Kekich, Mike 29, 41
Kellert, Frank 11
Kelly, Joe 259–60, 271
Kelly, Roberto 143–44, 148
Kemp, Matt 193, 218–19, 221, 227, 231, 242–43, 255–56, 260
Kendrick, Howie 240–241, 243, 247, 252
Kennedy, Adam 230, 236
Kennedy, Bob 66–67
Kennedy, John 27–29, 33–35
Kent, Jeff 199, 205, 220

Kershaw, Clayton 215, 235, 241, 246, 254–55, 268, 270, 273, 288, 291
Kessinger, Don 38
Ketchner, Ryan 20
Kickham, Mike 271
Kida, Masao 193, 201
Kiermaier, Kevin 293
Kimbrel, Craig 255, 273–74, 277, 281–82
Kiner, Ralph 28
Kinkade, Mike 189, 193
Kinzer, Paul 206
Kipp, Fred 5, 12
Kirby, Wayne 150, 153
Kittle, Ron 69, 74
Klippstein, Johnny 5, 7, 15
Knack, Landon 267
Knebel, Corey 267
Kolarek, Adam 262, 271, 287
Konerko, Paul 140, 156–57
Kopech, Michael 289–90
Koppe, Joe 17
Koranda, Jim 23
Kosco, Andy 41, 43, 46–47
Koufax, Sandy 5, 15, 25, 29–31, 33, 54, 89, 141, 167
Kozlowski, Ben 214
Krebs, Eric 222
Kremer, Dean 253, 257–58
Kreuter, Chad 175
Kroc, Ray 62
Krueger, Bill 103, 109
Kubenka, Jeff 150, 169
Kuhn, Bowie 89–90
Kuo, Hung-Chih 169, 230
Kuroda, Hiroki 216, 230

Labine, Clem 5, 14
Lackey, John 209, 259
Lacy, Lee 43, 59–60, 64–65, 71–72, 74
LaFever, Greg 109
LaGrow, Lerrin 77
Lajoie, Bill 10, 21
Lakey, Gordon 166
LaMabe, Jack 43
Lamb, Jake 277
Lamb, Ray 34, 45–46
Lambo, Andrew 216, 227
Lamet, Dinelson 294
LaMura, B.J. 214
Landestoy, Rafael 53, 71, 90, 91
Landreaux, Ken 80–81, 103
Landreth, Larry 74
Landrum, Tito 103, 110
Landry, Leon 227, 236
Lane, Frank 16, 46–47
Lankford, Frank 153
Lantigua, Eddie 140

Lara, Christian 219
Larker, Norm 5, 10, 19–20
Larkin, Barry 111
LaRoche, Andy 193, 217–18, 224
LaRussa, Tony 88
Lasorda, Tom 15, 58, 66–68, 71–73, 78–83, 89, 92–94, 101–02, 104, 110, 112–13, 119–21, 123–24, 126, 128, 133–34, 136, 138, 142–43, 148, 155–59, 161
Latham, Chris 145
Latos, Mat 245–47
Law, Rudy 61, 84
Leach, Brent 208, 227
Leach, Nick 169
League, Brandon 236, 250
Leary, Tim 97–98, 101, 111, 132
Leasure, Jordan 271, 281–82
Ledee, Ricky 201, 215
Lee, Bob 34, 39
Lee, Leron 61, 66
Lee, Zach 227, 252
Lefebvre, Jim 23, 33, 53
Lemmerman, Jake 227, 236
Leonard, Jeffrey 55, 71
Levinson, Seth 174
Lewallyn, Dennis 52, 79
Lewis, Darren 153
Leyritz, Jim 171–72
Liberatore, Adam 244, 262
Lieberthal, Mike 215–16
Lillis, Bob 13, 18, 19
Lilly, Ted 150, 158, 224–25, 232, 236, 238
Lima, José 201
Lincecum, Tim 237
Lincoln, Howard 200
Lindblom, Josh 220, 236
Lindsey, John 223, 230
Link, Jon 221, 230
Liranzo, Theyron 271, 291
Liriano, Nelson 150, 153
Little, Grady 205, 216
Littlefield, Dick 39
Loaiza, Esteban 216, 220
Locastro, Tim 249, 262
Lo Duca, Paul 139, 196, 198, 202
Lofton, Kenny 188, 20
Logue, Zach 294
Loney, James 189, 227, 233–34
Long, Matt 244
Looper, Aaron 200
Lopes, Davey 42, 60, 72, 81–83, 86, 89, 94
Lopez, Luis 90, 122
Loretta, Mark 220, 223
Lovelace, Vance 86–87
Lowe, Derek 203–04, 210, 220–21
Luccia, Rocky 130
Lugo, Julio 215

Lugo, Ruddy 177, 193, 215
Luke, Matt 153, 163–64
Lutz, Kenny 175
Lux, Gavin 253, 275
Lynch, Dave 122
Lynn, Fred 80
Lynn, Lance 281
Lyons, Barry 122, 132
Lyttle, Jim 66

Maas, Duke 14
MacDougal, Mike 236
Machado, Manny 255, 257–59, 270
MacPhail, Andy 174
MacPhail, Lee 16
Maddon, Joe 269
Maddux, Greg 212, 219–20, 269
Maddux, Mike 114, 122, 170
Madison, Scotti 86
Madlock, Bill 93–94, 103
Madson, Ryan 262
Maeda, Kenta 250, 264–65
Magadan, Dave 118
Magill, Matt 220, 244
Maholm, Paul 244, 250
Majewski, Gary 178, 181
Maldonado, Candy 74, 92, 95, 215
Mallette, Brian 188, 193
Malone, Kevin 143, 159, 161–165, 167–169, 171–74, 176–78
Maloney, Sean 164
Maness, Dwight 147
Mann, Devin 287
Mannion, Dennis 221, 225–26
Mantle, Mickey 41, 107
Manuel, Charlie 55
Margot, Manuel 284–85, 293
Marichal, Juan 61, 269
Marinan, James 257, 261
Marisnick, Jake 287
Marmol, Carlos 238, 244
Marrero, Oreste 147, 150
Marshall, Mike (outfielder) 77, 97, 110, 113–14
Marshall, Mike (pitcher) 53–54, 58, 64–65
Martin, Billy 50
Martin, Chris 277
Martin, Ethan 220, 236
Martin, Jarret 230
Martin, Russell 189, 210, 212, 226–27, 262–63
Martin, Tom 193, 198
Martínez, Edgar 146
Martinez, J.D. 276–78, 294
Martinez, Jonathan 243
Martínez, Pedro 109, 138–39, 149, 219
Martinez, Ramon (infielder) 215, 220

Martínez, Ramón (pitcher) 91, 113, 139, 151
Martínez, Ted 66, 79
Martinez, Tino 146
Masaoka, Onan 147, 181
Mattingly, Don 96, 222, 228, 232, 234, 248, 278
Matuszek, Len 95
Mauch, Gene 44, 53, 81
Maurer, Jonathan 222
May, Dustin 253, 270
May, Lucas 193, 227
Mayne, Brent 197–98
Mayo, Blake 169
Mays, Willie 137
Maza, Luis 216, 223
McBean, Al 43, 46
McCarthy, Brandon 241, 255–56
McClung, Scott 205
McCourt, Frank 193–94, 206, 220, 226, 230–31
McCourt, Jamie 193, 220
McDermott, Terry 43
McDevitt, Danny 5, 14
McDonald, James 189, 227
McDonald, Matt 147
McDowell, Roger 126, 133, 140
McDowell, Sam 45
McGee, Jake 267, 271
McGough, Scott 230–32
McGriff, Fred 189, 191, 201
McIlvaine, Joe 103, 137
McKinney, Billy 271
McKinstry, Zach 253, 277
McMichael, Greg 155–56, 163
McMullen, Ken 15, 27–28, 51–52, 66
McNally, Dave 62
Meeks, Tim 86, 103
Mejia, Erick 252, 261
Melhuse, Adam 170, 175
Meloan, Jon 208, 217
Melvin, Bob 251
Mercado, Orlando 103
Merricks, Matt 198
Merritt, Lloyd 10–11
Messersmith, Andy 51–52, 62, 77
Metcalfe, Mike 140, 175
Michael, Gene 33–34, 38–39, 42
Michel, Domingo 114
Mientkiewicz, Doug 223, 227
Mieses, Johan 261
Mikkelsen, Pete 42
Miles, Aaron 230
Miller, Andrew 255
Miller, Bobby 267, 291
Miller, John 30, 84–85
Miller, Justin 223, 227
Miller, Larry 11, 29

Index

Miller, Lemmie 82
Miller, Noah 293
Miller, Robert Lane "Bob" 23, 36–37
Miller, Shelby 277, 287
Miller, Trever 175
Miller, Tyson 287
Mills, Alan 164, 175
Milons, Jereme 181, 200
Milton, Eric 223
Minaya, Omar 184
Miranda, Willy 10
Mitchell, Bobby 69, 86
Mitchell, Ron 43
Mitchell, Russ 193, 236
Mlicki, Dave 155–56, 164–65
Moeller, Chad 216
Moeller, Joe 15, 42
Monasterios, Carlos 223, 236
Monday, Rick 66–67, 72, 91
Mondesi, Raul 109, 155, 159, 162, 165–67
Montalvo, Rafael 92–93
Montas, Frankie 248, 251–52
Moon, Wally 8–9, 30
Moorad, Jeff 159, 165–66
Moore, Dayton 211, 229
Moore, Gary 30
Moores, John 163
Morales, José 86, 91
Morgan, Mike 110–11, 123, 128–30
Morneau, Justin 233
Moronta, Reyes 277
Morris, Bryan 215, 218
Morris, Hal 131
Morrow, Brandon 257
Morse, Michael 245–46
Moses, Jerry 48
Moskau, Ryan 169
Moss, Brandon 218
Mota, Domingo 130
Mota, Guillermo 184, 196, 202, 223
Mota, José 103
Mota, Manny 42–43, 47, 77, 79, 86, 206
Moulder, Frederick 41
Moylan, Peter 238
Muegge, Daniel 202–03
Mueller, Bill 209
Mulholland, Terry 179, 185
Mullen, John 84–85
Mullen, Scott 193
Mulvey, James 5
Mulvey, Dearie 5
Muncy, Max 253–54
Munoz, Mike 98, 122
Muñoz, Noe 139
Munson, Thurman 74
Murakami, Masanori 141
Murdoch, Rupert 153, 163, 193

Murphy, Bill 196–98
Murphy, Jack 249
Murphy, Rob 147
Murray, Eddie 107–10, 115, 127, 131, 153
Musial, Stan 8
Myers, Rodney 189, 201
Myrow, Brian 200, 209

Nakamura, Norihiro 208–09
Nance, Shane 169, 188
Nastrini, Nick 271, 281–82
Naulty, Dan 169
Navarro, Dioner 202, 210, 227, 230
Neal, Charlie 5, 7, 20–21
Neal, Zach 261–62
Negray, Ron 5, 11
Negron, Kristopher 262–63
Neidlinger, Jim 109
Nelson, Jimmy 267, 277
Nen, Dick 21, 29
Neuse, Sheldon 271, 277
Newcombe, Don 5–6, 141
Nicasio, Juan 244, 250
Nichols, Rod 139
Niedenfuer, Tom 79, 95, 98–99
Niekro, Phil 130
Nina, Elvin 200
Nixon, Otis 151, 153
Noda, Ryan 267
Nolasco, Ricky 238
Nomo, Hideo 141, 155–57, 181, 204–05
Nomura, Don 156
Nootbar, Lars 286
Noren, Irv 15
Norman, Fred 39, 46
Norris, Bud 252–53
North, Bill 70, 72, 74
Núñez, Darien 262, 277
Núñez, Jhonny 193, 215
Nuñez, Jorge 165, 184
Nunez, Jose 175, 181
Nuno, Vidal 252

Oaks, Trevor 244, 261
Oates, Johnny 65, 79
O'Brien, Bob 43, 49–50
O'Donoghue, John 140
Oeltjen, Trent 227, 236
Oester, Ron 108, 112
Offerman, Jose 98, 103, 131, 146–47
Office, Roland 60
Ohman, Will 223
Ohtani, Shohei 282–284, 286–87
Ojeda, Bob 120–21, 127–28, 136
Olin, Steve 98
Oliver, Al 95
Oliver, Nate 11, 39, 43

Olivera, Héctor 245–46, 250
Olivo, Miguel 244
Olson, Gregg 175, 182
Olson, Matt 272
Olson, Tyler 249, 252
O'Malley, Peter 44–45, 48, 53, 57, 64, 76, 85, 104, 161
O'Malley, Walter 5, 33, 41, 44, 57, 76
O'Neill, Tyler 280
Oravetz, Ernie 21
Orosco, Jesse 101–03, 175–76, 189
Orta, Jorge 81–82, 86
Ortega, Carlos 178
Ortega, Phil 11, 19, 27–28
Ortiz, Ramón 227
Ortiz, Russ 202, 227
Osmond, Herb 62
Osoria, Franquelis 169, 215
Osteen, Claude 27–29, 47, 54
O'Sullivan, Ryan 230, 236
Osuna, Al 132, 140, 147
Osuna, Antonio 157, 178
Otáñez, Willis 145
Outman, James 262, 279
Owens, Paul 65
Ozuna, Pablo 220

Paciorek, Tom 42, 47, 55, 59–60
Padilla, Vicente 223, 230
Pages, Andy 262
Paine, Phil 8–9, 11
Palmquist, Ed 21
Pappas, Milt 16
Paredes, Edward 253, 262
Park, Chan Ho 140, 164, 180, 181, 220
Parker, Dave 112
Parker, Rick 147
Parker, Wes 26, 40, 43, 45, 55
Parra, José 114, 144–45
Parrish, Wade 181
Pascual, Camilo 46
Pasley, Kevin 51, 69
Pastorius, Jim 100
Patchin, Steve 66
Patterson, Arthur "Red" (executive) 30, 38
Patterson, Dave 66
Patterson, John "Red" (pitcher) 227, 253
Paul, Gabe 6
Paul, Xavier 193, 230
Paulson, Dillon 262, 267
Paxton, James 288
Pederson, Joc 227, 242, 247
Pederson, Stu 82
Pedroza, Sergio 208, 215
Peguero, Julio 136
Pelekoudas, Lou 146

Peña, Alejandro 74, 101, 113–14
Peña, Ángel 136, 182
Peña, José 43
Pendleton, Terry 183
Penny, Brad 196–97, 203 210, 219–21
Pepiot, Ryan 263, 284–85
Pepitone, Joe 22
Peralta, David 279–80, 294
Peralta, Jhonny 204
Peralta, Joel 250
Peraza, José 245–46, 248–49
Perconte, Jack 81–82
Pérez, Antonio 200, 205–06
Perez, Beltran 202–03
Pérez, Carlos 158, 164
Pérez, Chris 238
Pérez, Eduardo 219
Perez, Jeral 289–90
Pérez, Odalis 182–83, 196, 203, 211
Perranoski, Ron 12–13, 36–37, 40, 53
Perry, Gaylord 91
Perry, Pat 122
Peter, Jake 261
Peters, DJ 253, 271
Petersen, Michael 294
Pettitte, Andy 192
Pfeifer, Phil 250–52
Phillips, Adolfo 43
Phillips, Evan 271
Phillips, Jason 208–09
Phillips, Lefty 48
Phillips, Steve 162
Piazza, Mike 109, 136, 153–57, 161–62
Piedra, Jorge 175
Pierre, Juan 213, 218, 221
Pignatano, Joe 5, 15–16
Pillar, Kevin 277
Pimentel, Elisaul 215, 227
Pimentel, Jose 163
Pimentel, Julio 193, 211–12
Piniella, Lou 205
Plummer, Jarod 189, 214
Podres, Johnny 5, 15, 25, 31, 54
Podsednik, Scott 227
Pollock, AJ 263, 273–74
Poole, Jim 109, 122
Powell, Dennis 90
Powell, Paul 51
Power, Ted 86
Pop, Zach 257–58
Popovich, Paul 37–38, 42–43
Posada, Jorge 226
Powell, Boog 68–69
Powell, Dennis 96
Power, Ted 66
Prescott, Bobby 21
Price, David 245, 264–66, 270, 277

Prince, Tom 139, 164
Prior, Mark 264
Proctor, Scott 191–92, 216, 220
Prokopec, Luke 140, 181
Prouty, Scott 163
Puig, Yasiel 230–31, 242, 260–61
Pujols, Albert 211, 232, 269
Pujols, Luis 71
Punto, Nick 233–34, 238
Purdin, John 29, 42, 46
Pye, Eddie 109

Quackenbush, Kevin 262, 271
Quantrill, Paul 181, 185, 193
Quinn, Bob (Robert E. Quinn) 106, 142
Quinn, John 17

Rabe, Charlie 5
Rader, Doug 125
Radinsky, Scott 150, 157, 164
Rakow, Ed 29
Raley, Luke 253, 262, 264–65, 267
Ramírez, Hanley 231–32, 243
Ramírez, Manny 218–19, 221, 225–26, 231
Ramirez, Nick 293
Ramírez, Yefry 271, 277
Ramírez, Yohan 293
Ramsey, Mike (infielder) 96
Ramsey, Mike (outfielder) 86, 98–99
Randall, Bob 61
Randolph, Willie 108–09
Rasmussen, Rob 236, 238
Rath, Gary 140, 164
Rau, Doug 46, 54, 82
Rautzhan, Lance 46, 77
Ravin, Josh 238, 257
Reboulet, Jeff 181, 189
Reddick, Josh 251–52
Reed, Chris 230, 249
Reed, Howie 21, 34
Reed, Jake 271, 277
Reed, Jody 135–36, 138
Reese, Pee Wee 5, 9
Reeves, Matt 80
Regan, Phil 30, 40, 58, 110
Reich, Tom 100
Reiser, Pete 28
Reks, Zach 257, 271
Repko, Jason 169, 227
Repulski, Rip 9, 15
Reuss, Jerry 75, 76, 80, 89, 103
Reyes, Dennis 139, 156–57
Reyes, Gil 79, 114
Reyes, José 232
Reynolds, R.J. 79, 93
Rhame, Jacob 238, 257
Rhoden, Rick 51, 75

Ricciardi, J.P. 194
Richardson, Spec 54
Richert, Pete 9, 20, 27–28, 49–50, 55
Richy, John 244, 247–48
Ricketts, Chad 167, 181
Rickey, Branch 5–6
Riggleman, Jim 136–37
Riggs, Adam 140, 175
Rigney, Bill 102
Rijo, José 111
Rincon, Carlos 271
Rios, Edwin 250, 287
Ripken, Cal, Jr. 108, 176
Rivera, German 69, 93
Rivera, Juan (minor league shortstop) 219
Rivera, Juan (outfielder) 230
Rivera, Rene 243
Roberts, Dave 181, 189, 195, 198, 248, 258, 265–66, 269, 271, 273–74, 279–81, 283, 285, 291
Roberts, Rick 164–65
Robertson, Nick 263, 280
Robinson, Clint 238, 244
Robinson, Earl 9, 15
Robinson, Frank 49–52, 108, 269
Robinson, Jackie 20, 39
Robinson, Trayvon 208, 230
Robles, Benony 262, 293
Robles, Oscar 209, 216
Robles, Sergio 49–50
Rodas, Rick 77
Rodgers, Bob 120, 139
Rodriguez, Alex 181
Rodríguez, Ellie 66, 69
Rodriguez, Felix 114, 150
Rodríguez, Henry 96, 127, 143–44
Rodriguez, Juan 230
Rodriguez, Orlando 178
Rodríguez, Paco 236, 245–46
Rodríguez, Ricardo 150, 185–86
Rodríguez, Victor 193
Roebuck, Ed 5, 17, 24–25
Roenicke, Ron 69, 90, 236
Rogers, Randy 68
Rojas, Mel 160–61, 164–65
Rojas, Miguel 236, 239–40, 278–79
Rollins, Jimmy 243, 247
Romak, Jamie 238, 244
Romano, Jason 193, 200
Romo, Sergio 256 57
Romo, Vicente 39, 86
Rosario, Amed 276, 287, 293
Rose, Mike 201, 208
Rose, Pete 33, 73, 112, 226
Roseboro, John 5, 15, 31, 36–37, 39, 47, 94
Rosen, Al 73
Ross, Cody 200, 214

Ross, David 163, 198, 208
Rosscup, Zac 262–63
Rottino, Vinny 223
Rowe, Ken 29
Royster, Jerry 46, 59, 60
Ruan, Wilkin 184, 201
Ruf, Darin 252, 257
Ruggiano, Justin 201, 210, 249–50
Ruiz, Carlos 252
Ruiz, Keibert 244, 258, 270
Runnells, Tom 135
Russell, Bill 34, 48, 60, 72, 86–87, 93, 98, 101, 148, 151–52, 154, 156, 161, 168
Russo, Jim 49
Ruth, Babe 28, 47, 265, 282
Ryan, Nolan 52, 76, 97
Ryan, River 277
Ryan, Terry 145
Ryu, Hyun-Jin 234–35, 241, 263

Sabathia, CC 217
Sabean, Brian 155, 216
Saberhagen, Bret 144–45
Sadler, Casey 262, 267
Saenz, Olmedo 201, 216
Saito, Takashi 215, 220, 229
Salazar, Eduardo 287, 293
Salow, Logan 261
Sampen, Caleb 262
Samuel, Juan 113–14, 116, 136
Sánchez, Angel 227, 238
Sanchez, Duaner 193, 214
Sandberg, Ryne 88, 132
Sander, Richard 69
Sanders, Dick 12
Sanders, Reggie 188
Sands, Jerry 220, 233
Sanford, Chance 170
Santana, Carlos 217
Santana, Dennis 238, 271
Santangelo, F.P. 175, 182
Santiago, Benito 136
Santos, Sergio 250
Sasser, Mickey 118
Savage, Jack 96, 101, 103
Savage, Ted 40, 43
Sax, Dave 74, 96
Sax, Steve 74, 82–83, 106–09
Sborz, Josh 250, 271
Schaffer, Jimmie 40, 43, 46
Schebler, Scott 248–49
Scherzer, Max 270, 274
Schilling, Curt 203
Schlicting, Travis 216, 230
Schmidt, Jason 215, 23
Schmoll, Steve 193, 214
Schoendienst, Red 45

Schofield, Dick 31–32, 38–39
Schofield, Dick, Jr. 147
Schuerholz John 183
Schultz, Jaime 262
Schumaker, Skip 236, 238
Scioscia, Mike 94–95, 124, 130, 136–37
Scott, Dick 26–27
Scott, Tayler 287
Scrubb, Andre 253, 262
Seager, Corey 236, 271, 274
Seanez, Rudy 132, 136, 140, 150, 216
Searage, Ray 109, 122
Searcy, Steve 136
Seaver, Tom 54, 68
See, Larry 79, 103
Segedin, Rob 252
Seidler, Teresa O'Malley 76
Seitz, Peter 62
Sele, Aaron 215
Sellers, Justin 223, 244
Sells, Dave 27, 58–59
Semproch, Ray 14
Seo, Jae Weong 210, 214
Serritella, John 90
Sexson, Richie 199
Shanahan, Greg 46
Shantz, Bobby 14
Shapiro, Mark 195, 204
Shapiro, Ron 108
Sharperson, Mike 103, 140
Shaw, Jeff 156–58, 179, 182, 184
Sheehan, Emmett 271
Sheffield, Gary 153–54, 159, 162, 166, 182–83, 211
Shelby, John 81, 98–99, 110, 122
Sherfy, James 271
Sherill, George 223, 227
Sherry, Larry 5, 17, 26, 38
Sherry, Norm 15, 23
Shinjo, Tsuyoshi 188
Shipley, Craig 91, 109
Shirley, Bart 21
Shirley, Steve 56
Shuey, Paul 185–86
Siebern, Norm 36
Simpson, Andre 178
Simpson, Joe 55, 70
Sims, Duke 45–47, 50, 52
Singer, Bill 21, 47, 51–52
Sizemore, Ted 34, 44–45, 61, 63, 65
Skinner, Bob 44
Skowron, Bill 22–23, 25–26
Slocumb, Heathcliff 203
Smeltzer, Devin 253, 262
Smit, Kyle 215, 224
Smith, Ballard 85
Smith, Blake 223, 249

Smith, Dick 23, 29, 39
Smith, Don 68
Smith, Charley 17–18
Smith, Greg 122, 152
Smith, John 5
Smith, Lee 87, 134
Smith, Randy 165
Smith, Reggie 63, 72, 80–81
Smith, Tal 71
Smith, Will 253
Snell, Blake 292–93
Snider, Duke 5, 17, 24, 97
Snider, Kelly 80
Snyder, Cory 133, 138, 140
Snyder, Gene 9
Socarras, Tony 200
Sodders, Mike 133
Soler, Jorge 230
Solomon, Eddie 43, 58
Sopko, Andrew 250, 262
Soria, Joakim 229
Sosa, Elias 64–65, 74
Soto, Juan 292
South, Carl 150
Souza, Steven, Jr. 271
Spencer, Daryl 18, 26
Springer, Dennis 181
Stanhouse, Don 77, 80, 82
Stanky, Eddie 20
Stanley, Henri 198
Steinbrenner, George 73, 106–07
Stengel, Casey 20–21
Stephenson, Brian 167
Stephenson, Jerry 46
Stewart, Brock 244, 263
Stewart, Dave 61, 88, 103, 166
Stewart, Scott 200
Stillman, Royle 49–50
Stinson, Bob 34, 44–45
Stone, Gavin 267
Strahler, Mike 39, 52
Strawberry, Darryl 117–18, 120, 128, 140, 149, 166
Strayhorn, Kole 181, 189–90
Stripling, Ross 236, 267
Stuart, Dick 34
Stubbs, Franklin 86, 97, 110, 115–16
Stults, Eric 189, 227, 249
Sturtze, Tanyon 200, 216, 220
Sudakis, Bill 29, 52
Suero, Wander 287
Sulbaran, Miguel 238
Surkamp, Eric 249–50
Sutcliffe, Rick 56, 81–82
Sutton, Don 29, 31, 47, 79, 109–10
Sutton, Joe 169
Suzuki, Ichiro 213

Sweeney, Darnell 236, 247–48, 252, 257
Sweeney, Mark 215–16, 220
Sweeney, Trey 287, 291
Syndergaard, Noah 275–76, 287
Szekely, Joe 90

Tabata, Jose 246
Tallis, Cedric 74
Tamin, Alex 229
Tanaka, Masahiro 237
Tanner, Chuck 49
Tapani, Kevin 101, 103, 144–45
Tapia, German 277
Tarsovich, Jordan 250, 256
Taschner, Jack 227
Taveras, Alex 69
Taylor, Chris 252, 279
Tebbets, Birdie 6
Tekulve, Kent 94
Tellum, Am 207
Tepesch, Nick 253
Teufel, Tim 118
Thames, Marcus 230
Theriot, Ryan 224–25, 227
Thomas, Cody 253, 271
Thomas, Derrell 72–73, 89–91
Thomas, Ian 249, 252
Thomasson, Gary 74–75, 79
Thome, Jim 223, 269
Thompson, Derek 189, 201, 216
Thompson, Fresco 19–20
Thompson, Milt 150
Thompson, Ryan 143
Thompson, Trayce 248–49, 262, 277, 279, 281–82
Thurston, Joseph 169, 208
Tiffany, Chuck 193, 214
Tiffee, Terry 216, 220
Tillotson, Thad 15, 31–32
Tisdale, Freddie 63–64
Toles, Andrew 250
Tolleson, Shawn 227, 238
Tomko, Brett 215–16
Torborg, Jeff 26, 47–48
Torre, Joe 191, 216–18, 220, 222, 224–25, 228
Torres, Jaime 231
Torres, Jose 90
Torreyes, Ronald 250, 252
Toscano, Dian 252
Tovar, César 36
Towers, Kevin 155
Tracewski, Dick 20, 43
Tracy, Jim 175–76, 180, 186, 191, 195, 198–99, 203, 205, 214
Trammell, Taylor 293
Traxler, Brian 109

324 Index

Treadway, Jeff 139, 143–44
Treanor, Matt 230, 236
Trebelhorn, Tom 97
Treinen, Blake 263
Trevino, Alex 95, 110, 215
Triunfel, Carlos 244
Trlicek, Ricky 139
Trombley, Mike 179, 181, 189
Troncoso, Ramón 189, 236
Tsao, Chin-hui 216, 250
Tsutsugo, Yoshi 271
Tucker, Jon 158
Tudor, John 104–06, 114
Turner, Justin 238–39, 276, 278
Turner, Ted 62, 85
Turner, Trea 270–71, 274–75
Tyson, Mike 61

Uceta, Edwin 253, 271
Urias, Julio 236, 270
Uribe, Juan 227, 249
Utley, Chase 241, 247–48, 262

Vail, Mike 91
Valdez, Ismael 132, 164, 167–68, 179
Valdez, Jesus 262
Valdez, Luis 286
Valdez, Wilson 214, 219
Valentin, Jesmuel 236, 244
Valentin, José 201, 209
Valentine, Bobby 42, 48, 51–52, 162
Valenzuela, Fernando 77, 89, 101, 124–25, 141
Valera, Breyvic 257–58, 261
Valle, Hector 15
Valo, Elmer 5, 11
Vanasco, Ricky 286, 293
Vance, Dazzy 6
Vance, Sandy 42
Vande Berg, Ed 94–95, 98, 102
Van Ryn, Ben 140
Van Slyke, Scott 208, 257
Vargas, Claudio 223, 227
Vargas, Jason 237
Vargas, Miguel 257, 289–91
Varitek, Jason 203
Varland, Gus 271, 277, 287
Vasquez, Andrew 271
Vélez, Eugenio 227, 230
Venable, Will 253
Venafro, Mike 200
Venditte, Pat 257, 262
Ventura, Robin 191, 201
Verdugo, Alex 244, 254, 258, 265–66
Versalles, Zoilo 36–38, 41
Vesia, Alex 271
Victorino, Shane 236

Virdon, Bill 79
Vivas, Jorbit 286
Vizcaino, Jose 98, 122, 152, 154, 158, 171
Voigt, Paul 86
Volquez, Edinson 238
Von Schamann, Dalton 236, 243

Wade, Cory 201, 227
Wade, Ed 180
Waechter, Doug 205
Walker, Jerry 137
Walker, Rube 5, 9
Walker, Steve 90
Wall, Josh 208
Wall, Stan 43
Wallace, Dave 156, 178–79
Wallach, Brett 223–24
Wallach, Tim 135–36, 145, 148, 150
Walls, Lee 20–21, 29
Walsh, Dave 114, 123
Walsh, Dick 48
Walsh, Josh 238
Walter, Mark 230
Walters, Dan 137
Walters, Zach 253, 257
Walton, Danny 61, 69
Wang, Connor 265, 267
Ward, Daryle 193
Ward, Jay 21, 23
Warwick, Carl 18
Washburn, Jarrod 209
Washington, Ron 66, 79
Wathan, John 119
Watson, Tony 257, 262
Watt, Mike 216, 219
Watters, Mike 96
Wayne, Gary 140
Weaver, Earl 50, 163
Weaver, Eric 132
Weaver, Jeff 192, 203, 209, 223, 227
Weber, Neil 169
Webster, Allen 220, 233–34
Webster, Mitch 125–26, 140, 148
Wedge, Eric 195
Weeden, Brandon 192–93
Weiss, Gary 74
Weiss, George 24
Welch, Bob 69, 75, 88, 101–03
Wellman, Brad 98
Wells, David 216
Wells, Terry 115–16, 122
Werhas, Johnny 15, 35
Werth, Jayson 194, 215
West, Matt 250, 253
Westrum, Wes 32
Wetteland, John 96, 113, 127–29
White, Devon 159–60, 176–77

White, Larry 81–82
White, Mitch 253, 277
White, Myron 61
White, Roy 35
White, Tyler 262, 267
Whitehurst, Wally 101, 103
Whitfield, Terry 90, 98
Wieland, Joe 242–43, 252
Wilhelm, Hoyt 51, 53
Wilkins, Mike 122
Wilkins, Rick 170
Willhite, Nick 11, 29, 30, 34
Williams, Billy 86
Williams, Dick 85, 96
Williams, Eddie 150, 152
Williams, Jeff 150
Williams, Jim 37–38, 41
Williams, Kendall 267
Williams, Kenny 178
Williams, Luke 277, 287
Williams, Matt 133
Williams, Mitch 126
Williams, Reggie 81, 86, 109, 139, 147, 150
Williams, Stan 22–23
Williams, Todd 122, 147
Wills, Maury 12–13, 33–34, 37–38, 42, 53, 83
Wilson, Bob 11
Wilson, Brian 238, 241, 244
Wilson, Glenn 115
Wilson, Steve 132
Wilson, Tom 200
Windhorn, Gordon 12, 21
Windle, Tom 238, 242
Winfield, Dave 142
Winkles, Bobby 51, 70
Winslett, Dax 147

Wise, Brett 90
Withrow, Chris 216, 249
Witt, Nathan 257, 262
Wolf, Randy 215–16, 223
Wolters, Tony 271, 277
Wong, Connor 257, 265, 267
Wood, Alex 245–46, 254, 260–61, 267
Woodson, Tracy 91, 114
Workman, Widd 163
Worrell, Todd 134–35, 153
Wright, Jamey 236, 250, 253
Wright, Ricky 79, 88
Wrobleski, Justin 271
Wunsch, Kelly 201, 209
Wynn, Jim 54–55, 59–60
Wynns, Austin 287

Yamamoto, Yoshinobu 285–87
Yarbrough, Ryan 87, 293
Yeager, Steve 39, 63, 65, 68, 71, 87, 94–95
Yoshii, Masato 156
Young, Delwyn 189, 222
Young, Dick 11
Young, Eric, Sr. 114, 136, 151, 167–68, 172
Young, Matt 96–97, 101–02
Young, Michael 238
Yurchak, Justin 262

Zabala, Aneurys 261
Zachry, Pat 82, 86, 95
Zahn, Geoff 42, 58
Zaidi, Farhan 239, 251–52, 254, 258–59
Zambrano, Jhan 271
Zazueta, Christian 293
Zeile, Todd 149–50, 153–54
Zimmer, Don 5, 12–13, 25–26, 37
Zisk, Richie 69

www.ingramcontent.com/pod-product-compliance
Ingram Content Group UK Ltd.
Pitfield, Milton Keynes, MK11 3LW, UK
UKHW041829220426
5349IPUK00002B/33